Virgil and Renaissance Culture

MEDIEVAL AND RENAISSANCE
TEXTS AND STUDIES

VOLUME 510

ARIZONA STUDIES IN THE MIDDLE AGES
AND RENAISSANCE

VOLUME 42

Virgil and Renaissance Culture

Edited by

L. B. T. Houghton
Marco Sgarbi

ARIZONA CENTER FOR MEDIEVAL
ACMRS
AND RENAISSANCE STUDIES
Tempe, Arizona
in collaboration with
BREPOLS
2018

THE ARIZONA CENTER FOR
MEDIEVAL & RENAISSANCE
STUDIES

Published by ACMRS (Arizona Center for Medieval and Renaissance Studies)
Tempe, Arizona
and Brepols Publishers, n.v., Turnhout, Belgium.

ASMAR Volume 42: ISBN 978-2-503-58190-3 D/2018/0095/220

Library of Congress Cataloging-in-Publication Data
Names: Houghton, L. B. T., 1978- editor. | Sgarbi, Marco, 1982- editor.
Title: Virgil and renaissance culture / edited by L.B.T. Houghton, Marco Sgarbi.
Other titles: Medieval & Renaissance Texts & Studies (Series) ; v. 510.
Description: Tempe, Arizona : Published by ACMRS (Arizona Center for Medieval and Renaissance Studies), 2018. | Series: Medieval and renaissance texts and studies ; volume 510
Identifiers: LCCN 2018023335 | ISBN 9780866985659 (hardcover : alk. paper)
Subjects: LCSH: Virgil--Influence. | European literature--Renaissance, 1450-1600-- History and criticism.
Classification: LCC PA6826 .V574 2018 | DDC 871/.01--dc23
LC record available at https://lccn.loc.gov/2018023335

Cover Image:
Quos ego (1515–1516).
Neptune calming the tempest which Aeolus raised against Aeneas' fleet in central compartment surrounded by nine scenes (not shown) from Book I of the Aeneid
Engraving.
By permission of The Trustees of the British Museum.

∞
This book is made to last. It is set in Adobe Caslon Pro,
smyth-sewn and printed on acid-free paper to library specifications.
Printed in the United States of America

Contents

List of Illustrations

Foreword

With one exception, the papers collected in this volume were first presented (along with many others) at a conference of the same name held at the Accademia Nazionale Virgiliana di Scienze Lettere e Arti in Mantua in October 2012. A brief report on this event can be found in *Bruniana & Campanelliana* 19 (2013): 269–71. The conference was generously sponsored by the President of the Italian Republic and the Ministero per i Beni e le Attività Culturali, with collaboration from the province and commune of Mantua. The editors (who were also responsible for the organization of the conference) would also like to express their gratitude to the Accademia Nazionale Virgiliana and to all those who participated in the event, among them some of the most distinguished names in scholarship on Virgil, on the Renaissance, and on the intersection of the two. In assembling the present volume it has been our aim to offer a series of case studies illustrating the breadth and depth of Virgil's presence in the visual, intellectual, and imaginative worlds of the Renaissance. Constraints of space have meant that a large number of excellent papers from the conference could not be included here, and hopefully many of these will appear in print elsewhere in due course. For advice both during the conference and since, we would particularly like to thank Philip Hardie, Craig Kallendorf, and Peter Mack, and Roy Rukkila for accepting the volume for publication as part of the Medieval and Renaissance Texts and Studies series. It has been a pleasure to work with the contributors to this collection, who have supplied material promptly and responded to editorial queries with patience and good humor; our heartfelt thanks go to them all.

Neither the Mantua conference nor this volume would have happened without the Warburg Institute, where the enlightened policy of allocating shared office space to visiting fellows based on the compatibility of their interests first brought us together as Frances A. Yates fellows in early 2011. The Institute remains a crucial, unique, and internationally treasured resource for the study of the afterlife of antiquity, particularly during the period of the Renaissance, and we would like to join our voices with those of many other colleagues around the world in hoping that it will be able to continue to serve the needs of scholars in the way it has done so well for many years to come.

M. S. / L. B. T. H.

1

Introduction:
The Virgilian Panorama

L. B. T. Houghton
University of Reading

Of the four words that make up our title, at least three might be thought to require further explanation or qualification. It might seem relatively straightforward, for instance, to talk of Virgil, the ancient Roman poet, author of *Eclogues*, *Georgics*, and *Aeneid*, and it is as a shorthand for these works that the term is used in the title of this collection. But by the time of the historical period under consideration here, the name "Virgil" had grown to encompass a broad semantic field. It could be employed to refer to the figure of the poet, the creator of a corpus of poetry which had held unrivalled authority and prestige throughout later antiquity and the centuries following the fall of Rome. Around this figure there had developed an extensive tradition of literary "lives," or *vitae*, in which the ancient author featured as the protagonist of a series of more or less fanciful biographical episodes, many of them extrapolated from details contained in the poet's own works.[1] This tradition, which continued well into the period with which these essays are concerned (see Fabio Stok's chapter in this collection), attributed to Virgil a number of shorter juvenile works in addition to the canonical triad of his maturity. The authenticity of these accretions, now known collectively as the *Appendix Vergiliana*, was still generally accepted by editors and scholars of the Renaissance, and their circulation under the name of Virgil

[1] For the texts of the Virgilian *vitae*, see *The Virgilian Tradition: The First Fifteen Hundred Years*, ed. Jan M. Ziolkowski and Michael C. J. Putnam (New Haven and London: Yale University Press, 2008), 179–403. On the continuation of this biographical tradition into the Renaissance, see especially Fabio Stok, "Virgil between the Middle Ages and the Renaissance," *International Journal of the Classical Tradition* 1 (1994–1995): 15–22, and on Renaissance reception of the ancient lives, see David Scott Wilson-Okamura, *Virgil in the Renaissance* (Cambridge: Cambridge University Press, 2010), index s.v. "Virgil, biography"; Elisabeth Klecker, *Dichtung über Dichtung. Homer und Vergil in lateinischen Gedichten italienischer Humanisten des 15. und 16. Jahrhunderts* (Vienna: Verlag der Österreichischen Akademie der Wissenschaften, 1994), 164–88.

persisted for many years thereafter.[2] The addition of supplementary material to the Virgilian corpus evidently began at an early date; but in more recent times the figure of the poet had undergone yet more extraordinary transformations, appropriated for the Christian faith as a prophet of the incarnation,[3] revered in medieval legend as a sorcerer and sage,[4] and recruited by Dante as an authority for the doctrine of imperial monarchy and as the pilgrim's guide to the horrors of hell and the atonements of purgatory. With some justification, then, does Colin Burrow's chapter in *The Cambridge Companion to Virgil* refer not to a singular "Virgil," but rather to "Virgils, from Dante to Milton."[5]

Each of these various strands of assimilation, moreover, left its mark on subsequent readers' perceptions of and interactions with the texts of the "historical" Virgil, creating a vast field of associations which together shaped the interpretative climate in which those texts were read,[6] a climate to which the physical format of the editions in which Virgil's poems were presented also made

[2] On the *Appendix Vergiliana* in the Renaissance, see Colin Burrow, "English Renaissance Readers and the *Appendix Vergiliana*," *Proceedings of the Virgil Society* 26 (2008): 1–16; Wilson-Okamura, *Virgil in the Renaissance*, 80n18.

[3] On Christian interpretations of *Eclogue* 4, see especially Domenico Comparetti, *Vergil in the Middle Ages*, trans. E. F. M. Benecke (London: S. Sonnenschein, 1895; repr. Princeton: Princeton University Press, 1997), 96–103, 309–17, 360–61; Ella Bourne, "The Messianic Prophecy in Vergil's Fourth Eclogue," *The Classical Journal* 11 (1916): 390–400; Karl Prümm, "Das Prophetenamt der Sibyllen in kirchlicher Literatur, mit besonderer Rücksicht auf die Deutung der 4. Ekloge Virgils," *Scholastik* 4 (1929): 54–77, 221–46, 498–533; Karl Strecker, "'Iam nova progenies caelo demittitur alto'," *Studi medievali* n.s. 5 (1932): 167–86; Pierre Courcelle, "Les exégèses chrétiennes de la quatrième Eglogue," *Revue des études anciennes* 59 (1957): 294–319; Stephen Benko, "Virgil's Fourth Eclogue in Christian Interpretation," *Aufstieg und Niedergang der römischen Welt* II.31.1 (1980): 646–705; Ziolkowski and Putnam, *The Virgilian Tradition*, 487–503; Daniel Hadas, "Christians, Sibyls and *Eclogue* 4," *Recherches augustiniennes et patristiques* 37 (2013): 51–129; and most recently, Craig Kallendorf, *The Protean Virgil: Material Form and the Reception of the Classics* (Oxford: Oxford University Press, 2015), 48–58.

[4] On Virgil the magician, see, e.g., Comparetti, *Vergil in the Middle Ages*, 249–376; Joseph Salathiel Tunison, *Master Virgil: The author of the Aeneid, as he seemed in the Middle Ages* (Cincinnati: R. Clarke, 1890); John Webster Spargo, *Virgil the Necromancer: Studies in Virgilian Legends* (Cambridge, MA: Harvard University Press, 1934); Jean Céard, "Virgile, un grand homme soupçonné de magie," in *Présence de Virgile*, ed. Raymond Chevallier (Paris: Les Belles Lettres, 1978), 265–78; Ziolkowski and Putnam, *The Virgilian Tradition*, 829–74.

[5] Colin Burrow, "Virgils, from Dante to Milton," in *The Cambridge Companion to Virgil*, ed. Charles Martindale (Cambridge: Cambridge University Press, 1997), 79.

[6] For the principle, see Charles Martindale, *Redeeming the Text: Latin Poetry and the Hermeneutics of Reception* (Cambridge: Cambridge University Press, 1993), 54: "Instead of Virgil, 'Virgil', that is *all-the-forces-that-moulded-the text-plus-its-reception*" (original emphasis).

a significant contribution, as Craig Kallendorf has demonstrated.[7] Whilst it is true, then, of the Renaissance period, as of others, that "a single age can possess an almost mind-boggling diversity of Virgils,"[8] we might go even further: even such a formulation as *quot homines, tot Vergilii* can scarcely do justice to the kaleidoscopic variety of configurations to which Virgil's poetry was subjected;—for even across the multiple reading experiences of a single reader the ancient text continues to fashion itself anew each time, although of course only a relatively restricted number of these encounters leave any trace in the literary or artistic record. To determine the full range of associations that might have suggested themselves to the mind of a Renaissance reader or viewer at the mention of the name "Virgil" is thus not as straightforward a process as it might at first appear. If we are constrained to use "Virgil" as a convenient cipher for the poet's major works, that should by no means circumscribe our understanding of what that name might have evoked for past readers.

Again, if the name "Virgil" turns out to be more contentious than might have been supposed,[9] it is scarcely necessary to expatiate on the difficulties attendant on the use of the term "Renaissance," which has been the object of such intense scrutiny in scholarship on this period for so long.[10] The verdict of the ancient historian Arnaldo Momigliano was unequivocal: "We all know what a waste of time the word Renaissance has represented."[11] In the title here it is intended in a strictly chronological sense, to denote the period between the late fourteenth and the late sixteenth century. Despite the mass of tendentious implications attaching to this term, it is—and is likely to remain—difficult to find a satisfactory replacement; the popular (though not necessarily equivalent) alternative "early modern," with its evident teleological connotations, is not

---

[7] Kallendorf, *The Protean Virgil*; idem, *Virgil and the Myth of Venice: Books and Readers in the Italian Renaissance* (Oxford: Clarendon Press, 1999); idem, *The Virgilian Tradition: Book History and the History of Reading in Early Modern Europe* (Aldershot and Burlington, VT: Ashgate, 2007), especially chapters 3, 6, and 7.

[8] William M. Porter, "Review of Theodore Ziolkowski, *Virgil and the Moderns*," *Modern Philology* 94 (1996): 61, quoted in *Virgilian Identities in the French Renaissance*, ed. Phillip John Usher and Isabelle Fernbach (Cambridge: D. S. Brewer, 2012), 10n33.

[9] Indeed, the name aroused controversy at the time, in the form of the debate over the spelling *Vergilius / Virgilius*, in which the leading part was played by Angelo Poliziano: see Wilson-Okamura, *Virgil in the Renaissance*, 15–20.

[10] The bibliography on this subject is vast; for a wide-ranging historical survey, see Wallace K. Ferguson, *The Renaissance in Historical Thought: Five Centuries of Interpretation* (New York: Houghton Mifflin Co., 1948; repr. Toronto, Buffalo, and London: University of Toronto Press, 2006). A recent introduction to some of the major issues can be found in William Caferro, *Contesting the Renaissance* (Malden, MA and Oxford: Wiley-Blackwell, 2011).

[11] Arnaldo Momigliano, "J. G. Droysen between Greeks and Jews," *History and Theory* 9 (1970): 139.

obviously preferable, merely substituting one ideologically weighted expression for another.[12] Both terms are chiefly of value as vague but expedient chronological markers, and we have not sought to impose a consistent use of such terminology on our contributors. In one sense, however, the choice of "Renaissance" in our title might be considered entirely appropriate, since the final essay in this collection argues that the poetry of Virgil was crucial to writers of the period in their attempts to give expression to the concept of a Renaissance, attempts which have proved sufficiently successful that their consequences for the historiography of these centuries have been felt ever since, and continue to generate discussion.

In combination with the final word of the title, "culture," the use of the expression "Renaissance" risks becoming particularly inflammatory. Once again, the term "culture" serves here as a shorthand, in this case for the art, literature, music, and philosophy of the period in question. There are few (if any) scholars who would be willing to argue that there was one single, homogeneous, monolithic "Renaissance culture," and that is certainly not intended to be the implication here. Even if we accept—and again, there is no necessary implication that we should accept this proposition—that there was some identifiable historical phenomenon that could be isolated under the label "Renaissance," the period covered by that term is so wide and the geographical scope so broad that it is impossible to maintain that there can have been any universal "Renaissance culture" that remained essentially unchanged across time and space.[13] Rather, as we would expect, there was a multitude of cultures at different times and in different places—and even at the same time and in the same place—during the period traditionally identified as the Renaissance. Once we adopt the designation "Renaissance" to denote a defined chronological segment, moreover, it must immediately be acknowledged that "not everything that happened during the Renaissance was part of the Renaissance,"[14] and that the manifestations of

---

[12] Wilson-Okamura, *Virgil in the Renaissance*, 8, dispenses with the label "early modern" on different grounds: "*rinascimento*, 'rebirth,' is a term that was actually used in the Renaissance, whereas no one in any period has ever called him- or herself 'early modern.' If we want to understand an earlier period, it is helpful to employ at least some of the period's own vocabulary." Certainly we ought to *examine* the terminology that writers in the past used to characterize their own time, but to adopt that terminology in our own accounts as a matter of interpretative principle might be considered uncomfortably close to the historiographical practices that have been responsible for the contention over the term "Renaissance" and its equivalents that has so bedeviled study of this period.

[13] See, e.g., A. C. Spearing, *Medieval to Renaissance in English Poetry* (Cambridge: Cambridge University Press, 1985), 1–2: "There are several different Renaissances in the various cultural fields such as literature, the visual arts, architecture, philosophy and political thought, to which the term applies, and they begin at different moments, proceed at different paces, interact differently with earlier cultural traditions, and affect different parts of Europe at different times."

[14] Wilson-Okamura, *Virgil in the Renaissance*, 8.

"culture" with which we are here concerned were simply a number of different forms among many, in most cases the preserve of a small (though socially, financially, and intellectually influential) educated elite. In the frontispiece painted by Simone Martini for Petrarch's manuscript of the works of Virgil, now in the Biblioteca Ambrosiana in Milan, the late antique commentator Servius may be identified as *Servius altiloqui retegens archana Maronis | ut pateant ducibus pastoribus atque colonis* ("Servius, unveiling the secrets of eloquent Maro, so that they might be revealed to leaders, shepherds, and farmers"),[15] but it is hard to imagine that there was much serious perusal of the works of the ancient poet among the shepherds (whom Duke Guidobaldo, at least according to W. B. Yeats, did not consult "when he made | That grammar school of courtesies | Where wit and beauty learned their trade | Upon Urbino's windy hill"[16]) or farmers of the following centuries. In certain locations, perhaps—Mantua and Naples, in particular—the name "Virgil" may have commanded more recognition than elsewhere; but it is impossible to tell how many of those who passed beneath his effigy in the Piazza Broletto knew more of their poet than his name, any more than we can calculate the proportion of Londoners whose thoughts turn to Cape St. Vincent and the Nile as they struggle through the clouds of pigeons in Trafalgar Square.

The title under which the essays collected here are presented calls for some clarification, therefore, and perhaps for a certain amount of critical forbearance, but not, I think, for too much apology. Without the use of necessary (if questionable) terminological conveniences, it would be impossible to talk about the past at all, at least in a way that could make some claim to readability and concision, and it is our belief that the chapters which follow possess a value that does not depend on any one overarching definition of the Renaissance, of culture, or even of Virgil. It would be irresponsible, however, to leave the reader with the impression that any of these terms (not to mention that troublesome "and" that has crept in between them) cannot be, and has not been, contested, and that under

[15] MS Ambrosiana S.P. 10, 27; for analysis of the frontispiece see especially Nicholas Mann, *Pétrarque: Les voyages de l'esprit* (Grenoble: Jérôme Millon, 2004), 47–71; Enrico Fenzi, "Servio, Simone Martini, Petrarca: un percorso attraverso il Virgilio Ambrosiano," in *Servius et sa réception de l'Antiquité à la Renaissance*, ed. Monique Bouquet and Bruno Méniel (Rennes: Presses Universitaires de Rennes, 2011), 409–41. There is a magnificent reproduction of the painting in Giulietta Chelazzi Dini, Alessandro Angelini, and Bernardina Sani, *Five Centuries of Sienese Painting: From Duccio to the Birth of the Baroque* (London: Thames and Hudson, 1998), 97.

[16] William Butler Yeats, "To a Wealthy Man who Promised a Second Subscription to the Dublin Municipal Gallery if it were Proved the People Wanted Pictures," lines 14–17, in *W. B. Yeats: The Major Works*, ed. Edward Larrissy (Oxford: Oxford University Press, 2001), 50, quoted (with "mirror-school" for "grammar school") in relation to this point by Kenneth Clark, *Civilisation: A Personal View* (London: British Broadcasting Corporation and John Murray, 1969), 112.

the same heading there are not innumerable different stories that might be, and in some cases have been, told.

~

If the shepherds of the Renaissance, who presumably had other things to do (such as scratching likenesses of their sheep on rocks while awaiting discovery by some leading painter of the day), were less assiduous in their study of the classics than were some of their contemporaries, at a certain level of society—and it is not easy to determine at exactly what point that level began or ended—Virgil and his works enjoyed a pervasive presence in the life of the intellect and the imagination, as they did also in the elaborate machinery of courtly or civic pageantry and social ritual. The birth of the scion of a wealthy Florentine family might be celebrated with the presentation of a *desco da parto* (birth tray) featuring the legend of Virgil's humiliation at the hands of a princess, whose abandonment of the infatuated poet in a basket half-way up her tower was used alongside Aristotle's degradation at the hands of the courtesan Phyllis to illustrate the theme of female power.[17] His education and training in rhetoric in preparation for a career in civic life would involve study of the poet's texts and of particular examples from the Virgilian corpus used to illustrate specific rhetorical tropes (see the chapter by Peter Mack in this volume). His alliance in marriage with another prominent family might be marked by the commissioning of a *cassone*, or wedding chest, with scenes of Dido and Aeneas or the fall of Troy.[18] Guests at the tables of affluent and fashionable patrons could admire the glazed ceramic ware known as maiolica, which was frequently adorned with lively and colorful scenes from the *Aeneid* (see Lisa Boutin Vitela's essay in this collection), or they might cast a glance of erudite envy around the cycles of Virgilian frescoes stretching over the walls or across the ceiling.[19]

[17] For a reproduction of a tray with this subject matter, see Cecilia De Carli, *I deschi da parto e la pittura del primo rinascimento toscano* (Turin: Allemandi, 1997), 157, and on the legend of Virgil in the basket, see Ziolkowski and Putnam, *The Virgilian Tradition*, 457–59 (with further bibliography).

[18] For Virgilian subjects on *cassoni*, see, e.g., Jennifer Klein Morrison, "Apollonio di Giovanni's *Aeneid* Cassoni and the Virgil Commentators," *Yale University Art Gallery Bulletin* (1992): 26–47; Margaret Franklin, "Vergil and the *femina furens*: Reading the *Aeneid* in Renaissance Cassone Paintings," *Vergilius* 60 (2014): 127–44. The conference at which the majority of these papers were first presented featured a paper by Caroline Campbell (National Gallery, London) on the use of motifs from Virgil in *cassone* decoration, which unfortunately we have not been able to include here.

[19] On such schemes see especially Erika Langmuir, "*Arma virumque* . . . Nicolò dell'Abate's *Aeneid gabinetto* for Scandiano," *Journal of the Warburg and Courtauld Institutes* 39 (1976): 151–70; Marcello Fagiolo, *Virgilio nell'arte e nella cultura europea* (Rome: De Luca, 1981), 120–93; Vincenzo Farinella, "Raffigurare Virgilio, 'dolcissimo patre': dia-

The appearance of subjects from Virgil's poetry or from the wider Virgilian tradition in paintings and on luxury household objects gave the ancient texts an important function in the definition and projection of particular public and private identities and thus a central role in the process of what Stephen Greenblatt has called "Renaissance self-fashioning."[20] This practice of self-definition through exploitation of themes and motifs from the most prestigious poet of classical antiquity can be seen on both a collective and a personal level, from the promotion and reinforcement of the values of a community in its civic art to the adoption of Virgilian mottoes by individual grandees.[21] Such plundering of the classic texts for the purposes of public posturing meant that these borrowings were frequently harnessed to convey a message that could be understood within the context of its surroundings and did not necessarily require a profound familiarity with the poetry of Virgil or even an awareness of the source of the citation—although in their contribution on the use of Virgilian mottoes on medals and tokens, Cécile Arnould and Pierre Assenmaker argue that in certain cases an awareness of the original context from which these tags were derived is required for a full understanding of the artifacts concerned. Likewise, musical settings of a text from Virgil (such as those mentioned here by Evan A. MacCarthy) might be enjoyed on some level without a detailed knowledge of the origin of the lyrics, even if listeners without a solid grounding in classical literature are likely to have missed the nuances available to an audience with the benefit of a humanist education. The dissemination of Virgilian subjects, phrases, and imagery among spectators of the Renaissance therefore extended to recipients across the social spectrum who may not even have been conscious of the provenance of this material, in addition to all the other various gradations of knowledge and expertise within contemporary society. The same is not quite true—or is true to a lesser extent—of the literary culture of the time, for reasons which are not too difficult to fathom. Certainly readers approach texts with differing expectations, differing competences, and differing degrees of immersion in the literature of the past, but the centrality of Virgil's position within literate education ensured that authors could assume a thorough and long-standing acquaintance with the works of the ancient poet on the part of those whose training equipped them to engage

---

loghi tra arte e letteratura," in *Virgilio: Volti e immagini del poeta*, ed. Vincenzo Farinella (Milan: Skira, 2011), 27–83.

[20] Stephen Greenblatt, *Renaissance Self-Fashioning: From More to Shakespeare* (Chicago: The University of Chicago Press, 1980); the role of Virgil's poetry as a vehicle for identity formation is acknowledged in the title of Usher and Fernbach, eds., *Virgilian Identities*.

[21] As an example of the appropriation of the poet's works as an endorsement of civic values, we might adduce Craig Kallendorf's study of the use of Virgil's texts in the corroboration and propagation of a set of political, educational, and religious ideologies together constituting the "myth of Venice" (Kallendorf, *Virgil and the Myth of Venice*).

with works of literature.[22] The result is that in literary productions of the period, the steady stream of Virgilian adaptation and allusion that we have observed in other areas of Renaissance culture becomes an unstoppable torrent.

The degree of intimacy with the Virgilian oeuvre acquired by Renaissance writers and expected of their intended audiences is perhaps most strikingly apparent from the literary form known as the cento, a technique applied to Virgil's texts since antiquity, in which lines or sections of lines from a revered and familiar master-text are recombined and reordered to create a new text on a different subject; as George Hugo Tucker demonstrates in his chapter in this volume, this practice found notable exponents among Renaissance *littérateurs*, particularly the Capilupi brothers of Mantua. In more mainstream genres of literature, too, in both Latin and the vernacular, ambitious authors sought both to display their literary dexterity and to speak to an audience schooled in the ancient classics through their appropriation of Virgilian forms and their incorporation and reshaping of celebrated episodes from the poet's corpus (see, for example, the studies of Giovanna Laterza and Helen Lovatt among the chapters that follow). Perhaps the ultimate victory in this arena was won by the neo-Latin poet Maffeo Vegio, whose mastery of Virgilian style and spirit was judged so accomplished that his thirteenth book of the *Aeneid* (considered by Anne Rogerson in her essay in this collection) appeared after the twelve canonical books in several editions of Virgil's works printed in the fifteenth and sixteenth centuries, thereby becoming, like the marginal commentaries and *vitae* that accompanied the texts of the poems, a part of the many-sided prism through which Renaissance readers perceived and interpreted the works of the Roman poet (Gavin Douglas's Scots translation of the *Aeneid* included Vegio's supplement, as did the English translation by Thomas Phaer and Thomas Twyne).[23]

---

[22] On the place of Virgil in Renaissance education, see Paul F. Grendler, *Schooling in Renaissance Italy: Literacy and Learning, 1300–1600* (Baltimore and London: The Johns Hopkins University Press, 1989), 235–50; Robert Black, *Humanism and Education in Medieval and Renaissance Italy* (Cambridge: Cambridge University Press, 2001), index s.v. "Vergil," especially 256–60; Andrew Wallace, *Virgil's Schoolboys: The Poetics of Pedagogy in Renaissance England* (Oxford: Oxford University Press, 2010); Craig Kallendorf, "Virgil in the Renaissance Classroom: From Toscanella's *Osservationi . . . sopra l'opere di Virgilio* to the *Exercitationes rhetoricae*," in *The Classics in the Medieval and Renaissance Classroom: The Role of Ancient Texts in the Arts Curriculum as Revealed by Surviving Manuscripts and Early Printed Books*, ed. Juanita Feros Ruys, John O. Ward, and Melanie Heyworth (Turnhout: Brepols, 2013), 309–28.

[23] For a conveniently accessible text and translation, see Maffeo Vegio, *Short Epics*, ed. Michael C. J. Putnam with James Hankins, I Tatti Renaissance Library 15 (Cambridge, MA and London: Harvard University Press, 2004). Vegio's was not the only attempt at a "completion" of the narrative of the *Aeneid*: see bibliography cited in Wilson-Okamura, *Virgil in the Renaissance*, 239n174.

The Virgilian tendency in Renaissance literature was not confined, however, to such epic ventures as Vegio's *Aeneidos Liber XIII*, Marco Girolamo Vida's *Christiad*, Ugolino Verino's *Carlias*, and the host of panegyrical effusions directed towards dignitaries of the time, in which the presence of so illustrious a model as the *Aeneid* might naturally be expected; nor did it exhaust itself in the crowded pastures of pastoral poetry,[24] or in the more sporadically tilled fields of neo-Latin didactic.[25] Even beyond the principal subjects and the literary genres of his own compositions, the shadow of Virgil's influence infiltrated every corner of artistic and scholarly endeavor, and his poetic corpus was regarded as a repository of wisdom on medicine and mathematics,[26] on history and antiquarian learning,[27] on rhetoric and law, on theology and philosophy.[28] Leonardo Bruni, in the treatise on the study of literature which he dedicated to Battista Malatesta in the 1420s, quotes Virgil's famous lines on the animating spirit of creation at *Aeneid*, 6.724–31, before exclaiming *Quae cum legimus, quem philosophum non contemnimus? Aut quis umquam de natura animi tam enucleate scienterque locutus est?* ("When we read these things, what philosopher do we not hold cheap? Or who has ever spoken with such clarity and such knowledge on the nature of the soul?" *De studiis et litteris*, 22).[29] In this respect, it is surely significant that Cristoforo Landino, the

---

24 See especially W. Leonard Grant, *Neo-Latin Literature and the Pastoral* (Chapel Hill: University of North Carolina Press, 1965); also Marcial José Bayo, *Virgilio y la pastoral española del Renacimiento (1480–1550)*, 2nd ed. (Madrid: Gredos, 1970); Sukanta Chaudhuri, *Renaissance Pastoral and its English Developments* (Oxford: Clarendon Press, 1989); Nancy Lindheim, *The Virgilian Pastoral Tradition: From the Renaissance to the Modern Era* (Pittsburgh: Duquesne University Press, 2005).

25 On the fortunes of Virgil's *Georgics* during the Renaissance, see L. P. Wilkinson, *The Georgics of Virgil: A Critical Survey* (Cambridge: Cambridge University Press, 1969), 290–96; Wilson-Okamura, *Virgil in the Renaissance*, 83–85.

26 The composite fifteenth-century life of Virgil known as *Donatus auctus* (examined in this volume by Fabio Stok) includes the assertion *tandem omni cura omnique studio indulsit medicinae et mathematicis* ("finally he immersed himself with all diligence and all studiousness in medicine and mathematics [or "astronomy"]," chapter 7).

27 See Cristoforo Landino, *Disputationes Camaldulenses*, ed. Peter Lohe, Studi e Testi 6 (Florence: Sansoni, 1980), 117, quoted in translation by Wilson-Okamura, *Virgil in the Renaissance*, 94. The importance of Virgil for writers of history is displayed also in the frequency with which the poet is quoted in historiographical works such as Flavio Biondo's *Italia Illustrata*.

28 On Virgil as theologian, see especially Craig Kallendorf, "From Virgil to Vida: The *Poeta Theologus* in Italian Renaissance Commentary," *Journal of the History of Ideas* 56 (1995): 41–62.

29 Text from *Humanist Educational Treatises*, ed. Craig W. Kallendorf, I Tatti Renaissance Library 5 (Cambridge, MA and London: Harvard University Press, 2002), 114; see also Scaliger, *Poetices libri septem* 3.19 (Deitz 2:242—see below, note 39), *Nullis profecto philosophorum praeceptis aut melior aut civilior evadere potes quam ex Vergiliana lectione* ("Certainly you cannot come away either a better or a more civilized person through

author of one of the earliest Platonic dialogues of the Renaissance, *Disputationes Camaldulenses*—of which the third and fourth books are devoted to an allegorical exegesis of the first six books of the *Aeneid*—also produced influential commentaries on both Virgil's epic and Dante's *Commedia.* (Landino's reading of the *Aeneid* and its relationship with the Renaissance Neoplatonism of Marsilio Ficino are the subject of the essay here by Adam T. Foley.)

Landino's commentary on Dante brings together this varied array of specialisms attributed to the ancient author to assert the universal range of Virgil's interests and expertise. On *Inferno*, 7.3, where Dante's narrator refers to his guide as "quel savio gentil, che tutto seppe" ("that gentle sage, who knew all"), the Florentine commentator—who undoubtedly read the works of the classical poet through the lens of his characterization in Dante[30]—observes "gran lode di Virgilio degna di lui, imperoché che legge attentamente el suo poema vede quello essere refertissimo di tante et sí varie cose, che facilmente comprende lui essere stato universale in tutte le discipline degli antichi" ("great praise of Virgil, and worthy of him, insofar as whoever reads his poem carefully sees that it is absolutely packed with such great and so varied things, that he easily understands that he [Virgil] was universal in all branches of study belonging to the ancients").[31] Nor was Landino the first to conflate the prodigious intellect of Dante's Virgil with the all-encompassing wisdom traditionally ascribed to his Roman counterpart and to see the Italian poet's depiction of his learned predecessor as a representation of the multifarious knowledge contained in the latter's poetry. So the fourteenth-century commentator Guido da Pisa remarks on the narrator's description of Virgil at *Inferno*, 8.7 as "[i]l mar di tutto 'l senno" ("the sea of all wisdom"): *Magistrum suum mare totius sapientie autor appellat, quia, re vera, in omni mundana scientia profundissimus homo fuit* ("The author calls his master 'sea of all wisdom' because truly he was a man most profoundly versed in all earthly knowledge").[32] In all these cases, the medieval and Renaissance commentators on the later poem were merely following the lead of ancient literary criticism,

---

the teachings of philosophers than from a reading of Virgil"). The same passage from the *Aeneid* had been quoted (along with others from *Eclogues* and *Georgics*) by Boccaccio in his *Genealogia deorum gentilium* to illustrate Virgil's status as a philosopher: Ziolkowski and Putnam, *The Virgilian Tradition*, 466–67.

[30] See Kallendorf, *The Virgilian Tradition*, 1.144–46.

[31] Text from Cristoforo Landino, *Comento sopra la Comedia*, ed. Paolo Procaccioli, 4 vols. (Rome: Salerno Editrice, 2001), 2:490. See also Landino's comment on *Inferno*, 4.73 ("O tu ch'onori scïenzia ed arte": "O you who honor science and art"): "È adunque propia laude di tanto poeta, e poemi del quale son refertissimi d'ogni maniera di doctrina" ("It is therefore fitting praise of so great a poet, whose poems are absolutely packed with all manner of learning," Procaccioli 1:420).

[32] Text from Guido da Pisa, *Expositiones et Glose super Comediam Dantis, or Commentary on Dante's Inferno*, ed. Vincenzo Cioffari (Albany: State University of New York Press, 1974), 152.

which had detected an abundant erudition in the works of Virgil since at least the time of the late antique critics Servius, whose commentary on the sixth book of the *Aeneid* begins with the observation *Totus quidem Vergilius scientia plenus est, in qua hic liber possidet principatum* ("The whole of Virgil, indeed, is full of knowledge, in which this book holds first place"), and Macrobius, who called the poet *nullius disciplinae expers*, "not unacquainted with any branch of study," and *disciplinarum omnium peritissimus*, "most skilled in all branches of study."[33]

As heirs to this long-established critical discourse, for numerous Renaissance readers the Virgilian canon was in many respects a world in itself,[34] a reflection or embodiment of the wider universe. In lines from his *Manto*, a poetic introduction to a course of lectures on the *Eclogues* delivered at the Studium in Florence in 1482, Angelo Poliziano likens the wondrous variety of Virgil's eloquence to the boundless diversity of the natural world, in terms largely borrowed from the ancient poet's own formulations (*Manto*, 351–63):[35]

> Et quis, io, iuvenes, tanti miracula lustrans
> eloquii, non se immensos terraeque marisque
> prospectare putet tractus? Hic ubere largo
> luxuriant segetes, hic mollia gramina tondet
> armentum, hic lentis amicitur vitibus ulmus;
> illinc muscoso tollunt se robora trunco,
> hinc maria ampla patent, bibulis hoc squalet harenis
> litus, ab his gelidi decurrunt montibus amnes;
> huc vastae incumbunt rupes, hinc scrupea pandunt
> antra sinus, illinc valles cubuere reductae
> et discors pulchram facies ita temperat orbem.
> Sic varios sese in vultus facundia dives
> Induit. . . .

> And who, my young men, scanning the wonders of such great eloquence, would not think that he is surveying the limitless stretches of land and sea? Here crops abound in generous fertility, here the herd crops the soft

[33] See Ziolkowski and Putnam, *The Virgilian Tradition*, 463–65 (and 465–68 for later examples); Wilson-Okamura, *Virgil in the Renaissance*, 78–82, 99.

[34] For "Virgil as second nature" see Wilson-Okamura, *Virgil in the Renaissance*, 96–100 (as he notes, the comparison goes back to Macrobius, *Saturnalia*, 5.1.18–20); for the related notion of the Virgilian corpus as the embodiment of stylistic variety, see Wilson-Okamura, *Virgil in the Renaissance*, 93–96, and Perrine Galand-Hallyn, "Maître et victime de la «docte variété». L'exégèse virgilienne à la fin du Quattrocento," *Europe: Revue littéraire mensuelle* 765–766 (1993): 106–17.

[35] Text from Angelo Poliziano, *Silvae*, ed. and trans. Charles Fantazzi, I Tatti Renaissance Library 14 (Cambridge, MA and London: Harvard University Press, 2004), 26–28. For a catalogue of the Virgilian (and other) reminiscences in these lines, see Angelo Poliziano, *Silvae*, ed. Francesco Bausi (Florence: Olschki, 1996), 42–43.

> grasses, here the elm is clothed with pliant vines; on that side oak trees raise themselves with mossy trunk, on this side broad seas stretch out; this shore is rough with thirsty sands, from these mountains rush down chilly streams; in this direction vast crags overhang, on one side rocky caverns lay bare their folds, on the other recessed valleys sink down, and thus a discordant appearance regulates the world's beauty. Just so does rich eloquence put on different aspects. . . .

Even more expansively, Domenico di Bandino, in the *Life* of Virgil that appears in his encyclopedic compendium of knowledge from the late fourteenth-early fifteenth century, quotes as a testimony to the Roman poet's comprehensive learning a line, which he falsely attributes to *Ovidius in libro de remediis amorum* ("Ovid, in his book on the remedies for love"), stating that *omnia divino monstravit carmine vates* ("the bard revealed all things through his divine poetry").[36] The appositeness of this judgement to the subject of his biography is remarked by the compiler, who comments *Et vere laus ista Maroni competit, primo dicendo omnia, quia de caelestibus, terrestribus, visibilibus et invisibilibus scripsit* ("And truly that praise is fitting for Maro, through his speaking first of all of everything, since he wrote about things heavenly, earthly, visible, and invisible"). The reputation of Virgil as a conscious or unconscious prophet of Christianity, an exponent of Christian values and doctrines *avant la lettre*,[37] presumably goes some way towards explaining the obvious echo here of the words of the Nicene Creed (*factorem caeli et terrae, visibilium omnium et invisibilium*: "creator of heaven and earth, of all things visible and invisible"), which in turn justifies the epithet applied to his *divinum carmen* ("divine poetry")—although by this date the characterization of Virgil as *divinus poeta* was already firmly engrained in tradition.[38] With the scope of Virgil's writings equated with the infinite span of creation, there could be no ampler estimate of the cosmic compass of the poems' content.

Perhaps the fullest expression and most systematic manifestation of the conception of Virgil's poetry as a rival to or embodiment of nature is to be found in the *Poetices libri septem* of the Italian scholar Julius Caesar Scaliger, published posthumously in 1561,[39] in which the works of the Roman poet are used as an

---

36 Text in Ziolkowski and Putnam, *The Virgilian Tradition*, 305.

37 See above, note 3; also Pierre Courcelle, *Lecteurs païens et lecteurs chrétiens de l'Énéide*, 2 vols. (Paris: Institut de France, 1984–1989).

38 So, e.g., Dante, *Monarchia* 2.3, *divinus poeta noster Virgilius* ("Virgil, that divine poet of ours"); and see Ziolkowski and Putnam, *The Virgilian Tradition*, 467–68.

39 Quotations here are taken from Iulius Caesar Scaliger, *Poetices libri septem, Sieben Bücher über die Dichtkunst*, 6 vols., ed. Luc Deitz and Gregor Vogt-Spira (Stuttgart and Bad Cannstatt: Frommann and Holzboog, 1994–2011); in citations the first number refers to book and chapter numbers within the work, the second to volume and page numbers in Deitz's edition. On Scaliger's approach to Virgil, see Wilson-Okamura, *Virgil in the Renaissance*, index s.v. "Scaliger, Julius Caesar" (esp. 99–100, 129–33), and Vladimiro

exclusive quarry for examples of different literary techniques and as the ultimate model for the treatment of particular poetic subjects. The justifications given by Scaliger for this practice reveal the extent to which the view of Virgil's works as a universe in themselves still determined the way in which his poems were conceived in the mid-sixteenth century, and the enormous popularity attained by Scaliger's monumental treatise in the century and a half after its publication will have ensured that this attitude continued to enjoy currency well beyond the period with which we are concerned here. At times Scaliger can sound very much like the ancient commentators in his assessment of the Virgilian corpus as a treasure-house of universal wisdom (1.4; Deitz 1:112):[40]

> Vergilius propter vulgaria argumenta Silenum pinxit universa paene natura ac serie fatorum. . . . Sane veterum monumentorum praeter ceteros mortales scientissimum ubique divinum illum virum praedicavimus, atque ita verum est. Quo enim quis doctior est, eo maiorem in eius scriptis deprehendit eruditionem.

> Besides common subjects, Virgil depicted Silenus [in *Eclogue* 6] with almost the whole of nature and sequence of fate. . . . Certainly we have declared that divine man to be most knowledgeable everywhere, beyond all other mortals, in the monuments of antiquity, and such is the case; for the more learned someone is, the greater erudition he discovers in his [i.e., Virgil's] writings.

Elsewhere, the later critic goes beyond the parallel between nature and Virgil drawn by Macrobius and Poliziano in accounting for his choice of the classic poems as sole exemplar for illustrations of literary topics and motifs: not only is the ancient poet a match for nature herself (*is . . . non solum humana superavit ingenia, verum etiam sese quasi parem extulit naturae*, 6.1 [Deitz 5:44]: "he not only surpassed human genius, but even established himself, as it were, as nature's equal"), but the art of Virgil has reached such a pitch of perfection that his verses combine and crystallize in a concentrated form the diffuse and isolated qualities present in the natural world (3.24; Deitz 2:310).

> Hactenus rerum ideae, quemadmodum ex ipsa natura exciperentur, Vergilianis ostendimus exemplis. Ita enim eius poesi evenisse censeo sicut et picturis. Nam plastae et ii qui coloribus utuntur ex ipsis rebus capessunt notiones, quibus lineamenta, lucem, umbram, recessus imitentur. Quod

---

Zabughin, *Vergilio nel rinascimento italiano*, 2 vols. (Bologna: Zanichelli, 1921–1923; repr. Trento: Editrice Università degli studi di Trento, 2000), index s.v. "Scaligero Giulio Cesare" (esp. 2:14–19; "il culto dello Scaligero pel Mantovano si palesa sempre uguale, implacabile, fanatico," 2:16).

[40] For Virgil's *summa eruditio* see also 1.18 (Deitz 1:248).

> in quibusque praestantissimum inveniunt, e multis in unum opus suum transferunt, ita ut non a natura didicisse, sed cum ea certasse aut potius illi dare leges potuisse videantur . . . Itaque non ex ipsius naturae opere uno potuimus exempla capere, quae ex una Vergiliana idea mutuati sumus. Nunc reliquum est, ut tam divinas opes scite atque sapienter disponere conemur.
>
> Up to this point we have shown by means of examples from Virgil how the forms of things may be drawn from nature itself. For it is my view that things have turned out like this in his poetry just as they have in paintings. Sculptors and those who make use of colors take from actual things their impressions, by means of which they imitate outlines, light, shade, and background. What they find to be most outstanding in each thing, they transfer from many things to one work of their own, in such a way that they seem not to have learned from nature, but to have competed with her—or rather to have been able to give her laws. . . . And so we have not been able to take from any one work of nature herself the examples which we have borrowed from a single Virgilian form. Now it remains for us to attempt to deploy such divine resources with skill and understanding.

If the notion of art giving laws to nature seems somewhat reminiscent of Ovid (see *Metamorphoses*, 3.158–59, 11.235–36), it is to Virgil's successor that Scaliger, like Domenico di Bandino—but this time the quotation from Ovid is genuine—explicitly turns for his neatest articulation of the Virgil-as-nature topos. In view of the universal, even godlike, capacity we have seen imputed to the poet's corpus, it is perhaps no coincidence that the passage in question is one in which the subject is overtly cosmogonic: *Denique Homerus moles quidem, sed ut ait Ovidius rudis indigestaque, Vergilius autem eiusdem poetae deus et melior natura* (5.3 [Deitz, 4:142]: "Finally, Homer is indeed a mass, but, as Ovid says, 'rough and unordered' [*Met.*, 1.7]; whereas Virgil is the same poet's 'god and better nature' [*Met.*, 1.21]").

This emphasis on Virgilian versatility, on the poet as polymath, may help to explain, at least in part, how language, imagery, and narratives derived from the works of Rome's foremost literary figure came to permeate so many different aspects of Renaissance life and culture. One result of this is that the study of any one of the uses made of the poetry of Virgil during this period offers a valuable point of access to the world of the Renaissance itself. Without Virgil—or rather, the multiple versions of Virgil in circulation at the time—as our guide, it is impossible to trace adequately the contours of the landscape of learning and taste, of artistic and literary imagination, from which emerged so many of the most enduring achievements of western civilization.

There has probably never been a better time to attempt to chart the terrain of Virgil's fortunes during the period traditionally known as the Renaissance. Although the volume of the *Catalogus translationum et commentariorum* devoted to the poet's works has not yet appeared, the resources currently available to the student of this strand in European culture provide a solid and extensive foundation for pursuing research on the Renaissance reception of Virgil, his texts, and the mass of associated appendages that together constitute the Virgilian tradition. Craig Kallendorf has catalogued Renaissance Italian translations of Virgil's poetry, early printed editions of the poems, and editions of Virgil published in Venice in the fifteenth and sixteenth centuries,[41] and his three monographs on various aspects of Virgil's Renaissance *Nachleben* (now supplemented by *The Protean Virgil*) are essential reading for anyone working on the subject.[42] A number of Kallendorf's most influential essays have been collected in a volume entitled *The Virgilian Tradition*, published in Ashgate's Variorum series in 2007. An earlier census of Virgilian incunabula was produced by Martin Davies and John Goldfinch, while Mambelli's list of editions and translations remains useful, and sixteenth-century translations of the *Aeneid* have been surveyed by Luciana Borsetto.[43] Vladimiro Zabughin's classic study of the place occupied by Virgil in the scholarship, literature, art, and thought of the Italian Renaissance has been reprinted with helpful indices, and the recent overview by David Scott Wilson-Okamura, an attempt to do for Virgil's profile in the Renaissance what Domenico Comparetti famously did for the poet's afterlife in the Middle Ages, provides valuable orientation in the main areas of interpretation, although its focus is largely confined to literary criticism and adaptation and the commentary

[41] Craig Kallendorf, *A Bibliography of Renaissance Italian Translations of Virgil* (Florence: Olschki, 1994); idem, *A Bibliography of the Early Printed Editions of Virgil, 1469–1850* (New Castle, DE: Oak Knoll Press, 2012); idem, *A Bibliography of Venetian Editions of Virgil, 1470–1599* (Florence: Olschki, 1991).

[42] Craig Kallendorf, *In Praise of Aeneas: Virgil and Epideictic Rhetoric in the Early Italian Renaissance* (Hanover, NH and London: University Press of New England, 1989); idem, *Virgil and the Myth of Venice*; idem, *The Other Virgil: "Pessimistic" Readings of the Aeneid in Early Modern Culture* (Oxford: Oxford University Press, 2007); idem, *The Protean Virgil.* Unfortunately it was not possible to publish Kallendorf's opening address to the Mantua conference in this volume, to which it would have made an excellent introduction.

[43] *Vergil: A Census of Printed Editions 1469–1500*, ed. Martin Davies and John Goldfinch (London: Bibliographical Society, 1992); Giuliano Mambelli, *Gli annali delle edizioni virgiliane* (Florence: Olschki, 1954); Luciana Borsetto, *L'«Eneida» tradotta: riscritture poetiche del testo di Virgilio nel XVI secolo* (Milan: Edizioni Unicopli, 1989). Samples from a variety of English translations are available in *Virgil in English*, ed. K. W. Gransden (London: Penguin Books, 1996).

tradition.[44] If the mighty compendium of Ziolkowski and Putnam is fuller in its coverage of the earlier end of its chronological spectrum, it nonetheless includes a number of sources relevant to the period under discussion here, to say nothing of a wealth of material on responses to Virgil from earlier periods that furnish indispensable testimony on the background to the poet's Renaissance incarnations.[45]

New editions in the I Tatti Renaissance Library, published by Harvard University Press, offer convenient access to significant works by Latin writers of the period. For those interested in the appropriation and reworking of Virgilian material, the most relevant volumes issued so far are Charles Fantazzi's edition of Poliziano's *Silvae*, James Gardner's translations of Vida's *Christiad* and the poetry of Fracastoro, and Michael Putnam's translations of Vegio's short epics and the Latin poems of Sannazaro.[46] A collection of studies on the early Renaissance edited by Anthony L. Pellegrini features several contributions on Virgilian themes; a commemorative publication entitled *Vergil at 2000*, edited by John D. Bernard, boasts a handful of pieces on Renaissance subjects; and the volume on Virgil compiled by Craig Kallendorf for the series *The Classical Heritage* presents excerpts from some of the most important historical criticism on the poet's works.[47] The recent festschrift for Werner Suerbaum entitled *Vestigia Vergiliana* contains numerous items dealing with the Virgilian imprint on Renaissance literature;[48] and Suerbaum's own latest contribution to Virgilian scholarship (accompanied by a useful CD-ROM) guides the reader through illustrated editions of the poems from the early sixteenth to the mid-nineteenth century, complementing Bernadette Pasquier's analysis of Virgilian illustrations from the Renaissance onwards, and, most recently, the richly illustrated Italian catalogue *Virgilio: Volti e immagini del poeta*, edited by Vincenzo Farinella, from an

[44] Zabughin, *Vergilio nel rinascimento italiano*; Wilson-Okamura, *Virgil in the Renaissance*.

[45] Ziolkowski and Putnam, *The Virgilian Tradition*.

[46] Poliziano, *Silvae*, ed. and trans. Fantazzi; Marco Girolamo Vida, *Christiad*, trans. James Gardner, I Tatti Renaissance Library 39 (Cambridge, MA and London: Harvard University Press, 2009); Girolamo Fracastoro, *Latin Poetry*, trans. James Gardner, I Tatti Renaissance Library 57 (Cambridge, MA and London: Harvard University Press, 2013); Vegio, *Short Epics*, ed. and trans. Putnam with Hankins; Jacopo Sannazaro, *Latin Poetry*, trans. Michael C. J. Putnam, I Tatti Renaissance Library 38 (Cambridge, MA and London: Harvard University Press, 2009).

[47] *The Early Renaissance: Virgil and the Classical Tradition*, ed. Anthony L. Pellegrini (Binghamton, NY: The Center for Medieval and Early Renaissance Studies, 1984); *Vergil at 2000: Commemorative Essays on the Poet and his Influence*, ed. John D. Bernard (New York: AMS Press, 1986); *The Classical Heritage: Vergil*, ed. Craig Kallendorf (New York and London: Garland, 1993).

[48] *Vestigia Vergiliana: Vergil-Rezeption in der Neuzeit*, ed. Thorsten Burkard, Markus Schauer, and Claudia Wiener (Berlin and New York: De Gruyter, 2010).

exhibition of the same name held in the Palazzo Te in Mantua in 2011–2012.[49] Illustration, exegetical commentary, and literary adaptation all receive attention, with particular reference to the *Eclogues*, in Annabel Patterson's *Pastoral and Ideology*.[50]

On the Virgilian vein in particular national traditions and political contexts, a new collection of essays edited by Phillip John Usher and Isabelle Fernbach explores the uses made of *Eclogues*, *Georgics*, and *Aeneid* in Renaissance France, while Margaret Tudeau-Clayton's *Jonson, Shakespeare, and Early Modern Virgil* concentrates on the poet's fortunes in the English Renaissance, and Marie Tanner's *The Last Descendant of Aeneas* traces Virgilian threads in the court propaganda of the Holy Roman Empire.[51] The long and varied afterlife of one memorable episode from the *Aeneid* is revealed in Philip Hardie's magisterial survey of representations of *Fama*, beginning with Virgil's personification of the monstrous Rumor in the fourth book of his epic; the same scholar has recently completed a history of the countless transformations of the *Aeneid* in western culture, which naturally pays considerable attention to Renaissance engagements with this canonical text.[52] At the time of writing, *The Virgil Encyclopedia*, edited by Richard Thomas and Jan Ziolkowski, has recently joined the colossal six-volume *Enciclopedia Virgiliana*, which contains many articles of interest to students of the imitation and interpretation of Virgil's works in the Renaissance.[53]

---

[49] Werner Suerbaum, *Handbuch der illustrierten Vergil-Ausgaben 1502–1840* (Hildesheim, Zürich, and New York: Olms, 2008); Bernadette Pasquier, *Virgile illustré de la Renaissance à nos jours en France et en Italie* (Paris: Jean Touzot, 1992); *Virgilio: Volti e immagini del poeta*, ed. Farinella.

[50] Annabel Patterson, *Pastoral and Ideology: Virgil to Valéry* (Berkeley and Los Angeles: University of California Press, 1987), esp. 60–132.

[51] Usher and Fernbach, *Virgilian Identities* (see now also Phillip John Usher, *Epic Arts in Renaissance France* (Oxford: Oxford University Press, 2014)); Margaret Tudeau-Clayton, *Jonson, Shakespeare, and Early Modern Virgil* (Cambridge: Cambridge University Press, 1998); Marie Tanner, *The Last Descendant of Aeneas: The Hapsburgs and the Mythic Image of the Emperor* (New Haven and London: Yale University Press, 1993). For the Virgilian tradition in English literature, see also John Watkins, *The Specter of Dido: Spenser and Virgilian Epic* (New Haven and London: Yale University Press, 1995); Robin Sowerby, *The Classical Legacy in Renaissance Poetry* (London and New York: Longman, 1994), 29–57, 189–249; Christopher Baswell, *Virgil in Medieval England: Figuring the* Aeneid *from the Twelfth Century to Chaucer* (Cambridge: Cambridge University Press, 1995), 270–84.

[52] Philip Hardie, *Rumour and Renown: Representations of* Fama *in Western Literature* (Cambridge: Cambridge University Press, 2012); idem, *The Last Trojan Hero: A Cultural History of Virgil's* Aeneid (London: I. B. Tauris, 2014).

[53] *The Virgil Encyclopedia*, ed. Richard F. Thomas and Jan M. Ziolkowski, 3 vols. (Malden, MA, Oxford, and Chichester: Wiley-Blackwell, 2013); *Enciclopedia Virgiliana*, ed. Francesco Della Corte, 6 vols. (Rome: Istituto della Enciclopedia Italiana, 1984–1991).

Finally, among the rapidly proliferating ranks of handbooks, companions, and other reference works on the poems and their impact on later art and literature, Renaissance receptions of Virgil's epic are particularly prominent in *A Companion to Vergil's* Aeneid *and its Tradition*, edited by Joseph Farrell and Michael Putnam, the most recent of the current triad of companions to Virgil, following earlier forays into this territory from Brill and Cambridge.[54]

The profound and persistent diffusion of Virgilian elements in the intellectual, literate, and artistic spheres of the Renaissance means that a comprehensive account of the poet's place in the cultural life of the period is beyond the scope of a single volume, or even of many dozens of volumes. Each of the essays presented here seeks to contribute to the study of some aspect of that diffusion; together they touch on the key areas of rhetoric and education, court culture, the visual arts, music, philosophy, and Latin and vernacular literature, thereby offering a broader perspective, arguably, than any existing volume on the subject. It is hoped that, in the range and variety of their coverage, these studies will afford some impression of the expansive character of Renaissance Virgilianism and may point the way for future investigation of the part played by Virgil's poetry and the wider Virgilian tradition in the world of the humanists and their contemporaries, of other classical currents within Renaissance culture, and indeed of the reception of the Virgilian corpus in other times and places—for the story of Virgil's career in later ages (like the *Aeneid* itself, despite the best efforts of Maffeo Vegio and others) never really comes to an end.[55]

---

[54] *A Companion to Vergil's* Aeneid *and its Tradition*, ed. Joseph Farrell and Michael C. J. Putnam (Malden, MA, Oxford, and Chichester: Wiley-Blackwell, 2010); *A Companion to the Study of Virgil*, ed. Nicholas Horsfall, *Mnemosyne* supplementum 151 (Leiden: Brill, 1995; 2nd ed. 2000); *The Cambridge Companion to Virgil*, ed. Martindale.

[55] For the *Aeneid* as a text that "constantly works against its own closure," see Philip Hardie, *The Epic Successors of Virgil: A Study in the Dynamics of a Tradition* (Cambridge: Cambridge University Press, 1993), 2; also David Quint, *Epic and Empire: Politics and Generic Form from Virgil to Milton* (Princeton: Princeton University Press, 1993), 79, 82.

2

Virgil and Renaissance Rhetorical Theory

Peter Mack
University of Warwick

Rhetoric was one of the key preoccupations of Renaissance humanists, and Virgil was among their two or three favorite authors. In Renaissance schools the works of Virgil were a crucial element in the teaching of rhetoric. In this chapter I shall consider the ways in which reading and thinking about extracts from Virgil were used in teaching rhetoric and informed rhetorical theory in the Renaissance, especially in the work of Agricola, Erasmus, Melanchthon, and Ramus.

In the first place, much of Virgil's significance for Renaissance rhetoric is a consequence of the important place which his works occupied in the grammar school syllabus. The records of printing and the grammar school statutes indicate that Virgil's works, especially the *Eclogues* and the earlier books of the *Aeneid*, were required school texts throughout Europe.[1] When schoolteachers read the more advanced Latin texts with their pupils, they used those Latin texts to introduce and reinforce rhetorical teaching.

From the instructions given to teachers and from Renaissance commentaries we can conclude that when they read Virgil with their pupils, teachers were expected to point out the way in which the poet made use of rhetorical doctrines.[2] Teachers would have pointed out that particular passages showed Virgil using particular tropes or figures of speech. They would have indicated passages

---

[1] T. W. Baldwin, *William Shakspere's Small Latine and Lesse Greeke*, 2 vols. (Urbana: University of Illinois Press, 1944), 1:120–21, 124, 145, 168, 288, 291–92, 314, 343, 349, 355, 359–60, 425, 427; Craig Kallendorf, *A Bibliography of Early Printed Editions of Virgil, 1469–1850* (New Castle, DE: Oak Knoll Press, 2012), 1–36.

[2] William Lily, *Brevissima institutio* (London: R. Wolfe, 1573) STC 15616, sig. H5r–v; Erasmus, letter 56, in *Opus Epistolarum Erasmi*, ed. P. S. Allen, 12 vols., vol. 1 (Oxford: Clarendon Press, 1906), 171–73; Thomas Wolsey in John Colet, *Rudimenta grammatices* (London: Peter Treveris, 1529), STC 5542.3, sig. A4r–v; Peter Mack, *Elizabethan Rhetoric: Theory and Practice* (Cambridge: Cambridge University Press, 2002), 14–24.

where Virgil employed different types of amplification. In the sixteenth century many teachers would have pointed out passages in which Virgil was imitating Homer.[3] They would have discussed Virgil's characters as examples of particular virtues and vices and would have suggested ways in which figures like Aeneas, Dido, Drances, and Mezentius might be mentioned in pupils' own compositions. Reading Virgil was an important aspect of the way in which all pupils learned the craft of writing and obtained models of expression and ethical materials to reuse in their own writing.

Secondly, within the rhetoric manuals themselves quotations from Virgil appear most frequently in the treatment of style. Lists of the figures of speech and the tropes usually include many illustrative examples taken from Virgil. This pattern was established by Quintilian, who quotes Virgil more often than any author other than Cicero. For Quintilian Virgil was a principal model of elegant Latin style. Of the 157 quotations from Virgil which appear in the *Institutio oratoria*, 107 appear in Books 8 and 9, in which Quintilian discusses the tropes and the figures.[4] Almost all the references to Virgil in the first important rhetoric manual of the Renaissance, the *Rhetoricorum libri quinque* of 1433–1434, by George Trapezuntius of Crete, occur in the discussion of style in Book 5. George praises Virgil's composition of lines and sentences, commenting in some detail on his felicitous combinations of sounds and on his use of meter. Within his adaptation of Hermogenes's "Ideas" of style to Latin writing he includes many citations from Cicero and some from Virgil, particularly to illustrate grand and grave qualities of style.[5]

In Peter Schade's *Tabulae de schematibus et tropis* (1516; printed eighty-six times before 1590) the figures of speech are illustrated more often from Virgil than from any other author.[6] Virgil's status as a curriculum author made it appropriate that, where possible, rhetoric textbooks would provide examples from his texts. In this way the reading of Latin literature and the teaching of the figures of rhetoric in school reinforced each other. For the same reason we find many examples from Virgil in the rhetoric handbooks of Melanchthon, Susenbrotus, and Talon.[7] In the most frequently printed rhetoric textbooks of the sixteenth

[3] E.g., Virgil, *Opera* (London: Henry Middleton, 1580), STC 24789, sigs. C4r, D1r, G4r, I5r–8r, L1r–3r.

[4] Quintilian, *Institutio oratoria*, ed. M. Winterbottom (Oxford: Clarendon Press, 1970), 766–75.

[5] G. Trapezuntius, *Rhetoricorum libri V* (Paris: Chrétien Wechel, 1538; repr. Hildesheim: Olms, 2006), 480–89, 532, 583, 596.

[6] E.g., Petrus Mosellanus, *Tabulae de schematibus et tropis* (London: John Kingston, 1573), STC 21810.3, sigs. A3v–7v.

[7] E.g., P. Melanchthon, *Elementa rhetorices libri duo*, as at n.31 below, 476–78, 483, 490; J. Susenbrotus, *Epitome troporum ac schematum* (Zurich: Christoph Froschauer, n.d.), facsimile in J. X. Brennan, "The *Epitome Troporum* . . .: Text, Translation and

century numerous examples from Virgil were used to identify the tropes and figures and to show how they could be used effectively. This was the most important and ubiquitous use of Virgil in teaching rhetoric. As we have seen, it continued the approach that Quintilian established.

Thirdly, in strong contrast to this emphasis on style, examples from Virgil contribute to some of the important new doctrines of the most innovative rhetorical text of the Renaissance, Rudolph Agricola's *De inventione dialectica*, completed in 1479 and first printed in 1515. One of the key structuring features of Agricola's work is his proposal that all persuasive language can be considered to be either exposition or argumentation.[8] In exposition one sets out teaching a series of propositions or a narrative as clearly as possible in order to instruct someone who follows willingly. In argumentation one backs up a proposition so as to force an unwilling hearer to assent to it.[9] This distinction depends both on features of the language employed and on the speaker's response to the audience's likely reaction. In Book 2 chapter 16, Agricola explains the distinction between exposition and argumentation by comparing two passages from the start of Book 1 of the *Aeneid*. He contrasts the passage in which the poet sets out the reasons why Juno hates Aeneas (1.12–22) with Juno's soliloquy a little later in which she reminds herself of all the wrongs that have been done to her and encourages herself to cause trouble to Aeneas and his men (1.37–49). Agricola also shows how the former passage could be converted from exposition to argumentation by adding more connecting phrases.[10] In Virgil's text it is exposition because it takes it for granted that Juno hates Aeneas and explains why this should be the case; to become argumentation the same material could be cast into a slightly different form: the poet would aim to show that there was no doubt that Juno hated Aeneas because she loved Carthage, which Aeneas's offspring would destroy, and because in the Trojan war she had been on the side of the Greeks, and so on.

Basing his argument on Virgil rather than on examples from oratory has two important advantages for Agricola here. First it helps him to generalize the point. Rather than saying that all rhetorical orations have the characteristic of being either exposition or argument, he has wanted to claim from the begin-

Commentary," unpublished PhD diss., University of Illinois, 1953, sigs. A5r–7v, A8r, B1r–v, B4r–5r. Susenbrotus illustrates most of the figures with quotations from Virgil. Examples from Talon are listed below.

[8] Rudolph Agricola, *De inventione dialectica* (Cologne: Ioannes Gymnicus, 1539; repr. Nieuwkoop: De Graaf, 1967), 1–2.

[9] Agricola, *De inventione dialectica*, 2: "Expositionem voco orationem, quae solam dicentis mentem explicat, nullo, quo fides audienti fiat, adhibito. Argumentationem vero, orationem, qua quis rei de qua dicit, fidem facere conatur."

[10] Agricola, *De inventione dialectica*, 258–59.

ning of the book that this is a feature of language in general.[11] Citing poetry rather than oratory or philosophy helps him make this claim. The close relationship between the two passages prompts Agricola to a second perception, that although exposition and argumentation are the two possible categories, they are in fact closely related; the same material can be expressed in either form of discourse.[12]

Intense study of another passage from Virgil, Sinon's speech from Book 2, enables Agricola to develop this concept. Analyzing the way in which Sinon deceived the Trojans convinces Agricola of the persuasive power of exposition. In his view, the reason for the persuasive effectiveness of Sinon's speech is that Sinon makes no explicit arguments: rather he sets out a range of propositions and allows his hearers to make their own connections between the statements.

> Sinon, the character in Virgil, holds nothing in his words through which he can create belief in what he makes up about what happened to him and about the construction of the horse. From where then comes the belief in him?. . . Because everything is narrated in agreement with all these circumstances, the listener convinces himself that everything is so by gathering together and comparing the things and by their sequence and agreement, even though there is nothing in the address which proves that the truth is being told.[13]

According to Agricola, the Trojans convince themselves that Sinon is to be pitied and that the wooden horse should be brought within the city walls by drawing their own conclusions from the different statements Sinon makes, some of which are true, while others are close to the truth, and still others apparently unimportant. People are much more likely to believe conclusions that they reach themselves than conclusions that other people propose. If Sinon had made an argument his audience would have been led to question some of his propositions.[14] Later in the book Agricola further generalizes this conclusion, describing the technique of constructing expositions and explaining the importance of planting ideas in the exposition that audiences can think about for themselves.

---

[11] Agricola, *De inventione dialectica*, 2, 258. Peter Mack, *Renaissance Argument: Valla and Agricola in the Traditions of Rhetoric and Dialectic* (Leiden: Brill, 1993), 190–202.

[12] Agricola, *De inventione dialectica*, 259, 261–64, 296–306.

[13] Agricola, *De inventione dialectica*, 262: "Sinon ille Vergilianus nihil habet in verbis suis, quo fidem faciat eis, quae de casu suo, deque fabricatione equi confingit. Unde ergo fides illi venit? . . . Quia narrantur omnia consentanea istis, quanquam nihil sit in oratione, quo vera que dicuntur probentur, ipse tamen auditor collectione collationeque rerum, et earum inter se ordine et congruentia, sic esse sibi persuadet."

[14] Agricola, *De inventione dialectica*, 262–63. For a fuller discussion of this passage see Peter Mack, "Rudolph Agricola's Reading of Literature," *Journal of the Warburg and Courtauld Institutes* 48 (1985): 23–41, especially 31–33.

> Next, we must make an effort that the things which work in our favor give maximum support, and arguments must be uncovered and disclosed which constitute the heart of the matter, even if they are not connected with it at the time they are expressed. It will be through the reflection of the listener, who puts everything together in his mind, that they are the most advantageous to us, precisely because they do not give the impression of having been provided for that purpose.[15]

In this instance I would want to argue strongly that it was careful analysis of the passages in Virgil that led Agricola to a new theoretical understanding of how persuasion works, which in turn became a new contribution to rhetorical theory, namely, that exposition may sometimes be more effective than argumentation in persuasion, since listeners are less likely to doubt a conclusion that they have drawn themselves from the evidence provided. Agricola then elaborates and supports the perception reached through reading Virgil by analyzing examples taken from Cicero and other writers.

One of the key ideas in Agricola's discussion of the handling of emotion is his rejection of the position that argument and emotion are antithetical. In Book 2, chapter 2, he quotes Aristotle as stating that when one wants to move an audience, argumentation is redundant. While he agrees that syllogisms on their own will not be much use in arousing emotions, he then makes a distinction:

> But if we call argumentation everything by which we consider what is doubtful and uncertain, I would have thought that not only is it necessary for arousing emotions, but that it ought to be very dense and thickly packed. For force is necessary for the intellect to be seized and for the mind itself to be carried away as it were outside itself. This technique of argument is so much imitated by creative writers that if they are short of arguments, they pile on the same point, changing the words as if they were making several points. What else does Virgil express when Dido says in his work:
>
> Per ego has lachrymas, dextramque tuam te . . .
> Per connubia nostra, per inceptos Hymenaeos [*Aeneid* 4.314, 316]
>
> The right hand [*dextra*] and the marriage [*connubia*] and the nuptial rites [*Hymenaeos*] were the same thing: he means by these three things nothing other than the faith of married people. However, by repeating it in other words he has driven it home as if it were more than one thing.[16]

---

[15] Agricola, *De inventione dialectica*, 302: "Deinde quae prosunt, danda est opera, ut plurimum iuvent; et eruenda argumenta explicandaque, quae tum cum dicuntur, quamquam non cum summa rerum coniungantur, ut ipsam efficiant: ipsa tamen audientis cogitatione, colligentis apud animum suum, hoc ipso maxime prosunt tunc, quia minus in id parata videntur."

[16] Agricola, *De inventione dialectica*, 199: "Quod si omne id vocemus argumentationem, quo dubia incertaque colligimus, non modo opus ea esse ad affectus evocandos crediderim, sed crebriorem etiam densioremque esse oportere. Viribus enim opus est et

This is a crucial moment in Agricola's presentation of his material. It is very important to him to argue that the topics of invention are just as useful in gathering material for arousing emotions as they are in finding arguments. He justifies the argument with a quotation from Virgil. In fact the same point was implicit in his discussion of Juno's soliloquy: Juno uses arguments to work herself up into a state of emotion or of determination, in order to call down the storm on Aeneas. Having made the point, as a general point about language, through his analysis of Virgil, Agricola then provides a very detailed analysis of Cicero's use of arguments to arouse emotions at the end of *Pro Milone.*[17] Evidently Agricola analyzes passages from Cicero and Virgil in detail in order to justify his rhetorical theories to his audience. My argument is that it was the careful close reading of Virgil and Cicero and investigation of their practice that prompted Agricola to develop rhetorical theory in new ways.

Agricola followed Valla in insisting on the use of logic in everyday speech.[18] He went beyond him in using dramatic and poetic texts to explicate the topics of invention. His advocacy of a close connection between rhetoric and dialectic was to be of central importance to rhetorical thinking in the sixteenth century. Agricola's citation and analysis of quotations from Virgil was crucial to explaining these connections. Agricola cites Virgil in his discussion of five of the topics of invention: subject, place, time, comparisons, and similars.[19]

Within his discussion of argument Agricola cites eight quotations from the debates in the *Aeneid* in order to discuss the different ways in which arguments can be refuted, especially for cases in which the refutations involve attacking the person of the speaker or presenting the opponent's point as trivial.[20] These examples are not analyzed in detail, but they serve Agricola's polemical point of showing how the strategies of argument permeate many different types of text and that an understanding of dialectic is important to the interpretation of literary texts.

---

rapienda mens auferendusque ipse sibi animus et velut extra se ponendus. Imitantur hoc in eloquendo autores, ut si minus sint ipsis plura quae dicant, idem tamen mutatis subinde verbis velut plura ingerant. Quid aliud Virgilius expressit cum dicit apud eum Dido: Per ego has lachrymas, dextramque tuam te [4.314], Per connubia nostra, per inceptos Hymenaeos [316]. Idem erant dextra et connubium et Hymenaei. Non enim aliud quam fidem coniugii his tribus significat, repetendo tamen aliis verbis tanquam plura inculcavit."

[17] Agricola, *De inventione dialectica*, 200–1.

[18] Lorenzo Valla, *Repastinatio dialecticae et philosophiae*, ed. G. Zippel (Padua: Antenore, 1982), 329: "Dum ego ad consuetudinem eruditorum loquar, reprehendi non possum: quem si tu captionibus adorieris, leges loquendi ac mores, tanquam iura quaedam civilia apellabo." See Lodi Nauta, *In Defence of Common Sense* (Cambridge, MA: Harvard University Press, 2009).

[19] Agricola, *De inventione dialectica*, 75, 93–94, 99, 132–34, 146.

[20] Agricola, *De inventione dialectica*, 292–93.

One of Agricola's most fruitful innovations was his emphasis on *copia* and brevity as techniques for making an impression on an audience. In his discussion of *copia* he uses a quotation from Virgil as a starting point for showing how a compressed sentence could be elaborated by dwelling on many details implied but not stated. In the following chapter, on brevity, he cites Virgil seven times for examples of how ideas can be conveyed forcefully and pithily.[21]

Agricola quotes or cites Virgil sixty-three times, more often than any other author apart from Cicero. Because of Agricola's many quotations from the declamations formerly attributed to Quintilian, Quintilian is his third most cited author. But there is very little overlap between Agricola's use of Virgil and Quintilian's. Most of Agricola's quotations are taken from the *Aeneid*, mainly from Books 1, 2, and 4, which he quotes nine, nineteen, and ten times respectively. There are five quotations from Book 10, but only one each from the *Eclogues* and the *Georgics*.[22] Agricola also cites other Latin poets, especially Lucan and Terence, and the Roman historians. Many but not all of Agricola's most important innovations are associated with places in which he quotes and analyzes Virgil.

Fourthly, reading Virgil plays an important role in Erasmus's discussion of the copious style in what was unquestionably the most successful new rhetoric textbook of the Renaissance, Erasmus's *De duplici copia rerum ac verborum*, which was printed 168 times between 1512 and 1578. When Erasmus explains his reasons for teaching students to write copiously, he claims that the leading writers of antiquity practiced in order to achieve *copia* of style. The first example he gives is Virgil:

> We have a number of marvelous passages where Virgil tried his skill: descriptions of a mirror, a frozen river, a rainbow, a sunrise, the four seasons, the constellations.[23]

In the next chapter, in which he explains the delight which great writers took in demonstrating their powers of expression, he gives examples from Virgil only:

> What could be more concisely expressed than his phrase *campos ubi Troia fuit* ["the plains where Troy once stood," *Aeneid* 3.11]? As Macrobius says, in a very few words he has here consumed and swallowed up the city with-

[21] Agricola, *De inventione dialectica*, 408–10.

[22] Agricola, *De inventione dialectica*, ed. Lothar Mundt (Tübingen: Niemeyer, 1992), 750.

[23] Erasmus, *De copia*, ed. B. Knott, *Opera omnia*, I.6 (Amsterdam: North Holland Publishing Co., 1988), 28: "Siquidem extant etiamnum mirabiles aliquot Maronis experientiae de speculo, de fluvio gelu concreto, de Iride, de solis exortu, de quatuor anni partibus, de signis coelestibus." Translation by B. Knott, *Collected Works of Erasmus*, vol. 24 (Toronto: University of Toronto Press, 1978), 297. *Aeneid*, 8.22–24; *Georgics*, 3.360; *Aeneid*, 4.700–2; *Georgics*, 1.441–46, 2.315, 514, 3.354, 1.231. These references are from Knott's notes.

> out even allowing the ruins to remain. Now listen to the fullness of expression in the following passage:
>
> Venit summa dies et ineluctabile tempus
> Dardaniae. Fuimus Troes, fuit Ilium et ingens
> Gloria Teucrorum; ferus omnia Iuppiter Argos
> Transtulit; incensa Danai dominantur in urbe. [2.324–27][24]

And then he adds four lines from two passages elsewhere in Book 2 (2.241–42, 361–62) before commenting:

> What fountain, what torrent, what sea so swelled with waters as he with words?[25]

And then he adds another example, created by conflating two passages:

> Superatne et vescitur aura
> Aetheria, nec adhuc crudelibus occubat umbris.[26]

The last eight words of this quotation (*vescitur aura | Aetheria, nec adhuc crudelibus occubat umbris*) come from Book 1, lines 546–47, and are spoken by Ilioneus about Aeneas; the first four words (*Superatne et vescitur aura*) come from Book 3, line 339, and are from Aeneas's narration of Andromache's words questioning him about his son Ascanius. I suppose that the two words shared by both passages, *vescitur aura*, in some sense explain the conflation, but it is striking that while Virgil is Erasmus's model for the ability to write the copious style, he nevertheless feels the need to make Virgil's text more impressively copious by conflating different passages.

In Book 1 of *De copia*, on *copia* of words, Erasmus quotes Virgil fairly often in exemplifying the twenty techniques he describes. He includes quotations from Virgil among his examples of: variations of word form, apostrophe, antonomasia, metaphor, metonymy, synecdoche, hyperbole, meiosis, and methods of connecting sentences.[27] These uses of Virgil are strictly parallel to the widespread citation of Virgil in accounts of the tropes and figures that we have noted above. Virgil is also quoted in some of the examples of model phrases for different ideas in the second and longer part of Book 1, alongside frequent quotations from Terence,

---

[24] Erasmus, *De copia*, 28: "A quo quid brevius dici potuit quam illud: 'Et campos ubi Troia fuit'? [*Aeneid* 3.11] Paucissimis verbis, ut ait Macrobius, civitatem hausit et absorpsit, ne ruina quidem relicta. Rursum hoc ipsum audi quam copiose [quotes *Aeneid* 2.324–27]."

[25] Erasmus, *De copia*, 30: "Quis fons, quis torrens, quod mare tot fluctibus, quot hic verbis inundavit?"

[26] Erasmus, *De copia*, 30.

[27] Erasmus, *De copia*, 53, 56, 60, 63–64, 68, 70, 74, 76.

Horace, Ovid, Juvenal, Cicero, and Erasmus's own collection of proverbs, the *Adagia*.[28] In these cases I think we should say that Virgil is used as one of the key examples of Latin usage alongside the other grammar school curriculum authors.

When it comes to *copia* of things, in the second book, Erasmus does not refer to Virgil when he discusses the logical techniques for discovering more material to include. But few other literary texts are referred to there. Virgil comes into his own in method 5, descriptions, where he is mentioned for his descriptions of storms, shipwrecks, horses, oxen, bees, great Romans in Hades, the shield of Aeneas, and the personification of Rumor. Much the longest quotation in this whole section is Virgil's description of the night from *Aeneid*, 4.522–28.[29] Erasmus does not attempt to analyze the ways in which Virgil achieves his descriptions, but rather offers him as a well-known example of excellence in the many different types of description that pupils would do well to study. Erasmus also cites Virgil under method 6, digression; method 7, descriptive phrases; and in his discussion of different ways of using examples for the sake of persuasion, mentioning the golden bough, Virgil's use of historical figures in fiction, and school pupils' use of people or personifications described by Virgil as examples of virtues and vices in their own compositions.[30] Here I think that Virgil stands for the material that literature and poetry can provide for the pupil to use to make his own writing more impressive.

Virgil is certainly a continuing presence in *De copia*, as an example of effective writing to be imitated and in providing material for the pupil to use. It is possible that part of the inspiration for writing the whole book came from the example of Virgil, though the technical basis for the work probably derives more from Quintilian, the amplification practiced by the authors of the medieval *artes poetriae*, and Agricola's ideas about *copia* and brevity.

Fifthly, Melanchthon's 1525 commentary on Cicero's *De oratore* (2.41.176) shows the German humanist responding to Cicero's observation (at the end of his account of the topics) on the orator's need to master self-presentation and the arousal of emotions as well as the topics. Melanchthon's comment develops some ideas about the relationship between topics and emotions on the basis of his reading in Quintilian and Virgil:

> The method of handling emotions is largely taken from the topics of deliberative oratory—that is, from the honorable and the useful. For we love honorable and useful things and we hold in hatred and flee from disgraceful and harmful ones. But this same argument of rational and useful things

---

[28] E.g., Erasmus, *De copia*, 90, 112, 113, 115, 119, 121. The examples in these notes are taken from Knott's index, p. 314, which also gives other examples.

[29] Erasmus, *De copia*, 204, 206, 212, 214. *Aeneid*, 1.81; *Georgics*, 3.72, 3.51, 4; *Aeneid*, 4.173, 6.756, 8.626. These references are taken from Knott's notes.

[30] Erasmus, *De copia*, 216, 236, 238.

> needs to be clothed with circumstantial details, in which pictures, which rush into our eyes, and as Quintilian says, carry force to the eyes, have great effect. For example this passage from Virgil on the slaughter of Priam:
>
> He dragged him quivering to that same altar,
> Slipping in the pool of blood of his child. [*Aeneid*, 2.550–51]
>
> Here each individual word has an associated emotion. First he amplifies the savageness of the killing because it happened "at the altar," after the pathos invades the eyes with "quivering." Likewise "he dragged," likewise "falling" and rolling about "in blood," but the most appalling of all is that he rolls about in the blood "of his child." In this way he held back the highest point of emotion for the last place.[31]

Melanchthon here combines a new idea about the theory of arousing emotion with a close analysis of the impact of Virgil's word order on his audience. Thinking about what Cicero says leads him to want to add to it, with support from Quintilian and through his own close reading of Virgil. He gives his readers an example of how reading a major rhetorical text and reflecting on a well-known passage of poetry prompts him to refine his ideas about how language evokes emotion.

In his 1531 *Elementa rhetorices libri duo* Melanchthon develops this idea into a brief, somewhat Agricolan account of emotion. The emotions will be derived from the topics of things to be wished for and avoided in the deliberative genre: the honorable and the disgraceful, the useful and the useless. For the gentler emotions associated with ethos he gives the example of Aeneas's love for Ascanius from *Aeneid*, 1.646. For the stronger emotions, after discussing Livy's account of Pleminius, he cites the example of Mezentius lamenting the death of his son Lausus and seeking death himself at the end of *Aeneid* Book 10.[32] Reading Virgil evidently made an important contribution to Melanchthon's ideas about arousing emotions.

---

[31] Philip Melanchthon, *Scholia in Ciceronis De Oratore*, in Melanchthon, *Opera*, ed. C. G. Bretschneider and H. E. Bindsell, *Corpus Reformatorum* [hereafter *CR*], 16 (Halle: Schwetschke, 1850), 734: "Ratio tractandorum affectuum magna ex parte sumitur ex locis generis deliberativi, scilicet ex honesto et utili. Honesta enim et utilia amamus, turpia et damnosa odio habemus ac fugimus. Sed haec ipsa ratio honestorum utilium vestienda est circumstantiis, in quibus plurimum valent picturae, quae incurrunt in oculos, et ut Fabius ait, vim oculis afferunt: quale est Virgilii de caede Priami. Altaria ad ipsa trementem | Traxit et in multo lapsantem sanguine gnati. Hic enim in singulis verbis singuli affectus sunt. Primum auget atrocitatem caedis, quod ad aras fit. Postea πάθος est in oculos incurrens, Trementem. Item Traxit, item Lapsantem ac volutantem in sanguine, sed atrocissimum est, quod in gnati sanguine volutatur. Itaque quod summum erat, in postremum locum distulit."

[32] Philip Melanchthon, *Elementa rhetorices libri duo*, *CR*, 13 (Halle: Schwetschke, 1846), 454–55.

Sixthly, Virgil's place within Ramism can be stated quite briefly. Virgil was one of the authors whom Ramus read with his pupils. His aim in making his treatises on logic and Talon's treatise on rhetoric so brief was to move rapidly from the reading of theories about writing to studying how writers, especially Cicero and Virgil, used the techniques of rhetoric and logic in their writing. In their purest form the manuals of Ramus and Talon consist of concise definitions, subdivisions of each subject, and examples taken from literature to illustrate the meaning of a particular topic of invention and its use in the best authors.[33] In Ramus's accounts of the topics of invention and in Talon's discussion of the tropes and figures, their preference is to give examples from prose and poetry: the prose examples usually come from Cicero, though sometimes they are taken from the historians; the poetic quotations are usually taken from Virgil, though there are also examples from Ovid, Horace, and Catullus.[34] Ramus does not use examples from Virgil in his accounts of the proposition or the syllogism, but he does discuss the third book of the *Georgics* as an example of methodical organization.[35] It was important to Ramus to show that his doctrines could be exemplified from Virgil, and using examples from Virgil made a bridge between the textbooks and the classical texts which he expected his pupils to read better because they knew the elements of rhetorical theory. Ramus's commentaries on the *Eclogues* and the *Georgics* illustrate his appreciation of Virgil's knowledge, thought, and expression,[36] but the examples which Ramus uses in his textbooks very much illustrate doctrines that Ramus had developed independently of his reading of Virgil by simplifying the teaching of the manuals of rhetoric and logic; if a different poet had been at the center of sixteenth-century education, Ramus would have illustrated his textbooks from that author.

Finally, and even more briefly, the issue of imitation. In the mid sixteenth century, among those who most strongly promoted the teaching of Greek, Virgil became an important figure in the debate about imitation. Where earlier phases of the argument had centered on whether Cicero should be the sole model of Latin prose that students should follow, Johann Sturm and his followers insisted that Cicero had imitated Demosthenes, and more particularly that Virgil had imitated Homer in his epic and Theocritus and other Greek poets in the eclogues. For followers of Sturm, like Roger Ascham, this process

---

[33] Peter Mack, *A History of Renaissance Rhetoric, 1380–1620* (Oxford: Oxford University Press, 2011), 136–55.

[34] E.g., Ramus, *Dialecticae libri duo* (London: Thomas Vautrollier, 1576), STC 15242, sigs. A8v, B1v, B4r, B8v, C1r, C2r–v; Omer Talon, *Rhetorica* (Lyons: Thibaud Payen, 1557), sigs. A4r, A4v, A5v, A6v, A7r, A7v.

[35] Ramus, *Dialecticae libri duo*, sigs. I7v–8v.

[36] Peter Mack, "Ramus Reading: The Commentaries on Cicero's *Consular Orations* and Vergil's *Eclogues* and *Georgics*," *Journal of the Warburg and Courtauld Institutes* 61 (1991): 111–41.

of imitation both established the principal canon of their schools centered on these four authors, two Greek (Homer and Demosthenes) and two Latin (Virgil and Cicero), and suggested a program of writing instruction based on studying the ways in which the Roman authors had copied and altered their great Greek originals.[37] This approach seemed to offer a model for the way in which vernacular writers could enhance their native literature through creative imitation of classical authors. Following Macrobius, mid-sixteenth-century commentaries on Virgil identify and sometimes print the Greek sources that Virgil was copying at particular moments. This study of imitation led to a strong focus on the effect of the particular words that Virgil had chosen and on the ways in which he had altered the model he was copying.

Since Renaissance schools and scholars generally regarded Virgil as the most important Latin poet, and since rhetoric wished to extend its reach beyond the three genres of oratory to writing and literature in general, it is unsurprising that Renaissance teachers should have made so much use of Virgil's works to exemplify the practical use of rhetorical techniques. As we have seen, Renaissance rhetoric manuals mostly used Virgil as an example of fine style and to illustrate the tropes and figures. But I have also argued that reading Virgil was an important stimulus to the innovators in Renaissance rhetoric, above all to Rudolph Agricola, but also to Erasmus and Melanchthon. Reading and analyzing Virgil made a significant contribution to several of the major innovations of Renaissance rhetorical theory, especially in relation to the arousal of emotions, to the theory of persuasion, to *copia* and brevity, to ideas about description and exemplification, and in relation to imitation.

[37] Roger Ascham, *The Scholemaster*, in *English Works*, ed. W. A. Wright (Cambridge: Cambridge University Press, 1904), 264–68, 271–76.

3

Virgil in the Renaissance Court

Fabio Stok
Università di Roma Tor Vergata, Rome

The biography of Virgil that has had the largest diffusion since the Renaissance is the so-called "Donatus auctus" (hereafter DA),[1] an enhanced and interpolated version of the "Life of Virgil" compiled in the fourth century by the grammarian Aelius Donatus.[2] The diffusion of the DA is confirmed by at least forty manuscripts copied in the fifteenth century[3] and by several editions printed from 1471 until the nineteenth century. The first printed version is that included in the edition of Servius's commentary on Virgil published in Venice by Battista Guarini. Afterwards the DA was printed mostly in editions of Virgil, until those published by Heyne.[4]

In the manuscripts the DA is generally anonymous. In one late branch of the manuscript tradition there is an attribution to Servius, in another to Aelius Donatus; some copyists are undecided about the two possibilities. The rediscovery of the *Interpretationes Vergilianae* by Tiberius Claudius Donatus (fl. 430s) in the last decades of the fifteenth century suggested to Giano Parrasio in 1505 the

---

[1] I published a critical edition of DA in *Vitae Vergilianae antiquae*, ed. Georgius Brugnoli and Fabius Stok (Rome: Officina Polygraphica, 1997), 71–135. The Latin text and English translation are in *The Virgilian Tradition: The First Fifteen Hundred Years*, ed. Jan M. Ziolkowski and Michael C. J. Putnam (New Haven and London: Yale University Press, 2008), 345–69.

[2] On the Donatian *Life*, largely reproducing that written by Suetonius at the beginning of the second century, see Fabio Stok, "The Life of Vergil before Donatus," in *A Companion to Vergil's* Aeneid *and its Tradition*, ed. Joseph Farrell and Michael C. J. Putnam (Malden, MA and London: Wiley-Blackwell, 2010), 107–20.

[3] Manuscripts are listed in Fabio Stok, *Prolegomeni a una nuova edizione della* Vita Vergilii *di Svetonio-Donato* (Rome: Accademia Nazionale dei Lincei, 1991), 141–56.

[4] Christian Gottlieb Heyne, *Publius Vergilius Maro varietate lectionum et perpetua adnotatione illustratus*, editio quarta cur. G. Ph. E. Wagner (Leipzig and London: Libraria Hahniana—Black, Young & Young, 1830), LXXXI–CVI.

attribution of the DA to this commentator.[5] This attribution was retained by most of the subsequent printed editions.

The original version of the Donatian *Life*, without the additions of the DA, was printed only in 1600 by Pierre Daniel.[6] The *Life* was rediscovered at the end of the fourteenth century and had a large manuscript diffusion in the first half of the fifteenth.[7] It was later eclipsed by the DA.

After the edition of Daniel the Donatian *Life* was soon considered more ancient than the DA. Heyne was aware that the *Life* published by Daniel was written by Aelius Donatus; however, although he published the DA under the name of Tiberius Donatus, he considered the DA the result of interpolations accumulated during the Middle Ages.[8] This hypothesis was later abandoned, the prevailing opinion being that the DA must have been written by a compiler at the beginning of the fifteenth century.[9] Sabbadini observed that the DA had been used by Sicco Polenton in the biography of Virgil included in his *De scriptoribus illustribus Latinae linguae* (1437),[10] thus setting the *terminus ante quem* of its composition (Sabbadini also stated that he had an idea about the author of the DA, but he did not give his name, as he first wanted to verify his own hypothesis.[11]) I stated, years ago,[12] that since the DA uses the first redaction of Polenton's Virgilian biography, written in 1426,[13] it must have been compiled between 1426 and 1437.

It is possible to advance one step further by considering the manuscript tradition of the DA. One of the two oldest dated manuscripts is the Lat. Class. 61 of Oxford's Bodleian Library; it is a Virgilian manuscript copied in 1439 in the town of Rovigo by Leoninus Brembatus. Brembatus was a scholar of Guarino of Verona; in that year scholar and master had gone to Rovigo to escape from the

---

[5] See Aulo Giano Parrasio, *De rebus per epistolam quaesitis (Vat. Lat. 5233, ff. 1r–53r)*, ed. Luigi Ferreri (Rome: Edizioni di Storia e Letteratura, 2012), 47–48.

[6] In the edition of Servius printed in Paris *apud S. Nivellium* (it is also the first edition of the so-called "Servius Danielis").

[7] See Stok, *Prolegomeni*, 19–28.

[8] Heyne, *Publius Vergilius*, LXXXI–LXXXII. The idea that the DA was the result of several interpolations was also adopted by Domenico Comparetti, *Vergil in the Middle Ages* (London: S. Sonnenschein & Company, 1895), 140.

[9] C. Suetonius Tranquillus, *Praeter Caesarum libros reliquiae*, ed. August Reifferscheid (Leipzig: Teubner, 1860), 401; Remigio Sabbadini, "Le biografie di Virgilio antiche medievali umanistiche," *Studi Italiani di Filologia Classica* 15 (1907): 260–61.

[10] *Sicconis Polentoni Scriptorum illustrium Latinae linguae*, ed. B. L. Ullman (Rome: American Academy in Rome, 1928), 73–90.

[11] Sabbadini, "Le biografie," 261.

[12] Stok, *Prolegomeni*, 197–200.

[13] The first edition of the work of Polenton is available in MS 121 of the Biblioteca Riccardiana in Florence; for the text of the Virgilian biography, see Ziolkowski and Putnam, *The Virgilian Tradition*, 321–45.

plague that had struck Ferrara.[14] In the same months Brembatus also worked on another manuscript, containing Guarino's works and Cicero's *De legibus.*[15] The text of the DA was therefore copied under the supervision of Guarino. This copy is very close to the archetype and also the most correct of all the manuscript copies of DA.[16]

The other oldest dated manuscript was also copied in Ferrara in November 1438: it is MS Aedil. 168 of the Laurentian Library in Florence. It was brought to Florence, where it was used in 1464 by Pier Cennini[17] (another copy of it was made for the king of Hungary, Matthias Corvinus[18]). Other manuscripts of DA were also copied in Ferrara,[19] and from their family derives the copy used for the *editio princeps* by Battista Guarini, the son of Guarino of Verona.

The manuscript tradition suggests, therefore, that the diffusion of DA spread from Ferrara, where Guarino of Verona had settled since 1429 as the tutor of Leonello d'Este, the son of the Marquis Niccolò III, and then as a teacher in the studium of Ferrara. It seems therefore very probable that the compiler of the DA was Guarino himself or a member of his circle. The use of the first version of Polenton's Virgilian biography is not surprising, because in the preceding years Guarino had lived in Venice and Verona and was in correspondence with Sicco Polenton, who lived in Padua, near Venice.

It is very probable that the copy of the Donatian *Life* used by the compiler was anonymous: it was not in fact a recent copy of this text, like the copies which were at that time in circulation, but an exemplar of another textual family, of which there remain only a few medieval manuscripts copied in Germany, a family in which the *Life* is anonymous.[20] The compiler seems therefore to have acquired a medieval copy and amplified it with new additions. He was perhaps aware of the more recent tradition of the Donatian *Life*, which he also seems to use, but only for a few details: generally, he used only the medieval copy, from which he reproduces some omissions that would have been possible to fill in with the help of the other textual tradition.[21] It is possible that the compiler ignored the attribution of the *Life* to Donatus. Not all *recentiores*—that is, the fifteenth-century manuscript copies of the *Life*—give this attribution. Sicco Polenton, who used a recent copy

14 See Remigio Sabbadini, *Epistolario di Guarino Veronese*, 3 vols. (Venice: R. Deputazione di Storia Patria, 1915–1919; repr. Turin: Bottega d'Erasmo, 1959), 3:360–61.

15 Brescia, Bibl. Queriniana, A VII 1.

16 Stok, *Prolegomeni*, 189–90.

17 For the MS Florence, BN, Magl. XXVIII 51.

18 Milan, Bibl. Trivulziana, 817.

19 Wolfenbüttel Helmst. 338 (1460–1461); Vatican Barb. Lat. 43 (1466); Paris BNF Lat. 7965 (1469).

20 The manuscripts of Sankt Gallen 862 (C10th) and Oxford Bodl. Laud. Lat. 117 (C11th). Only in the Vatican lat. 1575 (C12th) is the *Life* attributed to Donatus.

21 Stok, *Prolegomeni*, 195 and 30.

of the *Life* for the first version of his biography of Virgil, seems to attribute the *Life* to Servius.[22] It seems therefore likely that the compiler of the DA found an anonymous copy of the *Life* and produced an enlarged version, likewise anonymous, but adapted to his own vision of Virgil's life.

However, the DA was soon attributed to Donatus. This attribution had been made already by Sicco Polenton in 1437 for the final version of his biography of Virgil.[23] We do not know what Polenton knew about the DA or its origin, but he seemed to consider it the original version of the Donatian *Life* (it should be remembered that he also knew the authentic Donatian *Life*, which he was perhaps still attributing to Servius). Lorenzo Valla, some years later, also attributed the DA to Donatus and criticized some aspects of its language,[24] wondering that such a renowned grammarian could write so badly.

The additions inserted by the compiler in the Donatian Life reflect the cultural interests of Guarino and his circle.

Several of the additions present Virgil as a political advisor of Augustus. The poet is represented twice in political interviews with the emperor. In the first passage Augustus asks Virgil by what arrangement the state is to be governed:

> Interroganti Augusto, quo pacto civitas feliciter gubernaretur, "si prudentiores—inquit—temonem tenuerint et boni malis praeponantur itaque optimi suos habeant honores, nulli tamen aliorum iniusti quicquam fiat." (113.6–10 S.)

> When Augustus asked him by what arrangement the civic state was most felicitously to be governed, he said: "If the most foresighted control the axle and the good are preferred to the wicked, then the best should hold the post of honor, but nothing unjust would happen to anyone of the other sort."[25]

It is a statement that is reminiscent of some political considerations by Isocrates, one of the Greek authors greatly admired by Guarino. The sentence echoes particularly the oration *Ad Nicoclem*, where we read that the king would be a good, popular leader if he would "neither permit the multitude to commit outrages nor allow them to suffer them, but contrive that, while the best men take the honors, the rest

---

[22] Stok, *Prolegomeni*, 81.

[23] Stok, *Prolegomeni*, 200.

[24] Elisabet Sandström, ed., *Laurentius Valla: De reciprocatione 'sui' et 'suus'* (Göteborg: Acta Universitatis Gothoburgensis, 1998), 40–43.

[25] Trans. by Philip Larratt-Smith in Ziolkowski and Putnam, *The Virgilian Tradition*, 256–69.

shall suffer no wrong" (§16, trans. by J. H. Freese). Guarino in 1431 recommended Leonello to read this oration, translated a year before by Bernardo Giustiniani[26] (and dedicated to Ludovico Gonzaga, the son of the marquis of Mantua). The oration was then translated in 1442 by the same Guarino.[27] Isocrates was a supporter of the monarchy: in another work, the *Panathenaicus*, Isocrates writes that monarchy is justified if the king who governs "preserves what is good and avoids what is disastrous" (§138), and if he is among "the wisest and the best" (§143).

The political view attributed to Virgil also becomes clearer in the second passage, in which the interlocutors of Virgil are Augustus, Maecenas, and Agrippa:[28]

> Posteaquam Augustus summa rerum omnium potitus est, venit sibi in mentem an conduceret tirannidem omittere et omnem potestatem annuis consulibus et senatui rempublicam reddere. In qua re diversae sententiae consultos habuit Maecenatem et Agrippam. Agrippa enim utile sibi fore, etiamsi honestum non esset, relinquere tirannidem longa oratione contendit, quod Maecenas dehortari magnopere conabatur. Quare Augusti animus et hinc ferebatur et illinc, erant enim diversae sententiae variis rationibus firmatae. Rogavit igitur Maronem, an conferat privato homini, se in sua republica tirannum facere. "Omnibus ferme—inquit—rempublicam occupantibus molesta ipsa tirannis fuit et civibus, quia necesse erat propter odia subditorum aut eorum iniustitiam magna suspicione magnoque timore vivere. Sed si cives iustum aliquem scirent, quem amarent plurimum, civitati id utile foret, si in eo uno omnis potestas esset. Quare si iustitiam, quod modo facis, omnibus in futurum nulla hominum facta compositione distribues, dominari te et tibi conducet et orbi. Benivolentiam enim ita omnium habes, ut deum te et adorent et credant." Eius sententiam secutus, Caesar principatum tenuit. (117.8–119.7 S.)

> After Augustus had attained supreme command of the entire world, the question came to his mind whether it would be of use to give up autocracy and to restore full power to the one-year consuls and the Republic to the Senate. In this matter he had Maecenas and Agrippa resolved on different opinions. For in a lengthy oration Agrippa had argued that it would be useful to him, even if it were not entirely honorable, to give up the dictatorship; but Maecenas tried to dissuade him from this with all his strength. Consequently, the mind of Augustus was tugged now this way, now that. For the divergent opinions had been backed up with vari-

[26] Sabbadini, *Epistolario*, 1:133–34.

[27] Sabbadini, *Epistolario*, 2:420–22.

[28] Maecenas is also understood to be present in the first dialogue: after Virgil's answer he in turn asks him how one can preserve his high and happy fortune. He replies in line with the other political statements: *si, quantum honore ac divitiis aliis praestantior sis, tanto liberalitate et iustitia alios superare nitaris* ("If you strive to exceed others as much in generosity and justice as you excel others in honor and wealth," 114.3–6 S.).

> ous reasons. He therefore asked Maro whether it was suitable for him, a private citizen, to make himself dictator in his republic. He answered, "For almost everyone who took hold of the republic and for the citizens tyranny itself was harmful, because it was necessary to live in great suspicion and great fear, on account of the hate of those subjected and the injustice they suffered. But if the citizens knew some just man, whom they loved deeply, it would be in the best interest of the civic body if all power were concentrated in that one person. Consequently, if you apportion in the future (as you do now) justice to everyone without causing any strife to be made between people, your sole domination will be useful to both you and the world. For you so have the goodwill of all that they both love you like a god and believe you are a god." Caesar followed his advice and took the principate. (trans. by Philip Larratt-Smith)

The dialogue was suggested to the author of DA by the story told by Cassius Dio in Book 52 of the *Roman History*, where Maecenas and Agrippa (but not Virgil) debate in 29 BCE with Augustus on monarchy and democracy (52.2–40).[29] In the dialogue Agrippa recommends that Augustus give power back to the Senate, while the position that the DA attributes to Virgil is taken by Maecenas in Cassius Dio. Also in this debate, Maecenas's preference for monarchy is conditioned on the virtue of the prince and his ability to appreciate the virtue of the citizens: "those to whom any task was entrusted would be appointed because of their merit and not as a result of the lot or rivalry for office; . . . the good would be honored without arousing jealousy and the bad punished without causing rebellion" (52.15.3). For Maecenas too the good prince becomes a god: "it is virtue that raises many men to the level of gods . . . if you are upright as a man, honorable as a ruler, the whole earth will be your allowed precinct, all cities your temples" (52.35.5).[30]

Cassius Dio's work was discovered by Giovanni Aurispa, who brought to Italy a manuscript of the *Roman History* from Constantinople in December 1423. One of the first to examine the new text was Francesco Barbaro, who asked Aurispa if he could borrow the codex.[31] Barbaro had been a student of Guarino, and it is very likely that Guarino had the chance of early access to the new text, thanks to Barbaro or to Aurispa himself.

Certainly Guarino knew Cassius Dio in 1435, when he argued with Poggio Bracciolini about the precedence of Caesar or Scipio.[32] Poggio affirmed the

[29] In the margins of three manuscripts of DA, Basel A.N. II 43, Madrid B.N. 3520, and Paris BN Lat. 16237, this note is copied: *hic copiose Dion graecus historicus tractat.*

[30] Trans. by E. Cary (Loeb Classical Library).

[31] Remigio Sabbadini, "Briciole filologiche," *Studi Italiani di Filologia Classica* 6 (1898): 397–406.

[32] See Marianne Pade, "Guarino and Caesar at the Court of the Este," in *La corte di Ferrara e il suo mecenatismo, 1441–1598 / The Court of Ferrara & its Patronage, 1441–1598*, ed. Marianne Pade, Lene Waage Petersen, and Daniela Quarta (Copenhagen: Museum

primacy of Scipio in a letter addressed in April 1435 to Scipione Mainente, one of the favorites of Pope Eugenius IV (Poggio was the pope's secretary). In the summer the letter was brought to Ferrara by Leonello d'Este, who had visited the pope in Florence. Guarino, who favored Caesar, explained his position in a long reply to Poggio, together with a letter addressed to Leonello, who was chosen by Guarino as the arbiter of the controversy. Among the criticisms directed against Caesar, Poggio charged him with having established a dictatorship by bringing down the Roman Republic. Guarino supported the correctness of Caesar's behavior and praised his virtues and clemency. Like Virgil in both dialogues with Augustus in the DA, Guarino qualifies the good prince as *iustus*: "He who has lived honestly, has not harmed anyone, has given to each his own, is a just man" (*qui honeste vixerit, alterum non laeserit, suum cuique tribuerit, iustus est*).[33] Among the various historical sources Guarino used was the work of Cassius Dio.[34] In his subsequent reply Poggio denied the reliability of Dio, whom he qualified as a "Greek adulator, a follower of emperors, a man devoted to kings, born a slave" (*Graeculum adulatorem, imperatorum adseclam, virum addictum regibus, natum in servitute*).[35]

The controversy is partly scholarly and rhetorical: comparisons of great personalities of antiquity had already been proposed by Petrarch.[36] However, it also had political implications because the Florentine humanists had praised the Roman Republic from the time of Coluccio Salutati, when the Republic of Florence was in conflict with the Visconti, the dukes of Milan. Florentine republicanism is highlighted by Leonardo Bruni's *Laudatio Florentinae urbis*, in which *Florentina libertas* is compared with the democracy of Athens as portrayed by Thucydides. In their republicanism the Florentine humanists obviously considered the political context in which they operated: Salutati, in the anti-monarchist polemic of his *De tyranno* (1400), nevertheless damned Caesar's killers, as Dante Alighieri had already done in his *Divina Commedia*, in which Brutus and Cassius are condemned to hell. On the contrary, Poggio justified the actions of Brutus and Cassius,[37] but his arguments in the controversy with Guarino also took into

Tusculanum Press, 1990), 71–92. The text of the controversy was published by Davide Canfora, *La controversia di Poggio Bracciolini e Guarino Veronese su Cesare e Scipione* (Florence: Olschki, 2001).

[33] Canfora, *La controversia*, 134.

[34] Canfora, *La controversia*, 135 and 138.

[35] Canfora, *La controversia*, 165.

[36] Petrarch compared Scipio and Caesar in the first version of the *Triumphus Fame*: see Giuliana Crevatin, "Scipione e la fortuna di Petrarca," *Rinascimento* 17 (1977): 9.

[37] Canfora, *La controversia*, 31.

account the political projects of Cosimo de' Medici, who in 1434 had returned from exile.[38]

The republicanism of the Florentine humanists is also demonstrated by their interest in the heroes of the Roman Republic, whose Plutarchan biographies were first translated by the students of Manuel Chrysoloras (c. 1355–1415) at the beginning of the fifteenth century. This interest in the republican age can perhaps explain their silence regarding the biography of the Augustan Virgil, a silence even more surprising if we consider that the Donatian *Life* had just reappeared in the Florentine scene at the end of the fourteenth century. But this *Life*, as Wilson-Okamura noted, was "a tale of patronage,"[39] not a witness of republican liberty.

Poggio, in his reply to Guarino, links the latter's admiration for Caesar to his relationship with Leonello d'Este: "I see however what this very learned man is following: Leonello d'Este, a very valiant and praiseworthy man, is a supporter of Caesar's party" (*Video tamen quid hoc vir eruditissimus sit secutus: praestantissimus atque omni laude vir dignus Leonellus Estensis, Caesaris partium est fautor*).[40] Leonello's interest in Caesar is documented by the letters of Guarino, who frequently refers to Caesar and to his own studies on Caesar. He worked in these years on the *Commentarii* and also planned a revision of the translation of Plutarch's *Life of Caesar*, which he had translated before 1414.[41] Here Poggio refers not only to Leonello's intellectual interest but also to the political implications of his admiration for Caesar and to the role of the same Guarino, who was in the service of the d'Este, the family which held power in Ferrara. The position of Guarino was similar to that of most of the humanists in their dealings with the princes and tyrants who dominated many Italian cities.

The political position assumed by Virgil in the DA is very similar to that defended by Guarino in his polemic against Poggio. Virgil is, moreover, quoted by Guarino to counter Poggio's assertion that Latin literature declined after the rise of Caesar. Denying this decline, Guarino quotes some praise of Virgil, including that attributed by Servius (on *Eclogues,* 6.11 Thilo) to Cicero, *magnae spes altera Romae* ("the second hope of great Rome"),[42] a compliment that Virgil would later incorporate in the *Aeneid* (12.167). Servius's story is fanciful (Cicero died before

[38] See John W. Oppel, "Peace vs. Liberty in the Quattrocento: Poggio, Guarino, and the Scipio-Caesar Controversy," *Journal of Medieval and Renaissance Studies* 4 (1974): 221–65.

[39] David Scott Wilson-Okamura, *Virgil in the Renaissance* (Cambridge: Cambridge University Press, 2010), 50.

[40] Canfora, *La controversia*, 142.

[41] Pade, "Guarino," 75–80.

[42] Canfora, *La controversia*, 121. Another endorsement of Virgil proposed by Guarino is Propertius 2.34.65–6, *Cedite, Romani scriptores, cedite Grai: | nescio quid maius nascitur Iliade*, quoted also by the Donatian *Life* (Ziolkowski and Putnam, *The Virgilian Tradition*, 349).

the recitations of the *Bucolics*). It is reproduced in an addition to the DA (something which had already been done by Polenton).

The political dialogues discussed above between Virgil and Augustus highlight an important innovation introduced by the compiler of the DA. In the Donatian *Life* the relationship between Virgil and Augustus is that of patronage: the prince supports the poet, favoring his poetical production. Augustus requires from Virgil "with supplicatory and even jokingly threatening letters"[43] the completion of the *Aeneid*, not political advice. In the DA, on the other hand, Virgil is not only a poet celebrating the prince but also an advisor. He supports Augustus's aspiration to monarchy, supplanting the role of Maecenas and Agrippa, an advisor who also professes a pedagogical function and who shares culture and friendship with the prince. It is not difficult to recognize in this image of the advisor the self-representation of many humanists in their relationship with political power, such as that of Guarino himself with Leonello d'Este.

The role of Virgil as Augustus's advisor is also detectable in the additions to the DA in which the poet is a victim of envy and slanders. The setting of these stories is the Augustan court. In the Donatian *Life* Virgil works under the protection of Augustus, but he does not live in his palace (in Suetonius / Donatus Virgil often lived in Naples and had his own house in Rome, on the Esquiline[44]). In the additions to the DA Virgil lives in Augustus's palace, competing with other poets and advisors. One of these is Bacillus, "a mediocre poet," who claimed to have composed a distich that Virgil posted anonymously on the folding-doors. The DA states that Virgil "was so much a despiser of glory that, when someone appropriated some of his verses and was deemed wise for the result, not only did he not take it badly, but it was even a pleasure to him."[45] In the case of Bacillus, however, he did not tolerate the plagiarism of verses praising Augustus: *Nocte pluit tota, redeunt spectacula mane. | Commune imperium cum Iove Caesar habet* ("It rained all night, the games return with the morning: | Caesar has joint rulership with Jove").[46]

The distich was well-known in the Middle Ages, and Guarino also quoted its second line in a letter sent to Leonello in September 1433.[47] Moreover, the story told by the DA was already known, as we can see in some "Lives" of the twelfth

[43] Ziolkowski and Putnam, *The Virgilian Tradition*, 192.

[44] Ziolkowski and Putnam, *The Virgilian Tradition*, 183.

[45] *non modo aegre non ferebat, immo voluptuosum id sibi erat* (111.22–4 S.).

[46] 112.2–113.2 Stok, trans. by Philip Larratt-Smith.

[47] Sabbadini, *Epistolario*, 2:165: the letter was written on the occasion of the visit of the Emperor Sigismund, who is presented by Guarino as the heir of Caesar and Augustus (see Pade, "Guarino," 74–75).

century.[48] But in these previous versions the name of the plagiarist is usually Cornificius (Virgil's detractor, according to the exegetical tradition). The name "Bacillus" is otherwise unknown, but in the later manuscripts copied in Ferrara and also in the edition published by Battista Guarini the name becomes "Bathyllus," as the freedman of Maecenas and a performer of pantomimes mentioned by Seneca (*Controversiae* 10, *praefatio* 8). The form "Bacillus" is perhaps due to a mistaken reading of the name Bathyllus in a manuscript of Seneca, later corrected in the same Guarinian circle.

In the story the plagiarist is in the end exposed in the presence of Augustus and Virgil "more honored" (*Maro vero exaltatior*, 113.2 S.). The same happy ending is to be found in the story of a certain Philistus, who "annoyed Virgil with curses and witticism whenever they happened to meet." Virgil generally did not reply, but on one occasion Philistus in the presence of Augustus "said that Virgil was incapable of eloquence and could not speak in his own defence, even if the cause was his own" (*elinguem illum diceret et causam, etiam si suam haberet, defendere nequire*). Virgil replied: "for this silence of mine has made Augustus and Maecenas the defenders of my cause, and I speak when I wish with that trumpet, which will be heard everywhere and for a very long time." After Augustus "rebuked Philistus with a grave look," Virgil explained the moral of the story: "For one should always keep silence [*tacendum enim semper est*], except when silence will hurt you or speech will benefit others. For wise men think that man who contends and whose contention has no useful goal is to be numbered among the foolish" (115.12–117.7 S.). This conclusion seems to have been influenced by the sentence *tempus tacendi, tempus loquendi* of Ecclesiastes (3.7), very popular in the Renaissance (it was also inscribed in the Malatesta Temple at Rimini).

The story was probably suggested by the statement of the Donatian *Life* that Virgil "argued a case before the judges, once and once only" and by the judgment, attributed to a certain Melissus, that Virgil "was very slow in speaking and almost like someone who had not been schooled" (*et in sermonem tardissimum ac paene indocto simile fuisse Melissus tradidit*).[49] The name of Philistus was instead taken from Cassius Dio, who recounts that the philosopher Philiscus consoled Cicero regarding his exile (*Roman History*, 38.18–29). This episode was translated into Latin by Aurispa in 1425 (*Consolatio Philisci ad Ciceronem*) and imitated by Guarino in a letter to Leonello d'Este in 1439.[50] It is not clear why the philosopher friend of Cicero becomes, in the DA, "a public speaker and a man of middling knowledge about poetry" (115.12–13 S.).

The Virgil of the DA, like the humanists of the Renaissance courts, is very interested in being remunerated by his prince. Several added passages point out this matter. To the section of the Donatian *Life* concerning Virgil's wealth DA

48 See Stok, *Prolegomeni*, 209–10.

49 Ziolkowski and Putnam, *The Virgilian Tradition*, 183.

50 Sabbadini, *Epistolario*, 2:371.

adds: "Whatever he asked from Augustus, he never received a rebuff" (*quaecumque ab Augusto peteret, repulsam numquam habuit*, 87.9–10 S.). Relating to Virgil's family this is added: "Every year he sent his relatives gold for ample support" (*parentibus quotanni aurum ad abundantem altum mittebat*, 87.11–12 S.). The DA adds that Asinius Pollio not only supported Virgil's recovery of his farms but was also very generous towards him: Virgil "received great gifts from him" (*et ab eo magna munera tulit*, 93.4–5 S.) In the Donatian *Life* Virgil receives as a gift from Pollio the boy-slave Alexander; in the DA this is only one example of Pollio's gifts. Particularly significant is the DA's addition to the scene of the *Aeneid*'s recitation in the presence of Augustus, where Octavia fainted on hearing the lines about her son Marcellus. After the reading Augustus "decreed that Virgil was to be given ten thousand sesterces for every verse he wrote" (*dena sestertia pro singulo verso Virgilio dari iussit*, 98.5 S.).[51]

The subject of remuneration is also present in the longest added passage of DA, namely the surprising story in which Virgil, after studying medicine and mathematics in Naples, becomes Augustus's veterinary surgeon:

> Quibus rebus cum ante alios eruditior peritiorque esset, se in Urbem contulit statimque magistri stabuli equorum Augusti amicitiam nactus multos variosque morbos incidentes equis curavit. [9] At ille in mercedem singulis diebus panes Virgilio ut uni ex stabulariis dari iussit. [10] Interea a Crotoniatis pullus equi mirae pulchritudinis Caesari missus dono fuit, qui omnium iudicio spem portendebat virtutis et celeritatis immensae. Hunc cum aspexisset Maro magistro stabuli dixit natum esse ex morbosa equa et nec viribus valiturum nec celeritate idque verum fuisse inventum est. Quod cum magister stabuli Augusto recitasset, duplicari sibi in mercedem panes iussit. [11] Cum item ex Hispania Augusto canes mitterentur et parentes eorum dixit Virgilius et animum celeritatemque futuram. Quo cognito mandat iterum augumentari Virgilio panes. [12] Dubitavit Augustus Octaviine filius fuerit an alterius idque Maronem aperire posse arbitratus est, quia canum et equi naturam parentesque cognorat. [13] Amotis ergo omnibus arbitris illum in penitiorem partem domi vocat et solum rogat an sciat quisnam esset et quam ad felicitandos homines facultatem haberet, [14] "Novi—inquit Maro—tu Caesarem Augustum et ferme aequam cum diis immortalibus potestatem habere ut quem vis felicem facias." "Eo animo sum—respondit Caesar—ut, si verum pro rogatu dixeris, beatum te felicemque reddam." "Utinam—ait Maro—interroganti tibi vera dicere queam!" [15] Tunc Augustus: "putant alii me natum Octavio, quidam suspicantur alio me

[51] The addition was suggested by Servius, on *Aeneid*, 6.861 Thilo: *pro hoc aere gravi donatus est, id est massis.*

genitum viro." Maro subridens "facile,—inquit—si impune licenterque quae sentio loqui iubeas, id dicam." Affirmat Caesar iureiurando nullum eius dictum aegre laturum immo non nisi donatum ab eo discessurum. [16] Ad haec oculos oculis Augusti infingens Maro "facilius—ait—in ceteris animalibus qualitates parentum mathematicis et philosophia cognosci possunt, in homine nequaquam possibile est. Sed de te coniecturam habeo similem veri, ut quid exercuerit pater tuus aperire possim." Attente expectabat Augustus quidnam diceret. [17] "Quantum rem ego intelligere possum, pistori filius es." Obstupuerat Caesar et statim quo id pacto fieri potuerit animo volvebat. Interrumpens Virgilius "audi—inquit—quo pacto id coniicio: cum quaedam enuntiarim praedixerimque, quae intelligi scirique non nisi ab eruditissimis summisque viris potuissent, tu, princeps orbis, item et item panes in mercedem dari iussisti, quod quidem aut pistoris aut nati pistore officium erat." [18] "At deinceps—inquit Caesar—non a pistore sed a rege magnanimo dona feres." Placuit Caesari facetia illumque plurimi fecit et Pollioni commendavit. (80.9–84.12 S.)

When he was more learned and more skilled in these subjects than other men, he betook himself to Rome and at once gained the friendship of Augustus's equerry and cured the many and various ills that had befallen the horses. And the master ordered bread to be given to Virgil for pay every day, as he would do for one of his stable-boys. Meanwhile a foal of wondrous beauty was sent by the men of Croton as a gift for Augustus; one which, in the judgment of all men, carried the hope of great strength and speed. When Maro saw it, he told the equerry that it had been born from an ill mother and would possess neither great strength nor great speed; and it was found that this had been the case. When the equerry repeated this to Augustus, the latter bade that the bread given to Virgil as pay be doubled. Similarly, when dogs were sent from Spain as a gift to Augustus, Virgil correctly told the state of their parents as well as what their spirits and their speed would be. When this became known Augustus again directed that the bread for Virgil be increased.

Augustus was uncertain as to whether he was the son of Octavius or of another, and he decided that Maro would be able to lay the matter open, because he had known the nature and the pedigree of the dogs and the foal. Therefore, after sending away all witnesses, Augustus summoned Maro into the innermost part of his house and, once they were alone, asked him whether he knew who Augustus really was and what capacity he had to make men happy. "I know," said Maro, "that you are Caesar Augustus and that you have a power nearly equal to that of the immortal gods, with the result that you can make whom you choose happy." "I am minded," answered Caesar, "to make you blessed and happy, if you have answered my questions truthfully." Said Maro, "I wish I might be able to answer your question with the truth!" Then Augustus: "Some think me the son of Octavius, while others suspect that I was born to another man." Maro, smiling, said, "It is easy; if you bid me speak my opinion freely and with impunity, I will say it." Caesar assured him

> by swearing an oath that he would take amiss nothing Virgil said—on the contrary, that Virgil would not depart without receiving a gift from him. Whereupon Maro locked his eyes with Augustus's eyes and said: "It is quite easy to discern the qualities of the parents in other creatures, by the use of philosophy and mathematics. In regard to a human being it is not in the least possible. However, I have a conjecture regarding you which is like the truth, that I may lay open that which your father did by profession." Augustus waited expectantly to hear what he would say. "Insofar as I am able to understand the matter," said Maro, "you are a baker's son." Caesar was stunned and at once began to consider to himself in what manner this could have happened. Virgil broke in and said: "Hear on what basis I make this conjecture. When I proclaimed and foretold things that could be understood and known by none but the most learned and superior minds, you, the prince of the world, again and again ordained that I receive bread as pay. And that was the action of a baker, or a baker's son." "But from now on," said Caesar, "you will receive gifts not from a baker, but from a magnanimous king." That little bit of raillery pleased Caesar, and he made much of Virgil and commended him to Pollio. (trans. by Philip Larratt-Smith)

Roth connected the story with the tradition of Virgil the magician,[52] but what it really attributed to Virgil were not magical powers, but scientific knowledge, a common topic even in late antiquity (Servius wrote that Virgil is *totus scientia plenus*, "overflowing with knowledge"[53]). This topic once again became prevalent in the Renaissance, when Virgil, considered adept in every branch of learning, was fashioned in the image of the universal scholar and the perfect courtier (Burckhardt's "uomo universale").[54]

The story, in the biographical outline of DA, occurs after Virgil's studies in medicine and mathematics, in which "he immersed himself with his full effort and enthusiasm" in Naples:[55] it is after these studies that he goes to Rome and is employed as a hostler. In the biographical approach of the compiler of the DA the story answers an important question: how did Virgil become an advisor of Augustus? In the Donatian *Life* we read that Virgil knew Maecenas, and we can only imagine that Maecenas introduced Virgil to Augustus. In the DA version Virgil

---

[52] Karl Ludwig Roth, "Über den Zauberer Virgilius," *Germania: Vierteljahrsschrift für deutsche Alterthumskunde* 4 (1859): 286–87, consequently attributed the DA to a Neapolitan scholar of the twelfth century.

[53] In the preface to Book 6 of his commentary on the *Aeneid* (1–2 Thilo).

[54] L. B. T. Houghton, "Virgil the 'Renaissance Man' and his Medieval Antecedents," *Proceedings of the Virgil Society* 26 (2008): 86; see also the Introduction to this volume.

[55] The Donatian *Life* states that Virgil studied medicine and mathematics, but not where he studied them. The localization in Naples was introduced by Sicco Polenton, on the basis of the information provided by Servius that Virgil studied in Cremona, Milan, and Naples.

knows Augustus without intermediaries, and it is on the contrary Augustus who introduces Virgil to Pollio. The pun in Virgil's reply is also noteworthy: appreciation of irony and *facetiae* is another feature of the story that reproduces the atmosphere of the Renaissance court, in which irony and humor were highly valued qualities in the behavior of the courtier.

The story develops the information given by Suetonius, who recounts some gossip broadcast by Mark Antony, that Augustus's great-grandfather was of African birth and first had a perfumery shop and then a bakery (*pistrinum*) at Aricia; Cassius of Parma also taunts Augustus with being the grandson both of a baker (*pistor*) and of a money-changer (Suet., *Augustus*, 4). Another source probably used by the DA compiler was Pliny the Elder, who emphasizes Virgil's veterinary expertise: "The making of good horses indeed, and their beauty, such as a man would chose for the best, has been most elegantly and absolutely described by the poet Virgil" (*Natural History*, 8.65).

Medicine and mathematics (also philosophy, as Virgil declares in the dialogue above) make the poet an expert not only in veterinary science, for curing horses, but also in physiognomics—that is, the ability to make diagnoses by observing the bodies and the faces of animals and men. Virgil recognizes that the foal was born from a sick mare when he sees the animal. In the presence of the prince he looked into Augustus's eyes. Ancient physiognomics became very popular in the fifteenth century, and one of the most renowned scholars of this pseudo-science was Michele Savonarola (grandfather of the preacher Girolamo), who taught in Padua and worked from 1440 in Ferrara. In his *Speculum phisionomie* (1442), dedicated to Leonello d'Este, he also deals with the physiognomy of horses and dogs.[56]

In the above-mentioned story of Philistus, Virgil presents himself as a Platonist philosopher, reproaching his rival for criticizing "everyone's every word, not so as to illuminate the truth, as Socrates was accustomed to do, but rather to seem more learned" (*omnium omnia dicta reprehendere conabatur, non ut verum dignosceret, quod Socrates facere consuevit, sed ut eruditior videretur*, 116.1–3 S.). This is a peculiar trait of Virgil in the DA, which portrays the poet not as Epicurean, in accordance with the ancient tradition, but as Platonic:

> Audivit a Silone praecepta Epicuri, cuius doctrina socium habuit Varum.[57] Et quamvis diversorum philosophorum opiniones libris suis

[56] Gabriella Zuccolin, "The Speculum phisionomie by Michele Savonarola," in *Universality of Reason. Plurality of philosophies in the Middle Ages*, ed. A. Musco (Palermo: Officina di Studi Medievali, 2012), II.2, 873–86.

[57] The forms Silo (instead of Siro) and Varus (instead of Varius) are misreadings by the compiler.

> inseruisset, de animo maxime videatur ipse Academicus: nam Platonis sententias omnibus aliis praetulit. (118.8–12 S.)
>
> From Silo he heard the precepts of Epicurus, in whose doctrine he had a companion in Varus. And although he inserted into his books the opinions of different philosophers, on questions about the soul he seems to be an Academic; for he preferred the opinions of Plato before all others. (trans. by Philip Larratt-Smith)

That Virgil and Varius frequented the Epicurean school of Siro was stated by Servius (on *Eclogues*, 6.13 Thilo), who also refers to the Platonic doctrine of the soul in his commentary on Book 6 of the *Aeneid*. But the resolute attribution to Virgil of a Platonic faith obviously reflects the spread of Platonism in the early Renaissance, starting from Manuel Chrysoloras and from the first translations of Plato's works.[58] Another reference to Virgil's Platonism is proposed by the DA in its rewriting of Donatus's moral portrait of Virgil, where we read that the poet "was sparing of food and wine. With regard to sexual pleasure, he was partial to boys" (*cibi vinique minimi, libidinis in pueros pronioris*). DA paraphrases and minimizes the source (*fama fuit libidinis pronioris in pueros fuisse*: "the rumor was that he was inclined in sexual desire towards boys"), and then adds: "the good think that he loved boys the way Socrates loved Alcibiades and Plato his favorites" (*boni ita eum pueros amare putaverunt ut Socrates Alcibiadem et Plato τὰ παιδικά*).

Guarino had frequented Chrysoloras, before refining his Greek in Constantinople. His interest in Plato is revealed by the MS Vatican Reg. lat. 1131, a copy of Plato's *Republic* with his annotations on Books 2–5.[59] In 1432, soon after his arrival in Ferrara, Guarino wrote a *Life of Plato* at the request of Filippo Pelliccioni, the physician of Niccolò III. This *Life* is based largely on Diogenes Laertius but also on Augustine and other sources:[60] in this respect it is an interesting document regarding Guarino's idea of writing a biography. On the basis of an ancient biography, the modern compiler adds information collected from other sources. This working method had already been used by Leonardo Bruni for his *Vita Ciceronis* (or *Cicero novus*), a biography based on that of Plutarch but expanded with additions from other sources.[61]

[58] Eduard Norden, "De vitis vergilianis," *Rheinisches Museum* 61 (1906): 166–67.

[59] James Hankins, "A Manuscript of Plato's 'Republic' in the Translation of Chrysoloras and Uberto Decembrio with Annotations of Guarino Veronese (Reg. lat. 1131)," in *Supplementum festivum: Studies in Honor of P. O. Kristeller*, ed. James Hankins (Binghamton, NY: Medieval and Renaissance Texts and Studies, 1987), 149–88.

[60] E. B. Fryde, *Humanism and Renaissance Historiography* (London: The Hambledon Press, 1983), 62–67.

[61] Brad L. Cook, "Plutarch, Cicero, and Leonardo Bruni's *Cicero novus*," in *Gli scritti di Plutarco: Tradizione, traduzione, ricezione, commento*, ed. Giovanna Pace and Paola Volpe Cacciatore (Naples: M. D'Auria, 2013), 119–25.

The method used by the compiler of the DA is very similar: an ancient biography, in this case Donatus's, is enlarged by additions and adjustments. What is peculiar to DA is the presence of additional material for which we cannot detect the source, which seems to be a creative amplification of ancient sources, such as the stories of Augustus asking Virgil about political matters, of Philistus, and of Virgil as a veterinary practitioner. A probable falsification is what the DA attributes to Asconius Pedianus, adding it to the information from this author included in the Donatian *Life*: "Pedianus also reports that he was kindly and a devotee of all good and learned men, and was so free of envy that, if he beheld a well-educated phrase from another, he was no less happy than if he had written it itself; that he disparaged no one, praised good men, and had such humanity that anyone, aside from an extremely disturbed individual, not only esteemed but loved him [*quisque illum non diligeret modo, sed amaret*]" (109.7–110.3 S.). The last sentence seems to have been influenced by Cicero (*Ad familiares* 13.47.1): *eum a me non diligi solum vero amari* ("a man whom I not only like, but even love"). In the first part, the compiler (if the falsification is to be attributed to him) imitates the *Life* of Virgil by Polenton, for whom the poet "was reserved and sparing of angers" and "no less a foe of avarice than of ambition."[62] The following statement that Virgil's library "was not less open to other men of learning than to himself" also seems to be an invention of the compiler. We do not read about Virgil's library in other sources, and the note seems to reflect a concern typical of the humanistic age, in which the access to books and libraries was a very deeply felt problem.

With regard to this and the other probable inventions, it should be borne in mind that there were very faint boundaries between imitation and falsification in early humanism, as may be seen in the fabricated letter from Virgil to Maecenas written (jokingly?[63]) in 1426 by Pier Candido Decembrio, which was, however, copied in several manuscripts.[64] There was also a change to the source in the above-mentioned controversy between Guarino and Poggio. In 1425 Aurispa translated into Latin the *Dialogue of the Dead* by Lucian (another Greek author he brought from Constantinople), in which Minos gives an evaluation of the greatest generals, assigning the first place to Alexander, the second to Scipio, and the third to Hannibal. In his translation Aurispa radically altered the Greek text, assigning, for patriotic purposes,[65] the first place to Scipio and flattering the Roman Battista

[62] Ziolkowski and Putnam, *The Virgilian Tradition*, 44.

[63] According to Luciano Barozzi and Remigio Sabbadini, *Studi sul Panormita e sul Valla* (Florence: Le Monnier, 1891), 23–24.

[64] Decembrio began to write a Book 13 of the *Aeneid* and then accused Maffeo Vegio of plagiarism with regard to his Book 13. Decembrio's supplement has been examined by Sonja Eckmann, "Das Aeneis-Supplement des Pier Candido Decembrio—die pessimistische Stimme der Aeneis?," *Neulateinisches Jahrbuch* 4 (2002): 55–88.

[65] David Marsh, *Lucian and the Latins: Humor and Humanism in the Early Renaissance* (Ann Arbor: University of Michigan Press, 1988), 30–31.

Capodiferro, governor of Bologna. Aurispa claimed the authority of Libanius for this innovation, but wrongly.[66] Poggio knew Aurispa's translation, but in his letter to Mainenti he quotes it imprecisely, attributing to Lucian praise of Caesar rather than Scipio, and Guarino denied this statement in his reply.[67] (A more accurate translation of the *Dialogue* than Decembrio's had been made some years earlier by the Veronese scholar Bartholomeus Landus, who dedicated it to Bartholomeus Cendratus, Guarino's brother-in-law.[68])

Finally, several clues suggest that the DA was compiled in Ferrara in the milieu of Guarino of Verona, around 1430–1435. The compiler's aim was to provide a more complete biography of Virgil than Donatus's. For his revision, he used a medieval manuscript of the Donatian Life in which the Life was anonymous. The compiler did not insert his own name in the Life and so the expanded version was also in an anonymous form. For the additions, the compiler used and reworked several sources, some of them recently discovered (such as Cassius Dio).

The enlargement of the Donatian Life realized by the DA produced an image of Virgil that reflected the culture of the humanists, particularly with regard to Virgil's relationship with Augustus, imagined as being like the one prevalent in several Renaissance courts (such as that of the Este in Ferrara), where the humanist was (or, better, aspired to be) a friend and adviser of the prince, who was also interested in, and supported, humanist culture. This historical and cultural context is reflected in most of the anecdoctal stories introduced by the compiler, partly derived from unknown sources. The culture of the Renaissance is also reflected by the qualification of Virgil as a Platonist, as a result of the rediscovery of Plato in the first decades of the fifteenth century.

[66] Canfora, *La controversia*, 49–51.

[67] Canfora, *La controversia*, 111 and 125.

[68] David Cast, "Aurispa, Petrarch, and Lucian: An Aspect of Renaissance Translation," *Renaissance Quarterly* 27 (1974): 164.

4

Virgilian Imagery and the Maiolica of the Mantuan Court

Lisa Boutin Vitela
Cerritos College

The residents and rulers of Mantua felt great pride in their connection to their most famous native son, Virgil. This pride was formalized in visual reminders of the poet that could be found throughout the city. Most prominent was a thirteenth-century sculpture of Virgil, carved within a niche on the façade of the Palazzo del Podestà, but other representations and reminders of the poet appeared throughout the city center and reinforced a message of Mantua's historical importance, and may have also possessed a protective function akin to a patron saint.[1]

Virgil provided Mantua, a city devoid of large-scale ancient Roman ruins, with significant cultural and historical relevancy.[2] Such relevancy was especially important in light of the relatively recent ascension of members of the Gonzaga family as rulers of the city in 1328, first at the rank of captain general and later at the rank of *marchese* (marquis).[3] While Mantua was a small city, its central location on the Italian peninsula and its link to the Holy Roman Emperor as a feudal vassal demanded deference from nearby courts and city-states. The Gonzaga court's impressive history of artistic patronage under Marchese Ludovico III Gonzaga (1412–1478) added to its fame, and this renown would only increase under the most famous Renaissance female patron, Marchesa Isabella d'Este Gonzaga (1474–1539).[4]

---

[1] Sarah Blake McHam, "Renaissance Monuments to Favourite Sons," *Renaissance Studies* 19 (2005): 458–86. A bust of Virgil was also installed in the Porta Nuova.

[2] Barbara Furlotti and Guido Rebecchini, *The Art of Mantua: Power and Patronage in the Renaissance* (Los Angeles: J. Paul Getty Museum, 2008), 15–16.

[3] M. J. Rodríguez-Salgado, "Terracotta and Iron: Mantuan Politics (c. 1450–c. 1550)," in *La Corte di Mantova nell'età di Andrea Mantegna: 1450–1550*, ed. Cesare Mozzarelli et al. (Rome: Bulzoni Editore, 1997), 24.

[4] Clifford M. Brown has been the principal scholar to publish on all aspects of Isabella's collection, including paintings, antiquities, and musical instruments. Clifford

When Isabella d'Este became the consort of Marchese Francesco II Gonzaga (1466–1519) in 1490, she assumed a multifaceted role within the court as diplomat, administrator, collector, and provider of heirs for the Gonzaga dynasty.[5] Focusing on Isabella's collecting and commissioning practices, art historians have noted that she deliberately cultivated a learned persona through the classical narratives she favored.[6] This essay argues that she had a particular affinity for Virgil and Virgilian narratives, which reflected her desire to advance the status of Mantua as well as to further her own distinction as a patron. The presence of three Virgilian narratives within the surviving twenty-three dishes of Isabella's *istoriato* (narrative-painted) maiolica service exemplifies the type of imagery that Isabella favored for her city and for herself. Her maiolica service, which has received little scholarly attention relative to other art objects in Isabella's collection, may have had an especially personal connection to Isabella, while also influencing the development of narrative-painted maiolica during the sixteenth century.[7] This essay advances these claims through analysis of three central

M. Brown, "'Lo insaciabile desidero nostro de cose antique': New Documents for Isabella d'Este's Collection of Antiquities," in *Cultural Aspects of the Renaissance*, ed. Cecil Clough (Manchester: Manchester University Press, 1976), 324–53; idem, "A Ferrarese Lady and a Mantuan Marchesa: The Art and Antiquities Collections of Isabella d'Este Gonzaga (1474–1539)," in *Women and Art in Early Modern Europe: Patrons, Collectors, and Connoisseurs*, ed. Cynthia Miller Lawrence (University Park: Penn State University Press, 1997), 53–71; idem, *Per dare qualche splendore a la gloriosa cità di Mantua: Documents for the Antiquarian Collection of Isabella d'Este* (Rome: Bulzoni, 2002); idem, *Isabella d'Este in the Ducal Palace in Mantua: An Overview of her Rooms in the Castello di San Giorgio and the Corte Vecchia* (Rome: Bulzoni, 2005). Other studies include *Isabella d'Este: Fürstin und Mäzenatin der Renaissance: "La Prima Donna del Mondo,"* ed. Sylvia Ferino-Pagden (Vienna: Kunsthistorisches Museum, 1994); Stephen Campbell, *The Cabinet of Eros: Renaissance Mythological Painting and the* studiolo *of Isabella d'Este* (New Haven: Yale University Press, 2004); Francis Ames-Lewis, *Isabella and Leonardo: The Artistic Relationship between Isabella d'Este and Leonardo da Vinci, 1500–1506* (New Haven: Yale University Press, 2012).

[5] Carolyn James, "Marriage by Correspondence: Politics and Domesticity in the Letters of Isabella d'Este and Francesco Gonzaga 1490–1519," *Renaissance Quarterly* 65 (2012): 321–52.

[6] See note 4 for literature about Isabella d'Este's collecting practices.

[7] This essay expands on a portion of my doctoral dissertation: Lisa Boutin, "Displaying Identity in the Mantuan Court: The Maiolica of Isabella d'Este, Federico II Gonzaga, and Margherita Paleologa," PhD dissertation, UCLA, 2011. Much initial dissertation research relied on the following studies of Gonzaga maiolica: Burr Wallen, "A Majolica Service for Isabella d'Este," MA thesis, Institute of Fine Arts, New York University, 1966; J. V. G. Mallet, "The Gonzaga and Ceramics," in *Splendours of the Gonzaga*, ed. D. Chambers and J. Martineau (London: Victoria and Albert Museum, 1981), 39–43; J. V. G. Mallet, "Mantua and Urbino: Gonzaga Patronage of Maiolica," *Apollo* 114 (1981): 162–69; Mariarosa Palvarini Gobio Casali, *La ceramica a Mantova* (Ferrara:

topics: Isabella d'Este's education and humanist interests, the Virgilian imagery within her maiolica service in the context of dining in her suburban palace, and, finally, later instances of maiolica with Virgilian imagery that may have been inspired by the examples in Isabella's service.

Isabella d'Este as Collector and Patron

Isabella d'Este's maiolica service survives as twenty-three painted dishes attributed to the workshop of the preeminent maiolica painter Nicola da Urbino (active c.1520–1537/8), although the original service may have included many more dishes.[8] The dishes were decorated with classical narratives that were inspired by circulating prints, including scenes from Virgil's *Aeneid* and Ovid's *Metamorphoses*. Isabella's *imprese* (emblems) and *stemma* (coat of arms), intended as clear representations of her identity and ownership, are incorporated into the painted narratives. Analysis of Isabella d'Este's education and particular interest in Virgil provides context for discussion of her maiolica.

Isabella d'Este received training in humanist literature at the court of Ferrara as the eldest child of Duke Ercole I d'Este (1431–1505). As a young woman of high social rank, Isabella had access to instruction in Latin and ancient texts. A sentimental note of March 25, 1490 from her tutor in Ferrara, following her departure for Mantua, provides details regarding the content of her lessons, which included reading Cicero, Terence, and Virgil's *Bucolics* and *Aeneid*.[9] In her

---

Belriguardo, 1987); Dora Thornton and Timothy Wilson, *Italian Renaissance Ceramics: A Catalogue of the British Museum Collection* (London: British Museum, 2009), 229–36; Carmen Ravanelli Guidotti, "Majoliken aus den Marken im Land der Gonzaga," *Keramos* 210 (2010): 29–43.

[8] For a discussion of the original number of the dishes in the service, see Thornton and Wilson, *Italian Renaissance Ceramics*, 232. Sets of dishes were often commissioned during the Renaissance in multiples of six, so twenty-four dishes or a higher multiple are likely possibilities for the original number. See Reino Liefkes, "Tableware," in *At Home in Renaissance Italy*, ed. Marta Ajmar-Wollheim and Flora Dennis (London: Victoria and Albert Museum, 2006), 258.

[9] ". . . I remember the accurate and deep memory that your ladyship has, who on Saturdays would translate for me . . . Virgil's *Bucolics*; the first, second, and part of the third book of Virgil; several of Cicero's epistles . . . and then with what charm and grace you explicated the lessons you heard me read, especially from Terence and Virgil." Virgil's first, second, and third books most likely refer to the first three books of the *Aeneid*. Translation by Deanna Shemek, "Isabella d'Este and the Properties of Persuasion," in *Form and Persuasion in Early Modern Women's Letters across Europe*, ed. Ann Crabb and Jane Couchman (Burlington, VT: Ashgate, 2005), 125. For the Italian transcription, see Alessandro Luzio, *I precettori di Isabella d'Este* (Ancona: Gustavo Morelli, 1887), 15: ". . . mi ricordo la fidelle et profunda memoria la quale tene V.S. la quale soleva rendermi el

reading and analysis of an ancient Roman orator, playwright, and poet, Isabella's instruction extended well beyond the basics of Latin grammar.

During the second half of the fifteenth century, humanist education had become a subject of vital importance among members of the courts and upper classes throughout the Italian peninsula. Treatises detailed the ideal manner in which classical literature should be taught.[10] The authors advocated close readings of the *Aeneid* to analyze the morality of the characters in stories. Aeneas was considered the perfect hero, endowed with every virtue.[11] The Latin text was accessible to humanists and educated individuals and became even more widely available by the end of the fifteenth century as translations of the *Aeneid* and other works by Virgil were produced in the vernacular with increasing frequency.[12]

In addition to Isabella's lessons, she would have found an example of an educated and discerning female patron in her mother, Eleonora of Aragon (1450–1493), duchess of Ferrara and daughter of the king of Naples.[13] Eleonora possessed an impressive collection of books and supported humanists.[14] Three paintings by Ercole de'Roberti representing ancient Roman women are believed to have been commissioned by Eleonora.[15] The artworks, depicting Lucretia, Portia, and the wife of Hasdrubal, would have created a gallery of famous, determined, and virtuous women of antiquity when hung as an ensemble. Isabella

---

sabato tuto questo: prima tuta la bucolica de Virgilio, il primo et il secundo et parte del terzo libro de Virgilio, parechie epistole de Tullio . . . Anchora cum quanta galanteria et gratia rendea al senno le lectioni oldiva da mi et maxime quella de Terentio et de Virgilio."

[10] Some of the most famous include Leonardo Bruni's *De studiis et litteris* (c. 1405), Battista Guarino's *De ordine docendi et studendi* (c. 1459), and Maffeo Vegio's *De educatione liberorum clarisque eorum moribus* (c. 1460). See Craig Kallendorf, *Virgil and the Myth of Venice: Books and Readers in the Italian Renaissance* (Oxford: Clarendon Press, 1999), 50.

[11] Kallendorf, *Virgil and the Myth of Venice*, 53.

[12] Craig Kallendorf has compiled the translations that were created between 1476 and the end of the sixteenth century. Of the ninety-one editions he chronicled, the vast majority were editions of the *Aeneid*, typically not in its twelve-book entirety, but one or two books. When only a few books were translated, the most frequent selections were made from the first six books. See Craig Kallendorf, *A Bibliography of Renaissance Italian Translations of Virgil* (Florence: Leo S. Olschki, 1994); idem, *Virgil and the Myth of Venice*.

[13] Luciano Chiappini, *Eleonora d'Aragona: prima Duchessa di Ferrara* (Rovigo: STER., 1956).

[14] Rose Marie San Juan, "The Court Lady's Dilemma: Isabella d'Este and Art Collecting in the Renaissance," *Oxford Art Journal* 14 (1991): 70.

[15] Ruth Wilkins Sullivan, "Three Ferrarese Panels on the Theme of 'Death rather than Dishonour' and the Neapolitan Connection," *Zeitschrift für Kunstgeschichte* 57 (1994): 610–25; Virginia Cox, "Gender and Eloquence in Ercole de'Roberti's 'Portia and Brutus'," *Renaissance Quarterly* 62 (2009): 61–101.

appears to have sought artworks that conveyed similar virtuous or moral messages through classical iconography.

Soon after becoming marchesa of Mantua, Isabella d'Este was engaged in her own patronage projects and attempted to glorify her new city through an important commission intended to replace a destroyed statue of Virgil. The destruction was said to have occurred when Carlo Malatesta of Rimini invaded Mantua in 1397 and had a sculpture of Virgil thrown into the Mincio River because the people of Mantua were worshipping it as if it were a representation of a Christian saint.[16] Although a surviving drawing of the proposed statue by an artist in the circle of Andrea Mantegna includes an inscription that gives only Virgil's name and the intention of the monument, namely to memorialize him for eternity, written exchanges give details of a plan to give Isabella full credit for the restoration within the inscription.[17] The project was never completed during Isabella's lifetime, but her interest in its early phases demonstrated her passion for promoting Virgil as well as her own humanist interests.

Isabella's desire to cultivate an erudite persona was also made visible by the presence of a book in the now-cropped portrait cartoon that she commissioned from Leonardo da Vinci when he visited Mantua in 1499.[18] According to scholars, a copy after Leonardo now in the Ashmolean Museum that includes Isabella pointing to a book represents an accurate source on which to base interpretation of Leonardo's original cartoon, now in the collection of the Musée du Louvre.[19] By commissioning this portrait with a book as her attribute, Isabella sought to publicize her enthusiasm for literature, her literary patronage, and her role as a literary muse.[20] Isabella would have had no shortage of books to study in the Mantuan court, as, according to inventories, numerous editions of Virgil with illustrations and commentaries were available in her own and her son Federico II Gonzaga's libraries.[21]

Although Isabella pursued humanist study throughout her life, her ability to find sufficient time for lessons became increasingly limited as her diplomatic

---

[16] Alan Fisher, "Three Meditations on the Destruction of Virgil's Statue: The Early Humanist Theory of Poetry," *Renaissance Quarterly* 40 (1987): 607–35; James Hankins, *Humanism and Platonism in the Italian Renaissance*, vol. 1 (Rome: Edizioni di Storia e Letteratura, 2003), 170.

[17] Chambers and Martineau, eds., *Splendours of the Gonzaga*, cat. no. 92; Catherine King, "Medieval and Renaissance Matrons, Italian-Style," *Zeitschrift für Kunstgeschichte* 55 (1992): 388–89; Ferino-Pagden, *Isabella d'Este: Fürstin und Mäzenatin der Renaissance*, cat. no. 57; Ames-Lewis, *Isabella and Leonardo*, 67–68.

[18] Ames-Lewis, *Isabella and Leonardo*, 101–62.

[19] David Alan Brown, "Leonardo and the Ladies with the Ermine and the Book," *Artibus et Historiae* 11 (1990): 57–58.

[20] Brown, "Leonardo and the Ladies," 57; Ames-Lewis, *Isabella and Leonardo*, 130.

[21] Campbell, *The Cabinet of Eros*, 270–79.

duties became more pressing with her husband's frequent departures. Isabella's desire to continue her studies led to the unusual decision to hire Mario Equicola d'Alveto (d. 1525) as her tutor when she was thirty-four. After years of attempting to woo the marchesa, including writing the treatise *Nec Spe Nec Metu* (No Hope, No Fear) about Isabella's motto, Equicola became a full-time fixture of the Mantuan court.[22] In addition to her scholarly motivation, however, the marchesa benefited from the prestige that accompanied having a private tutor, from Equicola's abilities to serve as a diplomat for the Gonzaga court, and from his assistance in her patronage of classicizing works of art.[23]

The *Istoriato* Maiolica Service of Isabella d'Este

Approximately twenty-five years after the Leonardo da Vinci cartoon and the design for the Virgil statue, Isabella received the maiolica service that celebrated Virgil's narratives and demonstrated her continuing zeal for classical studies. While the iconography of two of the dishes, namely the *Flight of Aeneas from Troy* (private collection) and *The Banquet of Dido and Aeneas* [Figure 1], is easily identifiable, scholars are less certain about the dish that has been identified as representing the founding of the city of Mantua, known as *Tiber and Manto* [Figure 2]. The service demonstrates Isabella's preference for classical and, at times, obscure iconography, which she established as a young patron when commissioning paintings by Andrea Mantegna, Pietro Perugino, and Lorenzo Costa for her *studiolo*.

Although none of the dishes in Isabella d'Este's maiolica service was signed, the service is attributed to the master painter and workshop owner Nicola da Urbino based on stylistic comparisons to examples of signed maiolica.[24] Urbino was a center of maiolica production, with many workshops and masters producing services in the *istoriato* (narrative-painted) style that proved to be popular among members of aristocratic courts. "Maiolica" describes ceramic vessels covered in a lead-glaze; this is made white through the addition of tin oxide.[25] Before the glaze could be added, a ceramic vessel was soft biscuit fired and then covered in the white glaze, called *bianco,* which resulted in a background color that resembled refined porcelain vessels. Once the white glaze had dried, painters could add glazes of colored oxides to create designs and narratives, followed by a clear glaze and another firing. Visitors at the Gonzaga court would have

[22] On Mario Equicola, see Stephen Kolsky, *Mario Equicola: The Real Courtier* (Geneva: Librairie Droz, 1991).

[23] Kolsky, *Mario Equicola*, 105.

[24] Thornton and Wilson, *Italian Renaissance Ceramics*, 229.

[25] Frank and Janet Hamer, *The Potter's Dictionary of Materials and Techniques*, 4th ed. (London: A. C. Black, 1997), s.v. "Maiolica."

been impressed by the visual effect of the brilliant white, tin-glazed surfaces decorated with vivid, pigment-rich glazes.

Isabella d'Este's maiolica service was probably a gift from her daughter Eleonora Gonzaga (1493–1555), duchess of Urbino. In a 1524 letter, Eleonora mentioned a service of "vasi di terra" (earthenware vessels) from Urbino, which she believed would be appropriate for Isabella's suburban palace, Palazzo di Porto.[26] Isabella's service of 1524 arrived at a time when Isabella was retreating from public court life in Mantua and spending more time at her suburban estate at Porto. Although we cannot be sure that the letter refers to Nicola da Urbino's maiolica service, given the 1524 date, the producer (a workshop in Urbino), and the intended owner (Isabella), we can conjecture that Eleonora sent a maiolica service for the purpose of serving at Isabella's gatherings at Porto.[27] Eleonora presumably did not send her a service of plain wares, but a service that best exemplified the high-quality maiolica being produced in Urbino. Should her mother choose to display and use the maiolica service, it would reflect well on the duchess of Urbino's taste, as well as serving as excellent publicity for the maiolica industry of Urbino. Furthermore, the three narratives from Virgil's *Aeneid* included in the service must have been created with Isabella's interest in the ancient author in mind.

The Flight of Aeneas from Troy interpreted Aeneas's dramatic escape from the burning city of Troy (*Aeneid*, 2.708ff.). The imagery decorating a shallow bowl on a low foot, now in a private collection, drew on well-established iconography from antiquity.[28] Following the standard composition, Nicola depicted Aeneas carrying his elderly father, Anchises, who clutches two large, bronze household

---

[26] For the Palazzo di Porto, see Clifford Brown with Anna Maria Lorenzoni, "'Al Suo Amenissimo Palazzo di Porto': Biagio Rossetti and Isabella d'Este," *Atti e Memorie della Accademia Virgiliana di Mantova* 58 (1990): 33–56; Alessia Muroni, "La villa di Porto, 'amenissimo palagio'," *Civiltà Mantovana* 112 (2001): 7–23; Amedeo Belluzzi, "Le residenze di campagna di Isabella d'Este," in *Maisons des Champs dans l'Europe de la Renaissance*, ed. Monique Chatenet (Paris: Picard, 2006), 105–16. For discussion of the Gonzaga suburban and country palaces, see Molly Bourne, *Francesco II Gonzaga: The Soldier-Prince as Patron* (Rome: Bulzoni, 2008), 103–82.

[27] Eleonora Gonzaga to Isabella d'Este, November 15, 1524, ASMn, AG, b. 1070, c. 410r. Published in Casali, *La ceramica a Mantova*, 211–12: "Ho facto fare una credenza de vasi di terra . . . per havere li maestri de questo nostro paese qualche nome di lavorar bene, et se piacerà alla Ex.tia v.mi sera di contento, et lei se ne fara servire a Porto per essere cosa da villa." For the English translation, see Thornton and Wilson, *Italian Renaissance Ceramics*, 231: "I have had made a credenza of earthenware vessels . . . since the *maestri* of this country of ours have some reputation for good work. And if it pleases Your Excellency I shall be happy, and you might make use of it at Porto, since it is a villa thing."

[28] For an illustration, see Jörg Rasmussen, *The Robert Lehman Collection, X, Italian Maiolica* (New York: Metropolitan Museum of Art, 1989), 251, fig. 67.18.

gods, while a cherubic Ascanius follows, grasping his father's garment, rather than Aeneas's hand, as stated in the text. The strength of Aeneas as a well-regarded hero was conveyed in his military cuirass, his visible musculature, and his determined gaze. This gaze contrasted with the outward, fearful gazes of Ascanius and Anchises that were intended to engage viewers. Nicola incorporated a fortress engulfed in flames and a ship prepared for departure in the background. The scene of three generations struggling through adversity gained popularity with Renaissance and Baroque artists, and it appeared in painting and sculpture throughout the sixteenth and seventeenth centuries.[29]

Nicola's version was based on a print by the Master of the Die (an unidentified engraver who worked in Marcantonio Raimondi's workshop), depicting the Aeneas group, which is almost identical in its composition to Nicola's work.[30] The print was a variation on *The Fire in the Borgo*, a fresco painted by Raphael's workshop in the Vatican Palace. In the fresco, Rome was equated with burning Troy by inserting the figures of Aeneas, Anchises, and Ascanius into the scene.[31]

Nicola da Urbino and other maiolica artists used circulating prints for artistic guidance in painting narratives but would also add coats of arms and emblems to personalize maiolica services. In the case of Isabella's service, each dish included her *stemma* (coat of arms), which combined Este and Gonzaga arms, and at least one *impresa* (emblem). For *The Flight of Aeneas from Troy*, the *stemma* was positioned on the left of the composition, while Isabella's XXVII *impresa* was illustrated at the base of the scene. The number XXVII, pronounced *ventisette*, was probably a pun on *vinti i saeti* (overcome the arrows).[32] These arrows may symbolize misfortune and challenges, and, in the case of this maiolica dish, may allude to the vicissitudes of fortune faced by both Aeneas and the marchesa.

Nicola da Urbino may have had Isabella and her court in mind when he created *The Banquet of Dido and Aeneas* [Figure 1]. The shallow bowl on a low foot was painted with the scene from the *Aeneid* during which Cupid takes the form of Ascanius. Cupid proceeds to crawl onto Dido's lap, inflaming her with

---

[29] See the painting by Federico Barocci (Galleria Borghese, Rome) and sculpture by Gian Lorenzo Bernini (Galleria Borghese, Rome). Peter Gillgren, *Siting Federico Barocci and the Renaissance Aesthetic* (Burlington, VT: Ashgate, 2011), 163–67. Carolina Mangone, "Like Father, Like Son: Bernini's Filial Imitation of Michelangelo," in *Theorizing Imitation in the Visual Arts: Global Contexts*, ed. Paul Duro (Hoboken: Wiley & Sons, 2015), 69–89.

[30] *The Illustrated Bartsch*, ed. Walter L. Strauss (New York: Abaris Books, 1978), 15 (224) no. 72.

[31] Ingrid D. Rowland, "The Vatican Stanze," in *The Cambridge Companion to Raphael*, ed. Marcia B. Hall (Cambridge: Cambridge University Press, 2005), 115–17; Patricia L. Reilly, "Raphael's *Fire in the Borgo* and the Italian Pictorial Vernacular," *The Art Bulletin* 92 (2010): 308–25.

[32] Campbell, *The Cabinet of Eros*, 67. J. V. G. Mallet suggests *vente sette* (factions defeated); see Mallet, "Mantua and Urbino," 167.

Fig. 1: Nicola da Urbino, *Banquet of Dido and Aeneas*, 1524. Diameter: 27 cm. Musée du Louvre, Paris. © RMN-Grand Palais / Art Resource, NY.

love for Aeneas and initiating the undoing of the queen of Carthage (*Aeneid*, 1.657ff.). The viewer would comprehend the story not only through the iconography, which features a banquet echoing the richness described in Book 1 with Dido seated in a grand chair while being served, entertained, and surrounded by Aeneas and Ascanius, but also through an inscription, which reads: CUI VENUS ASCANI SUB IMAGINE MITTIT AMOREM ("Venus sends love in the guise of Ascanius"). Nicola da Urbino probably used a print by Giovanni da Brescia that was a reversed copy of Marcantonio Raimondi's engraving *Quos Ego* when creating the iconography and adding the inscription.[33] *Quos Ego* was a 1516 engraving of ten scenes from the first book of the *Aeneid*, created in imitation of ancient Roman

[33] *Bartsch* 14 (264) no. 352.

relief sculpture, which likely served as a useful source of Virgilian stories for Nicola da Urbino and other maiolica artists.[34]

Nicola depicted the scene on a Renaissance stage-like setting that may have recalled popular Renaissance plays.[35] Representations of contemporary furniture placed the scene in the sixteenth century, but classically-inspired costume with heavy drapery reminded viewers of the story's ancient origins. Isabella's *imprese* were added along the base of the scene, functioning as appropriate symbols of female virtue and quiet fortitude. The *tempi e pausi* (musical repeats and rests), signifying the desirable virtue of silence, were represented on an unrolled scroll between the two tables, and the XXVII *imprese* appeared under the left foot of the musician. This scene of Dido's banquet was an especially popular and logical subject for maiolica due to its connections to dining. The same scene is repeated in later examples of *istoriato* maiolica.[36] Isabella may have appreciated this iconography due to the prominence of a female character within the narrative, as well as the "historic" Dido's renown as a virtuous widow.[37] The narrative may also have been a catalyst for discussion about correct behavior since the scene represents the beginning of Dido's demise.

The third Virgilian dish owned by Isabella d'Este may present the most explicit connection to Mantua. Nicola represented an encounter between a seated female figure and a male figure emerging from a river [Figure 2]. Art historians have identified this scene on a small plate with a broad rim as the meeting of the prophetess Manto and the river god Tiber.[38] The relationship between the prophetess and the river god would have been well known to Mantuans because the consummation of their relationship resulted in a son, Ocnus, who founded the city, as briefly recounted in Book 10 of the *Aeneid* (10.198–99).[39] The narrative included symbols of virtue on either side of the scene in the form of Isabella's alpha and omega *impresa*, an emblem with both humanist and Christian interpretations, and the *tempi e pausi impresa*. Manto is depicted as scantily covered and resting on the side of the river, while the muscular form of Tiber appears to leap from the water, an unusual contrast to the languid, reclining males typically

---

34 Lawrence Nees, "'Le Quos Ego' de Marc-Antoine Raimondi. L'Adaptation d'une source antique par Raphael," *Nouvelles de l'estampe* 40–41 (1978): 18–29.

35 For the relationship between painting and theater in Renaissance Italy, see Kristin Phillips-Court, *The Perfect Genre: Drama and Painting in Renaissance Italy* (Burlington, VT: Ashgate, 2011).

36 For comparable dishes, see 'In Castel Durante painter': *Dido, Aeneas, and Ascanius*, Shallow bowl on low foot, 1526, British Museum, no. 1855,12–1,97, and Francesco Xanto Avelli, *Dido Entertaining Aeneas*, Victoria and Albert Museum, C.2117–1910.

37 Jan L. De Jong, "Dido in Italian Renaissance Art: The Afterlife of a Tragic Heroine," *Artibus et Historiae* 30 (2009): 73–89.

38 See note 7 for literature about Isabella d'Este's maiolica service.

39 For Manto, see Statius, *Thebaid*, 4.463–68.

Fig. 2: Nicola da Urbino, *Tiber and Manto*, 1524. Diameter: 26.8 cm. Kunstgewerbemuseum, Berlin. © bpk, Berlin / Kunstgewerbemuseum, Berlin / Saturia Linke / Art Resource, NY.

representative of rivers. Nicola conveyed the dynamism of the scene through billowing drapery and windblown hair.

Nicola must have selected this story with Isabella in mind, since, based on the corpus of his surviving maiolica, he never repeated it for other patrons. In addition to the story's brief appearance in Virgil's *Aeneid*, Manto's role in the foundation of Mantua was known through references in Dante's *Inferno* (20.52–93) and in Mario Equicola's *Istoria di Mantova*.[40] Manto remained an important subject for the Gonzaga: the Sala di Manto in the Palazzo Ducale was created

[40] Mario Equicola, *Istoria di Mantova* (Bologna: Forni, 1968), 3–5.

in the second half of the sixteenth century under Duke Guglielmo Gonzaga, Isabella's grandson.[41]

Isabella's maiolica service included the scenes from Virgil discussed above as well as narratives from nearly every book of Ovid's *Metamorphoses*. Thus, the dishes reminded guests of both Isabella's knowledge and their own understanding of classical texts. Upon seeing a particular story, the viewer would think of the narrative and identify characters from his or her own reading. By the third decade of the sixteenth century, this mode of experiencing classical poetry through painted dishes had gained considerable momentum. Viewers may have also been familiar with visual renditions of these classical epics represented in painted cycles.[42] Most importantly, the scenes from the *Aeneid* reminded Isabella's guests that Virgil was Mantua's native son.

Although debate exists as to whether *istoriato* maiolica was used to hold and serve food, the variety of bowls, plates, platters, and ewers, has been used as evidence of actual use at the table.[43] Based on the accounts of visitors, discussions and dining were important and congenial experiences at Isabella's suburban palace, Palazzo di Porto, and therefore the elaborate and colorful dishes featuring Virgilian narratives would have suited the environment there.[44] While some scholars have hypothesized that the commissioners of this service did not significantly influence the imagery, the combination of Isabella's *imprese*, *stemma*, and the Virgilian stories reinforced the humanist identity that Isabella had diligently created since her arrival in Mantua.[45]

When Isabella received her *istoriato* service around 1524, she had settled into life as a dowager marchesa after enacting the role of marchesa for nearly thirty years. She frequented Palazzo di Porto with regularity as a widow. Indeed,

---

41 *Palazzo Ducale di Mantova*, ed. Giuliana Algeri (Mantua: Sometti, 2003).

42 Such as the Camerino dell'Eneide in the Rocca Nuova at Scandiano. See Katherine A. McIver, "Matrons as Patrons: Power and Influence in the Courts of Northern Italy in the Renaissance," *Artibus et Historiae* 22 (2001): 75–89. Dosso Dossi contributed ten scenes from the *Aeneid* for Duke Alfonso d'Este's Camerino d'Alabastro; see Charles Hope, "The 'Camerini d'Alabastro' of Alfonso d'Este-I," *Burlington Magazine* 113.824 (1971): 641–47, 649–50, and idem, "The 'Camerini d'Alabastro' of Alfonso d'Este-II," *Burlington Magazine* 113.825 (1971): 712, 714, 719, 721.

43 J. V. G. Mallet, "Mantua and Urbino," 167; Jacqueline Marie Musacchio, *Marvels of Maiolica from the Corcoran's William A. Clark Collection* (Charlestown, MA: Bunker Hill Publishing, 2004), 32.

44 See note 26 for literature about Palazzo di Porto.

45 See Luke Syson and Dora Thornton, *Objects of Virtue: Art in Renaissance Italy* (Los Angeles: J. Paul Getty Museum, 2001), 222–28. Reinforcing the idea that Nicola da Urbino did not tailor his narratives to specific patrons is the fact that he included narratives in Isabella's service in other maiolica services, such as the stories of Apollo and Marsyas, and Apollo, Pan, and Midas that represented popular courtly motifs relating to music. The exact compositions of the scenes were never precisely replicated, however.

her daughter, Eleonora, mentioned Porto as the proper place for the use of an earthenware service in the 1524 letter discussed above. At the Palazzo di Porto, Isabella could return to her lead role as hostess and orchestrate all the pleasurable activities there.

Later Maiolica with Virgilian Narratives

Although Isabella's dishes featuring Virgilian scenes would have resonated with her guests due to her interest in classical subjects and her significant role in the city of the poet's birth, the 1520s and 1530s were a golden age of *istoriato* maiolica production, and therefore other collectors also acquired dishes with scenes from Virgil's poetry. A large service by the maiolica painter Francesco Xanto Avelli created for the Pucci family of Florence in 1532 included dishes with family *imprese* and narratives from the *Aeneid*. The six surviving Virgilian narratives are *The Hunt of Aeneas and his Companions*, *Aeneas Contemplates the Trojan Battles, The Departure of Aeneas and Ascanius*, *Aeneas at the Tomb of Polydorus*, *Palinurus Falling Overboard*, and *Camilla's Rescue.*[46]

Later in the sixteenth century, Virgilian subject matter continued to be popular for maiolica decoration. A 1555 dish possibly commissioned for Vespasiano Gonzaga, founder of Sabbioneta, a Mantuan town, illustrates the scene in Book 8 of Aeneas awakening next to the Tiber following a dream, in which the river god predicts his founding of Rome (*Aeneid*, 8.26ff.). Following the dream, Aeneas and King Evander, who is pictured gesturing towards the reclining Aeneas, agree to join forces. The story would be especially appropriate for Vespasiano, the founder of a new town. [47] Although no coats of arms are included on the dish, curator Wendy Watson linked it to Vespasiano due to the presence of his *impresa* of lightning striking a mountain, and the *impresa* of the tree, which may belong to Vespasiano's first wife, Diana de Cardona.[48]

Maiolica dishes painted with Virgilian narratives provided collectors and patrons with a visually rich method of initiating conversation and encouraging reactions from guests when these dishes were on display or in use. The banquet participants could consider the moralizing messages of certain stories or debate the actions and judgments of the characters in the *Aeneid*. Isabella d'Este's guests

---

[46] Julia Triolo, "Francesco Xanto Avelli's Pucci service (1532–1533): A Catalogue," *Faenza* 74 (1988): part 1: 32–44; part 2: 228–84; eadem, "New Notes and Corrections to 'The Pucci Service: A Catalogue'," *Faenza* 78 (1992): 87–89.

[47] Wendy M. Watson, *Italian Renaissance Ceramics from the Howard I. and Janet H. Stein Collection and the Philadelphia Museum of Art* (Philadelphia: Philadelphia Museum of Art, 2001), 126–28.

[48] Giancarlo Malacarne, *Araldica Gonzaghesca: La storia attraverso i simboli* (Modena: Il Bulino, 1993), 226–27; Watson, *Italian Renaissance Ceramics*, 126–28.

would have been able to analyze closely the individual narratives and piece them together to create a complete story. The complex narratives of *istoriato* dishes seem to have encouraged dining participants to engage with them as though they were examining a beautifully illustrated text, which, given Isabella's humanist education and the classical interests of the Mantuan court, may have been the original intention.

5

Vergilius in nummis: Virgilian Quotations on Medals and Tokens Issued in the Low Countries during the Second Half of the Sixteenth Century

Cécile Arnould
Musée national d'histoire et d'art, Luxembourg

Pierre Assenmaker
Université de Namur

In the broad spectrum of studies regarding the reception of Virgil's works during the Renaissance, numismatics is still almost completely unexplored. With the exception of a brief study by Josèphe Jacquiot published in 1989,[1] the presence of Virgilian quotations on medals and tokens issued during the Renaissance has never been studied in a systematic way. This paper provides a first contribution to fill this void.

The medal, initiated in Italy during the fifteenth century, is an emblematic result of the Renaissance's willingness to carry on the cultural heritage of antiquity and to produce works inspired by and competing with antique models, in this case the coins issued under the Roman Empire. Unlike coins, however, medals had no monetary or exchange function. They were commissioned as gifts for princes, nobles, ambassadors, and other diplomatic or literary figures.[2] They primarily served the celebration of the famous and great of this world, whose portraits were almost always represented

---

[1] Josèphe Jacquiot, "Virgile dans les devises de médailles et de jetons de la Renaissance au XVIIIe siècle," *Revue belge de numismatique* 135 (1989): 97–107. Cf. T. Corey Brennan and Lee Fratantuono, "Coins and Medallions," in *The Virgil Encyclopedia*, ed. Richard F. Thomas and Jan M. Ziolkowski, 3 vols. (Chichester: Wiley-Blackwell, 2013), 282–83.

[2] On the production of medals in the Renaissance, see *The Currency of Fame: Portrait Medals of the Renaissance*, ed. Stephen K. Scher (London: Thames and Hudson, 1994), 13–28; John Graham Pollard et al., *Renaissance Medals, Volume One: Italy* (New York and Oxford: Oxford University Press, 2007), xv–xxvi.

on the obverse;[3] the two sides could also refer exclusively to one person, the reverse legend being often used, in that case, for a personal motto. Similar to the medals, but made of less precious metal, tokens—also called *jet(t)ons* or casting-counters—were produced for humbler users and used in a large variety of contexts (e.g., as presence tokens, receipts for tolls or taxes, etc.).[4] Medals and tokens were widely used to commemorate particular events—of a political, military, or dynastic nature—perpetuated by means of the images and legends.

A central feature of the art of the medal is the combination of image and text in the obverse and reverse "types" (i.e., the image and the inscription on each side of the medal).[5] Most of the legends consist of a titulature accompanying a portrait. Among the other inscriptions, we find not only original texts, specially composed for the medal's striking, but also a significant proportion of citations. These mottos are extracted mainly from two repertoires: the Bible, which provides the greatest number of quotes, and the classical authors, among whom Virgil enjoys an indisputable primacy, especially in Italy.[6]

Dealing with such a broad subject, we chose to focus our analysis on a restricted geographical and chronological context: the Low Countries during the second half of the sixteenth century, a crucial period in the history of these regions, which rebelled at that time for both political and religious reasons against the rule of Philip II of Spain (who was appointed to the government of the Low Countries in 1555, became king of Spain in 1556, and died in 1598).[7] If the history of the medal in the

---

[3] On the portrait medals of the Renaissance, see *The Currency of Fame*, ed. Scher; Pollard et al., *Renaissance Medals, Volume One*, xxvii–xxxviii; Walter Cupperi et al., *Wettstreit in Erz. Porträtmedaillen der Deutschen Renaissance* (Berlin and Munich: Deutscher Kunstverlag, 2013).

[4] On the various uses of tokens, see e.g., Tyll Kroha, *Grosses Lexikon der Numismatik* (Gütersloh: Bertelsmann Lexikon Verlag, 1997), 283–84, s.v. "Marken"; *Dictionnaire de numismatique*, ed. Michel Amandry (Paris: Larousse, 2001), 297.

[5] For a diachronic analysis of the thematic repertoire of the medal types of the Renaissance, see John Graham Pollard, "Text and Image," in *Perspectives on the Renaissance Medal*, ed. Stephen K. Scher (New York: Garland Publishing Inc. and The American Numismatic Society, 2000), 149–64.

[6] This can already be asserted after even a brief survey of the indexes of the catalogue of the Renaissance medals in the National Gallery of Art, Washington: Pollard et al., *Renaissance Medals, Volume One*, cvi–cxxxv; John Graham Pollard et al., *Renaissance Medals, Volume Two: France, Germany, the Netherlands, and England* (New York and Oxford: Oxford University Press, 2007), lxxxiii–cii.

[7] On the political and religious context, see, among others, the following standard works: Helmut Georg Koenigsberger, "Western Europe and the Power of Spain," in *The New Cambridge Modern History, Volume III. The Counter-Reformation and Price Revolution. 1559–1610*, ed. R. B. Wernham (Cambridge: Cambridge University Press, 1968), 234–318; Jonathan I. Israel, *The Dutch Republic: Its Rise, Greatness, and Fall, 1477–1806* (Oxford: Clarendon Press, 1995; paperback with corrections, 1998); Alain Tallon,

Low Countries in the sixteenth century has already been thoroughly studied,[8] an exhaustive and systematic corpus of the medals produced in this region is still lacking. In the absence of such an essential instrument, the main reference work for the period after 1555 remains the first volume of the *Histoire métallique des Pays-Bas* of Gerard Van Loon, a French translation published in 1732 of the original Dutch edition (1723).[9] Needless to say, this book cannot be used in the same way as a numismatic catalogue in the modern "scientific" sense of the word, as Luc Smolderen has rightly pointed out:

> These great works[10] have long served the function of a corpus, although properly speaking they cannot be called "numismatic": they are, to tell the truth, history books illustrated with medals rather than histories of the medal in the former Low Countries. Consequently, one finds in them, in no kind of order, various Italian, French, Spanish, English, and German pieces which, according to the needs of the story, are put there to fill the gaps in the local production, inflating our drawers at the expense of those to whom these foreign pieces really belong. If we rid Van Loon of these intruders, there remains only the chronological order.[11]

Therefore, if the first volume of Van Loon's book, which deals with the half century from the abdication of Charles V (1555) to the death of Queen Elizabeth I of England (1603), is necessarily the main documentary basis for the constitution of our corpus, the data must be systematically checked and updated with modern bibliography, and, as far as possible, completed with recent reference works.

L'Europe au XVIe siècle. États et relations internationales (Paris: Presses Universitaires de France, 2010).

[8] Liliane Wellens-De Donder, *Médailleurs et numismates de la Renaissance aux Pays-Bas* (Brussels: Bibliothèque royale, 1959); Pollard et al., *Renaissance Medals, Volume Two*, 759–76; Luc Smolderen, *La médaille en Belgique des origines à nos jours* (Wetteren: Cultura, 2009), 11–63.

[9] Gerard Van Loon, *Histoire métallique des XVII provinces des Pays-Bas depuis l'abdication de Charles-Quint jusqu'à la paix de Bade en MDCCXVI. Tome premier* (La Haye: P. Goose, J. Neaulme, P. de Hondt, 1732).

[10] Besides Van Loon's book, the author alludes to another contemporary reference work: Frans Van Mieris, *Histori der Nederlandsche Vorsten* (Gravenhage: P. De Hondt, 1732–1735).

[11] Smolderen, *La médaille en Belgique*, 6–7: "Ces grands ouvrages font depuis longtemps office de corpus, bien qu'ils ne puissent à proprement parler pas être qualifiés de numismatiques: ce sont, à vrai dire, des livres d'histoire illustrés par les médailles plutôt que des histoires de la médaille dans les anciens Pays-Bas. Il en résulte qu'on y trouve pêle-mêle quantité de pièces italiennes, françaises, espagnoles, anglaises et allemandes qui, au gré des besoins du récit, sont venues meubler les vides de la production locale, gonflant nos tiroirs au détriment de ceux auxquels ces pièces étrangères appartiennent réellement. Si l'on expurge Van Loon de ces intrus, il ne reste que l'ordre chronologique."

Toward a Corpus of the Medals and Tokens with Virgilian Quotations

In Van Loon's first volume, twenty-nine medals and tokens with a Virgilian quotation are mentioned. We were able to complete this list with several medals commissioned by Antoine Perrenot de Granvelle and bearing two legends extracted from the *Aeneid* (1.207 and, on only one medal, 9.279).

In the following table, medals and tokens are classified according to the Virgilian legends; since the starting point of this investigation is the reception of Virgil's works, we quote the Virgilian passages exactly, even if they happen to be modified in the legends, as we shall see. Concerning the dating of the objects, if they bear a date, we give it without special indication; for the few ones without dates, we mention the dates given either in Van Loon (indicated "VL") or in modern reference works if other dates have been proposed since then, in which case the reference is given in a footnote.

Reference to Virgil's works	Virgilian text and translation[12]	Object, date, reference[13]
Eclogae, 1.6	*Deus nobis haec otia fecit* ("It is a god who wrought for us this peace")	• Medal, after 1550 and before 1615[14] (Wynants 10 = Van Loon I, 5, no. 1)
Eclogae, 3.93	*Latet anguis in herba* ("A snake lurks in the grass")	• Token, 1592 (Van Loon I, 421, no. 2)

[12] All the translations of passages from Virgil cited in this paper are taken, sometimes slightly modified, from the edition and English translation of the Loeb Classical Library by Henry Rushton Fairclough, 2 vols. (Cambridge, MA: Harvard University Press; London: William Heinemann Ltd, 1935 [new and revised edition]; repr. 1986).

[13] Key to the shortened references:

Granvelle + Roman numeral refers to the catalogue compiled by Luc Smolderen, "Les médailles de Granvelle," in *Les Granvelle et les anciens Pays-Bas*, ed. Krista de Jonge and Gustaaf Janssens (Leuven: Universitaire Pers, 2000), 293–320.

Jonghelinck + Arabic numeral refers to the catalogue of Jonghelinck's medals and tokens compiled by Luc Smolderen, *Jacques Jonghelinck. Sculpteur, médailleur et graveur de sceaux (1530–1606)* (Louvain-la-Neuve: Séminaire de Numismatique Marcel Hoc, 1996), 207–442.

Van Loon I refers to Van Loon, *Histoire métallique . . . Tome premier*, page number, and number of the illustration according to the page layout.

Wynants + Arabic numeral refers to the catalogue of medals representing Maria of Hungary compiled by Benedicte Wynants, "Maria van Hongarije in medailles," *Jaarboek voor het Europees Genootschap voor Munt- en Penningkunde* (1997): 173–221.

[14] Wynants, "Maria van Hongarije," 194.

Reference to Virgil's works	Virgilian text and translation	Object, date, reference
Eclogae, 4.7	*Iam nova progenies* ("Now a new generation")	• Tokens, 1572 (Van Loon I, 142, no. 2 and 143, no. 1)
Eclogae, 4.34	*Et altera quae vehat Argo* ("And a second Argo to carry")	• Token, 1599 (Van Loon I, 519, no. 2)
Aeneid, 1.199	*Dabit deus his quoque finem* ("To this, too, God will grant an end")	• Token, 1597 (Van Loon I, 488, no. 1)
Aeneid, 1.203	*Olim meminisse iuvabit* ("It will someday be a joy to recall")	• Token, 1590 [VL] (Van Loon I, 409, no. 1)
Aeneid, 1.207	*Durate* ("Endure")	• Medals, around 1555[15] (*Granvelle* V–VI; cf. Van Loon I, 47, no. 3) • Medal, 1555 (*Granvelle* VIII = Van Loon I, 47, no. 4) • Medals, around 1555 (*Granvelle* IX–X = *Jonghelinck* 23-24; cf. Van Loon I, 47, no. 5) • Medal, around 1555 (*Granvelle* XI = *Jonghelinck* 22) • Medal, around 1555 (*Granvelle* XII = Van Loon I, 47, no. 2) • Medal, before 1560 (*Granvelle* XV = *Jonghelinck* 27) • Medal, before 1560 (*Granvelle* XVI = *Jonghelinck* 28) • Medals, 1561 (*Granvelle* XVII–XIX = *Jonghelinck* 31-33; cf. Van Loon I, 58, no. 1) • Medal, 1561/1564 (*Granvelle* XXI = *Jonghelinck* 35 = Van Loon I, 58, no. 4) • Medals, without date (around 1571?) (*Granvelle* XXVII–XXVIII; cf. Van Loon I, 58, no. 2)

[15] All medals and tokens bearing the motto *Durate* were commissioned by Antoine Perrenot de Granvelle (see below, n.40). The chronology assigned here to these medals is taken from Smolderen, *Granvelle*, 297-313.

Reference to Virgil's works	Virgilian text and translation	Object, date, reference
Aeneid, 1.207	*Durate* ("Endure")	• Medals, without date (around 1571?) (*Granvelle* XXXI = Van Loon I, 58, no. 3) • Numerous tokens[16] (cf. Van Loon I, 47, no. 6; 58, no. 5). See especially Smolderen, *Granvelle*, 314, fig. B; *Jonghelinck* J1 and J2, before and in (?) 1561.v[17]
Aeneid, 2.61	*In utrumque paratus* ("Ready for either event")	• Token, 1559 (Van Loon I, 26, no. 1)
Aeneid, 3.7	*Incerti quo fata ferant* ("Uncertain whither the Fates lead")	• Token, 1565 (Van Loon I, 71, no. 1)
Aeneid, 3.395 = 10.113	*Fata viam invenient* ("The Fates will find a way")	• Token, 1580 (Van Loon I, 278, no. 3) • Token, 1591 (Van Loon I, 418, no. 1)
Aeneid, 4.13	*Degeneres animos timor arguit* ("'Tis fear that proves souls base-born")	• Token, 1581 (Van Loon I, 288, no. 1)
Aeneid, 6.620	*Discite iustitiam moniti* ("Be warned; learn ye to be just")	• Token, 1570 (Van Loon I, 127, no. 1)
Aeneid, 8.641	*Caesa iungebant foedera porca* ("Each with each made covenant o'er sacrifice of swine")	• Token, 1596 (Van Loon I, 471, no. 3)
Aeneid, 9.279	*Seu pacem, seu bella geram* ("Be peace or be war on hand")	• Medal, 1557?[18] (*Granvelle* XIV = *Jonghelinck* 26) • Medal, 1589 [VL] (*Jonghelinck* 103 = Van Loon I, 398, no. 2)
Aeneid, 10.284	*Audentes fortuna iuvat* ("Fortune aids the daring")	• Medal, 1567 (Van Loon I, 126, no. 1) • Medal, 1572 [VL] (Van Loon I, 154, no. 1)
Aeneid, 11.362	*Te poscimus omnes* ("All of us pray thee")	• Token, 1579 (Van Loon I, 269, no. 1)

[16] See Smolderen, *Granvelle*, 314.

[17] Smolderen, *Jonghelinck*, 433.

[18] Smolderen, *Granvelle*, 303.

Reference to Virgil's works	Virgilian text and translation	Object, date, reference
Aeneid, 12.6	*Tum demum movet arma* ("Then only he wakes to war")	• Token, 1595 (Van Loon I, 448, no. 1)

Out of the thirty-one items constituting our corpus, seventeen Virgilian mottos are mentioned: thirteen extracted from the *Aeneid*, four from the *Eclogues*, and none from the *Georgics*. This distribution fully confirms what is known about the reception of Virgil's poetry during the Renaissance. The primacy of the *Aeneid* was to be expected, for the epic had always been regarded, since antiquity, as the supreme masterpiece of the poet. It should further be noted that Aeneas's speech after the storm in the first book (*Aeneid*, 1.198–207) seems to have been really famous at the time, since three quotations in our corpus come from this passage (see below, n.41). The absence of the *Georgics* is also not surprising, since in this period "there are fewer tangible signs of influence than one might expect, and they often prove to have only limited importance . . . . Most citations . . . come from just a few sections of the poem, primarily the nondidactic passages."[19]

On the basis of this corpus, which will have to be completed by further studies, we will now investigate the processes of quotation that are implemented in these medals and tokens. To this end, we will examine the relation these quotations bear to the original text. The first step consists of checking the textual accuracy of the quotation: did the designers of the medals and tokens quote exactly the Virgilian text or did they modify it? If so, what was the meaning of such a modification? The second step of our analysis concerns the absence or presence of a reference to the legend's original narrative context. Was the legend simply taken from a repertoire of famous classical mottos, or was it an actual quotation of a precise Virgilian passage with which the readers of the legend were invited to make a connection? If this is the case, did the understanding of the legend presuppose deep knowledge of the Virgilian context, or was a veneer of classical culture sufficient to grasp the meaning of the whole design?

Examining in this way what could be called the "level of consciousness" of the several Virgilian quotations will allow us to specify the place Virgil occupied in the cultural horizon of the persons who designed the medals and tokens as well as the circles they addressed.

[19] Craig Kallendorf, "Renaissance Literature," in *The Virgil Encyclopedia*, ed. Thomas and Ziolkowski, 1072–74, esp. 1073 for the citation.

Playing with the Text: Quotation and Adaptation

Of the seventeen Virgilian quotations in our corpus, eleven take up the exact words of Virgil's text, while six of them show more or less important and significant modifications. Among these adaptations of the original text, the case of the famous motto *Audaces fortuna iuvat* (see below), adapted from Virgil's *Audentes fortuna iuvat* (*Aeneid*, 10.284), is not relevant for the present research, since the substitution of *audaces* for *audentes* was not peculiar to the medals and already had a long history.[20] There are still five cases of "intentional" adaptation of the Virgilian original that are worth analyzing.

The first case is provided by the medal struck between 1550 and 1615 to commemorate the government of Mary of Hungary, Charles V's sister and governor of the Low Countries from 1531 to 1555 (Van Loon I, 5, no. 1). The reverse portrays a ship on a calm sea under a radiant sun and symbolizes the stability brought to the state by Mary. The iconographical message is completed by the legend *His Deus ocia fecit*, directly inspired by the famous sixth verse of the first Eclogue: *deus nobis haec otia fecit*. In Virgil, the personal pronoun *nobis* ("for us") designates the shepherd Tityrus, who pronounces these words. On the medal, it was replaced by the pronoun *his* ("for them"), a dative plural referring to the population of the Low Countries.[21] The reference to the *deus*, an encomiastic designation of Octavian in the eclogue, is obviously given a Christian meaning in the new context.

An interesting modification of the original text can also be found in two medals designed by Jacques Jonghelinck, the first one (Smolderen, *Granvelle*, XIV) around 1557 for Antoine Perrenot de Granvelle, bishop of Arras at that time, the second one (Van Loon I, 398, no. 2) in 1589 for Alexander Farnese, duke of Parma and Piacenza and governor of the Spanish Netherlands. Both medals show on the reverse an olive branch[22] and a palm branch tied up, with the words *Sive pacem, sive bella geras* ("whether you bring peace or war"). This legend is an adaptation of a sentence from the ninth book of the *Aeneid*, where it concludes a speech of Ascanius who is swearing loyalty to Euryalus: *Seu pacem, seu bella geram tibi maxima rerum | verborumque fides* (*Aeneid*, 9.279–80: "be peace

[20] This modification could have been inspired by the use of the adjective *audax* for Turnus a few verses before (*Aeneid*, 10.276: *audaci Turno*). The Virgilian hemistich was already an adaptation of the ancient proverb *Fortes fortuna adiuvat* (Terence, *Phormio*, 1.4.16; Cicero, *Tusculan Disputations*, 2.4.11), which was often quoted under an abbreviated form: *Fortuna fortes* (cf. Cicero, *De Finibus*, 3.4).

[21] The written form *ocia* for *otia* is common and simply reflects the pronunciation of the time. Cf. *paciencia* for *patientia* in another medal representing Mary of Hungary (Wynants, "Maria van Hongarije," 195, no. 11).

[22] According to Smolderen, *Jonghelinck*, 245 and *Granvelle*, 303, the reverse of Granvelle's medal shows a laurel branch and not an olive-branch.

or be war on hand, in thee shall be my chiefest trust in deed and in word"). The first-person *geram* of the Virgilian verse is transformed into the second-person *geras*, so that the legend appears to be aimed at the political opponents of the two men portrayed on the obverses, who are presented as equally talented for peace and war, for diplomatic and military matters.[23]

A token struck in 1565 (Van Loon I, 71, no. 1), at a time of "marked weakening of royal authority in the Netherlands,"[24] echoes the great difficulties encountered by the main officials of Philip II, especially the President of the Council, Viglius.[25] The obverse shows a vessel with broken masts on a rough sea—a clear symbol of the political crisis which then struck the state—and the legend *Incertum quo fata ferent*, directly inspired by *Aeneid*, 3.7: *incerti quo fata ferant, ubi sistere detur.* In Virgil, this line refers to the surviving Trojans who, after the destruction of their city, are building a fleet "without knowing either where the fates would bring them, or where they will be allowed to settle down." On the token, the phrase is given an impersonal structure (*incertum* [*est*]), which corresponds better to the use of this line as an accompanying legend. The future indicative *ferent* instead of the subjunctive *ferant* in the expression of indirect questions—a construction well attested in post-classical Latin—is a purely grammatical modification that has no consequence on the meaning and is perhaps not to be attributed to the designers of the token.

The two following tokens with modifications of the Virgilian text were issued in the last decade of the sixteenth century to commemorate some political and military events that marked the first years of the Dutch Republic. In 1596, with the conclusion of the Treaty of the Hague, the Seven United Provinces joined the alliance established by France and England against Spain. The commemorative token struck on this occasion (Van Loon I, 471, no. 3) shows on the obverse *Fides* and *Constantia* shaking hands under the name of Jehovah; on the reverse, a hand emerges from a cloud, holding a stone to hit a pig or a sow [Figure 3]. This image refers to the ancient Roman custom of sacrificing a pig or a sow to conclude a treaty. This custom was best known to the educated modern thanks to the description given by Livy of the mythical treaty between the Romans and the Albans. The ritual closes with the sacrifice of a pig killed by means of a stone: *id ubi dixit, porcum saxo silice percussit* (1.24.9). The mean-

---

[23] The warlike tone of the message conveyed by the medals is especially pronounced in the case of Granvelle's medal since the obverse shows the only portrait of Granvelle in armor. The reverse type of this medal is also analyzed by Claudia Banz, *Höfisches Mäzenatentum in Brüssel. Kardinal Antoine Perrenot de Granvelle (1517–1586) und die Erzherzöge Albrecht (1559–1621) und Isabella (1566–1633)* (Berlin: Gebr. Mann Verlag, 2000), 55. However, her commentary can hardly be used since she misses the Virgilian quotation (she refers instead to Horace, *Carmina*, 2.19.27–28: *sed idem pacis eras mediusque belli*).

[24] Israel, *The Dutch Republic*, 145.

[25] Cf. Jacquiot, "Virgile dans les devises," 104.

Fig. 3: *Caesa firmabant foedera porca*: Token struck in Dordrecht, 1596 (Van Loon I, 471, no. 3). Bronze, 29 mm. MPO Auctions, Auction 36, 3935.

ing of the scene depicted, which was certainly not obvious for all the users of the tokens, is cleared up by a quotation from the famous description of Aeneas's shield in the eighth book of the *Aeneid*, where Virgil mentions this antique custom in relation to the peace concluded between Romulus and Titus Tatius. The legend *Caesa firmabant foedera porca*, however, is not an exact quotation since the verb *iungebant* of the Virgilian verse (*Aeneid*, 8.641: *caesa iungebant foedera porca*) is replaced by *firmabant*. It is difficult to determine whether this modification should have a particular meaning, since the expression *foedus firmare* is attested in classical Latin, as well as *foedus iungere*, in the sense of "to conclude a treaty."[26]

The last piece in our corpus that presents a modified Virgilian quotation was struck in 1599 in commemoration of an expedition of the Dutch fleet against the Spanish possessions in Africa (Van Loon I, 519, no. 2). The reverse depicts a ship with the legend *En altera quae vehat Argo*, a nearly exact quotation of *Eclogues*, 4.34. Only the first word was changed: *et* becomes *en* ("here"), a slight modification which made the expression more emphatic and more adapted to its new function as a legend accompanying an image. It should also be noted that the object complement of the verb *vehat*, in Virgil the accusative *delectos heroas* ("chosen heroes") at the beginning of the following verse, was not felt to be indispensable, even if, grammatically speaking, the legend limited to these words is incomplete. The key point in this quotation was the emphasis on the mythic boat that carried the Argonauts. With reference to our token,[27] these few words were sufficient to make the recipients of the message understand that the

[26] It is interesting to observe that the expression is precisely used in a passage of Festus where the grammarian refers to the custom of killing a sow at the conclusion of treaties, without mentioning the stone (as Livy did) but using the same ablative absolute *caesa porca* as in Virgil: *confecto bello inter quos pax fieret, caesa porca foedus firmare solebant* (Festus, *De verborum significatu*, p. 267 Lindsay).

[27] The identically modified quotation *En altera quae vehat Argo* constitutes also the text of an emblem from the collection of Claude Paradin, *Devises heroïques* (Lyons: Jean de Tournes and Guillaume Gazeau, 1557; initially published in 1551), 104. In an augmented edition by François d'Amboise (*Devises héroïques et emblèmes*, Paris: Rolet Boutonné, 1621, 138), the legend is translated by "Une autre Argo pour nous porter en

ship depicted, which allegorically stood for the entire Dutch fleet, was "a second Argo."

This first "philological" approach to the corpus reveals that the designers of the medals and tokens had some latitude in the quotation of classical authors, even in the case of the great Virgil. The attitude towards this monument of classical literature was far from a kind of "religious" respect for the text. Virgil's verses were a still living cultural heritage that everyone was free to use and adapt in order to bring it closer to the political and ideological context of the time or merely to produce a coherent association of image and text.

Losing the Narrative Context: Virgil's Works as a Stock of Maxims

After having checked the textual accuracy of the quotations, we will now analyze the relationship between the legends inspired by Virgil and the narrative contexts from which they are extracted. As we might expect, the understanding of the legend often does not presuppose knowledge of the Virgilian context. This can be explained partly by the fact that many of the lines quoted on the medals and tokens seem to have been chosen precisely for their general, universal meaning. The *sententiae* are indeed one of the most characteristic stylistic features of Virgil's poetry, and many of them very quickly acquired a great celebrity, so that they were quoted and imitated for centuries. But this mode of extracting maxims from Virgil's poetry was not limited to the lines that were coined as actual *sententiae* by the poet. As Craig Kallendorf pointed out, "the general tendency was for the poem [i.e., the *Aeneid*] to be read slowly with a focus on language, style, and moral content, so that for many Renaissance readers the poem ended up being reduced to a series of memorable lines."[28]

---

mer." This translation makes clear that Virgil's object complement *delectos heroas* was not regarded as relevant for the "emblematic" use of this phrase.

[28] Kallendorf, "Renaissance Literature," 1073. On this process, see further Craig Kallendorf, *The Protean Virgil. Material Form and the Reception of the Classics* (Oxford: Oxford University Press, 2015), 88–106 ("From Marginalia to the Commonplace Book"). Cf. also R. R. Bolgar, "Education and Learning," in *The New Cambridge History*, vol. 3, ed. Wernham, 427–52, esp. 437: "Many of the classical references, not only in schoolboy themes, but in the best literature of the time, came from these miscellanies. By the close of the Renaissance, it was not unusual for the heritage of antiquity to reach its devotees second-hand, fragmented and alphabetically classified." For a collection of the main memorable lines from Virgil's works, see Michael von Albrecht, *Vergil:* Bucolica—Georgica—Aeneis. *Eine Einführung* (Heidelberg: Universitätsverlag Winter, 2006), 58 (*Eclogues*), 98–99 (*Georgics*), 187–89 (*Aeneid*).

In our corpus, the most evident example of such reduction is the citation of the famous—yet not authentically Virgilian (see above)—motto *Audaces fortuna iuvat*. It is not necessary to have in mind the speech in which Turnus urges the Latins to march against the Trojans, which closes with the incomplete verse *Audentes fortuna iuvat* (*Aeneid*, 10.284), to be able to understand fully the meaning of this maxim, which appears on the reverse of two medals issued in different contexts: the first, struck in 1567, shows the portrait of Charles, archduke of Austria (Van Loon I, 126, no. 1), while the second, dated to 1572 by Van Loon, was issued for William of Nassau (Van Loon I, 154, no. 1).

At least as famous as the previous instance was the maxim *Fata viam invenient*. A clear sign of the gnomic character of this phrase is that Virgil himself uses it twice in the *Aeneid*: first in the third book, when Helenus tries to comfort Aeneas (3.395), then in the tenth book, in the scene of the assembly of the gods, which is concluded by these words uttered by Jupiter (10.113). This maxim appears on two series of tokens. The first one (Van Loon I, 278, no. 3) was issued in 1580, soon after the Union of Utrecht (1579), which marked the real beginning of the Dutch Republic as a federal state encompassing the whole of the northern Low Countries, and a few months before the Act of Abjuration (July 1581), which repudiated Philip II and his heirs in perpetuity.[29] In this context, the Virgilian maxim gives utterance to the hopes of the people who had been in revolt against the Spanish power for more than fifteen years and were now witnessing the emergence of a new nation. The second token (Van Loon I, 418, no. 1) on which this legend appears was issued in 1591 by the Spanish authorities since it shows on the obverse the portrait of King Philip II. On the reverse, the legend is associated with a labyrinth, a symbol of the fates "finding their way."[30] The royal portrait, on the other hand, is linked with the legend *Dominus mihi adiutor*, which also proclaims the faith of the Spanish power in an auspicious future.

Another Virgilian *sententia* in our corpus comes from the fourth book of the *Aeneid*: *Degeneres animos timor arguit* (4.13). In Virgil, these words are uttered by Queen Dido to underline *a contrario* the bravery of Aeneas in all the great trials he suffered. There is no allusion to the Virgilian hero any more on the token where this maxim is quoted (Van Loon I, 288, no. 1). It was struck in 1581 to commemorate the defense of a Dutch fort against the Spanish troops, and this legend was chosen to praise the heroic resistance of the garrison. It was clear, however, to the designers of the token that the meaning of this phrase was the recognition of supreme bravery.

On the contrary, it can be doubted that the original meaning of the quotation was known to those who associated the legend *Olim meminisse iuvabit* with the coat of arms of the city of Vlissingen (in Zeeland) on a token (Van Loon

---

[29] See Israel, *The Dutch Republic*, 196–211.

[30] The same labyrinth is to be found in the emblem designed by Paradin, *Devises heroïques*, 94.

I, 409, no. 1) apparently issued on behalf of Maurice of Nassau (his blazon is depicted on the obverse). In the *Aeneid*, these are words of comfort and exhortation which Aeneas addresses to his men after the dreadful storm triggered by Juno (1.203). On the token, the quotation seems to be a message addressed by the *Stathouder* Maurice to the people of Vlissingen, the meaning of which, however, is far from being obvious.[31]

On the following medals or tokens, we find Virgilian phrases that originally do not have an especially gnomic character and are extracted without any allusion to the narrative context, so that they often acquire a totally new meaning.

On a token of 1559 (Van Loon I, 26, no. 1), the expression *In utrumque paratus* is associated with a portrait of Philip II holding a sword in his right hand and an olive-branch in his left hand. As a legend accompanying this image, the expression can be understood only as "ready for both war and peace." We are thus far from the scene of the second book of the *Aeneid* where the Greek prisoner Sinon, when he is brought to the Trojans, is said to be *in utrumque paratus, | seu versare dolos, seu certae occumbere morti* (2.61–62: "ready for either event, whether to ply his crafty wiles or to meet certain death").

Another Virgilian quotation was used as a motto by Philip II (and before him already by Charles V[32]): *Discite iustitiam moniti* (*Aeneid*, 6.620). This hemistich comes from the *katabasis*, Aeneas's descent to the underworld under the guidance of the Sibyl, who describes to him the damned locked in Tartarus. The injunction to justice and respect for the gods (*Discite iustitiam moniti et non temnere divos*) is delivered to the shadows by a king imprisoned among them, either Theseus or Phlegyas, king of the Lapiths.[33] Although its religious connotations may have determined the choice of this motto by Charles V, on the token issued

[31] Van Loon, *Histoire métallique . . . Tome premier*, 409 (who dates the token to 1590) feels uncomfortable about the exact meaning of this legend: "Cette sentence fait vraisemblablement allusion aux désastres passés, & peut-être aussi à la conduite de ceux de Flessingue, qui avoient autrefois refusé de reconnoitre Maurice solennellement pour Seigneur. Il est assez apparent que ce Prince leur en fait ici un reproche modéré, en témoignant qu'un jour il s'en souviendra."

[32] In commemoration of the battle of Mühlberg in 1547, Charles V's major victory over the Protestant princes of the Schmalkaldic League, Leone Leoni designed, presumably in 1549, a medal with a portrait of Charles V on the obverse and the scene of the fall of the Giants on the reverse, with the legend *Discite iustitiam moniti.* See Pollard et al., *Renaissance Medals, Volume One*, 493–94, no. 492, and Alfonso Rodríguez Ceballos, "Le medaglie spagnole di Leone Leoni e della sua cerchia: forma, clientela e iconografia," in *Leone Leoni tra Lombardia e Spagna. Atti del Convegno Internazionale. Menaggio 25–26 settembre 1993*, ed. Maria Luisa Gatti Perer (Milan: Istituto per la storia dell'arte lombarda, 1995), 87–95, esp. 89–90 and 88 (for the inscription *Discite iustitiam moniti* on a temporary triumphal arch erected for a solemn entrance of the prince Philip into a city).

[33] There is uncertainty about the identity of the figure who utters these words because of the serious problems of editing posed by this passage: see the comment of

Fig. 4: *Latet anguis in herba*: Token struck in Middelburg, 1592 (Van Loon I, 421, no. 2). Copper, 31.5 mm. Baldwin's Auctions Ltd., Auction 70, 744.

in 1570 with Philip II's portrait (Van Loon I, 127, no. 1), a connection with the underworld context does not seem necessary for the understanding of the reverse type. The sword and the rope depicted allude generally to the different forms of punishment for all crimes, not only the religious ones, perpetrated against the royal power.[34]

On a token (Figure 4) issued in 1592 in the Dutch Republic (Van Loon I, 421, no. 2), we find on the reverse a quotation from the amoebean singing performed by the shepherds Damoetas and Menalcas in the third Eclogue: *Latet anguis in herba* (*Eclogues*, 3.93). In his improvised poem, Damoetas warns the young boys who are picking flowers and strawberries against the snake which hides in the grass. The reference to the pastoral and bucolic world is totally missing in the reverse type of the token,[35] which conveys a purely political message: a Spanish ambassador holds out an olive-branch to an inhabitant of the Low Countries, who is showing with his finger a snake lurking in the grass, an obvious symbol of the ambassador's treachery. In a sense, the Virgilian phrase acquires in the legend a gnomic value that it did not possess in the original text: it becomes a maxim warning against all treacheries and unexpected dangers, at least in the political and diplomatic field.

Jacques Perret in his edition for the *Collection des Universités de France* (Paris: Les Belles Lettres, 1978), 174.

[34] Cf. Jacquiot, "Virgile dans les devises," 98–99, who sees in the legend a warning to the inhabitants of the Low Countries.

[35] On the other hand, there is a clear reference to Virgil's text in the emblem composed on this quotation and published by Claude Paradin, *Devises heroïques*, 70: the picture shows a serpent hiding under a strawberry plant.

Fig. 5: *Iam nova progenies*: Token struck in the Southern Netherlands, 1572 (Van Loon I, 142, no. 2). Copper, 29 mm. Jean Elsen et ses Fils SA, Auction 109, 1655.

Playing with the Virgilian Hypotext: Allusion and Reinterpretation

Other Virgilian legends in our corpus allude more or less directly to the original context of the quotation, so that the meaning of the type cannot be entirely grasped without knowledge of the original passage. A link to the mythical or historical background provided by the quotation conferred a higher symbolic value on the event commemorated by the medal or token.

This is particularly true for tokens (Figure 5) struck in 1572 (Van Loon I, 142, no. 2 and 143, no. 1), which jointly praise two events that occurred in the preceding year: the victory of Lepanto, which is referred to on the reverse by the depiction of a ship and a trophy as well as the legend *Turcae classe devicta*, and the birth of Fernando,[36] son of Philip II, who had been without a male heir since Don Carlos's death in 1568. The obverse of the tokens shows the goddess Juno, protecting deity of weddings and births, with a peacock and a child. This image is accompanied by the words *Iam nova progenies*, extracted from the famous fourth Eclogue (4.7), where they refer to a new generation that will see the return of the Golden Age. In his commentary on this token, Van Loon specially invites us to take the entire Virgilian verse (*iam nova progenies caelo demittitur alto*) into account to understand the sense of the allusion:

> We should understand "descended from Heaven," as it appears in the following part of the Latin verse in question. Certainly the already advanced age of the king, who was without male heir, could lead this young prince to be considered as a gift from Heaven.[37]

---

[36] Not Diego (born in 1575), as erroneously indicated by Van Loon, *Histoire métallique . . . Tome premier*, 142.

[37] Van Loon, *Histoire métallique . . . Tome premier*, 143: "Il faut sous-entendre, *descendu du Ciel*, comme il paroit par la suite du Vers Latin en question. Certainement, l'âge déjà avancé du Roi, qui étoit sans Hoir mâle, pouvoit faire considerer ce jeune Prince

It can be assumed that the allusion to the context of the fourth Eclogue was even more subtle. In Virgil, the new generation is symbolized by the birth of a child, whose identity is not made clear and who is destined to "rule the world pacified by his father's virtues" (*Eclogues*, 4.17: *pacatumque reget patriis virtutibus orbem*). Thus, quoting the fourth Eclogue in commemoration of Fernando's birth was a particularly sophisticated and erudite way (quite typical of the Renaissance) to praise indirectly the military success of Philip II. It is well known that the remarkable synchronism between the victory of Lepanto (7 October) and the birth of the Infante (4 December) was illustrated by Titian in his famous painting depicting Philip II presenting Fernando to Victory, who gives the newborn child a palm with the inscription *Maiora tibi* ("greater things await you").[38] The testimony of the tokens reveals that the link between these two auspicious events was exploited to enhance the prestige of the Spanish realm, not only at the court but also in the distant Low Countries. In a sense, despite the obvious artistic superiority of Titian's masterpiece, the reference to the fourth Eclogue makes the tokens convey an ideologically more elaborate and powerful message: instead of the vague *maiora* promised to the newborn Fernando in Titian's painting, the legend of the tokens, echoing the highly symbolic and messianic tones of Virgil's poem, shows the descendant of the victorious king as bringing a new Golden Age to Catholic Christendom.[39]

We find an even more explicit reference to the narrative context from which the Virgilian legend was extracted on numerous medals and tokens struck between c. 1555 and 1570 for Antoine Perrenot de Granvelle, a central figure of the Spanish administration in the Low Countries under Charles V and Philip II.[40] They bear the prelate's personal motto *Durate* ("Endure!"), inspired by a verse from the first book of the *Aeneid*: *Durate, et vosmet rebus servate secundis* (1.207). At the very beginning of the epic, this "programmatic" exhortation to endure the present sufferings and await better circumstances is uttered by Aeneas to his companions after they have barely escaped from a storm thanks to the

comme un présent du Ciel." Van Loon rightly interprets the word *progenies* in the legend of the token as referring to Philip II's child and not in the sense of "new race" or "new generation," as is very likely the case in Virgil's verse.

[38] Harold E. Wethey, *The Paintings of Titian, Complete Edition, II: The Portraits* (London: Phaidon Press, 1971), 132–33, no. 84.

[39] For more on uses of the fourth Eclogue in the Renaissance, see the final chapter of this volume.

[40] For the biography of Antoine Perrenot de Granvelle (1517–1586), see Maurice Van Durme, *Antoon Perrenot, bisschop van Atrecht, kardinaal van Granvelle, minister van Karel V en van Filips II (1517–1586)* (Brussels: Paleis der Academiën, 1953). For a detailed study of his activities as a patron of the arts and protector of artists, see Banz, *Höfisches Mäzenatentum*, 15–76; eadem, "Zwischen Repräsentation und Humanismus. Zu Funktion und Anspruch von Granvelles Mäzenatentum," in *Les Granvelle et les anciens Pays-Bas*, ed. de Jonge and Janssens, 389–409.

salutary intervention of Neptune. So, Granvelle's motto, which was also widely spread through media other than medals and tokens,[41] was both the symbol of Granvelle's own *constantia* and a general exhortation to steadfastness, as Claudia Banz rightly pointed out:

> [The motto] had a dual function: first, it was to be understood as an ideogram of the owner, who had the virtue of *constantia* raised to his moral "coat of arms"; on the other hand, it appealed to the viewer and thereby assumed a universal character. The ideal virtue of *constantia* was proclaimed as an obligatory standard, on the basis of which the success of Granvelle also ultimately rested.[42]

The first medals with the motto *Durate* were designed around 1555 by Leone Leoni,[43] who illustrated it with images referring directly to the storm in the *Aeneid*, an association which was then taken up for the design of most[44] of the

[41] It was inscribed on Granvelle's seal (Smolderen, *Granvelle*, 314–15) and on the courtyard and garden façades of his palace in Brussels (Banz, *Höfisches Mäzenatentum*, 34 and 181–82, figs. 4–5). Antoine Perrenot not only commissioned medals centered on his personal motto, but also a musical piece, a motet with the title *O socii durate*, which was composed in 1558 by the Flemish polyphonist Adriaan Willaert, chapel master at San Marco in Venice, on the (slightly adapted) text of *Aeneid*, 1.198–99 and 202–7. See Ignace Bossuyt, "*O socii durate*: A Musical Correspondence from the Time of Philip II," *Early Music* 26 (1998): 433–44, and idem, "*O socii durate*: Antoine Perrenot de Granvelle en de vlaamse polyfonist Adriaan Willaert (c. 1490–1562). Nieuwe gegevens op basis van de in Madrid bewaarde correspondentie van Granvelle," in *Les Granvelle et les anciens Pays-Bas*, ed. de Jonge and Janssens, 321–40.

[42] Banz, "Zwischen Repräsentation und Humanismus," 391: "[Die Devise] besaß eine doppelte Funktion: Zum einen war sie als Ideogramm des Besitzers zu begreifen, der die Tugend der 'constantia' zu seinem moralischen 'Wappenschild' erhoben hatte, zum anderen appellierte sie an den Betrachter und nahm dadurch einen allgemeingültigen Charakter an. Das Tugendideal der 'constantia' wurde zur verbindlichen Norm erklärt, auf deren Grundlage schließlich auch der Erfolg Granvelles basierte." Cf. eadem, *Höfisches Mäzenatentum*, 52–53. See also Smolderen, *Granvelle*, 314, who speaks of "portraits moraux."

[43] Smolderen, *Granvelle*, nos. v, vi, and viii. Leoni's medals pleased Granvelle so much that he purchased a chain worth 250 scudi to give to the artist: see Kelley Helmstutler Di Dio, *Leone Leoni and the Status of the Artist at the End of the Renaissance* (Farnham: Ashgate, 2011), 20. See further Maurice Van Durme, "Antoon Perrenot van Granvelle en Leone Leoni," *Revue belge de Philologie et d'Histoire* 27 (1949): 653–78.

[44] There are a few exceptions: two *Durate* medals show instead Granvelle's coat of arms (Smolderen, *Granvelle*, nos. ix and x) and another one (Smolderen, *Granvelle*, no. xi), designed by Jacques Jonghelinck, depicts Odysseus resisting the sirens' singing, another model of *constantia*. Tokens bearing Granvelle's motto in a cartouche show on the other side a ship with broken masts on a rough sea (Smolderen, *Granvelle*, 314, fig. B).

Fig. 6: *Durate*: Medal depicting the portrait of Antoine Perrenot de Granvelle, 1561 (Van Loon I, 58, no. 1). Silver, 59 mm. Royal Library of Belgium – Coins and Medals Department (photo: Cristof Weber).

medals and tokens bearing Granvelle's motto, many of which were struck by Jacques Jonghelinck and Giovanni Melon. Various scenes were depicted: a vessel with broken masts in the midst of a storm, Neptune's intervention to calm the winds and the rough sea (Figure 6),[45] and Scylla savagely wielding a rudder with both hands and threatening Aeneas's ships.[46] The choice of images referring explicitly to the Virgilian narrative is in itself not surprising, since this episode of the *Aeneid* had been very popular in the fine arts since the Quattrocento.[47] On the other hand, it appears that the prelate wanted to recall in a visual way the source of his personal motto. It was essential to the understanding of Granvelle's "moral portrait" presented on these medals that everyone made the connection with the figure of Aeneas and the episode of the storm, which was not only emblematic of the hero's *patientia* and *constantia* but could also be related in several ways to the political context in which Granvelle moved.[48]

---

[45] *Aeneid*, 1.124–56.

[46] The idea of depicting Scylla, who was primarily associated with Odysseus rather than with Aeneas, could have been suggested by the mention of the sea-monster a few lines after the verse with *Durate* (*Aeneid*, 1.200–1: *Vos et Scyllaeam rabiem penitusque sonantis | accestis scopulos*) and also by the famous description given in the third book of the *Aeneid*, where the seer Helenus warns Aeneas against this redoubtable obstacle (*Aeneid*, 3.424–32). The design of the type was very likely inspired by the reverse of some coins issued by Sextus Pompeius, last son of Pompeius Magnus: see Michael H. Crawford, *Roman Republican Coinage* (Cambridge: Cambridge University Press, 1974), 520–21, no. 511/4.

[47] See Jane Davidson Reid, *The Oxford Guide to Classical Mythology in the Arts, 1300–1990s*, 2 vols. (New York and Oxford: Oxford University Press, 1993), s.v. "Aeneas," 40–68, esp. 46–48; Marisa Bass, "*Quos ego* in Art," in *The Virgil Encyclopedia*, ed. Thomas and Ziolkowski, 1063–64.

[48] In a subtle analysis of the symbolism of the types with the motto *Durate*, Banz (*Höfisches Mäzenatentum*, 53–54 and 55–56) distinguishes several associations: the sail alluding to Granvelle's name ("*gran velum*"), Aeneas as incarnation of *pietas* and *con-*

Fig.7: *Tum demum movet arma*: Token struck in the Southern Netherlands, 1595 (Van Loon I, 448, no. 1). Copper, 27.5 mm. Baldwin's Auctions Ltd., Auction 70, 709.

We also find an image reminiscent of the Virgilian context from which the legend is extracted[49] on a token (Figure 7) struck in 1595 in Antwerp (Van Loon I, 448, no. 1), which bears a quotation from the twelfth book of the *Aeneid*: *Tum demum movet arma* (12.6). In the first lines of this book, Turnus, who has just seen the Latin army put to rout by the Trojans, decides to fight against Aeneas in single combat. He is compared to a lion who prepares for fighting only when he has been wounded (*Aeneid*, 12.4–9):

Poenorum qualis in arvis
saucius ille gravi venantum volnere pectus
tum demum movet arma leo gaudetque comantis
excutiens cervice toros fixumque latronis
impavidus frangit telum et fremit ore cruento:
haud secus accenso gliscit violentia Turno.

As in Punic fields a lion, when wounded, lo! with grievous stroke of huntsmen in the breast, then only wakes to war, joyously tosses from his neck his shaggy main, and snaps, undaunted, the robber's implanted dart, roaring with blood-stained mouth: even so in Turnus's kindling soul the fury swells.

---

stantia, the ship as metaphor for the state, and Neptune as a symbolic representation of Charles V or Philip II. We fully agree with the conclusion regarding the plurality of themes expressed in this type: "Das emblematische Motiv . . . vereinte persönliche Ambitionen und Repräsentationsansprüche Antoines mit Topoi der kaiserlichen Herrschersymbolik." Cf. Banz, "Zwischen Repräsentation und Humanismus," 405, n 9. The highly imaginative commentary on the *Durate* medals given by Jacquiot, "Virgile dans les devises," 99–106, lacks intellectual rigor and is therefore hardly useful; among other things, she maintains that some medals bearing the portrait of Granvelle convey the message that Philip II will soon condemn the presumptuous cardinal!

[49] For another example of this process of allusion, see the discussion above on the token with the legend *Caesa firmabant foedera porca* (Van Loon I, 471, no. 3).

In the legend, the subject of the phrase—*leo*—does not appear, but it is made present by the depiction of a roaring lion, whose leg is pierced by an arrow (*telum* in Virgil's text). Thanks to this image, the users of the token were reminded of the exact meaning of the legend. At the same time, the Virgilian passage was perfectly integrated into the contemporary political context, since the lion could easily be interpreted as the *leo Belgicus*.[50]

Another example of an accomplished complementarity of the text and the image is given by the tokens issued in 1597 (Van Loon I, 488, no. 1) with the legend *Dabit deus his quoque finem*.[51] The obverse shows a woman praying on a battlefield strewn with weapons and an angel coming down from heaven, evidently uttering the words of the legend. In Virgil (*Aeneid*, 1.199), the pronoun *his* refers to the *mala* ("sufferings," "evils") Aeneas and his companions have gone through. Here, it refers more generally to the harms of war.

Intellectually more demanding was the reverse type of a token struck in 1579 (Van Loon I, 269, no. 1), where the quotation *Te poscimus omnes* lacks the object complement *pacem* which we read in the famous verse: *nulla salus bello, pacem te poscimus omnes* (*Aeneid*, 11.362: "No safety is there in war; for peace we pray thee"). The female figure with a cornucopia depicted in the type, which was immediately interpreted as an allegory of Peace, helps in "decoding" the allusion. In this last example, it is almost necessary to have the entire Virgilian verse in mind in order to grasp the exact meaning of the legend.

~

This brief analysis of the Virgilian quotations on the medals and tokens issued in the Low Countries in the second half of the sixteenth century is intended to be a first step in a larger study of Virgil's reception in this art form typical of the erudite amusements of the Renaissance. The first results of this research, which brings a new documentation into the field of Virgilian reception studies, have fully confirmed what is known about the reading processes applied to Virgil's works in Renaissance culture. The more or less erudite displays of allusion and reinterpretation at work in the medals and tokens rested less on a deep knowledge of the entire works than on the mastering of the "classical" collection of the most famous Virgilian lines, which constituted a common cultural background.

An important issue that should be dealt with in future studies is specifically the question of the sources from which the designers of medals and tokens drew the Virgilian quotations. Parallels to collections of emblems, which were flour-

[50] For the context in which the token was issued, see Van Loon, *Histoire métallique . . . Tome premier*, 447–48.

[51] This famous Virgilian line had already been used as a legend on a medal made by Leone Leoni for the duke of Sessa; see Helmstutler Di Dio, *Leone Leoni*, 27.

ishing in this period, are obvious.[52] The design of *emblemata* required the same intellectual approach, resting on the association of a text and an image. But were emblem books the source of inspiration for the designing of medals and tokens? Or should we not rather regard these two artistic genres as different and parallel, even if certainly influencing one another, expressions of the same "cultural fashion"? In this case, from what kind of collections were the Virgilian quotations drawn?[53]

There is, however, a sociological distinction to be established between the emblems and the medals or tokens. If the *emblemata* may be regarded as a refined intellectual play confined to erudite circles, the latter were systematically connected to the political sphere, since they were issued on behalf of magnates or civic powers. The study of the legends, therefore, gives us a privileged means of access to the role that Virgil—and more generally the stock of classical literary knowledge—could play in the political life of the time.[54] Inserted in several ways in the types of medals and tokens, Virgil's most famous maxims exalted the glorious deeds and virtues of the kings and the nobles and, in the case of the Dutch Republic, could even contribute to the construction of a new state identity.

---

[52] On some *emblemata* of the sixteenth century designed on the basis of Virgilian lines, see Guy de Tervarent, *Présence de Virgile dans l'art* (Brussels: Académie royale de Belgique, 1965), 21–37.

[53] On the commonplace books of the Renaissance, see now Kallendorf, *The Protean Virgil*, 88–116. Cf. the suggestion of Rodríguez Ceballos, "Le medaglie spagnole di Leone Leoni," 88: "Non è sempre facile trovare la fonte e l'origine delle iscrizioni impresse sulle medaglie di Leoni. . . . La cosa più probabile è che le iscrizioni gli fossero suggerite dagli umanisti di corte che erano al servizio dei re, principi e governanti."

[54] Cf. Kallendorf, "Renaissance Literature," 1072: "*A*[*eneid*] provided a key part of the mental apparatus through which Renaissance decision makers made sense of their world. . . . Although most people alive in the Renaissance never read Virgil even in translation, his poetry had a great impact on their lives nonetheless."

6

The Song of Iopas in Renaissance Italy

Evan A. MacCarthy
West Virginia University

In a letter to Bernardo Bembo, Marsilio Ficino describes the importance of banquets (*convivia*) for rebuilding the body, reviving humors, restoring the spirit, delighting the senses, and fostering as well as awakening reason. A banquet, for Ficino, is "rest of labours, release from cares and nourishment of genius; it is the demonstration of love and splendour, the food of good will, the seasoning of friendship, the leavening of grace and the solace of life."[1] Ficino specifies the form of such banquets, noting in particular who should speak, and when, and which topics should be covered: "If divine matters are to be discussed, they should be discussed by those who are temperate; if the participants are to discuss subjects relating to nature, it should be after the table has been removed." At the end of this letter, Ficino invokes the model for banquet interlocutors: the Carthaginian bard Iopas, whom Dido called upon to perform for Aeneas and the assembled crowd of Carthaginians and Trojans in Virgil's *Aeneid* (1.740–47). Ficino pleads, "May long-haired Iopas with his cithara be constantly present at the feasts of the Graces and Muses."[2] This poet-musician Iopas, the subject of

---

[1] Marsilio Ficino, *Letters*, letter 3, line 42, trans. School of Economic Science, London, Language Department, 9 vols. (London: Shepheard-Walwyn, 1975-), 2:51–53. Ficino, *Epistolae* (Venice: Matteo Capcasa, 1495), fol. 73v: . . . *laborum requies, remissio curarum, ingenii pabulum, amoris et magnificentiae argumentum, esca benivolentiae* [sic], *amicitiae condimentum, fomentum gratiae, vitae solatium.*

[2] *Adsit omnino Gratiarum Musarumque mensae cithara crinitus Iopas*: Marsilio Ficino, *Opera omnia*, 2 vols. (Turin: Bottega Erasmo, 1959), vol. 1, part 2, 770. On Ficino's interests in music, see D. P. Walker, *Spiritual and Demonic Magic from Ficino to Campanella* (Notre Dame: Notre Dame University Press, 1958; repr. University Park, PA: The Pennsylvania State University Press, 2003), 3–29; Gary Tomlinson, *Music and Renaissance Magic: Toward a Historiography of Others* (Chicago: University of Chicago Press, 1993), 101–88; Angela Voss, "*Orpheus Redivivus*: The Musical Magic of Marsilio Ficino," in *Marsilio Ficino: His Theology, His Philosophy, His Legacy*, ed. Michael J. B. Allen and Valery Rees with Martin Davies, Brill's Studies in Intellectual History 108 (Leiden and Boston: Brill, 2002), 228–41; Brenno Boccadoro, "Marsilio Ficino: The Soul and the

his banquet song and the increased interest in him as a musician and poet by late medieval and early Renaissance writers, will be the focus of this essay.

The relationship of Virgil and his writings to music in the Renaissance has been studied at length. The *Aeneid* was a source of inspiration for generations of composers who chose to compose polyphonic settings of verses from Book 4, *Dulces exuviae, dum fata deusque sinebat* (4.651–58) or *Fama, malum qua non aliud velocius ullum* (4.174–77).[3] Others chose to allude to the epic poem or its characters in their music or lyrics.[4] Some manuscripts of Virgil, together with those of other ancient authors, were among the corpus of tenth- to twelfth-century sources featuring neumatic notation, offering evidence of the musical delivery

---

Body of Counterpoint," in *Number to Sound: The Musical Way to the Scientific Revolution*, ed. Paolo Gozza, The Western Ontario Series in Philosophy of Science 64 (Dordrecht: Kluwer Academic, 2000), 99–134; Michael J. B. Allen, "Eurydice in Hades: Florentine Platonism and an Orphic Mystery," in *Nuovi maestri e antichi testi: umanesimo e Rinascimento alle origini del pensiero moderno: atti del Convegno internazionale di studi in onore di Cesare Vasoli, Mantova, 1–3 dicembre 2010*, ed. Stefano Caroti and Vittoria Perrone Compagni, Ingenium 17 (Florence: L. S. Olschki, 2012), 19–40.

[3] Musical settings of *Dulces exuviae* (*Aeneid*, 4.651–54, or 4.651–58) and *Fama, malum* (*Aeneid*, 4.174–77) can be found in manuscript and print sources with attributions to Alexander Agricola, Johannes Ghiselin, Josquin Desprez, Jean Mouton, Marbrianus de Orto, Adrian Willaert, and others, as well as a handful of anonymous settings. Jacob Arcadelt composed a setting of *At trepida et coeptis immanibus effera Dido* (*Aeneid*, 4.642–54) and Cipriano de Rore composed *Dissimulare etiam sperasti, perfide, tantum* (*Aeneid*, 4.305–19). Bibliography on these settings and others includes Helmut Osthoff, "Vergils Aeneis in der Musik von Josquin des Prez bis Orlando di Lasso," *Archiv für Musikwissenschaft* 11 (1954): 85–102; Wendelin Müller-Blattau, "Der Humanismus in der Musikgeschichte Frankreichs und Deutschlands," in *Festschrift für Walter Wiora zum 30. Dezember 1966*, ed. Ludwig Finscher and Christoph-Hellmut Mahling (Kassel: Bärenreiter, 1967), 296–303; Allen B. Skei, "*Dulces exuviae*: Renaissance Settings of Dido's Last Words," *The Music Review* 37 (1976): 77–91; Leofranc Holford-Strevens, "'Her Eyes Became Two Spouts': Classical Antecedents of Renaissance Laments," *Early Music* 27 (1999): 379–93; Richard Sherr, "Three Settings of Italian Texts and Two Secular Motets," in *The Josquin Companion*, ed. Richard Sherr (Oxford: Oxford University Press, 2000), 423–30; Michael Zywietz, "*Dulces exuviae*: Die Vergil-Vertonungen des Josquin des Prez," *Archiv für Musikwissenschaft* 61 (2004): 245–54; Jaap van Benthem, "Ist Josquins *Dulces exuvie* eine Motette?," *Tijdschrift van de Koninklijke Vereniging voor Nederlandse Muziekgeschiedenis* 56 (2006): 77–95; Katelijne Schiltz, "Polyfone Dulces Exuviae-Zettingen (15de-16de eeuw)," in *Als Orpheus zingt . . . : De klassieke oudheid in de West-Europese muziek*, ed. Pieter Bergé and Mark Delaere (Leuven: Davidsfonds, 2008), 49–61.

[4] For a valuable fifteenth-century case study, see Sean Gallagher, "*Pater optime*: Vergilian Allusion in Obrecht's *Mille quingentis*," *The Journal of Musicology* 18 (2001): 406–57. See also William Fitzgerald, "Vergil in Music," in *A Companion to Vergil's* Aeneid *and its Tradition*, ed. Joseph Farrell and Michael C. J. Putnam (Malden, MA, Oxford, and Chichester: Wiley-Blackwell, 2010), 341–52.

of epic poetry in the medieval period.[5] In the Virgilian corpus, there are few substantive passages offering details of musical performance for citation by later scholars, such as music theorists or other scholars interested in music. The figure of Iopas stands out among the few musical moments in the *Aeneid*, which otherwise include references to Greek and Roman instruments as well as one brief specific passage about the plucking of a seven-string lyre (*Aeneid*, 6.644–47). Notwithstanding scattered references to instruments and occasional songs, the main musical passage in Virgil's *Georgics* is the lyre-playing and singing of Orpheus (4.464–66, 471–84), the mythological figure whose representations in music, literature, art, and on stage revolutionized music and the appreciation of its power in the Renaissance. While Virgil's telling of the Orpheus myth, alongside Ovid's, served as vital evidence for early modern adaptations of the myth of Orpheus, thus overshadowing the figure of Iopas and his own contributions to music-making, Iopas was not entirely forgotten by Renaissance writers and musicians.

Iopas at Carthage

Iopas appears at the end of Book 1 of the *Aeneid* just before Aeneas begins his account of how he and his fellow travelers came to land on the shores of Carthage. The noisy, joyful banquet welcoming the Trojans that Dido had arranged (1.695–756) is the scene for the song of Iopas. Amid the feasting, the tables were cleared and bowls of wine laid out. Silence fell upon the room as Queen Dido, already transfixed by Aeneas through Cupid's deception, lifted a cup of wine, called out to Jupiter, Bacchus, Juno, and her fellow Phoenicians, poured an offering of wine on the table, then drank from the bowl of wine before challenging Bitias to drink, which he did before passing it to other princes. It is at this point that Virgil introduces Iopas (*Aeneid*, 1.740–47):

> cithara crinitus Iopas
> personat aurata docuit quem maximus Atlas.
> hic canit errantem lunam solisque labores,
> unde hominum genus et pecudes unde imber et ignes,
> Arcturum pluviasque Hyadas geminosque Triones;
> quid tantum Oceano properent se tinguere soles
> hiberni vel quae tardis mora noctibus obstet.
> Ingeminant plausu Tyrii, Troesque sequuntur.

> Long-locked Iopas, whom mightiest Atlas taught, sounds his golden lyre. He sings of the wandering moon and the travailing sun, of the birth of man

[5] Jan M. Ziolkowski, *Nota Bene: Reading Classics and Writing Melodies in the Early Middle Ages*, Publications of the Journal of Medieval Latin 7 (Turnhout: Brepols, 2007).

> and beast, of rain and of fire, of Arcturus and the rainy Hyads, and of the twin Bears: why the wintry suns so hasten to lave themselves in ocean, and what delay impedes the laggard nights. The Tyrians peal with applause, and the Trojans follow.

The attributes given to Iopas, the subject of his song, and the response by the mixed audience are all details worthy of note, while the Apollonian hair of Iopas, his instruction by Atlas, and his golden instrument all become the common features of a bardic musician performing at table. The topics treated in his cosmogonic song are fascinating: the motions of the sun and moon, the origins of humans and animals, of weather and fire, constellations, and the seasons and lengths of days. Following this song, Dido poses to Aeneas three questions, then there begins the account of the travels heretofore of Aeneas and his companions, as Book 2 commences.

The details offered by Virgil in these lines about the appearance of Iopas and the subject of his song have generated much recent scholarship on his significance as a bardic figure performing at a court banquet, his role at this moment in the epic poem before Aeneas recounts his journeys, the content of his song representing ancient science (namely Lucretius), the didactic poetic style he represents, the models Virgil might have used in forming this character, even the distinction of response by the Carthaginians and the Trojans noted by Virgil.[6] Among the late antique commentators, Servius, Donatus, Macrobius (*Saturnalia*, 7.1.14),

---

[6] Modern scholarship has interpreted the song of Iopas toward several, often conflicting, ends. Analyses include Viktor Pöschl, *Die Dichtkunst Virgils: Bild und Symbol in der* Äneis (Wiesbaden: Rohrer, 1950), 246–53; Walther Kranz, "Das Lied des Kitharoeden von Jaffa (Virgil, *Aeneis* I 740ff.)," *Rheinisches Museum für Philologie* 96 (1953): 30–38; Charles Segal, "The Song of Iopas in the *Aeneid*," *Hermes* 99 (1971): 336–49; T. E. Kinsey, "The Song of Iopas," *Emerita* 47 (1979): 77–86; Charles Segal, "Iopas Revisited (*Aeneid* I 740 ff.)," *Emerita* 49 (1981): 17–25; T. E. Kinsey, "The Song of Iopas (II)," *Emerita* 52 (1984): 69–76; Charles Segal, "Iopas Again," *Emerita* 52 (1984): 77–82; Philip Russell Hardie, *Virgil's* Aeneid: *Cosmos and Imperium* (Oxford: Oxford University Press, 1986), 52–66; Robert D. Brown, "The Structural Form of the Song of Iopas," *Harvard Studies in Classical Philology* 93 (1990): 315–34; Douglas A. Little, "The Song of Iopas: *Aeneid* 1.740–746," *Prudentia* 24 (1992): 16–36; Robert Hannah, "The Stars of Iopas and Palinurus," *The American Journal of Philology* 114 (1993): 123–35; Giovanna Garbarino, "Mitici Cantori: Iopas nel I Libro dell'*Eneide*," *Voce di molte acque: Miscellanea di studi offerti a Eugenio Corsini*, ed. Giorgio Barberi Squarroti et al. (Turin: S. Zamorani, 1994), 183–97; Marco Scaffai, "Lunae labores e solis labores in Virgilio e oltre," *Paideia* 57 (2002): 448–65; Wendell V. Clausen, *Virgil's* Aeneid: *Decorum, Allusion, and Ideology*, Beiträge zur Altertumskunde 162 (Munich and Leipzig: Saur, 2002), 53–57.

and Fulgentius offer nothing substantial about the figure, beyond the potential origins of his name.[7]

Several models for Virgil's Iopas, his song, and the Carthaginian banquet have been identified.[8] One is the song of Phemius on the return of the Greeks from Troy in *Odyssey*, 1.150–55 and 1.325–44. Or later, at *Odyssey*, 8.62–83 and 8.266–369, one finds the songs of Demodokos at the Phaiakian banquet, regaling the story of the disagreement between Odysseus and Achilles, the love between Ares and Aphrodite, and the Trojan horse at the sack of Troy.[9] The song of Orpheus in Book 1 of the *Argonautica* concerning the creation of the world draws direct parallel with Iopas's song.[10]

The aforementioned account by Virgil of the Orpheus myth, in the Aristaeus episode of *Georgics* 4, has been compared to Iopas's music-making, while the most remarkable parallel from Virgil's own writings with the Iopas scene is found earlier at *Georgics*, 2.475–82, where there is an instance of text repetition (*Aeneid*, 1.745–46 and *Georgics*, 2.481–82).[11] The constellations about which Iopas sings have been noted on the shield of Achilles in *Iliad*, 18.483–89.[12] Lastly, the cosmogonic song of Silenus in *Eclogues*, 6.31–40, has perhaps the

[7] Fulgentius, *Expositio Virgilianae continentiae*, I: *Dehinc ad epulas accipitur et citharae sono mulcetur; parvulorum quippe mos est nihil amplius quaerere quam delectari sono et saturari cibo. Nam denique nomen eiusdem citharedantis considera; Iopas enim Grece quasi siopas dictus est, id est taciturnitas puerilis*. Cited in *The Virgilian Tradition: The First Fifteen Hundred Years*, ed. Jan M. Ziolkowski and Michael C. J. Putnam (New Haven and London: Yale University Press, 2008), 667: "Next he is invited to dinner and is lulled by the sound of the cithara. For it is typical of small children that they want only to be pleased by sounds and filled with food. And consider the name of the cithara-player. For Iopas in Greek is, as it were, *siopas*, that is, the 'silence' of a child."

[8] David J. White, "Iopas," in *The Virgil Encyclopedia*, ed. Richard F. Thomas and Jan M. Ziolkowski, 3 vols. (Malden, MA, Oxford, and Chichester: Wiley-Blackwell, 2013), 1:664.

[9] On the topic of Homeric modeling, see Georg Nicolaus Knauer, *Die* Aeneis *und Homer: Studien zur poetischen Technik Vergils mit Listen der Homerzitate in der* Aeneis, Hypomnemata 7 (Göttingen: Vandenhoeck & Ruprecht, 1964; repr. 1979), 410; Damien P. Nelis, "Vergil's Library," in *A Companion to Virgil's* Aeneid *and its Tradition*, 13–25; Hardie, *Virgil's* Aeneid*:* Cosmos *and* Imperium, 52–66.

[10] Apollonius of Rhodes, *Argonautica*, 1.494–518.

[11] *quid tantum Oceano properent se tinguere soles | hiberni, vel quae tardis mora noctibus obstet*. Also, *Aeneid*, 1.742 can be compared with *Georgics*, 2.478. For a comparison of the Iopas and Aristaeus episodes, see David J. White, "Iopas and Orpheus: Vergil's Rejection of Cosmological Poetry" (paper presented at the Classical Association of the Middle West and South, Gainesville, FL, April 1, 2006).

[12] Robert D. Brown, "The Homeric Background to a Vergilian Repetition (*Aeneid* 1.744 = 3.516)," *American Journal of Philology* 111 (1990): 183–84.

clearest correspondence to the song of Iopas, with its descriptions of the earth, sea, sun, weather, forests, and animals.[13]

The strongest model, however, for the cosmogonic content of the song of Iopas can be seen in the *De rerum natura* of Lucretius, especially Books 5 and 6, which are explicitly dedicated to natural philosophy.[14] In Book 5, Lucretius covers the mortality of the planet, the movements of the stars, the origins of humanity, while Book 6 offers explanations of physical phenomena such as earthquakes and lightning, removing the involvement of divine power. Lucretius even highlights the value of music-making while reclining after a meal, "for at such times everything is enjoyable."[15] Iopas's observations on the sun, the moon, and the revolving seasons can be found in Lucretius.[16] In fact, each of the topics given to Iopas by Virgil finds a parallel in Book 5 of Lucretius: moon, sun, birth of men and beasts, rain, fire, constellations, and seasons.[17] The circulation of *De rerum natura*, as well as its influence on scholars, during the early Italian Renaissance has been debated recently, leaving open to question whether this relationship between Virgil's figure of Iopas and Lucretian models was recognized in the fifteenth and early sixteenth centuries.[18] Instead perhaps, as shown in the examples below, the frequent references to Iopas during this period suggest that it was his didactic song that was celebrated as the model for investigating and discussing natural phenomena.

---

[13] Alexander McKay, "Dido's Court Philosopher," in *Daimonopylai: Essays in Classics and the Classical Tradition presented to Edmund G. Berry*, ed. Rory B. Egan and Mark Joyal (Winnipeg: University of Manitoba Centre for Hellenic Civilization, 2004), 297–307 at 302–3, compares Silenus's song to Iopas's: "a celebratory banquet-symposium with high-spirited guests, brings me back to *Eclogues*, 6.31–40, whose verses are lodged precariously in an entertainment."

[14] Hesiod's *Works and Days* is another digest of cosmological lore.

[15] Lucretius, *De rerum natura*, 5.1379–91.

[16] Lucretius, *De rerum natura*, 5.1436–39.

[17] See McKay, "Dido's Court Philosopher," 300–1. Michael C. J. Putnam, *Virgil's Epic Designs: Ekphrasis in the* Aeneid (New Haven: Yale University Press, 1998), 48, calls the song of Iopas "a brief *De Rerum Natura*."

[18] Recent scholarship on the reception of Lucretius during the Italian Renaissance includes Ada Palmer, *Reading Lucretius in the Renaissance* (Cambridge, MA: Harvard University Press, 2014); Gerard Paul Passannante, *The Lucretian Renaissance: Philology and the Afterlife of Tradition* (Chicago: University of Chicago Press, 2011); Stephen Greenblatt, *The Swerve: How the World Became Modern* (New York: W. W. Norton, 2011); Alison Brown, *The Return of Lucretius to Renaissance Florence* (Cambridge, MA: Harvard University Press, 2010).

Iopas among the Italians

By the Trecento, Italian writers counted Iopas among celebrated poetic figures. Boccaccio's *Expositions on the Divine Comedy* singles out Iopas as the example of a true poet whose "versi" could be distinguished from the "canzoni" of Boccaccio's contemporaries. For Boccaccio, Iopas demonstrates that singing of distinguished themes or noble deeds, including topics of nature and our origins, is far more fitting for a poet than recounting frivolous matters, and perhaps that such performances contain the genuine character of true poetic verses:

> E non erano li loro canti di cose vane, come il piu delle canzoni odierne sono, anzi erano versi poetici, ne' quali d'altissime materie o di laudevoli operazioni da valenti uomini adoperate [si trattava], si come noi possiam vedere nella fine del primo dello Eneida di Virgilio, dove, dopo la notabile cena di Didone fatta ad Enea, Iopa, sonando la cetera, canta gli errori del sole e della luna e la prima generazione degli uomini e degli altri animali e donde fosse l'origine delle piove e del fuoco e altre simili cose: dal quale atto pote nascere il dirsi che i poetici versi si cantino.[19]
>
> And their songs were not of frivolous things, like most of today's songs, but rather, they were poetic verses, which treated lofty matters or praiseworthy deeds carried out by gifted men, as we can see at the end of the first book of Virgil's *Aeneid*, where, after Dido's noteworthy dinner for Aeneas, Iopas, playing the *cithara*, sings of the wanderings of the sun and the moon, and of the first generation of men and animals, and of the origin of rain and fire and other similar things, an act based on which one could say that poetic verses are sung.

By the middle of the fifteenth century, the status of Iopas had grown greater. Cristoforo Landino's commentary on the *Aeneid*, published in March 1488 in Florence alongside the ancient commentaries of Servius and Donatus, includes notes on the song of Iopas, citing Quintilian's *Institutio oratoria*, 1.10.9.[20] There, Landino makes reference to his Horace commentary and its discussion of music, where one finds Landino's *laus musicae*, in which the place of Iopas in the history of music is addressed. For Quintilian, and for Landino, musicians are endowed with a knowledge of divine things, which Iopas powerfully exemplifies:

---

[19] Boccaccio, *Esposizioni sopra la Comedia*, ed. Giorgio Petrocchi (Milan: Mondadori, 1965), 44. On this passage, see Paul Carranza, "Philosophical Songs: The 'Song of Iopas' in the *Aeneid* and the Francesca Episode in *Inferno* 5," *Dante Studies* 120 (2002): 35–51. Carranza observes that Boccaccio focuses on Iopas as an important figure who distinguished singing from composing.

[20] *Vergilius cum commentariis quinque: Servii, Landini, Ant. Mancinelli, Donati, Domitii* (Venice: Bartolomeo de Zanis de Portesio, 1495), fols. 144r–145r.

> Quod animadvertens praestantissimus ille poeta Maro hiopam cythara canentem inducit non res leves: sed errantem lunam: solisque labores: et caetera illa omnia: quae non nisi ex intimis philosophiae: penetralibus promi possunt.[21]
>
> Observing this, that outstanding poet Virgil introduces Iopas, with the *cithara*, singing not of trivial matters, but the wandering moon, the labors of the sun, and all the rest of those things, which can be taken from none other than the innermost chambers of philosophy.

Landino's writings on music are not limited to this passage. The relative of the celebrated fourteenth-century composer and organist Francesco Landino, Cristoforo Landino offers his views on music and cosmology throughout his writings. Many of them are concentrated in his *Disputationes Camaldulenses*, published in 1480, which discusses cosmic music and harmony of the spheres, and Books 3 and 4 of which offer a moral allegorization of the first six books of the *Aeneid*.[22]

Landino followed the tradition of the quadrivium in his definition of music that harmony is united to number.[23] On a cosmological level, Landino claimed that in order to recognize our powerful bond with the harmony of the spheres, one must be able to appreciate its harmonic resonances in earthly music heard with our earthly bodies. Drawing on Plato's *Timaeus*, Landino describes the var-

---

[21] Commentary of Landino on Horace, *Opera*, ed. Joannes F. Philomusus, with commentaries by Porphyrion, Acron, and Cristoforo Landino (Venice: Georgius Arrivabenus, 1490), fols. 6v–7r.

[22] See Craig Kallendorf, *In Praise of Aeneas: Virgil and Epideictic Rhetoric in the Early Italian Renaissance* (Hanover, NH and London: University Press of New England, 1989), 129–65. See also Craig Kallendorf, "Cristoforo Landino's *Aeneid* and the Humanist Critical Tradition," *Renaissance Quarterly* 36 (1983): 519–46; Arthur Field, "A Manuscript of Cristoforo Landino's First Lectures on Virgil, 1462–63," *Renaissance Quarterly* 31 (1978): 17–20; Arthur Field, "An Inaugural Oration by Cristoforo Landino in Praise of Virgil (From Codex «2», Casa Cavalli, Ravenna)," *Rinascimento* 2nd ser. 21 (1981): 235–45; Thomas H. Stahel, "Cristoforo Landino's Allegorization of the *Aeneid*: Books III and IV of the *Camaldolese Disputations*," PhD diss., Johns Hopkins University, 1968; David Scott Wilson-Okamura, *Virgil in the Renaissance* (Cambridge: Cambridge University Press, 2010); and Adam T. Foley in this volume.

[23] Cristoforo Landino, *De vera nobilitate*, in *Knowledge, Goodness, and Power: The Debate over Nobility among Quattrocento Italian Humanists*, ed. and trans. Albert Rabil, Jr. (Binghamton, NY: Medieval and Renaissance Texts and Studies, 1991), 96–97, 248: *Mathematice vero, ni fallor, quoniam quantam respicit, et aut illud continuum aut divisum considerat, geometriam arithmeticamque complectitur. Si vero ad quantum prospectum addas, eam quam prospectivam nominant, si vero vocem, musicam gignit; astrologia denique ex geometria arithmeticaque rationem ducit. Atque his absolvitur physice, quae ut graecum verbum indicat, naturam ipsam rerum complectitur.*

ied success of our musical imitations of the divine, praising certain musicians who have had success at this imitation, beyond mere caressing of the ears. These successful musicians are capable of expressing in refined song the profound and inner understandings of the mind:

> Interim vero, quoad per molestissimum corporis carcerem nobis licet, hac nostra illam imitari contendimus: non vocum modulationibus, veluti vulgares quidam et leviores musici consueverunt, quos aurium sensus demulcere posse non negaverim, quicquam autem propterea praestare posse non concedo, sed graviori quodam iudicio divinam harmoniam imitati profundos intimosque mentis sensus eleganti carmine exprimunt atque divino furore concitati res saepe adeo mirabiles adeoque supra humanas vires constitutas grandi spiritu proferunt, ut, cum paulo post furor ille iam resederit, se ipsos admirentur atque obstupescant.[24]

> In the meantime, insofar as it is permitted to us through that most troublesome prison of the body, we strive to imitate that divine music with this music of ours; and not with the melodies of the voice, as certain common and rather frivolous musicians were accustomed to doing (I would not deny that they could caress the ears, but I do not concede that they can be distinguished for anything else besides); but [other musicians], having imitated the divine harmony with more serious judgment, express in refined song the profound and inner understandings of the mind, and, inspired by the divine madness, bring forth in full-blown spirit such wondrous things, things so surpassing human powers, that afterwards when that madness has withdrawn, they are amazed and astounded at themselves.[25]

Landino then offers some insight into what this divine music created by these *vates* sounded like:

> Quapropter non solum auribus adulantur, sed suavi nectare et divina ambrosia mentes demulcent. Hi igitur divini vates sunt et sacri Musarum sacerdotes. Hi iure optimo sancti ab Ennio appellantur. His solum divinitus concessum est, ut carmine modo iocunde suaviterque labenti, modo graviter alteque surgenti, modo vehementi impetu ruenti, modo in sedati amnis morem fluenti, nonnunquam copiose exundanti, nonnunquam breviter atque compresse progredienti quocunque velint auditorem rapiant. Quam ob rem quoniam divinior vehementiorque in illis spiritus insurgit, ab huiuscemodi vehementia vates appellantur. Graeci autem ipsos poetas dixerunt, eo quod apud illos *poiein* facere significet.[26]

---

[24] Cristoforo Landino, *Disputationes Camaldulenses*, ed. Peter Lohe (Florence: Sansoni, 1980), 112.

[25] Translation from Stahel, *Landino's Allegorization of the* Aeneid, 42.

[26] Landino, *Disputationes Camaldulenses*, 111–12.

> Wherefore [these latter] serve not the ear alone; but they soothe the mind with sweet Nectar and divine Ambrosia. They are the divine poet-prophets and sacred priests of the Muses; and they are very rightly called "holy" by Ennius. Only to them has it been divinely granted that—by means of a song now pleasantly and sweetly falling, now solemnly surging on high, now rushing with a headlong impetus, now flowing in the manner of a calm river, sometimes overflowing copiously, sometimes proceeding briefly and concisely—they take the listener wherever they wish. And it is because a more divine and vehement spirit rises up in them that they are called, from this kind of vehemence, prophets. The Greeks, however, called them "makers" because among them *poiein* means "to make."[27]

These lengthy passages on music are also found in Landino's 1462–1463 Florentine lectures on Virgil, highlighting his long-standing interest in music and the power of the *vates*.[28] Furthermore, equating Iopas with a noble or even divinely inspired vatic figure, as Boccaccio, Landino, and others did, serves as strong evidence for the regular citation of him as a model figure for singing at philosophical banquets.[29] The location of Iopas's cosmogonic song at Dido's banquet, the convivial scene of eating, drinking, and discussion, is critical to the musical power of Iopas, and one that was not ignored in the Renaissance.

Iopas and Music at the Renaissance Banquet

The celebration of Iopas as the model bard for banquets goes back as far as Quintilian, who turned to Virgil and Iopas amidst his *laus musicae* (*Inst. orat.*, 1.10.10), particularly his consideration of the antiquity of music and its affiliation with divine matters. Calling Virgil the "greatest of poets," Quintilian observes that in Virgil's verses "we read that the praises of heroes and of gods were sung to the music of the cithara at the feasts of kings." Quintilian proceeds to pose the question: "Does not Iopas, the Virgilian bard, sing, 'The wandering moon and labors of the sun' and the like, whereby the supreme poet manifests most clearly that music is united with the knowledge even of things divine?"[30] This places Iopas

[27] Translation from Stahel, *Landino's Allegorization of the* Aeneid, 43.

[28] Field, "A Manuscript of Cristoforo Landino's First Lectures on Virgil," 19; Kallendorf, "Cristoforo Landino's *Aeneid* and the Humanist Critical Tradition," 520–21.

[29] David M. Gaunt, "The Creation-Theme in Epic Poetry," *Comparative Literature* 29 (1977): 213–20 at 219: "It is not that Iopas is consciously aware of these things; but, as a true vates, he is conscious . . . that great things are in the air, and he sings, like Silenus, for the future as well as the present."

[30] Quintilian, *Inst. orat.*, 1.10.10: *Itaque et Timagenes auctor est omnium in litteris studiorum antiquissimam musicen extitisse, et testimonio sunt clarissimi poetae, apud quos inter regalia convivia laudes heroum ac deorum ad citharam canebantur. Iopas vero ille Vergili nonne*

squarely within the history of music and oft-repeated praises of its power. Later writers, including Enea Silvio Piccolomini and the composer and music theorist Adam de Fulda, borrowed Quintilian in their treatment of Iopas.[31]

The appropriate intellectual topics for banquet singing are considered regularly in the fifteenth century. A 1424 letter of Guarino of Verona to Vitaliano Faella expands the treatment of music performed at banquets beyond the model of Iopas to include additional ancient examples from Homer, Plato, and Scriptures (namely King David):

> . . . praesto fuere tibicines, qui arte atque harmonia ita sensus delinibant, ut ex Timothei schola exisse apparerent. Solebant vero maiores nostri non lascivientem, sed sobriam conviviis adhibere musicam; quocirca nullas fere festas apud prius saeculum epulas legis, quibus cantores ipsi non interfuissent. Castae adhuc Didoni "cithara crinitus Iopas personat aurata"; Homerus vates sane primarius Ulixem apud Alcinoum convivam cantu ac fidibus exhilarat; Platonis quoque Symposium inducta non caret psaltria. Quid totiens gentiles? an David divinorum poeta carminum sacros eius psalmos non psalterio modulatur et cithara?[32]

> . . . pipers were present, who charmed the senses with their art and their harmony in such a way that they appeared to have come from the school of Timotheus. Indeed, our ancestors were accustomed to include not wanton but sober music at their banquets; for this reason you read of almost no celebratory feasts in an earlier age at which singers were not in attendance. To Dido, while she still retained her virtue, "long-haired Iopas sounds his songs on a gilded lyre"; Homer, certainly the foremost of poets, gladdens Ulysses as a guest of Alcinous with singing and the lyre; the Symposium of Plato, too, is not without the introduction of a music-girl. Why all these

---

canit "errantem lunam solisque labores" et cetera? Quibus certe palam confirmat auctor eminentissimus musicen cum divinarum etiam rerum cognitione esse coniunctam.

[31] Enea Silvio Piccolomini, *De institutione liberorum*, in *Humanist Educational Treatises,* ed. Craig Kallendorf, I Tatti Renaissance Library 5 (Cambridge, MA: Harvard University Press, 2002), 248. See also Reinhard Strohm, "Enea Silvio Piccolomini and Music," in *Uno gentile et subtile ingenio: Studies in Renaissance Music in Honour of Bonnie J. Blackburn*, ed. M. Jennifer Bloxam, Gioia Filocamo, and Leofranc Holford-Strevens (Turnhout: Brepols, 2009), 719–27, esp. 723, 727. Adam de Fulda, *Musica*, part 1, chap. 2, in *Scriptores ecclesiastici de musica sacra potissimum*, ed. Martin Gerbert, 3 vols. (St. Blaise: Typis San-Blasianis, 1784; reprint ed., Hildesheim: Olms, 1963), 3:329–41 at 334.

[32] *Epistolario di Guarino Veronese*, ed. Remigio Sabbadini, 3 vols., Miscellanea di storia Veneta, ser. 3, 8 (Venice: A spese della Società, 1915–1919), 1:405. Cited in F. Alberto Gallo, *Music in the Castle: Troubadours, Books, and Orators in Italian Courts of the Thirteenth, Fourteenth, and Fifteenth Centuries*, trans. Anna Herklotz and Kathryn Krug (Chicago: University of Chicago Press, 1995), 71.

> examples from the pagans? Does not David, the poet of divine songs, tune his holy psalms on the harp and the lyre?

The same examples from Homer and Virgil are also cited by Francesco Filelfo in his *Convivia mediolanensia* as the foundational individuals in establishing the art of singing at banquets.[33] Angelo Decembrio inserts excerpts of the opening lines of the song of Iopas (*Aeneid*, 1.740–42) into a discussion of joyous music-making.[34] Along a similar vein, Polydore Vergil cites Iopas among those associated with music's origins, confirming his place on the roster of excellent musicians.[35] The composer and poet Juan del Encina's *El triunfo de amor* does the same.[36]

The praise offered for banquets and the invocation of Iopas in the passage by Ficino cited at the opening of this essay are further developed with considerable commentary by Raffaele Brandolini in his *De musica et poetica* (1513), while

---

[33] Francesco Filelfo, *Convivia mediolanensia* (Milan: Simon Magniagus, 1483), 57: *Itaque et Virgilius Maro talem hyopam citharaedum apud Didonem figit canere in convivio et homerus apud Alcinoum Phaeacum regem Demodocum illum Corcyraeum de quo modo sermo est habitus convivas facit cithara delectare.* Leofranc Holford-Strevens observes that, on the whole, much of Filelfo's praises of music are derived from pseudo-Plutarch's *De musica.* On this, see Leofranc Holford-Strevens, "The *laudes musicae* in Renaissance Music Treatises," in *Essays on Renaissance Music in honour of David Fallows: bon jour, bon mois et bonne estrenne*, ed. Fabrice Fitch and Jacobijn Kiel, Studies in Medieval and Renaissance Music, 11 (Woodbridge: Boydell Press, 2011), 338–48 at 342. See also Anthony M. Cummings, "Music and feasts in the fifteenth century," in *The Cambridge History of Fifteenth-Century Music*, ed. Anna Maria Busse Berger and Jesse Rodin (Cambridge and New York: Cambridge University Press, 2015), 361–73, at 365–66.

[34] Angelo Decembrio, *De politia litteraria*, 1.11, ed. Norbert Witten (Munich: K. G. Saur, 2002), 181, lines 21–23: *Igitur sublatis protinus mensis, cum iocandi psallendique tempus intersit, ecce: cithara crinitus Iopas / personat aurata; hic canit errantem lunam solisque labores, ac caeteram cum plausu fremituque convivarum cantilenam* ("Therefore at once, behold, with the meal removed, time for both jesting and musicking intervenes: Long-locked Iopas sounds his golden lyre; he sings of the wandering moon and the travailing sun, and with applause and roaring the other song of banquets").

[35] Polydore Vergil, *On Discovery*, 1.14, ed. Brian Copenhaver, I Tatti Renaissance Library 6 (Cambridge, MA: Harvard University Press, 2002), 116–23. On this passage, see also Brian Copenhaver, "The Historiography of Discovery in the Renaissance: The Sources and Composition of Polydore Vergil's *De Inventoribus Rerum, I–III*," *Journal of the Warburg and Courtauld Institutes* 41 (1978): 192–214 at 201. The others in this list are Orpheus, Linus, Amphion, Dionysius, Zethus, the Dactyls of Ida, the Arcadians, Mercury, and the oldest (according to Polydore Vergil) Jubal. See also Holford-Strevens, "The *laudes musicae* in Renaissance Music Treatises," 343.

[36] *El Cancionero de todas las obras de Juan del Enzina* (Salamanca: [N.p.], 1496), fol. 50: "Vi la saltacion armada de los curetes sin ropas tambien al crinado Yopas con su citara dorada: y a Licinio vi que estava con su flauta de marfil, con la qua se moderava Braco quando concionava y vi mas otros dos mill . . . ."

admiring the lyre's power. There Brandolini celebrates Iopas for the seriousness of his song at the Carthaginian banquet:

> An non Iopam illum Virgilianum regium Didonis convivium lyricis decorantem numeris quam saepissime lectitasti? Cui poeta tum Apollineos crines, tum inauratam cytharam, tum maxime gravissimarum rerum tribuit argumentum, ut usitatissimum antiquitus morem planius indicaret, utque optimum personarum discrimen haberet. Neque enim par erat apud hominem externum, apud heroem in regio praesertim convivio scurrile aliquid adhibere. Servavit, inquam, poeta, quod phylosophi imprimis exigunt, decorum, ut apud Aeneam Romanae sobolis authorem, apud Didonem Punici regni moderatricem, peractis illis lautissimis epulis, Iopas et Apollini corporis cultu habituque non dissimilis et Apollineo instrumento altissimas naturae quaestiones elegantissimis versibus decantaret, ne a vilissimo scurra, sed ab optimo vate Aeneae sermo duceretur. Itaque vides quam sit lyricum instrumentum tempestivis conviviis oportunum, immo quanto caeteris, quae ad exprimendam laetitiam adhiberi possent, praestantius.

> Have you not read often how that Virgilian singer Iopas adorned the royal banquet of Dido with lyric verse? The Poet granted him not only Apollonian hair and a golden cithara, but above all granted him a subject matter of momentous events, in order to display plainly a custom so familiar from ancient times and to have the highest distinction for his characters. It was surely not proper to employ anything ludicrous at a royal banquet with a foreigner, with a hero. The poet preserved decorum, I say, something that philosophers particularly demand. So after the splendid banquet, in the presence of Aeneas, the originator of the Roman race, and of Dido, the ruler of the Punic Kingdom, Iopas, himself not unlike the figure of Apollo in habit and appearance and with Apollo's instrument, declaimed the most profound problems of nature in elegant verses, so Aeneas's speech was not introduced by some vile buffoon, but by the most accomplished prophet. Thus you see how suitable the lyric instrument is for proper dinner gatherings; in fact, how much more outstanding than other [instruments] that might be used for expressing happiness.[37]

Brandolini identifies the distinguishing characteristics of Iopas as a bard, which influenced so many later generations of musicians: his Apollonian hair and instrument, his prophetic nature, and the subject matter of his song. Avoiding anything ludicrous and preserving decorum are his primary objectives amidst such regal company, while performing on the appropriate instrument for the occasion. For Brandolini, the most profound problems of nature are appropriate

[37] Raffaele Brandolini, *De musica et poetica*, ed. Ann E. Moyer (Tempe: Arizona Center for Medieval and Renaissance Studies, 2001), 30–31.

themes for song after a meal. Singing of the deeds of heroes and gods is not encouraged by Brandolini, nor by Ficino in his letter to Bembo.

Music theorists of the fifteenth and sixteenth centuries regularly cited Iopas as the model musician for banquets, particularly for the spread of merriment, which seems at great distance from the serious songs of the natural world. In his *Complexus musices effectuum*, Johannes Tinctoris (c. 1435–1511) designates his eighteenth chapter "Music increases the merriment of a feast," citing passages from Ecclesiasticus (32), Horace (*Odes*, 1.32.13–16), Quintilian (*Inst. orat.*, 1.10.20), and Isaiah (5:12), as well as the *Aeneid*, namely the figure of "long-haired Iopas" and his cithara:

> But from of old it has been quite usual for famous men to introduce music at their banquets. So when Virgil recounts what happened at the sumptuous feast mounted by Dido for Aeneas and his comrades, he mentions that Iopas, a superb lyre-player, played his lyre to make the feast merrier. This is in the *Aeneid* (Book 1): ". . . long-haired Iopas / Set his gilded lyre a-ringing," and so on.[38]

It should be noted that the lyre-playing of Iopas is highlighted by Tinctoris, not the singing or its song's contents. In a similar passage on the effects of music, written near Milan in the second quarter of the fifteenth century, another theorist, Johannes de Olomons, glosses the opening lines of the song of Iopas (*Aeneid*, 1.740–41) after citing Isidore of Seville's *Etymologies* on the playing of a lyre or cithara at banquets: *Sic ergo in singulis ordinabatur genus condescens musicorum.*[39] The Ferrarese professor Lodovico Carbone accompanied his own singing on his "Apollonian cithara," which might be a nod to either the Apollonian hairstyle of Iopas or the golden hue of his lyre.[40]

Returning to the art of festive music, consider the account of the origins of music found in Franchino Gafori's *Theorica Musice* of 1492, which connects ancient practices with those of Gafori's day, particularly passing around instru-

[38] Johannes Tinctoris, *Complexus effectuum musices*, chap. 18, in *"That Liberal and virtuous art": Three Humanist Treatises on Music*, ed. J. Donald Cullington (Newtownabbey: University of Ulster, 2001), 64–65, 82: *Verum ab antiquo claros homines epulantes, assumere musicam non insolitum est. Unde Virgilius recitans ea quae in opiparo convivio, ab Elissa Aeneae suisque sociis preparato, gesta fuerunt, adducit Yopam citharoedum peritissimum, quo iucundius esset, citharam increpuisse, de quo Aeneidos libro primo: . . . cithara crinitas Yopas / personat aurata, et ceterea.*

[39] Johannes de Olomons (i.e., Johann von Olmütz), *Palma choralis*, ed. Albert Seay, Critical Texts, no. 6 (Colorado Springs: Colorado College Music Press, 1977), fol. 1v; cited in Holford-Strevens, "The *laudes musicae* in Renaissance Music Treatises," 338–39.

[40] *Ego certe versus meos ut plurimum facio apolleneam cytharam in manu tenens*: Bologna, Biblioteca Universitaria, MS 2948, t. 23, 371; cited in Gallo, *Music in the Castle*, 70. Pindar's Apollonian lyre was golden as well (Pindar, *Pythian Odes*, 1.1–4).

ments, sharing songs, and reciting the achievements of illustrious people to the accompaniment of musical instruments. Gafori remarks that it is the musical accompaniment that encourages young listeners to imitate the heroic accomplishments being commemorated. At the center of this is the model Iopas:

> Ut enim in veneratione divina hymni sic et in nuptiis hymenei atque in conviviis lyra vel cythara circumferebatur accubantibusque singulis ordinabatur convivale canticorum genus: fuitque apud Romanos in morem in conviviis egregia ad tibias superiorum opera carmine comprehensa pangere quo ad ea imitanda iuvenum virtutem redderent alacriorem quod in convivio Didonis decantat musa Maronis. Post alii proceres cythara crinitus Iopas Personat aurata docuit quae maximus Athlas Hic canit errantem lunam solisque labores. Id quoque ad nostra usque tempora celebratum conspicimus.[41]

> As in divine worship the hymns, so also in weddings the wedding-songs and in drinking parties the lyre or kithara were passed around and a convivial type of song was prescribed for those individuals who reclined at table. Among the Romans it was the custom at the banquets to recite to the tibiae the noble deeds of distinguished people, expressed in song, so that they gave youth a more eager inclination to imitate them, as the Muse of [Virgil] Maro sang at the banquet of Dido. "After other leading men, the long-haired Iopas sounded on his golden cithara what the greatest Atlas teaches. He sings about the labors of the revolving moon and sun." We perceive that this feast has also been celebrated until our times.[42]

Like Gafori, Johannes Cochlaeus was fascinated by the linking of poetry and music, connecting words with the lyre's harmonies. He believed this linkage achieved a recollection, or recreation, of antiquity, not unlike Landino's yearned-for union with a more perfect past. Glareanus even dedicated a panegyric to Cochlaeus, in which music's greatest artisans are celebrated, among them "pleasing Iopas."[43] In his *Tetrachordum musices*, Cochlaeus seems most interested in achieving metrical perfection in the accompanied recitation of poetry, as the ancients must have, and less interested in the content of this powerful musical medium since he considers both the songs of Phemius and Iopas to be songs of heroes.

> Iucundum est tamen carmen melo coniungere, antiquitatisque simulacrum referre. Quis enim nescit a canendo carmina dicta quasi canimina:

---

[41] *Theorica musice Franchini Gafuri Laudensis* (Milan: Ioannes Petrus de Lomatio, 1492; repr., New York: Broude Bros., 1967), fol. aiiiv.

[42] Franchino Gaffurio, *The Theory of Music*, trans. Walter Kreyszig, ed. Claude V. Palisca (New Haven: Yale University Press, 1993), 18–19.

[43] Henricus Glareanus, *Dodecachordon, Liber tertius* [Dodekachordon] (Basel: Henrichus Petri, 1547; repr., New York: Broude Bros., 1967), 470.

> Quid? Nonne lyrica carmina ad lyrae strepitum verba iungebant? Quid ille Phemius Homeri. Ioppasque Vergilii? Nonne ad doctissima heroum carmina harmonicos concentus applicuere? Non ab re itaque hos metris donamus concentus. Veruntamen pedum quantitates non vbique custodiuimus, melodiae hic potius quam metrice indulgentes.[44]

> But it is pleasant to join poetry and music, and to recreate a conception of antiquity. For who does not know that *carmina* are delivered by singing (*canendo*), as if *canimina*? How? Did not lyric poems join their words to the sound of the lyre? What about Phemius in Homer and Iopas in Virgil? Did not they apply harmonious strains to the most distinguished heroic poems? Therefore, it is with good reason that we present these metrical compositions. But we have not observed the metric feet in every place, favoring the melodies rather than the meters.[45]

At the time of these writings, several contemporary luminaries served as present-day models for the musical ideals found in the figure of Iopas. The singer and viol player Francesco Malacise was paid by the Este court in Ferrara for his singing of the deeds of Roman history, "just as they do for the Duke of Milan."[46] Antonio di Guido's singing in Florence in 1459 impressed the young Galeazzo Maria Sforza because of his skill at "combining so many ancient stories, the names of innumerable ancient Roman fables, poets, and the names of all the muses."[47] In addition, Marsilio Ficino, Angelo Poliziano, Angelo Maturanzio, Giles of Viterbo, Serafino dall'Aquila, and others were celebrated for their improvised and inspired songs, entertaining courts across Italy with tales of noble deeds of a serious nature not unlike the philosophical banquet song of Iopas.

Perhaps the most celebrated performer of plucked and bowed instruments in the second half of the fifteenth century was Pietrobono de Burzellis (c. 1417–1497). A cosmopolitan career brought him to nearly every important court in Europe to perform and teach music, earning him medals, lavish gifts, and honorific epigrams. Tinctoris counted Pietrobono as the preferred *lyricen* over others, while the brother of Raffaele Brandolini and fellow singer, Angelo Brandolini, composed verses in Pietrobono's honor, such as: "May princes desire you, kings and dukes praise you, and may anyone in the whole world who sees you

---

[44] Johannes Cochlaeus, *Tetrachordum musices*, tractatus quartus (Nuremberg: Fridericus Peypus, 1514), fol. Fiir.

[45] Cochlaeus, *Tetrachordum musices*, trans. Clement A. Miller (Münster: American Institute of Musicology, 1970), 83.

[46] Archivio di Stato di Ferrara, Camera Ducale Estense, Amministrazioni dei Principi, A), Regnanti, 14, Zornale de Intrada (1466), fol. 38 (2 luglio 1466).

[47] Cited in Timothy McGee, *The Ceremonial Musicians of Late Medieval Florence* (Bloomington: Indiana University Press, 2009), 87.

marvel."[48] The Bolognese orator Filippo Beroaldo, writing an epigram in honor of Pietrobono in 1473, described Pietrobono's incomparable skill and dexterity, controlling his instrument to the point that it could "speak at his whim." Hailing Pietrobono as the "new glory of our age," Beroaldo opens the epigram with a list of the finest ancient musicians, including Thamyras, Arion, Amphion, Timotheus, Linus, and Iopas, all of whom must be considered inferior now that Pietrobono has achieved such fame.[49] The captivating power of Iopas, his *cithara*, and his banquet song, which thrilled both the Carthaginians and the Trojans, could be heard in the stunning performances of Pietrobono at courts across Europe during the second half of the fifteenth century.

Celebrated in many banquet scenes of literature and the visual arts around the year 1500, this improvisatory manner of singing with lyre accompaniment became known widely as *cantare ad lyram*. Regrettably, much of the notated music of this period captured the mere fingerprints of this improvised art. Taking inspiration, as we have seen, from the model of Iopas, although unlikely to involve performing on a golden-hued cithara, this style of singing became the desired medium for banquet music-making and the focus of many literary works.[50]

The different rhetorical purposes for which the figure of Iopas was employed by writers in the late medieval and early modern period demonstrate the many roles and agendas his image and performance could serve, reflecting differences in genre, location, and audience: divinely inspired *vates*, highbrow poet elevating the topic of discussion, merry-maker, and charismatic musician. From the content of his song to his instrumental accompaniment, from the festive context of his singing to the philosophical and scientific nature of his verses, Iopas and his

---

[48] Johannes Tinctoris, *De inventione et usu musice*, 4.5, ed. Ronald Woodley et al. <http://earlymusictheory.org/Tinctoris/texts/deinventioneetusumusice/#> (accessed 30 March 2016), Birmingham Conservatoire, Birmingham City University, Birmingham, UK; Lucca, Biblioteca Capitolare, MS 525, fol. 181v; ed. and trans. in Gallo, *Music in the Castle*, 128–29: *Te cupiant proceres, laudent regesque ducesque, | miretur toto quisquis in orbe videt.*

[49] Filippo Beroaldo the Elder, *Epigramma ad Petrum bonum Citharedum*, lines 1–8, edited in Paul White, "Foolish Pleasures: The *Stultiferae naves* of Jodocus Badius Ascensius and the Poetry of Filippo Beroaldo the Elder," *Humanistica Lovaniensia* 60 (2011): 65–83 at 76. White demonstrates borrowing of these verses by Badius in his *Celeusma auditionis fatuae* (75–76). Lines 9–16 edited and translated in Gallo, *Music in the Castle*, 87–88. Final three lines found in *Varia opuscula* (Basel: Adam Petri, 1517), fol. 84v.

[50] Blake Wilson, "Feasting the Ear: 'Cantare ad lyram' at Renaissance Banquets," paper read at the 2014 Annual Meeting of the Renaissance Society of America in New York City. See also James Hankins, "Humanism and Music in Italy," in *The Cambridge History of Fifteenth-Century Music*, ed. Anna Maria Busse Berger and Jesse Rodin (Cambridge and New York: Cambridge University Press, 2015), 231–62.

song promoted a different, didactic power of music than that of the more famous singing of Orpheus as a supernatural force.

The figure of Iopas must have been significant for Virgil and his contemporaries as representing Virgil's engagement with cosmological and didactic poetry in his *Aeneid*, in the vein of Lucretius's *De rerum natura*. Over the next fifteen hundred years, as Virgil's writings were read and interpreted, this brief moment of celebrating "nature's greatest problems," as Raffaele Brandolini put it, was the source of inspiration for many. While the Orphic lyre of Ficino inspired generations of scholars, singers, artists, and poets, the consistent references to the fitting and divinely inspired banquet song of Iopas and its probing ideas about our origins and natural phenomena appear to have been equally stimulating for the "feasts of the Graces and Muses."

7

Pathetic Fallacy: A Virgilian Case Study

Giovanna Laterza[1]
Université de Strasbourg

The Pathetic Fallacy: Origin and Critical History

The transfer of personal emotions to the physical word, and specifically to landscapes, is a widespread artistic device that helps to increase the level of participation in a given scene by the external users, that is, the readers or spectators. On a rhetorical level, the transposition of emotions into the physical world is mirrored by an interesting and often discussed figure of speech, the pathetic fallacy, which is defined as "the poetic convention whereby natural phenomena which cannot feel as humans do are described as if they could: thus rainclouds may 'weep' or flowers may be 'joyful' in sympathy with the poet's (or imagined speaker's) mood."[2] This linguistic humanization of nature was formalized as a rhetorical device and discussed extensively by the critic John Ruskin,[3] whose theory of art was founded on the concept of truth. Ruskin considers the pathetic fallacy to be an effective instrument for tracing the line between good and bad poetry. Supposing that the quality of a poet is determined by his concern for the truth and by the authenticity of his emotions, Ruskin judges as negative and improper an excessive recourse to the pathetic fallacy: a great poet, even if overwhelmed by strong affections, will be able to control them, in order to preserve his ability of seeing truly.[4] Over time, the term pathetic fallacy lost its pejorative meaning

---

[1] I would like to thank Prof. Wolfgang Kofler, Prof. Yves Lehmann, Prof. Laurent Pernot, and Prof. Alessandro Schiesaro for comments on earlier drafts of this manuscript. I would also like to thank the editors, Luke Houghton and Marco Sgarbi, for inviting me to contribute to this volume. All errors are my own.

[2] Chris Baldick, *The Concise Oxford Dictionary of Literary Terms*, 2nd ed. (New York: Oxford University Press, 2001), 187.

[3] John Ruskin, *Modern Painters*, vol. 3 (New York: John Wiley, 1863; first pub. 1856), 156–72.

[4] Ruskin, *Modern Painters*, 163: "And thus, in full, there are four classes: the men who feel nothing, and therefore see truly; the men who feel strongly, think weakly, and

and has now been analyzed as a neutral literary device with an autonomous pre-Ruskinian history, starting at the very beginning of western literature. In the Homeric poems the pathetic fallacy occurs just occasionally and never occupies a central role in the text.[5] Instead, "the individualistic seventh and sixth centuries [BCE] carry the pathetic fallacy much farther in a poetry which deals intimately with men's thoughts and feelings."[6] Apollonius also uses the figure several times in his epic poem.[7] In Latin literature, the pathetic fallacy is well represented in the work of the Augustan poets.[8] It is therefore evident that, even if this figure of speech "never received a specific title in ancient rhetoric,"[9] it was used in ancient times. How has the status of the pathetic fallacy changed in its journey from the ancient to the modern world?

Mind the Gap: Pathetic Fallacy in Antiquity and Modernity

Classical poetry bores us, admits Paul Veyne, with a brave and ironic glimpse of intellectual honesty, in the final chapter of his book on Roman elegy.[10] On this basis, he successfully constructs two opposing aesthetic models, clearly pointing out some substantial aspects that divide modern and ancient poetry. Modern poetry is founded on the correspondence of intensity and authenticity: the experience of the poet is true because it is intense. The aesthetic of intensity needs the pragmatics of sincerity: the poet expresses his feeling sincerely and instinctively. This attitude produces an emotional tension that automatically cor-

see untruly (second order of poets); the men who feel strongly, think strongly, and see truly (first order of poets); and the men who, strong as human creatures can be, are yet submitted to influences stronger than they, and see in a sort untruly, because what they see is inconceivably above them. This last is the usual condition of prophetic inspiration."

[5] Frank Olin Copley, "The Pathetic Fallacy in Early Greek Poetry," *The American Journal of Philology* 58 (1937): 196; Richard Jenkyns, *Virgil's Experience: Nature and History; Times, Names and Places* (Oxford: Oxford University Press, 1998), 25: Jenkyns points out that, according to Ruskin's opinion, Homer "could thus fill his landscape with spiritual presences and still depict nature itself exactly as it is, without recourse to fantasy. Modern man desires to invest nature with a large and deep significance, but cannot believe in the nymph or god; he is thus driven to the fancy of attributing sentience to the trees and water themselves."

[6] Copley, "The Pathetic Fallacy in Early Greek Poetry," 202–3.

[7] Jenkyns, *Virgil's Experience*, 44.

[8] Arthur Stanley Pease, "Notes on the Pathetic Fallacy in Latin Poetry," *The Classical Journal* 22 (1927): 645–57, cites examples from Virgil, Ovid, and Propertius.

[9] Bernard F. Dick, "Ancient Pastoral and the Pathetic Fallacy," *Comparative Literature* 20 (1968): 27. See also Copley, "The Pathetic Fallacy in Early Greek Poetry," 195.

[10] Paul Veyne, *L'élégie érotique romaine*, 2nd ed. (Paris: Seuil, 2003), 292–305.

responds to a deeper comprehension of reality and through which the poet can more easily gain the sympathy of the reader. Classical poetry, on the other hand, is characterized by a constant and programmatic insincerity:[11] the poet speaks not to share with the public his personal emotions but to embody the experience and values of the collectivity, all the while respecting the rules of a specific literary genre.

The evolution of the meaning of the pathetic fallacy exemplifies well the transition from the artistic practice of insincerity to that of sincerity. As Jenkyns notes, "the pathetic fallacy, in Ruskin's sense, arises when the mind allows itself to be overborne by strong and genuine feeling into attributing to nature a sentience that it does not in reality possess: it is an instinctive rather than an artificial response."[12] The pathetic fallacy concretizes the dialogue between a poet with a strongly intensified emotional state and nature.[13] In Latin literature the pathetic fallacy is to be understood in a completely different way: the authors employed it as "a technical device, analogous in the literary field to what elaborate effects of stage lighting or orchestral accompaniment are in the dramatic."[14] In ancient literature, the pathetic fallacy is a rhetorical tool used within the frame of a codified relationship between man and nature, and is used to construct topical natural scenes of different kinds. Let us now see how this happens.

The Pathetic Fallacies

The pathetic fallacy can be understood as a linguistic procedure that occupies a very limited segment of text (e.g., the flowers are joyful) or as a practice that encompasses an entire scene, built around the interrelation of a character's emotions with the surrounding nature. In this case, as Pease noted,[15] the pathetic fallacy can be divided into two opposing subcategories. The sympathetic fallacy describes a situation in which human feelings are mirrored in nature: the emotion expressed, no matter whether it is positive or negative, is set in a homologous context, which has the effect of intensifying that emotion. The sympathetic fallacy seems to be often present in the context of pastoral consolation, in

---

[11] It is necessary to make an effort to detach the concept of insincerity from its negative modern perception.

[12] Jenkyns, *Virgil's Experience*, 196–97.

[13] Ruskin, *Modern Painters*, 162: "The temperament which admits the pathetic fallacy, is, as I said above, that of a mind and body in some sort too weak to deal fully with what is before them or upon them; borne away, or over-clouded, or over-dazzled by emotion; and it is a more or less noble state, according to the force of the emotion which has induced it."

[14] Pease, "Notes on the Pathetic Fallacy in Latin Poetry," 650.

[15] Pease, "Notes on the Pathetic Fallacy in Latin Poetry," 651–52.

which nature responds to the grief of a man faced with a sad death. The antipathetic fallacy, on the other hand, defines a pattern in which human emotions are supposed to stand in contrast to the external landscape: this contrast produces a strong dramatic effect. The antipathetic fallacy often presents a negative human experience inscribed on to a positive landscape in order to reconstruct the tragic *topos* of nature's indifference in the face of human affliction.

I want to suggest that we have to take into account another kind of pathetic fallacy, one that logically derives from the antipathetic one: the case in which a happy moment is set in a negative landscape. I argue that this fallacy, which I label counter-pathetic, based on the opposition between a positive moment and a negative landscape, is effectively employed in Virgilian epic.

Virgil's Pathetic Fallacies

As Conte has noted, the poetry of Virgil owes its originality to its pathetic tone,[16] which is brought about by the conscious employment of various expressive techniques. Above all, the style of Virgil is characterized by a programmatic deviance from the norm, voluntarily hidden by an apparent harmonious and structured linguistic form. In this sense, *enallage* should be considered highly representative of Virgil's epic technique: the act of referring to an element of the phrase and not to the logically expected word but to another component of the sentence produces an effect of intensification.[17] In this context, the pathetic fallacy can almost be considered as an enallage:[18] it manifests itself as the unexpected attribution of an emotional adjective to surrounding elements of the physical world.

---

[16] Gian Biagio Conte, *Virgilio: L'epica del sentimento*, 2nd ed. (Turin: Einaudi, 2007), 1: "Insomma che si tratti della strutturazione drammatica dei contenuti o dell'elaborazione artistica dell'espressione, la poesia dell'Eneide rivela constantemente un'impronta patetica. Questo è l'aspetto che anche qui ho cercato di analizzare, persuaso che in esso consista il valore più originale di un'esperienza poetica ineguagliabile." ("In short, whether in relation to the dramatic structure of the contents or to the artistic elaboration of the expression, the poetry of the *Aeneid* constantly reveals an imprint of pathos. This is the aspect that I have sought to analyze here, convinced that in this lies the most original value of an unmatched poetic experience.")

[17] Conte, *Virgilio: L'epica del sentimento*, 18.

[18] Heinrich Lausberg, *Elemente der literarischen Rhetorik: eine Einführung für Studierende der klassischen, romanischen, englischen und deutschen Philologie* (Ismaning: Hueber, 1990), §315, 102, speaks indifferently of hypallage or *enallage adiectivi*. I also consider the two denominations to be synonyms: both terms are etymologically related to the idea of "exchange" and both focus on the idea of semantic discontinuity. For an overview of the interrelation (and possible differentiation) between enallage and hypallage, consult the lemma "Hypallage" by Sonia Branca Rosoff and Thomas Zinsmaier in *Historisches*

Let us consider some examples selected from the instances of enallage identified by Conte.[19] In *Aeneid*, 7.343,[20] [*Allecto*] . . . *tacitumque obsedit limen Amatae* ("Allecto . . . sits down before the silent threshold of Amata"), the adjective *tacitum* improperly qualifies *limen* but it clearly concerns Allecto: the danger represented by Allecto is stronger because it is directly transposed on to Amata's house. In a similar way, in *Aeneid*, 6.520–21, *tum me . . . infelix habuit thalamus* ("I was then inside our ill-starred bridal chamber"), Deiphobus's unhappiness is objectified through the attribution of the adjective *infelix* to *thalamus*. The same effect is to be found in *Aeneid*, 5.48, *maestasque sacravimus aras* ("and [we] hallowed the altars of grief"), where the expected predicative *maesti* is replaced by *maestas* and thus qualifies *aras*.

Furthermore, Virgil makes use of the pathetic fallacy in entire scenes and constructs (to use Pease's terms of analysis) sympathetic and antipathetic landscapes according to his particular needs. Different authors have remarked upon the importance of the pathetic fallacy in Virgil's works and especially in the *Aeneid*: in the *Eclogues* and the *Georgics*, most of the instances may be explained as standard elements of bucolic scenery, while in the *Aeneid* they are not a "cliché of thought or language"[21] and "seem to be a part of Virgil's habits of thought."[22] In the *Aeneid*, Virgil often has recourse to the traditional use of the pathetic fallacy, to underscore the sympathy or the indifference of nature toward human experiences. In some instances, the text displays what I call the 'counter-pathetic fallacy'. In particular, I argue that these passages represent key narrative moments that prefigure the development of the plot.[23] I will support this idea through a concrete case study, the analysis of some significant instances of pathetic fallacies in Virgil's Dido episode.

Wörterbuch der Rhetorik Band 4 Hu - K., ed. G. Kalivoda, L. Keinath, F. Robling, et al. (Berlin and Boston: De Gruyter, 2012), 106–9.

[19] Conte, *Virgilio: L'epica del sentimento*, 1–63.

[20] Quotations and English translations of the *Aeneid* are taken from the Loeb Classical Library edition (vols. 63 and 64).

[21] Jenkyns, *Virgil's Experience*, 69.

[22] Pease, "Notes on the Pathetic Fallacy in Latin Poetry," 656.

[23] On the possible narrative value of the pathetic fallacy see also Dick, "Ancient Pastoral and the Pathetic Fallacy," 30: "Since the pathetic fallacy in its highest form (as symbol or leitmotiv) is a metaphor through which is distilled a way of looking at reality, it will not always be explicit and expressions like 'raging waves' or 'the cruel, crawling foam' will not in themselves constitute successful usage. The pathetic fallacy achieves artistic status when it is subtly worked throughout a poem, entering and leaving unobtrusively, and always standing for something more than mere ornament."

Pathetic Fallacies in the Dido Episode

In the first and fourth books, the emotions of the Carthaginian queen are often mirrored in surrounding spaces such as the city, the countryside, and the palace. First, I will analyze some instances of pathetic and antipathetic fallacies in order to specify their function in the Dido episode. In the verses 4.80–89, Dido has fallen in love with Aeneas because of Juno's will and, after having shown the heroes her Sidonian wealth, torments herself in the palace (*maeret*, 4.82), while outside a peaceful night falls (*suadentque cadentia sidera somnos*, 4.81: "the setting stars invite to sleep"). The calmness of the night opposes itself antipathetically to the suffering of the queen. The same situation is to be found in 4.522–32:[24] the description of the night is even more elaborate here (after the cosmic elements, Virgil describes the earthly creatures that are falling asleep) and represents a strong counterpoint to Dido's love madness (*ingeminant curae rursusque resurgens | saevit amor magnoque irarum fluctuat aestu*, 4.531–32: "her pangs redouble, and her love, swelling up, surges afresh, as she heaves with a mighty tide of passion"). Once again, nature is completely indifferent to the sorrows of the queen. In contrast, the space of the palace seems to mimic directly Dido's emotional state: in 4.82 the loneliness of Dido, who is described as *sola* ("alone"), materializes itself in the empty palace (*domo vacua*) and in the abandoned carpets (*stratisque relictis*). Even the psychological landscape of the nightmare in 4.465–68 is constructed around the feeling of loneliness: if the queen is *sola* ("alone," 4.467) and *incomitata* ("companionless," 4.467), the land becomes *deserta* ("forlorn," 4.468). Dido's solitude is a symptom of her more general inactivity: now, she appears to us as a simple woman who has forgotten her own identity as queen. In the name of love, she has given up her political engagement, the first prerequisite for the prosperity of Carthage.

The description of her vain grief in the palace (4.80–83) is followed by a description of Carthage (4.86–89),[25] which appears to be sympathetically influenced by the attitude of the queen: it is a phantom city, where all activities have apparently been put on stand-by. This new, unproductive rhythm of life is also effectively mirrored by the juxtaposition of multiple spondaic sequences, which characterize the verses. Looking at these various examples we can confirm that Virgil uses the pathetic and antipathetic fallacies as active agents of pathos. The

[24] On this passage see Arthur Stanley Pease, *Publi Vergili Maronis Aeneidos liber quartus* (Darmstadt: Wissenschaftliche Buchgesellschaft, 1967), 434.

[25] *Aeneid*, 4.86–89: *non coeptae adsurgunt turres, non arma iuventus | exercet portusve aut propugnacula bello | tuta parant: pendent opera interrupta minaeque | murorum ingentes aequataque machina caelo* ("No longer rise the towers begun, no longer do the youth exercise in arms, or toil at havens or bulwarks for safety in war; the works are broken off and idle—great menacing walls and cranes that touch the sky").

response or the indifference of landscape represents two different ways that both aim to intensify Dido's emotional state.

The third category, which, as said before, I label the counter-pathetic fallacy, to distinguish it from the antipathetic one, seems however to have a different goal. A scene that is supposed to be characterized by a positive atmosphere is set in a landscape with some ambivalent features that could potentially be interpreted as negative. In the Dido episode it is possible to isolate three instances of a counter-pathetic fallacy: the arrival in the Punic harbor (1.159–69); the construction of Carthage (1.418–29); and the marriage cave (4.160–72). These landscapes are all systematically based on a linguistic ambivalence, which portrays the apparently positive relations between Punics and Romans as extremely dangerous.

The first two scenes present multiple similarities. The safety of the Trojans after the storm is first guaranteed by the protection of the natural harbor and later increased by the presence of civilized inhabitants, observed by the hidden Aeneas. However, these two passages are strongly marked by some ambiguous linguistic expressions that do not embody the feelings of the Trojans. First of all, they have an almost "spectacular" appearance: in the harbor, the natural scenery is described with the theatrical word *scaena* ("background," 1.164), which is repeated in 1.429 in reference to the new Carthaginian theatre. Jenkyns considers the passage on the harbor, and in particular the expression *silvis scaena coruscis* ("a background of shimmering woods," 1.164), as strongly theatrical and pathetic.[26] Even if he tends to consider the scene as an imaginary landscape that sympathetically responds to the relief of sailors,[27] he also notices the possible presence in the reader's eyes of troubling overtones. This has the effect of making the landscape both beautiful and strange at the same time. In the two scenes we should notice the presence of verbs that suggest threatening and oppression (1.162, *minantur* "loom"; 1.165, *imminet* "overhanging"; 1.166, *pendentibus* "hanging"; 1.420, *imminent* "looms"; 1.423, *instant* "press on") and of adjectives which have an etymologically negative connotation (1.162, *vastae* "huge" or "devastated"; 1.165, *atrum* "black"—a typical chthonic adjective; 1.166, *adversa* "fronting"—facing or opposing as an enemy; 1.420, *adversas* "confronting"; 1.428, *immanis* "vast"—enormous, monstrous). In these two cases a skeptical reading of the *Aeneid* suggests that the only possible future is the one dominated by Rome: even if the Carthaginians seem to be friendly, their negative potential becomes transparent in the description of natural spaces. These ambiguous details in the text are the superficial symptoms of a deeper meaning: these scenes, even if they should be conceived as positive in the present, will have dramatic, negative consequences for the future.

The scene of the cave is constructed along the same lines, a contrast between a supposed positive moment and a setting that is "ominous of an impending

[26] Jenkyns, *Virgil's Experience*, 63 and 69.

[27] Jenkyns, *Virgil's Experience*, 70.

change."[28] Let us see exactly the terms in which this opposition is deployed and how it was reworked in Renaissance literature.

The Cave: From Virgil to the Renaissance

> Interea magno misceri murmure caelum
> incipit; insequitur commixta grandine nimbus,
> et Tyrii comites passim et Troiana iuventus
> Dardaniusque nepos Veneris diversa per agros
> tecta metu petiere; ruunt de montibus amnes.
> speluncam Dido dux et Troianus eandem
> deveniunt. prima et Tellus et pronuba Iuno
> dant signum; fulsere ignes et conscius Aether
> conubiis, summoque ulularunt vertice Nymphae.
> ille dies primus leti primusque malorum
> causa fuit. neque enim specie famave movetur
> nec iam furtivum Dido meditatur amorem;
> coniugium vocat; hoc praetexit nomine culpam.
> (*Aeneid*, 4.160–72)[29]

> Meanwhile in the sky begins the turmoil of a wild uproar; rain follows, mingled with hail. The scattered Tyrian train and the Trojan youth, with the Dardan grandson of Venus, in their fear seek shelter here and there over the fields; torrents rush down from the heights. To the same cave come Dido and the Trojan chief. Primal Earth and nuptial Juno give the sign; fires flashed in Heaven, the witness to their bridal, and on the mountain-top screamed the Nymphs. That day the first of death, the first of calamity was cause. For no more is Dido swayed by fair show or fair fame, no more does she dream of a secret love: she calls it marriage and with that name veils her sin!

The background to the cave scene is one of troubled nature, designed around some key natural elements that are, at the same time, formal *signa* from the goddess Juno: the prophetic tone of the scene is also more evident than in the harbor scene or in the construction of Carthage. Even Servius is aware that these *signa* can be interpreted alternatively as positive or negative.[30] Juno has planned the encounter between Dido and Aeneas in 4.120–27: the two scenes are dramatic,

---

[28] Pease, "Notes on the Pathetic Fallacy in Latin Poetry," 656.

[29] For the cave scene, consult the online bibliography of Niklas Holzberg on 4.160–72: http://www.niklasholzberg.com/Homepage/Bibliographien.html. For further literary parallels see Pease, *Aeneidos liber quartus*, 201–10.

[30] Maurus Servius Honoratus, *Servii Grammatici qui feruntur in Vergili carmina commentarii*, ed. Georgius Thilo and Hermannus Hagen (Leipzig: Teubner, 1881), ad *Aen.*,

but all the elements subsequently added in 4.160–72 are extremely ambiguous. Instead of proper wedding torches we have the more generic *ignes*,[31] which have no religious value; the *ululatus* of the nymphs can be interpreted as both a nuptial and a funeral song.[32] The expression *conscius aether conubiis* (167–68) is also significant: the adjective *conscius* in the sense of "aware of" relates to deities or elements of the cosmos to underscore their presence in a religious ritual as a witness;[33] however, it is relevant that this same adjective can also suggest the idea of participating in a crime.[34]

The Virgilian scene is thus comparable to the typology of the tragic wedding born of an extra-marital union, as defined by Richard Seaford. Seaford argues that the wedding ritual has by nature both positive and negative elements. In a normal context, the negative elements are overcome; in tragedy, however, they prevail and close linguistic analysis will reveal traces of this in the text.[35] In the cave scene we witness a failure of the wedding ritual: the verses 4.169–70 (*ille dies primus leti primusque malorum | causa fuit*) confirm the need to interpret the previous *signa* as negative. Furthermore, a "wedding expresses not only the victory of a positive over a negative tendency, but also in a sense the victory of culture over nature."[36] The cave seems to provide a contrast to the cultural scene of the hunt, as Schiesaro has noted:[37] Aeneas and Dido are protagonists of a primordial flood, and their union must be taken out of the historical cultural time and placed into a frame that is oblivious to the prescribed destiny of Rome. In my opinion, the linguistic and narrative two-fold nature of the cave allows us to classify the scene as a counter-pathetic fallacy. Furthermore, the contrast between the supposedly positive moment of the wedding[38] and the troubled landscape is

4.166: Servius argues that in the Etruscan tradition earthquakes and storms are inauspicious for weddings.

[31] Servius ad *Aen.*, 4.167: the light can also be interpreted as a bad omen (*malum omen*).

[32] Servius ad *Aen.*, 4.168: *ululari* is defined as a *vox media* (*medius sermo*); compare Ovid, *Heroides*, 7.93–96.

[33] Pease, *Aeneidos liber quartus*, 205: "the elements are all witnesses at this wedding; Earth, Juno (representing the air, with which Hera is often etymologically associated, . . . fire, aether . . . and the nymphs as representing water, . . . unless the *amnes* are considered in that function."

[34] *TLL* 4.0.370.80. For the semantic field of guilt in the Virgilian passage, see *Aen.*, 4.172, *culpam*.

[35] Richard Seaford, "The Tragic Wedding," *The Journal of Hellenic Studies* 107 (1987): 123–30.

[36] Seaford, "The Tragic Wedding," 106.

[37] Alessandro Schiesaro, "Under the sign of Saturn: Dido's Kulturkampf," in *La représentation du temps dans la poésie augustéenne. Zur Poetik der Zeit in augusteischer Dichtung*, ed. Jürgen P. Schwindt (Heidelberg: Universitätsverlag Winter, 2005), 102.

[38] See the words of Juno in *Aeneid*, 4.126 (*conubio iungam stabili propriamque dicabo*).

consistently perceived by the later tradition. This sequence is one of the most popular Virgilian scenes in the Renaissance. The passages that discuss or rewrite the cave suggest that their authors were aware of the ambivalence of the Virgilian original: starting from this assumption, we will focus on how they proceed to the activation or deactivation of the aforementioned ambiguous potential of the cave. In the Renaissance, as in modernity, we also witness a direct confrontation between an optimistic and a pessimistic interpretation of the *Aeneid*: the detection or the neglect of textually ambiguous details has a relevant impact on the overall interpretation of the poem, which can appear either as a coherent glorification of Augustan ideology or as a contradictory story profoundly marked by the "further voices" of Rome's enemies. The pessimistic tendency seems not to be ahistorical or particular to modern times; as Craig Kallendorf has pointed out, "there is a continuous tradition of pessimistic readings,"[39] and the analysis of the cave scene and its Renaissance reworking makes this even more evident.

The Virgilian scene, insofar as it is a counter-pathetic fallacy, proposed to the Renaissance interpreters a series of contradictions, which they in turn tried to solve with different approaches. The aim of this paper is not to give a full list of Renaissance Virgilian caves; I have chosen instead a selection of these rewritings and ordered it thematically. It is important to note that these rewritings respond to the ambiguities of the Virgilian counter-pathetic fallacy without necessarily depending on the pathetic fallacy rhetorical pattern and are adapted to the narrative necessities of the author;[40] in addition, an author's approach is not monolithic and can shift within the corpus of his works.

For example, in Boccaccio we can notice two opposite attitudes towards the cave episode, well represented by the following two works: in *Amorosa visione*, 28.34–60, he reproduces the cave scene with the ambivalence typical of the Virgilian text; in his *De mulieribus claris*, he completely eliminates it from the queen's biography, in order to restore the image of the historical (and not mythical) Dido, whose main quality becomes chastity.[41]

---

[39] Craig Kallendorf, *The Other Virgil: Pessimistic Readings of the* Aeneid *in Early Modern Culture* (New York: Oxford University Press, 2007), viii.

[40] The positive and negative polarizations of the cave need to be understood in their specific narrative context: a positive image can be set as a model for a negative character or a negative image can be presented as something to avoid for a positive character.

[41] Craig Kallendorf, "Boccaccio's Dido and the Rhetorical Criticism of Virgil's 'Aeneid'," *Studies in Philology* 82 (1985): 404.

Furthermore, there are several authors who ignore the Virgilian ambiguities. This is the case with Tasso[42] and Vida.[43] They focus their discussion on the highly appropriate Virgilian stylistic choice of narrating the lovers' sexual experience with tact and discretion, that is to say, only via symbolic, natural *signa*. The case of Dante's *De Monarchia*[44] is even more telling: the direct citation of the Virgilian passage does not prevent Dante from suggesting that the lawful

---

[42] Torquato Tasso, *Discorsi del poema eroico*, in *Prose*, ed. Ettore Mazzali (Milan and Naples: Ricciardi, 1959), 501: "Ma Virgilio ne gli amori d'Enea con Didone fu modestissimo, e accenna con brevi parole quel che seguisse dopo la pioggia mandata da Giunone: 'Speluncam Dido dux et trojanus eandem deveniunt'." Torquato Tasso, *Discourses on the Heroic Poem*, trans. Mariella Cavalchini and Irene Samuel (Oxford: Clarendon Press, 1973), 12: "Virgil is decidedly modest about the love-making of Aeneas and Dido, and only briefly mentions what followed the rain sent by Juno: 'To the same cave came Dido and the Trojan chief, etc.'"

[43] Marco Girolamo Vida, *De arte poetica*, ed. and trans. Ralph G. Williams (New York: Columbia University Press, 1976), 2.526–34: *Postremo, tibi siqua instant dicenda, ruborem | Quae tenerum incuterent Musis adaperta, chorisque | Virgineis, molli vel praeterlabere tactu | Dissimulans, vel verte alio, et rem suffice fictam. | Si pater omnipotens tonitru caelum omne ciebit, | Speluncam Dido, dux et Trojanus eandem | Deveniant: pudor ulterius nihil addere curet. | Nam sat erit, Tellus si prima, et conscius aether | Connubii dent signum, ululentque in vertice Nymphae* ("Finally, if you find yourself faced with an episode whose telling would bring even a faint blush to the (cheeks of) the virgin chorus of the Muses, conceal it, and either glide by it with a light touch only, or turn your narrative elsewhere and put fictitious material in its place. If the omnipotent father is to shake all heaven with his thunder, let Dido and the prince of Troy take shelter in the same cave; but modesty must take care to add nothing further. For it will suffice if primal Earth and the witnessing Air give the signal of the marriage, and the nymphs keen on the peaks of the hills"). On these texts of Tasso and Vida see also David Scott Wilson-Okamura, *Virgil in the Renaissance* (Cambridge: Cambridge University Press, 2010), 106.

[44] Dante, *Monarchia*, ed. Pier Giorgio Ricci (Milan: Mondadori 1965), 2.3.14–17: *Similiter etiam coniugio nobilitatum fuisse reperio . . . . Secunda Dido fuit, regina et mater Cartaginensium in Affrica; et quod fuerit coniunx, Idem noster vaticinatur in quarto; inquit enim de Didone: 'Nec iam furtivum Dido meditatur amorem: | coniugium vocat; hoc pretexit nomine culpam.'* [. . .] *Aut quem in illo duplici concursu sanguinis a qualibet mundi parte in unum virum praedestinatio divina latebit?* English translation by Aurelia Henry (Boston and New York: Houghton, Mifflin and Company, 1904), 82: "I find also that nobility accrued to Aeneas through marriage . . . . His second wife was Dido, queen and mother of the Carthaginians in Africa, of whom as Aeneas's wife the poet sings in the fourth book: 'No longer Dido dreams of secret love; she calls it marriage, hiding her sin beneath a name.'. . . Or from whom will still be hidden divine predestination in the twofold meeting in one man of blood from every part of the world?" On the contrast between *De Monarchia* and *Inferno*, 5.61–62, see Marilynn Desmond, *Reading Dido: Gender, Textuality, and the Medieval* Aeneid (Minneapolis: University of Minnesota Press, 1994), 94–98.

marriage between Aeneas and Dido legitimated the supremacy of Romans in the African territories.

Some literary Renaissance rewritings of the scene further support the deactivation of the ambiguities via a polarization of the cave's adjectives: in Ariosto's *Orlando furioso*[45] Angelica loses her virginity with Medoro, they marry (*Fêrsi le nozze sotto all'umil tetto | le più solenni che vi potean farsi*, 19.34: "And you must know the | honeymoon was spent | in royal style beneath | that humble roof"), and only afterwards find themselves in a grotto, which is explicitly paralleled to the one of Dido and Aeneas, here described as *commodo e grato* (19.35). As Garrison has already pointed out, [46] Ariosto rewrites *Aeneid* 4 in terms of a pastoral romance, in which "the potential tragic analogy between Angelica and Dido is rendered as a comedy of reconciliation." Shakespeare, as well, in his *Titus Andronicus*,[47] lets Tamora speak of the Virgilian event in positive terms ("happy storm . . . a counsel-keeping cave"). Tamora would like to reproduce the Aeneas-Dido situation with her illegitimate lover Aaron, who asks her instead to focus on their revenge plan. In this case, tragedy prevails, allowing no place for reconciliation: the cave is a desired *locus amoenus* that cannot be reached in the plot.

Finally, we shall consider the cases in which the negativity of the cave is formally recognized or even enhanced. Poliziano in his *Manto* celebrates the poet Virgil:[48] in his summary of the *Aeneid*, he rewrites the scene of the cave but

[45] Ludovico Ariosto, *Orlando furioso*, 19.35, ed. C. Zampese, trans. Emilio Bigi (Milan: Rizzoli, 2012), 1146: "Se stava all'ombra o se del tetto usciva, | avea dì e notte il bel giovine a lato: | matino e sera or questa or quella riva | cercando andava, o qualche verde prato: | nel mezzo giorno un antro li copriva, | forse non men di quel commodo e grato, | ch'ebber, fuggendo l'acque, Enea e Dido, | de' lor secreti testimonio fido." Ariosto, *Orlando Furioso: A Romantic Epic*, trans. Barbara Reynolds (London: Penguin, 1973), 592: "Whether in shade or in the open air, | She has the youth beside her night and day. | Morning and eve, together everywhere, | By stream, by fields, the lovers make their way. | Within a cave at noontide they repair, | As welcoming perhaps in every way | As one which gave Aeneas and the queen | From storm a shelter and for love a screen."

[46] James D. Garrison, *Pietas from Vergil to Dryden* (Cambridge: The Pennsylvania State University Press, 1992), 148–50.

[47] William Shakespeare, *Titus Andronicus*, Act 2, Scene 3, 21–26, in *The Oxford Shakespeare: The Complete Works*, ed. Stanley Wells and Gary Taylor (New York: Oxford University Press, 1986), 163: "And after conflict such as was supposed | The wand'ring prince and Dido once enjoyed | When with a happy storm they were surprised | And curtained with a counsel-keeping cave, | We may, each wreathed in the other's arms | Our pastimes done, possess a golden slumber . . . ."

[48] Angelo Poliziano, *Manto*, 224–27, in *Silvae*, ed. and trans. Charles Fantazzi (Cambridge, MA and London: Harvard University Press, 2004), 18–21: *Venatu tandem in medio Saturnia nimbum | Pronuba diffundet, soloque Hymenaeus in antro | Adfuerit nullasque faces, maestum, afferet, omen, | Fulgoresque dabit nymphis ululantibus aether* ("Finally, in the midst of the hunt the daughter of Saturn, as *pronuba*, will unleash a storm and

maintains the Virgilian landscape features (the thunder, the lights in the sky). However, he goes into more detail about what in Virgil was only implicit: the absence of proper nuptial torches in the solitary cave is definitely a *maestum omen*. If the sexual experience in the cave has nothing to do with a proper marriage, Dido can become the victim of Aeneas, now a contradictory hero charged with betrayal, seduction, and impiety. This is evident in Lionardo Salviati's letter to Giovanni de' Bardi da Vernio.[49] Here Salviati accuses Aeneas of having committed a sin against history (*commettendo ancor qui un peccato gravissimo contro la storia*). In a similar fashion, Chaucer in his *Legend of Good Women*[50] transforms the scene into one of courtly romance and depicts Aeneas as "a false lover, who acts while the storm rages outside . . . . Consequently, when Aeneas betrays

Hymen will be present in the solitary cave, but (gloomy omen!) will not bring any torches. The upper air will send forth lightning as the nymphs howl").

[49] Lionardo Salviati, letter to Giovanni de' Bardi da Vernio; text in Craig Kallendorf, "Historicizing the 'Harvard School': Pessimistic Readings of the *Aeneid* in Italian Renaissance Scholarship," *Harvard Studies in Classical Philology* 99 (1999): 399:

> Direi oltr'a questo, che Virgilio havesse peccato nel costume d'Enea in due modi, contra 'l comandamento d'Aristotile prima dipignendolo coraggioso, contr'a quel, che gl'era prima stato descritto dagl'autori, di poi facendolo diseguale a se stesso, col fare a colui, che egli ci haveva preposto per esempio di pietà, e di virtù morale, fare una impietà, et una scelleratezza detestabile qual fu il violar la castità d'una donna reale, a cui egli doveva la vita stessa, a poi esserle traditore e spergiuro, e cagionarle morte di sempiterna infamia commettendo ancor qui un peccato gravissimo contro la storia.
>
> I would say, besides this, that Virgil erred in the character of Aeneas in two ways, against the precept of Aristotle, first in depicting him as courageous, contrary to the way he had first been described by the author, afterward making him inconsistent with himself, in making one whom he had set forth for us as an example of piety and of moral virtue do something impious and detestable in its wickedness, which was to violate the chastity of a queenly woman to whom he owed his very life, then to betray and perjure her and to be the cause of her eternally disgraceful death, also committing here a grave violation against history. (Trans. C. Kallendorf)

[50] Chaucer, *Legend of Good Women*, 1224–1241, in *The Works of Geoffrey Chaucer*, ed. F. N. Robinson, 2nd ed. (London: Oxford University Press, 1957), 503: "And shortly, from the tempest hire to save, | She fledde hireself into a litel cave | And with hire wente this Eneas also. | I not, with hem if there wente any mo; | the autour maketh of it no mencioun. | And here began the depe affeccioun | . . . And, as a fals lovere so wel can pleyne | That sely Dido rewede on his peyne, | And tok hym for husbonde and becom his wyf | For everemo, whil that hem laste lyf. | And after this, whan that the tempest stente, | With myrthe out as they comen, hom they wente."

Dido's fate he betrays the convention of this courtly world."[51] In the same way, in Shakespeare's *Tempest* Ferdinand deploys the negativity of the scene and integrates into his speech to Prospero a reference to Aeneas and Dido's cave, defined as "the murkiest den."[52] In front of Prospero, he wants to emphasize that he will not be a new Aeneas nor Miranda a new Dido. He wants to avoid the error of the Virgilian hero and promises not to sleep with Miranda before their marriage.[53]

Our last example is particularly telling, even if the author does not mention directly the Virgilian model, as the others so far have done. In *Paradise Lost* Milton seems to use the Virgilian intertext for three new scenes:[54] the union of Adam and Eve (*PL*, 8.513–14), and the two scenes of Eve and Adam eating the apple of sin (*PL*, 9.782–84; *PL*, 9.1000–4). The pattern of ambiguity evident in the cave is inactive in the first scene but comes to the fore in the two others. The dramatic response of nature is interpreted as the logical consequence of the pagan sin of Dido and Aeneas, which is transposed by Milton into a Christian context: love leads to the failure of Adam and Aeneas.[55]

The pessimistic reading of the *Aeneid* was not just recognized by the authors I have cited; it also constituted an important point of departure for constructing new scenes, which programmatically either avoided or enhanced the negativity of the cave episode.

---

[51] Desmond, *Reading Dido*, 158–59; see also, ibidem, the whole chapter on Dido in Chaucer, 128–62.

[52] William Shakespeare, *The Tempest*, Act 4, Scene 1, 23–31, in *The Oxford Shakespeare*, ed. Wells and Taylor, 1237: "Ferdinand: As I hope | For quiet days, fair issue, and long life, | With such love as 'tis now, the murkiest den, | The most opportune place, the strong'st suggestion | Our worser genius can, shall never melt | Mine honour into lust, to take away | The edge of that day's celebration, | When I shall think, or Phoebus' steeds are foundered, | Or Night kept chained below."

[53] See Kallendorf, *The Other Virgil*, 108–26.

[54] John Milton, *Paradise Lost*, 8.510–14, ed. S. Orgel and J. Goldberg (New York: Oxford University Press, 2005): "To the nuptial bower | I led her blushing like the morn; all heaven, | And happy constellations, on that hour | Shed their selectest influence; the earth | Gave sign of gratulation, and each hill . . ."; 9.782–84: "Earth felt the wound, and nature from her seat, | Sighing through all her works, gave signs of woe | That all was lost"; 9.1000–4, "Earth trembled from her entrails, as again | In pangs; and Nature gave a second groan; | Sky loured; and, muttering thunder, some sad drops | Wept at completing of the mortal sin | Original . . . ." On these passages see Pease, *Aeneidos liber quartus*, 202 and 205; Kallendorf, *The Other Virgil*, 156–61.

[55] Kallendorf, *The Other Virgil*, 161: "Adam's love for Eve led to his fall, which parallels Aeneas's inappropriate affair with Dido. Both poems, in other words, stress the failure of their hero and the consequences of that failure."

The retrospective history of the pathetic fallacy allows us to measure on a concrete linguistic level the difference between two paradigms of poetry, the ancient and the modern: the pathetic fallacy, identified by Ruskin as a spontaneous reaction of a sensitive and poetic soul, has differences from and connections with a linguistic procedure born in ancient literature.

The study of the pathetic fallacy becomes particularly relevant in Virgil, who is an active mediator between the past and the modern aesthetics of poetry through his innovative pathetic style. In Virgil's *Aeneid* the pathetic fallacy is a proper rhetorical tool, through which he can technically fulfill his pathetic ambitions and include and emphasize in the story the emotions of different internal figures. In this paper I have tried to underscore the importance of what I have called the counter-pathetic fallacy, which associates a supposedly positive moment with some negative landscape features. I argue that the counter-pathetic fallacy is particularly relevant on the narrative level: it prefigures the future negative development of episodes that are perceived as positive in the present. The scene of the cave belongs to this category and represents an interesting case study because of its multiple rewritings during the Renaissance. This scene represents a concrete starting point for reconstructing a part of Virgilian reception history: the constant oscillations of Virgilian criticism between an optimistic or pessimistic interpretation of the *Aeneid* are tightly connected to the choice of making active or inactive the contradictory patterns of the text.

In conclusion, the pathetic fallacy seems to be representative of two important aspects of Virgilian poetry: on one hand, the art of re-editing materials from tradition and linguistic approaches in terms of pathos; on the other hand, the pleasure of valorizing consonances and contradictions, in the belief that the investigation of meaning necessarily occurs via the experience of contrasts.

8

Re-evaluating Turnus: Multiple Voices in Vegio's *Supplement*

Anne Rogerson
University of Sydney

Maffeo Vegio's 1428 *Supplement* to Virgil's *Aeneid*, the extraordinarily successful "*Aeneid* 13,"[1] opens with a temporal clause evoking two quite different times, the suspenseful beginning of *Aeneid* 12 and its traumatic end (*Supplement*, 1–2):[2]

> **Turnus ut** extremo devictus **Marte** profudit
> effugientem animam . . .
>
> When Turnus, decisively defeated in his final battle, spilled out his fleeing soul . . .

Turnus's fleeing soul (*effugientem animam*, 2) recalls his departure to the underworld in the last line of the *Aeneid*,[3] indicating that the *Supplement* continues on directly from where Virgil's narrative left off. At the same time, the phrase *Turnus ut . . . Marte* closely echoes the first line of *Aeneid* 12, where Turnus was alive, fighting against the Trojan invasion and yet to face his final battle (*Aeneid*, 12.1–2):

> **Turnus ut** infractos adverso **Marte** Latinos
> defecisse videt . . .

---

[1] On the success of the *Supplement* see Craig Kallendorf and Virginia Brown, "Maffeo Vegio's *Book XIII* to Virgil's *Aeneid*: A Checklist of Manuscripts," *Scriptorium* 44 (1990): 107–25.

[2] All quotations from the *Supplement* are from *Maffeo Vegio, Short Epics*, ed. Michael C. J. Putnam with James Hankins (Cambridge, MA: Harvard University Press, 2004). Translations are my own.

[3] *vitaque cum gemitu fugit indignata sub umbras* (Virgil, *Aeneid*, 12.952): "And his life flees aggrieved and with a groan down beneath the shades." Text from *P. Vergilius Maro: Aeneis*, ed. Gian Biagio Conte (Berlin: de Gruyter, 2011); translations are my own.

> When Turnus saw that the Latins had given up, their spirits broken because the battle had turned against them . . .

Vegio's double-edged opening performs a number of closuring functions,[4] but its most important and surprising feature is how, by placing Turnus's name first, it suggests that he is to be as central a figure to the *Supplement* as he was to *Aeneid* 12.[5] While the dead hero cannot be the protagonist of Vegio's text, which does not deal in ghosts, Turnus is nonetheless a major focus of attention in the first half of the *Supplement* and, I argue, a more complex figure in Vegio's work than has been formerly appreciated.

In this argument, I run counter to the current consensus on Vegio's Turnus. In focusing on ways in which Vegio's text imposes closure on Virgil's, modern scholarship frequently stresses how central the vituperation of Turnus is to the process of resolving Virgil's ambiguities.[6] A recent summary is forceful but characteristic:

> Vegio's Book 13 provides all the closure that Vergil denies us: eager surrender by the Latins, who blame Turnus (who was very, very bad) with no one among the Rutulians wanting revenge, the meeting of Aeneas with Latinus, who blames Turnus (who was very, very bad), and then with Lavinia, whom he marries in a ceremony followed by a joyful feast.[7]

There is some justification for expecting the *Supplement* to present Aeneas and Turnus as opposed representations of good and evil. Vegio himself, in a later treatise on education, described Aeneas as "a man endowed with every virtue,"[8] and later still published an allegorizing interpretation of the *Aeneid* in which he claimed that "Turnus is identifiable with the accursed devil."[9] Such assertions

---

[4] Vegio, *Short Epics*, xix–xx.

[5] On the importance of Turnus to *Aeneid* 12, see *Virgil,* Aeneid *12*, ed. Richard Tarrant (Cambridge: Cambridge University Press, 2012), 9–16.

[6] E.g., Richard F. Thomas, *Virgil and the Augustan Reception* (Cambridge: Cambridge University Press, 2001), 282. The most detailed discussions of Turnus are by B. L. Hijmans Jr., "*Aeneia Virtus*: Vegio's *Supplementum* to the *Aeneid*," *Classical Journal* 67 (1971): 144–55, and Craig Kallendorf, *In Praise of Aeneas: Virgil and Epideictic Rhetoric in the Early Italian Renaissance* (Hanover, NH: University of New England Press, 1989), 100–28. See also Margaret Tudeau-Clayton, "Supplementing the *Aeneid* in Early Modern England: Translation, Imitation, Commentary," *International Journal of the Classical Tradition* 4 (1998): 507–25, especially at 517–19 on how translators enlarged upon the criticisms of Turnus expressed in the *Supplement.*

[7] James J. O'Hara, "The Unfinished *Aeneid*?", in *A Companion to Vergil's* Aeneid *and its Tradition*, ed. Joseph Farrell and Michael C. J. Putnam (Malden, MA: Wiley-Blackwell, 2010), 96–106, at 104.

[8] *virum omni virtute praeditum* (*De educatione*, 2.18).

[9] *Turnum idem dyabolum infestum* (*De perseverantia religionis libri septem*, 1.4.10).

were, however, still in Vegio's future when he wrote the *Supplement* and are to a certain extent challenged by his earlier work.[10] There is, indeed, more than one perspective on Turnus in the *Supplement*: he is blamed and criticized, but he is also widely mourned and even praised before finally being laid to rest. The *Supplement* does not present him as an unambiguous villain, a straightforward foil for the virtuous Aeneas, and Vegio's characters, whose lengthy speeches make up nearly forty-five percent of the text,[11] do not unanimously hold a "very, very bad" Turnus responsible for the war between the Trojans and the Latin peoples. Instead, allowing multiple voices to speak, it offers a nuanced view of Turnus's character, thus reflecting concerns in Renaissance Italy about the age-old question of how to interpret the end of the *Aeneid*.

That there was debate about the *Aeneid*'s final moments and Aeneas's character in Vegio's time is clear. Craig Kallendorf has recently demonstrated how some Renaissance readers of Virgil questioned "the idea that the *Aeneid* must be read as simple, straightforward praise of a morally perfect hero."[12] While this was never a majority view, it was a recurring one. In the fourteenth century, for example, Petrarch doubted Aeneas's *pietas* towards his country, gods, and fellow man, and suggested that his treatment of Dido was immoral.[13] Similar sentiments were expressed in the fifteenth century by Francesco Filelfo, who criticized the way in which Aeneas gave in to anger at the end of the *Aeneid*,[14] while in the sixteenth century Lionardo Salviati claimed that Aeneas's behavior towards Dido was wicked and inconsistent with his characteristic *pietas*.[15] A contemporary of Salviati's, Antonio Possevino, wrote a dialogue that debated the propriety of Aeneas's killing of Turnus, concluding that it was indefensible and that Virgil would have altered the ending had he lived.[16] Marginalia written by one Andrea Tordi in a late fifteenth-century Florentine edition of the *Aeneid*

---

[10] Hijmans, "*Aeneia Virtus*," 154. See also Charles S. Ross, "Maffeo Vegio's 'schort Cristyn wark,' with a Note on the Thirteenth Book in Early Editions of Vergil," *Modern Philology* 78 (1981): 215–26, at 219–20.

[11] The importance of these speeches is discussed by Kallendorf, *In Praise of Aeneas*, 106–28. Previously, the speeches had been viewed with disdain: see e.g., *Mapheus Vegius and his Thirteenth Book of the* Aeneid, ed. Anna Cox Brinton (Stanford, CA: Stanford University Press, 1930), 4, and George E. Duckworth, "Maphaeus Vegius and Vergil's *Aeneid*: A Metrical Comparison," *Classical Philology* 64 (1969): 1–6, at 2.

[12] Craig Kallendorf, *The Other Virgil: Pessimistic Readings of the* Aeneid *in Early Modern Culture* (Oxford: Oxford University Press, 2007), 38. See also Craig Kallendorf, "Historicizing the 'Harvard School': Pessimistic Readings of the *Aeneid* in Italian Renaissance Scholarship," *Harvard Studies in Classical Philology* 99 (1999): 391–403.

[13] Kallendorf, *The Other Virgil*, 38–41.

[14] Kallendorf, *The Other Virgil*, 36–38.

[15] Kallendorf, *The Other Virgil*, 45–47; see also the previous chapter in this volume by Giovanna Laterza.

[16] Kallendorf, *The Other Virgil*, 48.

also strongly criticized Aeneas for failing to spare the suppliant Turnus.[17] An earlier dialogue by a connection of Vegio's, Angelo Camillo Decembrio, had similarly discussed the propriety of Aeneas's behavior, this time in the vexed Helen episode.[18] Decembrio has his chief speaker, Leonello, declare that Aeneas acted there in an understandable, human, and princely way. Nonetheless, the presence of the lengthy discussion, in which Leonello's interlocutor takes on the influential and highly respected fourth-century commentator Servius as well as his contemporaries, is further evidence for the live nature of Renaissance dispute regarding Aeneas's virtue.[19]

Alongside differences of opinion about Aeneas run conflicting views regarding his enemies. In the late fifteenth century, Giovanni Pontano wrote a treatise on virtue, which described both Mezentius and Turnus as brave, and presented Turnus as an example of the guileless and virtuous individual capable of controlling his emotions in a praiseworthy manner.[20] And most significantly for understanding the *Supplement*, Vegio's contemporary, Pier Candido Decembrio (brother of the Decembrio who wrote the *De Politia Litteraria* referred to above) also began a thirteenth book to the *Aeneid* in 1419. Never completed, this 89-line work is openly sympathetic to Turnus, describing him as "Italy's great avenger" (*magnum | ultorem Italiae*, 52–53).[21] It narrates the rebuilding of Latinus's city, the king's great grief at Turnus's death, and the devastating rumor that reaches Ardea, Turnus's home town, and Daunus, his wretched father, before his body arrives and inspires frenzied and pitiable lamentation. At this point the text breaks off, but its tenor is unmistakable: it is a sorrowful coda to the *Aeneid*, not a celebration, and its focus is entirely on Aeneas's opponents.[22]

There are some obvious differences between Decembrio's *Supplement* and Vegio's. In his first line, Decembrio describes Turnus as *magnanimus* ("greathearted'), while Vegio applies the epithet more conventionally to Aeneas at a

---

[17] Kallendorf, *The Other Virgil*, 220–21 and Fig. 12.

[18] Decembrio, *De Politia Litteraria*, 2.13.2–11. See *Angelo Camillo Decembrio, De politia litteraria*, ed. Norbert Witten (Munich: K. G. Saur, 2002).

[19] On this passage in the *Politia* as evidence for a Renaissance reading culture, see Anthony Grafton, *Commerce with the Classics: Ancient Books and Renaissance Readers* (Ann Arbor: University of Michigan Press, 1997), 46–48.

[20] Kallendorf, *The Other Virgil*, 43–44. On positive readings of Turnus in the Renaissance, see also David Scott Wilson-Okamura, *Virgil in the Renaissance* (Cambridge: Cambridge University Press, 2010), 191–203.

[21] Decembrio's *Supplement* has been discussed briefly by Kallendorf, *The Other Virgil*, 42–43, and at greater length by Sonja Eckmann, "Das Aeneis-Supplement des Pier Candido Decembrio: die pessimistische "Stimme" der Aeneis?," *Neulateinisches Jahrbuch* 4 (2000): 55–88. The text is printed in *Das Aeneissupplement des Maffeo Vegio*, ed. Bernd Schneider (Weinheim: VCH Verlagsgesellschaft, 1985), 136–38.

[22] Grief is a recurrent theme in Pier Candido Decembrio's *Supplement*, particularly at 19–24, 35, 52–57, 64–66, 77–78, 83, and 86–87.

similarly early and programmatic point in his text: *magnanimus stetit Aeneas, Mavortius heros* ("great-hearted stood Aeneas, war's hero," *Supplement*, 3). Vegio's *Supplement* could, then, be seen as a corrective to Decembrio's, as well as to the *Aeneid* itself, where Aeneas's magnanimity is questionable in the epic's final moments.[23] There are, however, also significant similarities between Decembrio's and Vegio's continuations of the *Aeneid*, not least in the stress that each lays on mourning, and I argue here that Vegio's poem shows elements of the sympathetic view of Turnus discernible in Decembrio's earlier work. It seems clear that Vegio knew the earlier *Supplement*, and certainly Decembrio himself thought that Vegio had read his work and plagiarized it. In an undated letter to a friend, he complains:

> Non enim solum Virgilio addictus est, cuius versus omnibus fere in locis circumcidit, sed meos etiam quosdam versiculos, quos adulescentior edidi, consectatur. [24]
>
> Not only did he [Vegio] knock off Virgil, whose lines he used in abridged fashion practically throughout, but he copied some little verses of mine too, which I composed when younger.

From the long list of parallels that Decembrio claims he could provide between his work and Vegio's, he offers only two. Firstly, he says that Vegio appropriated the name of Turnus's charioteer Metiscus from him, stating incorrectly that there is no mention of Metiscus in the *Aeneid*. The second parallel concerns a phrase from his work echoed in Vegio's, in the description of Turnus's funeral procession:

> Item alio loco dixi:
>
> principio currus **raptorum insignia Teucrum**
> vexilla et clipei.
>
> Hic autem Veggius scripsit:

[23] Vegio's Aeneas is not only great-hearted but "speaks with measured calm" (*placido ore profatur*, 23), in stark contrast to his frenzy at the end of the *Aeneid*. Verbal echoes of Virgil's epic encourage us to compare the description of Aeneas standing like a noble hero in line 3 of the *Supplement*, quoted above, to the more ominous image of him at the end of the *Aeneid* as he "stood fierce in his arms" (*stetit acer in armis*, Virgil, *Aeneid*, 12.938). His calm early in, and throughout, the *Supplement* is also quite different to the emotions we see in Virgil's work, where he is "inflamed by fury and horrifying in his anger" (*furiis accensus et ira | terribilis*, Virgil, *Aeneid*, 12.946–47).

[24] The text of the letter is printed in Remigio Sabbadini, "Due Supplementi all'*Eneide*," *Rivista Etnea di Lettere, Arti e Scienze* 1 (1893): 137–39.

multa super **Teucrum raptorum insignia** secum
et galeas et equos.

Quae quidem aliis in locis plura sunt, sed a me consulto praetermissa.

Moreover in another place I said: "in the front was the chariot, the trappings plundered from the Trojans, the standards and the shields." But this fellow Vegius has written: "and besides they had with them many trappings plundered from the Trojans, and helmets and horses." Indeed there are many examples in other places, but I've deliberately passed over them.

Decembrio does not make the case for plagiarism as convincingly as he might have, with only these two examples to support it, and one of them erroneous, but there is nonetheless reason to think that Vegio read the work that Decembrio says he later tried to suppress and was responding to it among other contemporary readings of the *Aeneid*, both pro- and anti-Turnus.

The variety of ways of reading the *Aeneid* in Vegio's world, and in particular the arguments in Renaissance Italy about the characters of both Aeneas and Turnus, suggest that it would be neither surprising nor anachronistic to find some positive elements in the depiction of Turnus in the *Supplement*. And indeed, Vegio's Turnus is by no means as shrouded in blame in the *Supplement* as the *communis opinio* holds.

After the opening lines describing Turnus's soul fleeing his defeated body and Aeneas standing over him, Vegio's focus turns to the Latins, who have witnessed this spectacle. Their immediate reaction to Turnus's death is not joy but stunned sorrow (*Supplement*, 4–7):

obstupuere omnes gemitumque dedere Latini,
et durum ex alto revomentes corde dolorem
concussis cecidere animis, ceu **frondibus** ingens
silva solet lapsis **boreali** impulsa tumultu.

All were paralyzed by amazement—the Latins groaned and spewed out again from the depths of their hearts bitter grief—their spirits shattered, they sank down, like a massive forest pummeled by the onslaught of the north wind, its foliage fallen to the ground.

Sinking to the ground, buffeted by emotion, the Latins closely resemble Aeneas himself troubled by conflicting emotions in Carthage, though knowing he has to move on.[25] Indeed, Vegio's Latins do move on, as they must under the compul-

[25] Verbal parallels encourage comparison of the effects of grief on Vegio's Latins to the action of the *Boreae* (north winds) on the troubled Aeneas-tree in Virgil's epic: *et altae | consternunt terram concusso stipite frondes* (Virgil, *Aeneid,* 4.443–44: "and the high-up leaves strew the ground when the trunk is buffeted").

sion of the destiny sketched in the *Aeneid* and which Vegio's *Supplement* shows us playing out in detail. Even Turnus's own Rutulians accept the inevitable and sue for peace, despite their grief and fear, preferring the stability of peace to the chaos of war (*Supplement*, 19–22):

> non aliter Rutuli, licet ingens maeror adhausit
> pectora pulsa metu caesi ducis, inclita malunt
> arma sequi et Phrygium Aeneam foedusque precari
> pacis et aeternam rebus belloque quietem.

> In exactly the same way—though great sorrow clung fast in their hearts, hearts which had been battered by the fear generated by the slaughter of their general—the Rutulians prefer to follow famous arms and Aeneas the Trojan, and to pray for a peace treaty and enduring respite from the business of war.

This is not, however, the last we hear of grief felt at Turnus's death.[26] The first half of the *Supplement* abounds with sorrow at Turnus's passing.[27] The Rutulians mourn their dead leader repeatedly, and it is notable that they are much more grief-stricken at Turnus's funeral than the business-like Trojans are at the funeral of their compatriots earlier in Vegio's text.[28] Latinus weeps copiously and is made wretched by Turnus's death,[29] Metiscus weeps,[30] Turnus's horse weeps,[31] the Latin people fill Latinus's unhappy city with lament,[32] and lastly Daunus mourns,[33] along with the beleaguered citizens of Ardea.[34] Even Aeneas laments Turnus's death, addressing him sympathetically with the phrase

---

[26] *Contra* Emma Buckley, "Ending the *Aeneid*? Closure and Continuation in Maffeo Vegio's *Supplementum*," *Vergilius* 52 (2006): 108–37, at 114, who suggests that *dolor* is purged in line 5 of the *Supplement*. The noun recurs several times (18, 180, 204, 253, 257, 287, and 298), and the participle *revomentes* seems to imply not purging but repetition of the earlier *dolores* of the *Aeneid*.

[27] The only voice, which readers of the *Aeneid* might anticipate, not raised in mourning in the *Supplement*, is that of Turnus's half-sister Juturna, who doesn't appear in Vegio's text. Lavinia, as can be expected, makes no remark.

[28] Elizabeth M. McCahill, "Rewriting Vergil, Rereading Rome: Maffeo Vegio, Poggio Bracciolini, Flavio Biondo and Early Quattrocento Antiquarianism," *Memoirs of the American Academy in Rome* 54 (2009): 165–99, at 174 and n. 49. Stress on the sorrowful Rutulians can be seen in Vegio, *Supplement*, 18, 19, 125–26, 127, 130, 132, 197–98, 206–7.

[29] Vegio, *Supplement*, 132, 142, 185, 186, 201.

[30] Vegio, *Supplement*, 194.

[31] Vegio, *Supplement*, 195.

[32] Vegio, *Supplement*, 202–3.

[33] Vegio, *Supplement*, 180, 253–54, 257, 265, 270, 279, 284, 287–88, 297–98.

[34] Vegio, *Supplement*, 181, 251.

"alas, noble corpse" (*heu, nobile corpus*, 36), and grants him full funeral honors, acknowledging that his death is indeed worth mourning.[35]

This preponderance of mourning voices in the first half of the Renaissance poem speaks forcibly against the notion that the characters in Vegio's *Supplement* are unanimous in viewing Turnus as "very, very bad." What, then, are we to make of the fact that Turnus is mourned so lavishly? Earlier epic offers precedent for several different interpretations.

Firstly, mourning and tears at the end of an epic have the potential to act as a catalyst for yet another war. In the *Odyssey*, the firm guidance of the gods was the only thing that stopped conflict continuing until Odysseus had murdered all the Greeks.[36] A text less respectful to the future promised in the *Aeneid* might have taken this direction, but in Vegio's Italy there seems, from the beginning, no possibility of blood feuds and further violence. The amazed and unhappy Latins do not cry for vengeance but beg for peace (*Supplement*, 8–12):

> tum tela infigunt terrae, et mucronibus haerent,
> scutaque deponunt umeris, et proelia damnant,
> insanumque horrent optati Martis amorem.
> nec frenum nec colla pati captiva recusant
> et veniam orare et requiem finemque malorum.

> Then they stab their weapons into the ground and droop over their swords and shrug off their shields and curse all battles, and they recoil from what they now realize was a crazy passion for the war they once desired. They don't balk at suffering the bridle or yoke of captives nor at humbly begging forgiveness and peace and an end of their sufferings.

Turnus's mourning Rutulians do the same, as we have already seen, and even in the face of contemptuous insult from the victorious Trojan troops none of the Italians show any desire for further fighting. Throughout his epic Vegio continues to stress how happy everyone is that the war is over and that the Trojans and Italians are to become one people. One example among many is provided by the emphasis on the willingness with which both groups are ruled by Aeneas after Latinus's death. It is their mutual desire for peace that finally unites them, without any need for divine interference (*Supplement*, 587–92):

> . . . et iam decedens sceptra Latinus
> liquerat, et pius Aeneas successerat, omnem
> Ausoniam lataque potens dicione tenebat.
> iam paribus Phryges atque Itali se moribus ultro

[35] Vegio, *Supplement*, 40.
[36] Homer, *Odyssey*, 24.484–86.

et socia ingenti firmabant pectora amore
concordique aequas miscebant foedere leges.

> And then when Latinus had passed away, giving up the scepter, and Aeneas the Pious had succeeded him, he held sway over all Italy, ruling with far-reaching authority. Then the Trojans and Italians needed no persuasion to strengthen hearts already allied in deep affection with shared customs, and in harmony they commingled mutual laws with a binding treaty.

Mourning in the *Supplement* is, then, not allowed to spark vengeance and another blood-bathed epic. A second option, which also has Homeric precedent, is to see the mourning of Turnus as simply being part of the closuring agenda of Vegio's text. Funerals are standard closuring devices, as we see at the end of the *Iliad*, for example, and the burial of Turnus and its associated lament in the *Supplement* might be viewed as a way of drawing a line under his part in Aeneas's story.

This is, in fact, the argument made by Emma Buckley, who proposes that the first three hundred lines of the *Supplement* offer an Iliadic resolution lacking in Virgil's text.[37] In support of this proposition, she cites the Virgilian echoes in Vegio's mourning voices and suggests that a kind of karmic payback is at work. As she shows, the lament and funeral for Turnus replay the burial and mourning of his victim Pallas, right down to the mourning horse seen on both occasions. These echoes, Buckley claims, close the circle, suggesting that "the loss of Pallas is balanced and righted with Turnus' death and burial."[38] This interpretation is not implausible: the fact that Turnus has exactly the sort of funeral that his victim had could indeed be seen as his just deserts and the satisfactory end of the story, particularly by those who view him as "very, very bad."

However, recognizing that Turnus is the *Supplement*'s new Pallas can cut the opposite way. If Vegio's Turnus is reminiscent of Pallas, he is also reminiscent of Lausus, of Euryalus, of Camilla, indeed of all of the victims of the *Aeneid*'s progress towards Rome. Seen in this light, his death and the sorrow it causes do not draw a line under the melancholy parade of sacrificed young warriors from the *Aeneid* but rather continue it. In this way, Vegio's text seems to suggest caution against adopting a triumphal attitude towards Turnus's death rather than to endorse uncomplicated exultation at Aeneas's victory. Such an interpretation was suggested by Hijmans in the early 1970s, who qualified his own argument that the *Supplement* presents Aeneas and Turnus as opposed symbols of virtue and vice with the statement that it is marked by a "curious mixture of sorrow and anger" with regard to Turnus, not the "relief one would expect," causing him to "wonder whether Vegio has not caught something of the Vergilian sympathy."[39]

---

[37] Buckley, "Ending the *Aeneid*?" 113.
[38] Buckley, "Ending the *Aeneid*?" 121.
[39] Hijmans, "*Aeneia Virtus*," 153.

Hijmans takes the argument no further, but if we look more closely at Turnus in the *Supplement* we can see that a number of ambiguities trouble the alleged certainties of Vegio's text. On the one hand, there are repeated assertions that Turnus's madness was responsible for the war between the Trojans and the Italians. Aeneas, for example, speaks of his insanity and contempt of the gods and says that Pallas's bereaved father Evander should be elated by Turnus's death.[40] Latinus also mentions Turnus's impatience and madness, claiming that, though he tried to rein him in, the headstrong young hero could not be controlled and describing him as the instigator of the conflict.[41] Lastly, Drances, Turnus's opponent and fiercest critic among the Italians in the *Aeneid*, makes it plain that he is glad that Turnus is dead and characterizes him as wholly to blame for every act that might be viewed with disapprobation in the second half of the *Aeneid* (*Supplement*, 339–42):

> sed quicquid tanto armorum flagrante tumultu
> tantorum furiisque operum atque laboribus actum est,
> id rapidus Turni et stimulis incensus iniquis
> correptusque odiis furor attulit . . .
>
> But whatever was done in such wild blazing uproar of fighting—and what fighting!—whatever happened in the frenzy and toil of those epic battles, it was brought about by Turnus's galloping frenzy, inflamed without just cause and consumed by hatred.

However, alongside such statements of blame we also see acknowledgments of Turnus's nobility, and throughout the first half of the *Supplement* condemnation is mitigated by praise for Turnus's virtues. Aeneas claims that his enemy was motivated by overweening insanity but also acknowledges his nobility and sympathizes with his sufferings.[42] Latinus says that Turnus was mad and unstoppable and was the instigator of the rebellion, but also mourns the great glory of his youth and his outstanding spirit.[43] Turnus's father, Daunus, expands on this theme with a pathetic catalogue of his excellence and achievements, which include "superior steadfastness of spirit" (*praestans animi constantia*, 260), among other heroic qualities.[44]

Not only, then, does Vegio's *Supplement* show us that many people mourn Turnus, it also suggests that they are not wrong to do so. Turnus's nobility and heroic qualities are reiterated repeatedly and not just by his father, whom we might expect to say such things. Similarly, if we look at the reasons that Vegio's

[40] Vegio, *Supplement*, 24, 30–32, 34–35, 43.

[41] Vegio, *Supplement*, 161–70, 434–35.

[42] Vegio, *Supplement*, 36, 40, 471.

[43] Vegio, *Supplement*, 177–79.

[44] Vegio, *Supplement*, 267–68, 271–73, 274–76.

characters advance for why Turnus acted the way that he did, we see a number of answers suggested. While "madness" and its variations dominate, there are also other, less opprobrious, possibilities, such as desire for Lavinia or military glory.[45] It is noteworthy, too, that Turnus's father Daunus blames the gods and inexorable fate as well as Turnus's own ungoverned emotions for his doom, reminding us that in the *Aeneid* supernatural forces are largely, if not wholly, responsible for much human suffering.[46] In this, Daunus is also reminiscent of Latinus in Decembrio's earlier *Supplement*, who similarly points to divine factors beyond human control when lamenting Turnus's death.[47]

A certain amount of sympathy and even admiration for Turnus is also discernible in the similes that describe him. His father Daunus, for example, is compared to a doe whose small fawn has been ripped to pieces by an eagle (*Supplement*, 299–301):

> qualis ubi incubuit validis Iovis unguibus ales
> et parvum effuso divulsit sanguine fetum,
> cerva videns miseri tristatur funere nati.

> As when Jupiter's eagle has swooped upon a little baby and torn it apart with its strong talons, spraying blood everywhere: the watching deer laments the death of her wretched child.

The view of Turnus as a "little baby" and a "wretched child" is undoubtedly focalized by his father, as Hijmans points out,[48] but it is also important to note that presenting the point of view of the victim in a sympathetic light is a typically Virgilian tactic, rather than that of a poet concerned to hammer home a blunt

---

[45] Aeneas lists a number of motivations driving Turnus: *dementia* (24), *furor* (31), desire for Lavinia (37), *violentia* (378), youthful love of praise (380), and misguided hope of winning Lavinia (472–73). Latinus similarly offers a range of options for understanding the young hero's actions: *superbia* (145), *furor* (146), *cupido* (146), *gloria* (147), worldliness (152), perversity (158–66), *insania* (166). Drances says it was all due to *furor* (342).

[46] Daunus claims several times that divine forces drove his son to his death, blaming the gods (289–90), the hate-filled gods (294–95), and fate (296), which cannot be avoided or controlled by its human victims. He too offers some other options: *gloria Martis* (276) and a desire for vengeance (279).

[47] Decembrio's Latinus ascribes Turnus's death to *Fortuna* and the powers above (29), the destiny of the Trojans (31), and a hostile Fury (40). Like Daunus in Vegio's *Supplement*, he also muses on the unknowability of human destiny (42–46), controlled by "hostile fate" (*laeva Fortuna*, 45).

[48] Hijmans, "*Aeneia Virtus*," 150 is concerned by the sympathy for Turnus implicit in the simile: "If the element fawn = Turnus may, to our objective (?) eye, seem quite out of place, it must be remembered that old Daunus has just been mourning over Turnus' corpse."

moral message.[49] Moreover, the stress on the eagle's violence as it rips the fawn apart (*divulsit*, 300), the detail of the spurting blood (*effuso . . . sanguine*, 300), and the way that the pitiful adjective *parvum* is widely separated from the noun it describes (*parvum . . . fetum*, 300), mirroring the tearing apart of the fawn's body, combine to give a vivid impression of the horrific brutality of Turnus's death. Such details cast a shadow over the picture of Aeneas as a calmly righteous hero presented elsewhere in the *Supplement*, and thus the simile suggests a degree of ambivalence in Vegio's text regarding the polarization of good hero (Aeneas) and evil villain (Turnus), which is urged both by Vegio's modern readers and by some of the characters in the *Supplement*, such as Drances.

Further ambivalence is implicit in an earlier simile, where Vegio compares Latinus speaking to the Rutulians to a huntsman calming a pack of dogs, the best of which has just been slaughtered by a boar (*Supplement*, 134–36):

> ceu spumantis apri quando per viscera dentes
> fulmineos canis excepit praestantior omni
> ex numero . . .

> Like when the most outstanding hound in the whole pack has taken the thundering tusks of a foaming boar through its vitals.

This simile has been criticized by Vegio's modern readers. Anna Cox Brinton thought that it had little relation to its narrative frame,[50] while Hijmans worried about its implications:

> One may, of course, feel that the comparison of Aeneas with a boar, Latinus with a hunter is wrong, but it should be pointed out that Vegio does not say that Latinus is a hunter who hunts a boar, but rather that he is the master who controls his pack of frightened dogs.[51]

Though Hijmans was reluctant to acknowledge it, the simile could be read as an acknowledgment that Latinus was more implicated in the war against Aeneas than he is prepared to admit. It also presents Turnus as not only a passionate figure but also a heroic one, at least in the eyes of the Rutulians and Latinus, by giving him the role of a hunting dog, which was awarded to Aeneas in the *Aeneid*.[52]

---

[49] Don Fowler, "Deviant Focalisation in Virgil's *Aeneid*," *Proceedings of the Cambridge Philological Society* 36 (1990): 42–63.

[50] Brinton, ed., *Mapheus Vegius and his Thirteenth Book*, 154.

[51] Hijmans, "*Aeneia Virtus*," 149.

[52] Aeneas appears as *venator canis* in Virgil, *Aeneid*, 12.751.

Vegio's Aeneas, by contrast, is less straightforwardly heroic here, taking the role of the infuriated boar given to Mezentius by Virgil.[53]

Against all such ambiguities stands Vegio's Drances, as hostile to Turnus dead as he was to Turnus living. He is given a lengthy speech vituperating Turnus and praising Aeneas as the new ruler of a combined Trojan and Italian race, which receives unanimous applause. Despite this, and despite the fact that Vegio's Drances, like Virgil's, has much to say in sympathy with the glorious future towards which both poems look, the multiple perspectives on Turnus already introduced leave a way open to resist the dominant, closuring momentum of his speech.

Furthermore, Drances is revealed as a somewhat untrustworthy speaker. He is, for example, described as excessive in his exultation over Turnus's death (*Supplement*, 329–31):

> tunc senior sic incipiens ardentia Drances
> verba movet nimium erepti pro funere Turni
> exultans . . .

> Then old Drances started speaking, producing inflammatory words as he exulted too much in the death of Turnus who had been snatched away.

His tendency to excess is demonstrated in his exaggerated portrayal of the dead hero as a monstrous, Cacus-like figure, belching fire and summoning war:[54] *quin acrius ignem | spumabat ferus ore vomens bellumque ciebat* ("instead, even more fiercely the beast foamed fire vomitously from his mouth, and war, war was still his cry," *Supplement*, 350–51). His speech, too, is "inflammatory" (*ardentia*, 329), suggesting that he himself is as fiery and unrestrained as the *Aeneid*'s worst offenders, Cacus among them. Indeed, the very fieriness of Drances's speech highlights the similarities between him and the Turnus whom he criticizes, repeatedly, for frenzied hot-headedness, as well as setting him at odds with the message of peace that the *Supplement* promotes.[55]

Moreover, concerns about Drances's message grow as he gloats that Turnus has, like the unsympathetic Pyrrhus and Dolon in the *Aeneid*, finally met his

---

[53] Virgil, *Aeneid*, 10.707–18. Vegio's description of the boar's tusks as being "like lightning" (*fulmineos*, 135) also aligns the animal (and thus Aeneas) with Jupiter, a connection later reinforced by the description of the eagle as "Jupiter's bird" (*Iovis . . . ales*, 299). This does not, however, negate the sympathy for the victims suggested in either passage.

[54] Cf. Virgil, *Aeneid*, 8.198–99.

[55] See Tarrant, *Virgil,* Aeneid *Book XII*, 85 for Turnus's fieriness in *Aeneid* 12.

deserved end gnawing at the ground darkened by his life blood (*Supplement*, 352–54):[56]

> at vero dignum invenit pro talibus ausis
> exitium, qui te tandem victore momordit
> nigrantem prostratus humum. . . .

> But indeed he has found an end worthy of such great daring, and at last—defeated by you—has gnawed at the blood-blackened earth, prostrate.

This gruesome recollection of the end of the *Aeneid* is far more shocking than the calm and bloodless picture that Vegio presents at the beginning of the *Supplement*, suggesting that narrator and character do not altogether see eye to eye. It is also an echo of Turnus's dramatic statement in the debate in *Aeneid* 11 that those who died biting the ground were more fortunate than those who lived to see the Latin forces wavering in the struggle against Aeneas.[57] This sardonic repetition twists the knife in Drances's dead enemy, demonstrating again his personal hostility to Turnus, and while it may suggest that Turnus deserves the death that Drances gloatingly recounts here, it also aligns Drances with the dark side of his opponent's character and makes us question whether we, as readers, can be comfortable with the point of view he espouses.

In the lines immediately following, Drances dismisses Turnus to Acheron, wishing him luck chasing war and marriage in hell (*Supplement*, 354–56):

> nunc improbus aedes
> Tartareas visurus eat quaeratque sub imo
> nunc alias Acheronte acies aliosque hymenaeos.

> Now let that very, very bad man go take a look at the halls of hell, and seek other armies, and other marriages down in the depths of the underworld.

Here the aged Italian sounds like notable disdainful warriors of the *Aeneid*, Pyrrhus in Book 2, and Turnus himself in Book 9, who similarly tell their opponents to go, literally, to hell.[58] While one could understand this as the curse that a Pyrrhus-like Turnus merited, it also exposes the vituperative Drances as being just as bad as he says his enemy was and again opens up the possibility that readers could question the truth of his accentuations of the negative.

---

[56] Death is presented as just deserts "for villainous daring" (*pro talibus ausis*) for some of the *Aeneid*'s worst offenders: Pyrrhus (Virgil, *Aeneid,* 2.535) and Dolon (Virgil, *Aeneid,* 12.351).

[57] Virgil, *Aeneid,* 11.416–18.

[58] Pyrrhus: Virgil, *Aeneid,* 2.547–49; Turnus: Virgil, *Aeneid,* 9.742.

That Vegio's Drances is questionable is evident when he says that everyone unanimously exults in Turnus's death at Aeneas's hands, ascribing his own emotion to the wider community:[59] *unanimes aequo ore volunt Turnumque sub armis | exultant cecidisse tuis* ("They all with equal voice yearn for [you, Aeneas] and exult that Turnus has been slain by your might," *Supplement*, 365–66). The weeping for Turnus in the *Supplement* is enough to contradict him, and the praise of Turnus, however modified, that we have heard from Latinus, Daunus, and even Aeneas underlines the contradiction. Drances would like us to think that his is the only point of view, but Vegio suggests otherwise. As in the *Aeneid*, Drances is a complex figure, whose speech is, on the one hand, intertwined with the poet's message but who is, on the other hand, characterized as overheated and unsympathetic.[60] The *Supplement* does not question that the hatchet needs to be buried between the Trojan and Latin forces, but neither does it fully endorse the burial of the hatchet where Drances urges, in the bleeding remains of Turnus's memory.

Thus we can see that Vegio's Turnus is both very, very bad and not so bad. Some blame him for the war, others do not. He is represented variously as unsympathetic monster and sympathetic victim. Some of those who blame him are admirable figures, while others are questionable. While the ambiguities in the representation of Turnus are not perhaps as agonizingly equally weighted as they are in the *Aeneid*, they are nonetheless plainly discernible. Even Vegio's Aeneas appears to acknowledge different perspectives on the character and actions of his dead enemy, in his response to the vehement and polarizing speech delivered by Drances (*Supplement*, 377–82):

> nec vos nec placida solitum sub pace Latinum
> arguerim, verum infesti violentia Turni
> tantum opus, haud dubito, et tanti discrimina Martis
> concivit, iuvenili autem plus laudis amore.
> quicquid id est tamen, Ausonii, nil pacta recuso
> conubia . . .

> I wouldn't blame you [Drances and the Italian people], nor Latinus who is accustomed to the reign of gentle peace, but rather the violent spirit of hateful Turnus, I'm sure, was responsible for the whole epic battle, and the struggles of such great war, and moreover more responsible than youthful love of glory. But whatever the case, Ausonians, I'm not going to draw back from the arranged marriage.

Here, we seem at first to see simple acceptance of the picture Drances has drawn. Turnus is described as "hateful" (*infestus*, 378) and characterized by *violentia*

59 Remember that Drances was earlier described as "exulting" (*exultans*, 331).

60 Philip Hardie, *Rumour and Renown: Representations of* Fama *in Western Literature* (Cambridge: Cambridge University Press, 2012), 126–49.

(378), and said to be solely responsible for the war that raged through the second half of the *Aeneid* (379–80). When Aeneas qualifies this conclusion with *haud dubito* ("I'm sure," 379), however, he reveals that his interpretation is a choice, as becomes even clearer when he discusses a less negative, if to him less preferable, view of Turnus's behavior: perhaps Turnus was really motivated by a youthful love of glory like Euryalus in *Aeneid* 9 (380).[61] The debate could continue further, but Vegio's Aeneas declares that it is time to move on. Whatever the truth about Turnus, he says (*quicquid id est tamen*, 381), he is eager for the marriage and peace treaty that await.

As Philip Hardie has demonstrated, the phrase *quidquid est* is Lucretian, a philosophical marker of a conclusion to a list of alternate possibilities.[62] It is particularly reminiscent of the doomed prophet Laocoon in *Aeneid* 2, where it refers both to a number of evils that the Trojan horse might be designed for and to a number of different explanations of the horse in circulation in antiquity (*Aeneid*, 2.45–49):

aut hoc inclusi ligno occultantur Achivi,
aut haec in nostros fabricata est machina muros
inspectura domos venturaque desuper urbi,
aut aliquis latet error: equo ne credite, Teucri.
quidquid id est, timeo Danaos et dona ferentis.

Either the Achaeans lie hidden inside this wood, or this is an engine built—a trick designed—to lay siege to our walls, to spy on our homes and come down upon the city from above, or some other deception remains yet to be perceived; don't trust that horse, Trojans. Whatever it is, I am afraid of the Greeks, even when they bear gifts.

In the mouth of Aeneas, *quicquid id est* reminds Vegio's readers of the possibility that more than one interpretation of Turnus's actions in the *Aeneid* is possible. Even more than Laocoon, who gives the right advice but is not heeded, Vegio's Aeneas is an authoritative speaker. Earlier he had appropriated the poet's famous opening words to describe his own action in granting Turnus's body to his people for burial:[63] *nunc, Rutuli, hinc auferte ducem vestrum;* ***arma virumque*** *| largior atque omnem deflendae mortis honorem* ("Now, Rutulians, bear your leader hence; arms and a man I bestow and every honor of a death worth mourning," *Supplement*, 39–40). With such authority vested in its speaker, the phrase *quicquid id est*

[61] Euryalus was "struck by love of glory" (*laudum percussus amore,* Virgil, *Aeneid,* 9.197).

[62] Philip Hardie, *Lucretian Receptions: History, the Sublime, Knowledge* (Cambridge: Cambridge University Press, 2009), 231–63.

[63] Anne Rogerson, "Vegio's Ascanius: Problems in the Continuation of the *Aeneid,*" *Classical Receptions Journal* 5 (2013): 106–25, at 111.

acts as a decisive footnote in the *Supplement*, a stamp of the author's awareness of the multiple perspectives on Turnus in circulation in his day, even as he throws most of his weight behind the first interpretation he offers. The view that Turnus was a very, very bad man, particularly in contrast to the pious hero Aeneas, which dominated Renaissance understandings of the *Aeneid*, is certainly given the loudest voice in Vegio's *Supplement*. It is also, however, quietly but firmly qualified. Vegio, through the voice of his hero Aeneas, demonstrates that other perspectives are possible, before attempting to close the discussion down, to move on to the marriage and the union of two peoples that still awaits.

Aeneas's speech almost puts an end to the debate about Turnus, and when Latinus speaks later of the Italian resistance to the Trojans, he mentions no names (*Supplement*, 424, 428–36):

> venisti tandem . . .
> quamquam humana furens nimis ausa licentia sanctas
> turbarit leges et divum exciverit iras,
> quin etiam invitum totiens meque arma negantem
> crediderit duri perferre pericula Martis.
> factum etenim, sed nec parvo: sat numina iustas
> indignata animis misere ultricia poenas.
> nunc age, magne Phrygum ductor, quando omnis origo
> seditionis abest et tanti criminis auctor,
> conubiis succede et promissis hymenaeis.

> You have come at last . . . though it be the case that human lawlessness, raging, dared too much and upset holy laws and provoked the wrath of the gods, and indeed even imagined that I—though I so often expressed unwillingness and refused to take up arms—would endure the dangers of harsh warfare. It is over, that's certainly true, though at no small price: sufficiently have the passionately outraged, avenging heavenly powers sent appropriate punishments. Come now, great leader of the Trojans, since the source and the instigator of all rebellion and such a great offence has passed away, enter into the state of matrimony and the promised marriage bonds.

Although it cannot be doubted whom Latinus means as "source and instigator" of the rebellion, his earlier vague reference to personified lawlessness (*licentia*, 428) blurs the apportioning of blame somewhat. His speech also suggests that he has heard Aeneas's attempt to draw a line under the debate around Turnus: though he cannot restrain himself from musing on the punishments meted out by the avenging gods, he acknowledges that "the fact is, the past is past" (*factum etenim*, 432).[64] Moreover, while still apportioning blame, he soon starts, as

[64] The adverb *sat* ("sufficiently," 432) also implies finality.

Aeneas did earlier, to look forward rather than back and talk about the Trojan hero's marriage to Lavinia.

It is at the moment when Aeneas sees Lavinia for the first time that the final mention of Turnus in the *Supplement* comes. Dumbstruck by her beauty, Aeneas's first conscious thought is pity for Turnus (*Supplement*, 471–73):

> et secum Turni casus miseratus acerbos,
> qui haud parva spe ductus ovans in proelia tantos
> civisset motus durisque arsisset in armis.

> And in interior monologue he noted that he pitied the bitter misfortunes of Turnus, who had been led triumphantly into battle by no small hope and had stirred up such great disturbances and had blazed under harsh arms.

Here, in a nutshell, we again see Vegio's ambiguous Turnus: to blame for stirring up the war, yet also pitiable, driven by forces out of his control, though also "triumphing" (*ovans*, 472) and apparently considering himself in charge and invincible. This Turnus is a tough and fiery warrior, and yet also—such is the multivalence of *duris . . . in armis* (472)—trapped within the hard-biting embrace of the weapons that love for Lavinia had forced him to assume.

Vegio's Turnus is not, then, simply to be dismissed as "very, very bad," nor does his funeral draw a line under the problems that he poses for the Renaissance reader of the *Aeneid*. The *Supplement* presents a number of points of view on the Italian hero and in the end brings in its greatest authority, Aeneas himself, to clear the way forward as the text accelerates to its end. Aeneas's enigmatic "whatever" more or less does the job. However, it also acknowledges that "very, very bad" need not be the last word on Turnus, even though it might need to be if the debate in the Renaissance, and later, on the Italian hero's posthumous reputation is not to derail progress towards closure altogether.[65] Even Aeneas retains a complex understanding of his dead opponent, and the *Supplement* provides no final answer as to how we might interpret the troubling young Rutulian who has long divided Virgil's readers. Vegio's *Supplement*, in other words, shows us his and his hero's awareness that while closure may demand the polarization of good and evil, the rewriting of history by the victor never gives the whole story. Other voices echo still, and the case regarding Turnus is not really closed when Vegio's Aeneas says so.

Vegio's subtle and nuanced representation of Turnus has significant implications for our understanding of the role played by the *Aeneid* in Renaissance thought and culture. The popular *Supplement* reveals itself as a more sophis-

[65] In this way, it could be argued, Vegio's Turnus also retains some of the qualities of delay that characterize him in the *Aeneid*, where he is often associated with the retardation of narrative progress.

ticated and ambivalent work than many have realized; its reading of the politics and ethics of Virgil's epic is deep and complex. Debates about literature are shaped according to the culture in which they take place: Vegio gave us not a commentary or scholarly article but a new end to the *Aeneid*, his Renaissance contribution to a literary-critical debate that was as alive then as it remains now. He uses Turnus to bring into focus a number of vital issues—the relationship of anger and violence to nobility, the achievement of reconciliation after war—issues that matter not simply in the *Aeneid* but also, and perhaps particularly, for its Renaissance readers in the strife-torn Italy of the fifteenth century. Thus literary debates become cultural ones, and Vegio's engagement with the *Aeneid* offers insight into both his perceptive reading of Virgil's text and the ways in which Renaissance thinkers might grapple with vexed questions around history, conflict, politics, and memory with Virgil as their guide.[66]

[66] I am grateful to audiences in Mantua and Sydney who listened to and commented on earlier versions of this argument, and in particular to Bob Cowan, Philip Hardie, Craig Kallendorf, Helen Lovatt, Frances Muecke, and Paul Roche.

9

Aeneas Interpres: Landino's Earliest Allegory of the *Aeneid* and Ficino's First Ten Dialogues

Adam T. Foley
University of Notre Dame

Der Unterschied zwischen einer hermeneutica sacra
und profana ist demnach ganz unstatthaft.
Philip August Boeckh (1886)[1]

During the academic year of 1462 Cristoforo Landino (1424–1498) offered a course on Virgil's *Aeneid* at the Florentine studium.[2] In these lectures he presented to his students an allegorical interpretation of Aeneas's journey from Troy to Rome. Landino believed that Virgil had been "dedicated to Platonic teachings" and that he had adorned Aeneas with the highest virtues so that his readers might imitate him in their pursuit of the blessed life.[3] As he says in his lecture

---

[1] I would like to thank Professor Craig Kallendorf for his kind feedback at the "Virgilio e la Cultura del Rinascimento" conference in Mantua and his willingness to read drafts of this chapter afterward. For the quotation, see Philip August Boeckh, *Encyklopädie und Methodologie der philologischen Wissenschaften* (Leipzig: Teubner, 1886), 8.

[2] For Landino's earliest allegory of the *Aeneid*, see Arthur Field, "A Manuscript of Cristoforo Landino's First Lectures on Virgil, 1462–63 (Codex 1368, Biblioteca Casanatense, Rome)," *Renaissance Quarterly* 31 (1978): 17–20, and Arthur Field, *The Origins of the Platonic Academy of Florence* (Princeton: Princeton University Press, 1988), 250–56. For Landino's inaugural speech in praise of poetry, addressed to the Florentine Studio to commence his lectures on Virgil, see Arthur Field, "An Inaugural Oration by Cristoforo Landino in Praise of Virgil (From Codex «2», Casa Cavalli, Ravenna)," *Rinascimento* ser. 2, 21 (1981): 235–45.

[3] Landino writes in MS Casanatense (hereafter MS Cas.) 1368, fol. 2v that Virgil was *vir plane bonus et Platonicis dogmatibus deditus*. See also MS Laur. 53.32 fol. 2v. For Landino's reliance on the tradition of laudatory interpretations of the *Aeneid*, see Craig Kallendorf, *In Praise of Aeneas: Virgil and Epideictic Rhetoric in the Early Italian Renaissance* (Hanover, NH and London: University Press of New England, 1989).

notes, the *propositio* or design of the *Aeneid* is threefold: Aeneas's maritime peregrinations are an allegory of the soul's journey from cupidity in Troy to avarice in Thrace and then to insolence in Carthage.[4] After shedding these vices Aeneas arrives at the shores of Latium where he seeks out the Sibyl, descends to hell, and emerges at last endowed with the virtue of philosophical wisdom in Rome. The *Aeneid* represented for Landino a moral allegory of the soul's progression from "childhood and that first period of life" in Troy to the "speculative life" of manly virtue in Rome.[5] According to Landino, Virgil had been steeped in Platonic philosophy, and he embroidered his narrative of Aeneas's journey with an allegory for the life-stages of the soul in its triumph over vice. This commentary breaks off after the seventh book of the *Aeneid* and is now extant in only two manuscripts.[6] By 1473 Landino returned to these lecture notes and used them to write a full commentary on Books 1–6 of the *Aeneid* in the form of a dialogue.

This dialogue took the form of his famous *Disputationes Camaldulenses*, a conversation on the *summum bonum* held between leading Florentine intellectuals on four summer days at the Camaldoli monastery outside of Florence.[7] In the third and fourth books of this dialogue Landino has Leon Battista Alberti expound the first six books of the *Aeneid* to Lorenzo de' Medici. The interpretation Alberti delivers is drawn substantially from Landino's 1462 commentary with a few innovations. Although Alberti tweaks the semantic valence of each

---

[4] In the *accessus* to Virgil in MS Cas. 1368, fol. 3r, where he treats the *intentio auctoris* Landino divides the *propositio* of the *Aeneid* into three themes: *Debitum etiam notari quod est tripartita propositio et in propositione cavendum est, ne species generi admisceatur, ut est, dicam de cupiditate, de insolentia, de avaritia, et avaritia est species cupiditatis.*

[5] MS Cas. 1368, fols. 203v–204r: *Illi itaque primo fuit ex Troia abeundum, quam pro pueritia et prima illa aetate intelligere debemus.*

[6] There are three manuscripts containing Landino's Virgil commentary from 1462–1463. The first and most comprehensive is MS Cas. 1368 at the Biblioteca Casanatense in Rome; see Field, "A Manuscript," 39–45; the second is MS Laur. 52.32 at the Biblioteca Laurenziana in Florence; and the third is MS Vat. Lat. 5129, which includes only the beginning of the sixth book and was written independently of the other two. For a detailed description of MS Cas. 1368, see Valerio Sanzotta, *I manoscritti classici latini della Biblioteca Casanatense di Roma* (Rome: Istituto Poligrafico e Zecca dello Stato, 2015), 112–13 and table 78.

[7] Those present in the dialogue are Landino, Ficino, Leon Battista Alberti, Lorenzo de' Medici, Giuliano de' Medici, Antonio Canigiani, Alamanno Rinuccini, Marco Parenti, Pietro Landino, Donato and Pietro Acciaiuoli. For the dating of the *Disputationes* I follow Kallendorf, "Cristoforo Landino's *Aeneid* and the Humanist Critical Tradition," *Renaissance Quarterly* 36 (1983): 519–46. Peter Lohe argues for a date of composition in the middle of 1472 in his "Die Datierung der *Disputationes Camaldulenses* des Cristoforo Landino," *Rinascimento* 9 (1969): 291–99. Eugenio Garin places it in the year 1475 in his *Testi inediti e rari di Cristoforo Landino e Francesco Filelfo* (Florence: Fussi, 1949), 6.

geographical juncture in Aeneas's journey, the allegorical structure of the soul's ascent remains intact. For instance, Troy now represents Venus (*voluptas*), Carthage Juno (*ambitio*), and Rome Minerva (*contemplatio*).[8] But the contours of the interpretation are still defined by the soul's ascent to philosophical contemplation:

> Aeneas rises from Troy, by which city I think we should rightly understand the first period in a person's life [*primam hominis aetatem*], in which all reason up to that point has been stupefied and only the senses rule. And mortals themselves, since they do not even pursue wisdom in that age, consider those things alone which philosophers call the early stages of nature.[9]

The framework of a life course thus remained a constant organizing principle for Landino and provided a basis for his claim to originality.[10]

Landino's interpretive framework is a curious one. In order to maintain Aeneas's journey as an allegory of the soul's ascent to wisdom, Landino had to read the *Aeneid* against the grain and interpret the events in the story not in the order in which Virgil presented them, but in the order in which they actually occurred. Because the *Aeneid* commences *in medias res*, Landino had to begin his commentary with Books 2 and 3 in Troy and then move to Books 1 and 4 in Carthage, while finishing with Books 5 and 6 in Rome. This way Landino could interpret the narrative in the sequence in which the events actually happened rather than as Virgil relates them. Once stitched together in its proper order, Aeneas's life-course represents a ritual purgation of the soul that culminates in the initiation into divine mysteries in Rome. Some scholars have described the Neoplatonic psychology that informs Landino's allegory as "Plotinian."[11] Landino was able to engage in the debate of the earlier Quattrocento over the respective merits of the *vita activa civilis* and the *vita contemplativa* by having Aeneas advance through the civic and purgative virtues to the pleasure of philosophical contemplation. Landino thus transformed Plotinus's three virtues—civic, pur-

---

[8] For a more detailed discussion of Landino's allegorical thought, see Kallendorf, "Cristoforo Landino's *Aeneid*," 519–46.

[9] Landino, *Disputationes Camaldulenses*, ed. Peter Lohe (Florence: Sansoni, 1980), 120: *Troiae igitur oritur Aeneas, per quam urbem recte, ut puto, primam hominis aetatem intelligimus, in qua, cum ratio adhuc omnis consopita sit, solus sensus regnat. Atque ipsi mortales, quia ea aetate sapientiam ne suspicantur quidem, ea sola sibi proponunt, quae philosophi prima naturae appellant.*

[10] For Landino's use of order as an organizing principle in his Virgil interpretations, see Kallendorf, "Cristoforo Landino's *Aeneid*," 532.

[11] See Garin, *Testi inediti e rari*, 5. Garin claims that Landino inherited his Plotinian division of virtue from Matteo Palmieri's poem *Città di vita*, a division that also finds expression in his funeral oration for Donato Acciaiuoli. See also Field, *Origins*, 259–60.

gatorial, and contemplative—into a geo-moral allegory of the every-soul in its journey towards beatitude.

It is an interesting coincidence that at the same time Landino was developing his allegory of the *Aeneid*, his younger colleague and friend Marsilio Ficino (1433–1499) was applying a similar interpretive scheme to the corpus of Platonic dialogues.[12] What both their interpretations have in common is that each read his chosen text out of its original sequence in order to repurpose material read to different ends in antiquity. For instance, when Ficino translated the first ten dialogues attributed to Plato for Cosimo de' Medici in 1464, he arranged them into a *cursus aetatis* similar to Landino's allegory of the *Aeneid*. Ficino's decade is as follows: *Hipparchus*, *Amatores*, *Theages*, *Meno*, *Alcibiades Major*, *Alcibiades Minor*, *Minos*, *Euthyphro*, *Parmenides*, *Philebus*.[13] In the preface to the decade Ficino claims to have selected these dialogues according to principles of arrangement, which, like Landino's Aeneas, follow the life-stages in the soul's ascent to wisdom. He commences the decade with the *Hipparchus* or "the desire for wealth," because as he says:

> At a young age [*tenera aetate*] people are deceived by their senses and by common opinion, and they suppose the good to be the possession of material things, so that their whole impulse is directed toward their possession. Hence I have placed the book *De lucri cupiditate* [*Hipparchus*] first in order. When people have progressed in age and been incited by reason, they begin to love the understanding of divine things as a good. The love of wisdom is "philosophy," therefore the book *De philosophia* [*Amatores*] is given the next place, second in order.[14]

---

[12] See James Hankins, *Plato in the Italian Renaissance*, vol. 1 (New York: Brill, 1991), 306–8; Field, *Origins*, 190–91.

[13] Ficino's earliest translation of these ten dialogues is contained in two manuscripts, MS Canonicianus Latinus Classicus 163 at the Bodleian Library, Oxford, and MS Carteggio di Lucca, Cassetta 5 at the Biblioteca Palatina in Parma. The Parma manuscript along with Nouv. acq. 1633 at the Bibliothèque Nationale de France (once one and the same manuscript) are both autographs and not only include the translations but also the argumentum to each dialogue.

[14] From the *Proemium in Primos Decem Dialogos ad Cosmum Medicem* in MS Canonicianus Latinus 163 at the Bodleian Library, fol. 1v: *Verum in tenera aetate homines sensibus et opinione decepti rerum mobilium possessionem bonum existimant, unde ad illam toto impetu perferuntur, quo fit ut de lucri cupiditate primus sit in ordine liber. Quoniam vero aetate provecti ac ratione quandoque admoniti divinorum cognitionem tamquam bonum amare incipiunt, amor autem sapientiae philosophia est, secundum ordinem est sortitus.*

The thrust of the sequence is protreptic: the *Hipparchus* is meant to turn vulnerable youths away from "common opinion" and towards the love of wisdom which is the subject of *Amatores*.[15]

After the *Amatores* follows the *Theages* or *De sapientia* "since we also seek wisdom through love before we actually possess it." Ficino places the *Meno* or *De virtute* next, "since when the light of wisdom first arises it exemplifies its beauty in particular powers and motions of the soul, which clearly receives the name of virtue." When the light of wisdom floods the mind it awakens the virtues (*virtutes*) to the three Plotinian powers (*vires*) of the soul—to return to oneself, to return to one's cause, and to guide lesser things. The two *Alcibiades* and the *Minos* treat these powers of the soul, after which the *Euthyphro* teaches us how to preserve these powers with piety:

> But when divine light flows into the mind now purged by holiness and it knows God himself in this passion, the discussion on the one beginning of all things rightly follows the book on holiness—that is, the *Parmenides* follows the *Euthyphro*. And since our blessedness consists in the vision of God, the *Philebus*, "On the highest good" of man, seems to be placed after the *Parmenides* on the highest good of all of nature.[16]

Finally purged of vice and prepared to receive divine wisdom, the reader-soul moves on to the *Parmenides* and, at last, apprehends God himself in the *Philebus* or *De summo bono*.

According to this rather complex rationale Ficino decided that the group of ten dialogues should commence with the *Hipparchus* which, like Landino's Troy, represents the lower faculties of bodily sense. He ended the decade with the *Philebus,* which, like Landino's Rome, represents the *summum bonum* or divine wisdom. In Ficino's schema the dialogues start with *tenera aetas* of immediate sense perception and advance through the soul's acquisition of reason to the maturity of the contemplative life. The principles according to which Ficino arranged these dialogues, as Michael Allen has argued, have much in common with the "Iamblichean" arrangement of dialogues in antiquity.[17] Iamblichus had constructed a curriculum of ten dialogues to initiate students into the basics of

---

[15] Field refers to Ficino, who insisted that philosophy require a transformed spirit and a new way of life, as a "philosopher for youth" (*Origins*, 195).

[16] MS Canon. Lat. 163, fol. 1v: *Cum vero in mentem iam sanctitate purgatam divinum lumen influat eiusque fulgore deus ipse cernatur, merito librum de sanctitate disputatio de uno rerum omnium principio sequitur, ideoque Parmenides Euthyphroni succedit. Cumque in Dei visione beatitudo nostra consistat, iure Philebus de summo bono hominis post Parmenidem de summo totius nature bono locatus esse videtur.*

[17] See Michael Allen, *Marsilio Ficino: The Philebus Commentary* (Los Angeles: Center for Medieval and Renaissance Studies, 1975), 1–15, and Allen, "Ficino's Lecture on the Good?", *Renaissance Quarterly* 30 (1977): 160–71.

philosophy before they embarked on the secrets of Platonic wisdom.[18] Just like Iamblichus's decade, Ficino's was arranged for pedagogical purposes according to the sequence of life-stages in the soul's ascent to wisdom.[19] Yet Ficino's program of study suffers not the least in originality since it bears at best only vague similarity to Iamblichus's curriculum of dialogues.

Scholars have noted some structural similarities between Ficino's principles of arrangement and Landino's allegorical interpretation of the *Aeneid*, but the question of influence has seldom been raised explicitly.[20] They both rejected the traditional principle of arranging the books that made up their respective texts, and it is this rearrangement in the sequence of books that underscores their shared commitment to a certain sequence of philosophical education. In this chapter I do not attempt to draw any line of influence between Landino's earliest commentary (1462) and Ficino's first decade of dialogues (1464), but I do put the two in much closer proximity by drawing attention to Landino and Ficino's respective appreciation for *as well as* insouciance towards traditional canons of order. Each abandoned the notion of linear organization, preferring to view the Platonic corpus and Aeneas's journey cyclically and holistically. In this view the destination recapitulates the point of departure at a higher level, so that the position of each component along the way remains relative while the sequential framework as a whole retains symbolic meaning. Each begins with pleasure and ends in contemplation, but it is the pleasure of contemplation that culminates the sequence and is thus a recapitulation of the beginning at a higher level of abstraction. Though order as such was still the chief hermeneutical principle for both Ficino and Landino, the particular sequence of elements in their interpretive schemes remained fairly flexible. Landino, for his part, cast his allegory in the form of a dialogue and always proposed a number of possible interpretations to choose from. Ficino, for his part, claimed to have arranged his dialogues "in a kind of human order."[21]

---

[18] Iamblichus's curriculum consisted of a decade of dialogues: *Alcibiades*, *Gorgias*, *Phaedo*, *Cratylus*, *Theaetetus*, *Sophist*, *Statesman*, *Phaedrus*, *Symposium*, *Philebus*. The decade was meant to prepare students to embark on the dyad of dialogues that followed: *Timaeus* and *Parmenides*. For a comparison of various canons of arrangement in antiquity, see Carol Poster, "The Idea(s) of Order of Platonic Dialogues and Their Hermeneutic Consequences," *Phoenix* 52 (1998): 282–98.

[19] Iamblichus's rationale for arranging his decade would have been known through an anonymous introduction to Platonic philosophy attributed to Elias in the sixth century CE. See *Anonymous Prolegomenon to Platonic Philosophy*, ed. L. G. Westerink (Amsterdam: North Holland Publishing Company, 1962), 47–49. Elias's rationale is determined by the pedagogical requirement of lecturing on the dialogues, which raises the question of Ficino's access to this Prolegomenon or information he may have had about it through other authors.

[20] See Hankins, *Plato in the Italian Renaissance*, 301; Field, *Origins*, 192.

[21] See Hankins. *Plato in the Italian Renaissance*, 309.

Yet the idea of order nevertheless supplied each with his chief interpretive principle. How do we explain their respective regard for and nonchalance towards traditional canons of arrangement for their respective texts? In Ficino's decade the reader arrives at the *Philebus*, and in Landino's allegory Aeneas arrives at Rome. In both interpretive frameworks the destination repeats or brings to fulfilment the point of departure—that is, pleasure or immediate sense perception. In antiquity the *Philebus* was often associated with pleasure, not with wisdom, while Landino's Rome represents not pure contemplation but the reconciliation of divine and human wisdom.[22] In other words, Ficino's reader, just like Landino's Aeneas, comes full circle to the pleasure of philosophical speculation. What is more, both Ficino and Landino cast Aeneas's descent to the underworld as a purgative rite required to interpret divine mysteries. Aeneas is an exemplary interpreter who, like the reader of Ficino's first ten dialogues, must be initiated by a series of trials before entering the sanctuary of wisdom. Ficino's arrangement of ten dialogues thus invites us to ask to what extent he intended these dialogues to act as a primer or *ianua* into the rest of the Platonic corpus. Only after being initiated into the central core of Platonic philosophy in the *Philebus* could the reader, like *Aeneas iam purgatus*, make good sense of the rest of the corpus.[23] What this means is that, as will be shown below, the figure of Aeneas for both Ficino and Landino represented the ideal philosophical exegete.

The idea of order thus held a preeminent place in the exegetical practices of both Landino and Ficino. Yet they both meddled with their texts. Each seemed

---

[22] In Ficino's codex of Platonic dialogues (MS Laur. 85.9) on fol. 105r the *Philebus* is given the σκοπὸς "περὶ ἡδονῆς" ("On Pleasure"). Landino explains why the grove of Diana lay near the temple of Apollo in Book 6 because the moon represents corporeal and the sun celestial knowledge and thus the union of human and divine wisdom: *Templum vero Phoebo Dianaeque ponit, quia, ut modo dicebam, et divinarum et humanarum rerum cognitio est sapientia*. See *Disputationes*, ed. Lohe, 208.

[23] Ficino considered the *Philebus* to be a dialogue intended to "refute" an "unteachable" sophist or fraud (Philebus wants to argue on behalf of a life of pleasure). The dialogue thus fell under the category of "purification" for Ficino. For Ficino's division of the Platonic corpus according to the age and character of the interlocutors in each dialogue, see MS Laur. 82.06, fol. 4r: *Tres vero sunt Platonicorum species dialogorum, aut enim Sophistas confutat, aut adolescentes adhortatur, aut docet adultos. Quae in epistolis vel in libris de legibus et epinomi Plato ipse suo disserit ore certissima vult haberi, quae vero in caeteris libris Socratis, Timei, Parmenidis, Xenonis ore disputat verisimilia*. For a discussion of this arrangement see Hankins, *Plato in the Italian Renaissance*, 330; Hankins shows that Ficino classified each dialogue in an ascending hierarchy from the conversion of disciples and well-disposed youths who are "teachable" to the purification of sophists and other frauds who are "unteachable." The *Hipparchus* is thus meant to convert a well-disposed disciple, while the *Philebus* falls under the category of "refutation." It would therefore be understandable that Ficino considered it necessary for readers to obtain a purged mind in order to facilitate the correct interpretation of the rest of the corpus.

more concerned with performing invasive interpretive operations upon their text rather than removing obstacles to understanding. They respected the organization of the original work while taking liberties with the disposition of its elements at the same time. Landino, for his part, believed that Virgil had cloaked divine mysteries of Platonic wisdom under a veil of allegory. The goal of the exegete was to lift this veil by distorting the original arrangement of events and by penetrating the *aenigmata* occluded by poetic figures. Ficino, for his part, may have borrowed the principles that Iamblichus used to construct a curriculum of dialogues for "initiating" pupils into the secrets of Platonic philosophy.[24] Yet when he translated his first ten dialogues he chose Platonic works that would not only be considered perverse by today's standards but were also unprecedented in any canon of antiquity, including that of Iamblichus.[25] Like Landino, Ficino invested the idea of sequential organization with philosophical importance

[24] There were a number of similar rationales in antiquity for arranging a sequence of dialogues, usually a decade, according to didactic principles. It still remains to be determined which Ficino relied on. Hankins, *Plato in the Italian Renaissance*, 301, argues that there were only two sources for Ficino's view of the canon: Diogenes Laertius's *Lives* (3.62) and Thrasyllus's canon of nine tetralogies preserved in his Greek codex (MS Laur. 85.09). According to Hankins, Ficino would have rejected internal evidence from the *Clitophon* and Letter 13, attributed to Plato, because Leonardo Bruni had dismissed their authenticity. There were further sources of the canon, however, including the introduction to Platonic philosophy attributed to Elias, in *Prolegomena*, ed. Westerink, 47–49; Albinus's *Prologos* (MS Laur. 85.09, fols. 32v–33v); Proclus's commentary on the *Alcibiades*, in *On the Alcibiades*, ed. L. G. Westerink (Amsterdam: North Holland Publishing Company, 1954); and Olympiodorus's commentary on the *Alcibiades*, in *On the Alcibiades*, ed. L. G. Westerink (Amsterdam: North Holland Publishing Company, 1956). The Olympiodorus commentary has been excluded by Westerink, who says that, even though Ficino annotated a manuscript of Olympiodorus's works, there are no traces of Olympiodorus in his *Philebus* commentary: see L. G. Westerink, "Ficino's Marginal Notes on Olympiodorus in Riccardi Greek MS. 37," *Traditio* 24 (1968): 351–78. Though Thrasyllus's tetralogical arrangement could not be further from Ficino's decade, Thrasyllus did wish to convert students to Platonic philosophy and instruct their souls, and should not, therefore, be dismissed *tout court* as a source of influence.

[25] That Ficino was familiar with Iamblichus at least as early as 1458 is clear from his *Di Dio et anima*, a compendium of philosophical opinions about God and the soul in the vernacular addressed to Francesco Capponi. In this work Ficino draws on Iamblichus along with Hermes, Plotinus, Proclus, Calcidius, Apuleius, and Plato. See Paul O. Kristeller, *Supplementum Ficinianum*, 2 vols. (Florence: Leo S. Oschki, 1966), 1.159–60 and 2.128–57. However, in 1458 Ficino still had not learned Greek and must have relied on indirect sources, e.g., in the Latin Church Fathers, for his knowledge of Iamblichus. Ficino also translated the *De Mysteriis* of Iamblichus c. 1488–1489 for Giovanni de' Medici while working on his translation of Plotinus, which is now in MS Strozzi 97 at the Biblioteca Laurenziana as well as MS Laur. 82.15, along with his *Argumentum in librum Iamblichi*.

while deviating significantly from the very model he was imitating. Order thus remained the primary hermeneutical framework for Landino and Ficino while each departed in his own way from established canonical arrangements.

Scholars have drawn attention to the uncomfortable relationship both Landino and Ficino had to the canonical arrangement of texts. Craig Kallendorf has explained Landino's confusing claim to originality in the *Disputationes* by calling attention to his sensitivity to the sequence of events in the *Aeneid*.[26] In his *Disputationes* Landino distanced himself from other quite similar humanist allegories, scattered in the writings of Petrarch, Salutati, Filelfo, Poggio, and others, as well as from the medieval tradition of moralizing allegory on the basis of sequence:

> Yet they have been explicated by many eminent men of learning. However, what you seek is more divine and much more hidden in obscurity and has not been explicated until now by anyone in its proper order [*a nullo . . . hactenus sua serie patefactum*], which no grammarian nor teacher of rhetoric would know of, but must be rooted out from the deepest secrets of philosophy.[27]

Though he relied significantly on the Latin medieval commentary tradition, Landino claimed that no one until him had interpreted the *Aeneid sua serie*, "in its proper order."[28] Arthur Field has also contributed greatly to Landino scholarship with his identification of codex 1368 at the Biblioteca Casanatense in Rome as Landino's earliest commentary on the *Aeneid*.[29] An examination of this codex reveals that Landino was concerned with the problem of sequence as early as 1462. In fact, the passage in the *Disputationes* to which Kallendorf called attention is a reworking of a similar passage from his 1462 commentary. We are thus now in a position to draw Landino's earliest explication of the *Aeneid* into a closer relation with the course of ten dialogues Ficino was confecting in the same year.

---

26 Kallendorf, "Cristoforo Landino's *Aeneid*," 519–46; for similarities between Landino's juxtaposition of "contemplative" and "active" lives and the Virgilian reflections of Salutati and Filelfo, see Eugene Wolf, "Die allegorische Vergilerklärung des Cristoforo Landino," *Neue Jahrbücher für das klassische Altertum Geschichte und deutsche Litteratur und Pädagogik* 22 (1919): 471.

27 *Disputationes*, ed. Lohe, 117–18: *Sed sunt tamen a multis iisdemque doctis viris patefacta. Quod autem petis, id et multo divinius est et magis in obscuro latet et a nullo, quod ego quidem sciam, hactenus sua serie patefactum, quod neque grammaticus neque rhetor noverit, sed sit ex intimis philosophiae arcanis eruendum.*

28 Kallendorf, "Cristoforo Landino's *Aeneid*," 532.

29 See Field, "A Manuscript of Cristoforo Landino's First Lectures," 17–20.

By examining MS Cas. 1368 we now know that Landino was concerned with the sequence of events in the life of Aeneas and the hidden, philosophical meaning behind them as early as 1462. In both works—his lectures of 1462 and the *Disputationes* of 1473—Landino voices his departure from the grammarians who think Virgil's only intention was to imitate Homer and praise the times of Augustus. In the preface to this commentary Landino says that the grammarians wished to rearrange the sequence of books in the *Aeneid* to put them back in order:

> Nevertheless there are some grammarians who say that his intention was to imitate Homer and praise the times of Augustus, but this was not the chief intention of so great a man—rather, that which I said. The number and order was [then] as it appears in the text [now]. Yet there are those who say that the number of books was changed by Varius, because the one which is now third used to be the second book. There are even those who say that the order should not be placed as it is but the second and third book should be placed before the first since events that happen later are contained in that book.[30]

Landino defends the number and order of books against the grammarians who would rearrange them to correspond to the historical progression of events in the life of Aeneas.[31]

If Virgil really was a Platonically pious poet inspired by divine madness, it was crucial that he cloak his true message by narrating the events in the life of Aeneas out of order, that is, by starting in Carthage (sequence two), then moving to Troy (sequence one), and finally ending in Rome (sequence three).[32] It was

---

[30] MS Cas. 1368, fol. 2v, under the heading *intentio auctoris*: *Sunt tamen nonnulli grammatici qui eius intentionem fuisse dicant ut Homerum imitaretur utque Augusti tempora laudaret, sed haec tanti viri non fuisset prima intentio, sed ea quam dixi. Numerus vero et ordo esset ut in textu apparet. Sunt tamen qui dicant numerum librorum a Vario immutatum, nam qui nunc tertius est secundus erat. Sunt etiam qui dicant eum ordinem non esse ponendum qui est, sed secundum et tertium librum ante primum ponendum, cum in eo res postea gestae contineantur.* Cf. the commentary attributed to Bernardus Silvestris of Chartres, who likewise declares his departure from the "historical" interpretation of Frigius: [*Vergilius*] *intendit itaque casus Enee aliorumque Troianorum errantium labores evolvere atque hoc non usque secundum historie veritatem, quo Frigius describit; sed ubique ut Augusti Cesaris gratiam lucraretur, Enee facta fugamque ficmentis extollit*, in *Commentum quod dicitur Bernardi Silvestris super sex libros Eneidos Virgilii*, ed. Julian and Elizabeth Jones (Lincoln: University of Nebraska Press, 1977), 1.

[31] Cf. MS Laur. 52.32, fol. 2v.

[32] Cf. the commentary attributed to Bernardus of Chartres, in *Commentum*, ed. Jones and Jones, who also allegorized the first six books of the *Aeneid* but did so "in order," starting from Book 1 and ending with Book 6. Like Landino, Bernardus obviated "historical" interpretations, but his order of exposition still followed the order of books.

the job of a philosophically minded exegete, according to Landino, to reveal the allegory of the soul's ascent refracted through Virgil's muddling of the natural, historical sequence of events. The actual sequence advanced from Troy (Books 2 and 3) to Carthage (Books 1 and 4) and finally to Rome (Books 5 and 6). This required suspending "grammatical," "historical," or "natural" modes of interpretation to detect what he calls "artificial" narrative here and "allegory" in his *Disputationes.*[33]

When he deals with "narrative," Landino discloses the "artificial" narrative of the *Aeneid* as an allegory of the soul's growth from *pueritia et prima illa aetas* in Troy to the speculative felicity of manly virtue in Rome:

> So it was at the start that he had to depart from Troy, which we should understand as childhood and that first period of life [*pueritia et prima illa aetate*] in which the soul has not yet been befouled by anything. . . . But Aeneas first became enamored with that which is called "active," in which he dwelled praiseworthily fighting like a man on behalf of his fatherland. Then when Troy was taken—for the life of pleasure is finally destroyed—he is directed to Italy, that is, to that speculative life, for thus was the appetite of his excellent soul, and he set out on the sea, that is, into those commotions [of adolescence] since all the forces of his soul and all his appetites were not yet obedient to reason. He turned to Thrace where, caught by avarice, he turned to Africa where he was seized by ambition and, for this reason, the active life is revealed.[34]

Aeneas's journey from "childhood and that first period of life" represents the soul's purgative life-course in preparation, ultimately, to receive divine mysteries in Rome. By *sua serie* Landino thus meant the actual sequence of events as they unraveled in Aeneas's life. Virgil cloaked this historical progression of events with the veil of "artificial narrative," thereby elevating his epic to the level of allegory and Landino's interpretation to that of philosophy.

It was also in this year, 1462, that Cosimo de' Medici enjoined Ficino to translate ten dialogues of Plato. There has been considerable debate over the

---

[33] MS Cas. 1368 fols. 2v–3r: *Sed hi non norunt duplicem esse narrationem imam quidem naturalem, in qua res narramus prout gestae sunt, altera vero artificiosa qua nunc utitur, de qua infra dicemus, et ea utimur praesertim cum apud doctos nostra habenda sunt* [. . .] *illa vero minus doctis et rudiori ingenio praeditis viris adhibetur.*

[34] MS Cas. 1368, fols. 203v–204r: *Illi itaque primo fuit ex Troia abeundum, quam pro pueritia et prima illa aetate intelligere debemus, in quo animus ipse nullo adhuc coinquinatus est. . . . Aeneas autem primo adamavit illam quae activa dicitur, in qua cum laude versatus est viriliter pugnando pro patria. Deinde iam capta Troia, nam voluptuosa vita tandem pessundatur in Italiam, se dirigit, id est ad ipsam vitam speculativam, sic enim egregii animi appetitus est et ingressus mare, id est in ipsas perturbationes, quoniam omnes animi vires et omnes appetitus rationi obtemperantes non erant, deflexit in Thraciam ubi, ab avaritia deprehensus, deflexit in Africam ubi ab ambitione comprehensus est et per hoc vita activa demonstratur.*

principles according to which Ficino selected which dialogues to translate and in what order to arrange them upon completion. Kristeller believed there was no underlying plan to the sequence and that Ficino arranged the dialogues in the chronological order in which he translated them.[35] According to Kristeller he chose dialogues that were relatively short and easy or otherwise unavailable in Latin. As we have seen, Michael Allen argues that such or similar arrangements constituted a didactic cycle with a long history in the Neoplatonic tradition.[36] Associated with the work of Iamblichus, this tradition often placed the *Philebus* at the end of a decade of dialogues. Allen points out that the *Philebus*, which treats the highest good of man, logically follows the *Parmenides*, which treats the highest good of nature (see above). The arrangement proceeds serially from the soul's search for a contingent, sense-oriented good, through the ethical good of nature, and finally to the metaphysical good of man or human felicity.[37]

Although it is most likely that Ficino's selection of dialogues was guided by the necessity of establishing the most authentic text, he made a virtue of necessity and rationalized his selection after the fact.[38] The question that concerns me is not what Ficino's actual principles of selection were, but the rationale he fabricated in the preface to the dialogues he presented to Cosimo in 1464. This rationale, as Allen has demonstrated, has much in common with Iamblichus's

[35] Paul O. Kristeller, "Marsilio Ficino as a Beginning Student of Plato," *Scriptorium* 20 (1966): 41–54.

[36] Allen, *Marsilio Ficino*, 1–15; idem, "Ficino's Lecture on the Good?" 160–71.

[37] Another view is offered by Raymond Marcel, who claims that Ficino was able to establish a summa of Platonic thought by forming such disparate dialogues into a coherent unity. Though Marcel suggests that such an arrangement constitutes a *summa platonica* of sorts, it seems that he has misapplied the phrase *summa quadam* (MS Canon. Lat. 163, fol. 2r), which Ficino intended only in reference to the minor works by Speusippus and Alcinous that he appended to the decade, and not the decade itself. See Raymond Marcel, *Marsile Ficin, 1433–1499* (Paris: Les Belles Lettres, 1958).

[38] For the Greek manuscripts at Ficino's disposal and his reluctance to translate works for which he did not have the best text, see Sebastiano Gentile, "Note sui manoscritti greci di Platone utilizzati da Marsilio Ficino," in *Scritti in onore di Eugenio Garin* (Pisa: Scuola Normale Superiore, 1987), 51–84. See also Ernesto Berti, "Osservazioni filologiche alla versione del Filebo di Marsilio Ficino," in *Il Filebo di Platone e la sua fortuna: Atti del convegno di Napoli (4–6 novembre 1993)*, ed. Paolo Cosenza (Naples: M. D'Auria, 1996), 93–167; idem, "Marsilio Ficino e il testo greco del Fedone di Platone," in *Les traducteurs au travail: Leurs manuscrits et leurs méthodes, Actes du Colloque international organisé par le Ettore Majorana Centre for Scientific Culture (Erice, 30 septembre–6 octobre 1999)*, ed. Jacqueline Hamesse (Turnhout: Brepols, 2001), 349–425; Stefano Martinelli Tempesta, *La tradizione testuale del Liside di Platone* (Florence: La Nuova Italia, 1997), 155–77; Antonio Carlini, "Marsilio Ficino e il testo di Platone," in *Marsilio Ficino: Fonti, Testi, Fortuna, Atti del Convegno (Firenze, 1–3 ottobre 1999)*, ed. Sebastiano Gentile and Stéphane Toussaint (Rome: Edizioni di storia e letteratura, 2006), 25–64.

paideutic arrangement of ten dialogues. The most notable similarity between Ficino's decade and Iamblichus's is, as Allen has shown, the ultimate position of the *Philebus*. Furthermore, Ficino must have been aware of Iamblichus's interpretation of the *Philebus* as a dialogue that was primarily concerned with the "highest good," because he obviated the tradition preserved in his manuscript that equates the dialogue with "pleasure." As noted above, in the codex gifted to him (MS Laur. 85.9, fol. 105r) the *Philebus* appears with the title περὶ ἡδονῆς, "on pleasure." However, Ficino deviated from this tradition, preferring Iamblichus's association of the *Philebus* with "the highest good" instead. Yet what is most striking about Ficino's decade are not the continuities with but the departures from Iamblichus's didactic cursus.

If Ficino was imitating Iamblichus's arrangement, we are burdened to explain why Ficino departed so significantly from his selection of dialogues, especially when he claims to have taken such pains to dispose them according to metaphysical principles quite similar to Iamblichus's didactic cursus. It seems that Ficino was more concerned with the paideutic *principles* of Iamblichus's arrangement than with the actual content, a preference that was reinforced by his peculiar understanding of the Platonic corpus. On folios 32v–33v of MS Laur. 85.9, immediately following Diogenes Laertius's *Lives of the Philosophers*, is Albinus's *Prologos*.[39] Though these folios lack annotations in Ficino's hand, this was likely due to the quality of the text rather than his level of interest in the work, because he owned and studied the work in another codex.[40] Albinus's *Prologos* merges Middle Platonic thought with subsequent Neoplatonism by transforming the "diairetic," or classifying, organization of dialogues introduced by Theon of Smyrna and offering an additional abbreviated course of four dialogues for "laymen."[41] Addressing the order in which the dialogues should appear, Albinus raises the question of which dialogue should commence the corpus. There are many opinions, he says: some begin with the *Epistles*; others with the *Theages*; still others divide the corpus into tetralogies.[42] In these tetralogies some begin with the *Euthyphro*, others with the *Apology*, *Crito*, or *Phaedo*. However, he says,

---

[39] Olaf Nüsser, *Albins Prolog und die Dialogtheorie des Platonismus* (Stuttgart: Teubner, 1991); Burkhard Reis, *Der Platoniker Albinos und sein sogenannter Prologos: Prolegomena, Überlieferungsgeschichte, kritische Edition und Übersetzung* (Wiesbaden: Ludwig Reichert Verlag, 1999).

[40] Reis, *Der Platoniker Albinos*, 193–94: "Das Fehlen von Bearbeitungsspuren im Prologos des Laurentianus 85,9 könnte ein Hinweis darauf sein, daß Ficino den für wenig attraktiven Text bereits anderswo studiert hatte und in einer eigenen Abschrift besaß."

[41] Nüsser, *Albins Prolog*, 32: the order is as follows: *Alcibiades*, *Phaedo*, *Republic*, *Timaeus*.

[42] Nüsser, *Albins Prolog*, 32.

these elaborate schemes were arranged not for pedagogical purposes but on the basis of dialogic personas, in other words, for purely intratextual reasons.[43]

Contrary to the Thrasyllan canon preserved in Ficino's Greek codex, Albinus wanted to establish the most appropriate dialogue with which to commence a canon of Platonic writings arranged for the purpose of instruction in Platonic wisdom, just as in Ficino. Yet any organizational strategy must be arbitrary, says Albinus, because the Platonic corpus is similar to a circle. Without beginning or end, infinite, perfectly harmonious, symmetrical, and endlessly repeating itself, the universe of Platonic writings cuts a "perfect" figure: "Because it is perfect it is similar to the perfect figure of a circle; just as there is no one definite beginning to a circle, so there is no one definite beginning to his teaching."[44] There are as many ways of concocting a curriculum of Platonic writings, says Albinus, as there are different stations in life that render readers more or less prepared for philosophy: "If we must draw a circle, we do not draw the circle by beginning from any point whatsoever; rather, each of us commences in various ways from the point at which he stands in relation to the lesson."[45]

A curriculum should take into consideration the natural endowments of the students and, significantly, their age (ἡλικίαν). It should also be adjusted to whether the student has been initiated or is ignorant (προτετελεσμένος ἢ ἀμαθής) and whether the students have leisure for philosophy or are distracted by their surroundings. It is well known that Ficino shared a similar view of the Platonic corpus. Ficino considered each work of Plato to participate in a holistic unity greater than the sum of its parts. Each work acted, as James Hankins has illustrated, as a *tessera* in a grand mosaic assembled from Plato's singular aim to instruct initiates into the divine secrets of his philosophy.[46] Ficino's holistic vision of the Platonic corpus and of Plato's unity of purpose militated against too strict an adherence to any one arrangement of dialogues, while he also recognized the need for incremental instruction for lay readers such as Cosimo.

Landino likewise compared Aeneas's journey to a circle. In the preface to his dedication copy of the *Disputationes Camaldulenses* (MS Laur. 53.28) addressed to Federico, duke of Urbino, Landino likens Aeneas's arrival at the shores of Latium to his completion of a circular journey. The τέλος, or goal, of human felicity in Rome signifies the soul's closing of a circle: *Ad quem veluti ad extremam*

---

[43] Nüsser, *Albins Prolog*, 32.

[44] Nüsser, *Albins Prolog*, 32: ἐοικέναι γὰρ αὐτὸν τέλειον ὄντα τελείῳ σχήματι κύκλου· ὥσπερ οὖν κύκλου μία καὶ ὡρισμένη οὔκ ἐστιν ἀρχή, οὕτως οὐδὲ τοῦ λόγου.

[45] Nüsser, *Albins Prolog*, 32: οὐδὲ γὰρ, εἰ δέοι κύκλον γράφειν, ἀφ' οὑτινοσοῦν σημείου ἀρχόμενός τις γράφει τὸν κύκλον· ἀλλ' ἀφ' ἧς ἂν ἕκαστος ἡμῶν σχέσεως ἔχῃ πρὸς τὸν λόγον ἀρχόμενος.

[46] Hankins, *Plato in the Italian Renaissance*, 336.

circuli metam devenientibus nobis in tuto tranquilloque acquiescere liceat.[47] Whether it was Landino's confabulation on the *aetates hominis* that supplied Ficino with a model for this incremental instruction remains to be substantiated with stronger evidence. It is most likely that Ficino was aware of Iamblichus's principles of arrangement but did not wish to translate the same dialogues, either because they had already been translated into Latin or because he did not have at his disposal another manuscript by which he could establish the *lectio vera.*[48] Albinus's *Prologos* then conveyed to him a holistic vision of the Platonic corpus, thereby granting him greater flexibility in the selection of which dialogues to translate.

Ficino's arrangement of dialogues was at once the product of his interpretation of each dialogue and a strategy for facilitating a certain interpretation of the whole. His interpretive procedures were therefore part of a hermeneutical circle involving the process of textual emendation, translation, and the rearrangement of texts in the Platonic corpus as much as promoting Platonic philosophy itself. Oftentimes Ficino's philosophical convictions informed his editorial decisions as a philologist and vice versa.[49] Traditional categories such as "philosophy" on the one hand and "exegesis" or "philology" on the other came to be blurred for Ficino as much as for Landino. Landino defended poetry as a "universal" discipline transcending the mere "liberal" arts. According to him, the poet achieves by vatic inspiration what dialecticians arrive at by argument. Not only did poets, such as Virgil and Dante, achieve by divine madness what philosophers achieved by dialectic, but one who correctly expounded divinely inspired poetry was himself a kind of philosopher.[50] Ficino proved to be as studious a philologist as a

[47] MS Laur. 53.28, fol. 1r: "When we reach it, as if reaching the final goal of a circle, we may rest in safety and in calm."

[48] Gentile demonstrates that Ficino collated MS Laur. 85.9 with at least one other manuscript besides its exemplar, MS Laur. 59.1, and that this manuscript was Laur. Conventi Soppressi 180. MS Laur. Conv. Sopp. 180 contains seven of the ten dialogues Ficino translated in 1464, with the exception of *Euthyphro*, *Parmenides*, and *Philebus*. See Gentile, "Note sui manoscritti," 60–70.

[49] For a study of Ficino's work as a philologist informing his philosophy, see Denis Robichaud, "Marsilio Ficino's 'Si Deus Fiat Homo' and Augustine's 'Non Ibi Legi': The Incarnation and Plato's *Persona* in the Scholia to the *Laws*," *Journal of the Warburg and Courtauld Institutes* 77 (2014): 87–114; idem, "Working with Plotinus: A Study of Marsilio Ficino's Philological Conjectures and Textual Practices," in *From Florence to Europe: Teachers, Students, and Scholars of Greek in the Renaissance,* Brill Studies in Intellectual History, ed. F. Ciccolella and L. Silvano (Leiden: Brill, 2014).

[50] See Landino's *Praefatio in Virgilio*, a laudation of the *ars poetica* delivered in 1462, in which Landino quotes from Ficino's *De divino furore* (1457) verbatim, in *Scritti Critici e Teorici*, ed. Roberto Cardini, 2 vols. (Rome: Bulzoni, 1974), 1:21.

philosopher, whose textual emendations were as often guided by manuscript variants as *ingenio eius platonico*. What is more, the life of Aeneas came to represent for Ficino and Landino the heroic act of philosophical exegesis and therefore embodied this synthesis of philosophy and philology.

In a letter to Giovanni Pannonio (c. 1491), Ficino comments on Aeneas's descent to the underworld. In this letter Ficino presents Aeneas in quasi-sacerdotal terms. His descent to the underworld symbolizes an initiatory sacrament of sorts that prepares his soul to receive the divine mysteries. Shriven of his sins, Aeneas has been purged of vice and can now, according to Ficino, "penetrate the secret mysteries of divine things":

> Aeneas, that is, the heroic soul, in order to descend to the underworld and then ascend again, that is, to penetrate the secret mysteries of divine things and to bring to light obscure things, is led by divine providence to this very same thing, since he "whom fair Jupiter fostered" [*quem et aequus amabat Iuppiter*] was born as from a god, and divine oracles provoked him to the same thing. Furthermore he was incited to this by a kind of free decision, where his "ardent virtue bore him to heaven" [*ardens evehit ad aethera virtus*] and where he deliberates about what should be done most of all and he conveys oracles voluntarily and is always quite willingly in harmony with divine sentiment.[51]

The language Ficino uses to describe Aeneas's descent in this letter closely resembles the language he used to describe Landino's *Disputationes* in his letter to Bartolomeo Scala—Landino "penetrated the inner sanctuary" of Virgil—yet it is also clearly taken from the language of exegesis.[52] Aeneas is not only a moral athlete and thus prepared spiritually to enter the divine rites, but he is also an exemplary interpreter who "brings to light obscure things."

What is striking in Ficino's letter to Pannonio is that the words he uses to describe what Aeneas is led to interpret—"secret mysteries of divine things"—are nearly identical to the words he used to describe the final, culminating point of

---

[51] Marsilio Ficino, *Opera omnia*, ed. Mario Sancipriano and Paul O. Kristeller, 4 vols. (Turin: Bottega d'Erasmo, 1959), 1:901–2: *Aeneas, id est, heroicus animus descensurus ad inferos et iterum ascensurus, id est, secreta divinorum mysteria penetraturus, et obscura editurus in lucem, divina ad hoc ipsum providentia ducitur, tanquam et divinitus, (ut ait) genitus quem et 'aequus amabat Iuppiter', et divina ad idem oracula provocabant. Incedit rursus ad idem, libero quodam arbitrio, ubi eum 'ardens evehit ad aethera virtus', et ubi consultat, quid potissimum sit agendum, et sponte oracula contulit et semper libentissime cum sententia divina consentit.*

[52] Ficino, *Lettere*, ed. Sebastiano Gentile (Florence: L.S. Olschki, 1990), 1:218: *Legi Questiones Christophori Landini Camauldulenses. In iis libris Maronis adyta penetrat.* For the metaphor of entering a temple as a symbol for interpreting a text philosophically, see Robichaud, "Marsilio Ficino's 'Si Deus Fiat Homo'."

the first ten dialogues in the *Philebus*. Cosimo requested that Ficino translate ten dialogues containing "all the precepts of life, all the principles of nature, and all the *sacred mysteries of divine things*."[53] Ficino fulfilled Cosimo's request by arranging ten dialogues into a progressive advancement from the lowest ethical good and the acquisition of virtue to the arrival at the one good of nature in the *Parmenides* and finally to the "sacred mysteries of divine things" in the *Philebus*. For Landino and Ficino, Aeneas's journey from Troy to Rome was not only a moral allegory for the soul's sloughing off turpitude but also for a purgatorial rite of initiation preparing the soul to "penetrate the innermost sanctuary" of divine wisdom, that is, for the heroic feat of interpretation.[54] Aeneas is the exemplary exegete. Like Aeneas, the reader could finally "bring to light obscure things"—that is, interpret the rest of the Platonic corpus—only after being initiated into the inner sanctuary of Platonic philosophy in the *Philebus*.[55]

---

[53] Ficino, *Opera*, 1:1965: [*Cosmus*] *divi Platonis libros decem, et unum Mercurii e graeca lingua in Latinam a nobis transferri iussit, quibus omnia vitae praecepta, omnia naturae principia, omnia* ***divinarum rerum mysteria sancta*** *panduntur.*

[54] Cf. Landino's interpretation of Aeneas's *descensus ad infernum* in MS Cas. 1368, fol. 215r: *Plato autem infernum esse dicit descensum animorum nostrum in corpora, quae ex loco purissimo in feculentum decidunt et illuc excluduntur et gravantur corporum contagione. . . . Quatuor modis in infernum homines descendunt: uno modo ut platonici dicunt cum animus a stellis purissimis descendit, persepitae exularione dedit se vitio relicta virtute et ob id animae peccantes ad ignem aeternum mutuntur ubi est luctus et fletus ut sacri theologi dicunt. Tertius est, dubito tamen verus an falsus sit, cum per quaedam carmina agitae umbrae revocantur ad corpus. Quartus est quotiens homines ipsi descendunt in speculationem vitiorum ut illa reliquant et virtutem sequantur: per speciem hanc . . . Aeneas nunc ad infernum descendere vult. Cum enim homo sapiens sit et tendere velit ad ipsam speculationem opus est ut ad infernum descendat id est ad contemplationem vitiorum et illis cognitis ea relinquat et virtutes omnibus viribus sequatur.*

[55] The only trouble with this claim is that Ficino seems to have prioritized the *Parmenides*, referring to it and not the *Philebus* as the inner sanctuary and chapel of Plato's divine mind. See Ficino's *Argumentum in Parmenidem* in Laur. MS 82.06 fol. 45v: *In hoc tandem se ipsum superasse videtur et ex divinae mentis adytis intimoque philosophiae sacrario celeste hoc opus divinitus deprompsisse: Ad cuius sacram lectionem quisquis accedere prius sobrietate animi mentisque libertate se praeparet quam attrectare mysteria caelestis operis audeat.* Cf. Raymond Klibansky, "Plato's *Parmenides* in the Middle Ages and the Renaissance," in *The Continuity of the Platonic Tradition during the Middle Ages, and Plato's 'Parmenides' in the Middle Ages and the Renaissance* (Munich: Kraus International Publications, 1981), 313: "With Proclus and Olympiodorus he [Ficino] holds that the *Parmenides* enshrines the essence of Plato's theology and that it is the innermost sanctuary of Platonic thought." Perhaps we should refer to the *Euthyphro*, *Parmenides*, and *Philebus* together as the culminating point of Ficino's decade, each of which is not included in MS Conv. Sopp. 180, and which he selected, arguably, for its philosophical content rather than from philological necessity.

Appendix

Canons of Arranging the Platonic Corpus

Trilogical	Tetralogical	Dodecalogical	Decalogical
Aristophanes	Thrasyllus	Iamblichus	Ficino
Republic	Euthyphro	Alcibiades	Hipparchus
Timaeus	Apology	Gorgias	Amatores
Critias	Crito	Phaedo	Theages
Sophist	Phaedo	Cratylus	Meno
Statesman	Cratylus	Theaetetus	Alcibiades I
Cratylus	Theaetetus	Sophist	Alcibiades II
Laws	Sophist	Statesman	Minos
Minos	Statesman	Phaedrus	Euthyphro
Epinomis		Symposium	Parmenides
Theaetetus	Parmenides	Philebus	Philebus
Euthyphro	Philebus	Timaeus	
Apology	Symposium	Parmenides	
Crito	Phaedrus		
Phaedo			
Epistles			

Diairetic Systems
Diogenes Laertius/ Albinus

ὑφηγητικός			
θεωρηματικός		πρακτικός	
φυσικός	λογικός	ἠθικός	πολιτικός
Timaeus	Statesman Cratylus Parmenides Sophist	Apology Crito Phaedo Phaedrus Symposium Menexenus Clitophon Epistles Philebus Hipparchus	Republic Laws Minos Epinomis
ζητητικός			
γυμναστικός		ἀγωνιστικός	
μαιευτικός	πειραστικός	ἐνδεικτικός	ἀνατρεπτικός
Alcibiades Theages Lysis Laches	Euthyphro Meno Io Charmides Theaetetus	Protagoras	Euthydemus Gorgias Hippias I & II

10

Reading Virgil through Dante: Literary Ancestry in Ugolino Verino, *Carlias* 6–8[1]

Helen Lovatt
University of Nottingham

Virgil's underworld is the perfect place in which to contact your literary ancestors: in particular, Dante's use of Virgil as guide and exemplar in the *Divine Comedy* changed the underworld of *Aeneid* 6 into a fantasy of connecting emotionally with poetic predecessors. This paper explores the use of Virgil in Renaissance Florence by Ugolino Verino in his epic poem the *Carlias*. Its three-book reworking of Dante investigates the interactions between Virgil's underworld and Dante in Verino's construction of his own literary ancestry.

Ugolino Verino (1438–1516) was writing in Florence at the end of the fifteenth century; according to his biographer, Lazzari, Verino was the third-best poet of quattrocento Florence, after Landino and Poliziano.[2] There is evidence of his interactions with better-known writers of his day: he was a pupil of Landino;[3] a literary exchange with Poliziano is extant; Marsilio Ficino wrote him a letter of consolation on the death of his son.[4] He was perpetually struggling for money in his attempt to support a large family; as well as writing prolifically, he taught various Medici offspring, probably including the future Pope Leo X,

[1] I would like to thank the editors for organizing the conference and their patience and hard work on this project, the audience for their encouragement, Philip Hardie for reading an earlier draft, and the anonymous referees for their constructive and stimulating comments.

[2] Alfonso Lazzari, *Ugolino e Michele Verino: Studii Biografici e Critici* (Turin: Libreria C. Clausen, 1897), 211. Lazzari's work draws on the seventeenth-century biography of Bartolozzi, as well as independent research in the libraries of Florence.

[3] Lazzari, *Ugolino e Michele Verino*, 34.

[4] Lazzari, *Ugolino e Michele Verino*, 44.

and also held down an administrative job.[5] In his herculean struggles to obtain patronage, he wrote a poem on the death of Cosimo de' Medici, a panegyric for Ferdinand and Isabella on the expulsion of the Moors from Spain, and a set of epigrams for King Matthias Corvinus of Hungary. The *Carlias*, Verino's *Hauptwerk* according to Thurn, is a Latin hexameter epic in fifteen books extolling the exploits of Charlemagne, a work optimistically intended for King Charles VIII of France, who unfortunately died before it was completed,.[6] It has recently been made accessible by Thurn's edition and commentary.[7] Six different versions of the poem or parts of the poem exist; the first full version was produced in 1480. The changes between versions are themselves fascinating, but for now I shall concentrate on the later revised version (R), the "finished" text, as Thurn (1995) presents it.

In his prose preface to the *Carlias*, Verino makes a specific claim to be following in the footsteps of Homer, Virgil, and Dante: *Huius sum gesta heroico carmine prosecutus, poetarum principes Homerum, Virgilium compatriotamque meum Dantem immitatus* ("I have followed the deeds of this man in a heroic song, imitating those princes among poets, Homer, Virgil, and my compatriot Dante").[8] Here we see the importance of Dante, whom Verino claims as his fellow countryman. Verino imagines himself as following his central character, using what is often a metaphor for literary discipleship for his relationship with his subject matter, while he does not soften the impact of the word "imitation" with metaphors, but claims it in a straightforward fashion. He presents Homer, Virgil, and Dante in chronological order, but this also has the effect of making Dante the climax, as if he regards the three as rungs on a ladder of literary sublimity. It is worth noting here that Verino's teacher Landino treats all three poets in a similar way: he reads the *Odyssey*, *Aeneid*, and *Divine Comedy* allegorically, each forming a progression from vice to virtue, from the human to the divine.[9]

---

[5] Nikolaus Thurn, *Ugolino Verino Carlias: Ein Epos des 15. Jahrhunderts erstmals herausgegeben* (Munich: Wilhelm Fink, 1995), 11; Lazzari, *Ugolino e Michele Verino*, 99–100.

[6] Nikolaus Thurn, *Kommentar zur 'Carlias' des Ugolino Verino* (Munich: Wilhelm Fink, 2002), 13.

[7] Thurn, *Ugolino Verino Carlias*, and Thurn, *Kommentar zur 'Carlias' des Ugolino Verino*.

[8] *Preface*, 7–9. Lazzari, *Ugolino e Michele Verino*, 152, dismisses this as a "conventional paying of tribute at the shrine of Virgil" and is keen to play up his originality, sincerity, and Christianity.

[9] Simon Gilson, *Dante and Renaissance Florence* (Cambridge: Cambridge University Press, 2005), 199, citing Landino's opening gloss to the commentary on *Inferno* 1: "It is likely therefore that Dante set himself the same end as that which Homer and Virgil had set themselves amongst the Greeks and the Latins respectively. And as the former uses Ulysses and the latter Aeneas in order to show how, by acquiring knowledge of the vices and having understood them, and by purging oneself from them, one comes finally to contemplate divine things, so too does Dante demonstrate the same by means of this

In his proem, too, Verino alludes to both Virgil and Dante (*Carlias*, 1.1–11):

Proelia magnanimi canimus victricia Carli
armaque Francorum nullis impervia terris
edomitumque orbem Longobardosque feroces
impiaque horrendis miserorum Tartara poenis
Elysiumque nemus civesque ardentis Olympi.
insuetum per iter ferimur, nullisque priorum
orbita currenti monstrat vestigia signis.
Christe, potens rerum, aeterni sapientia patris,
aspira coeptis, vatem nec, diva, precantem,
Calliope, spernas (res ardua), pande recessum
Parnasi memorans breviter compendia rerum.

We sing the victorious battles of great-hearted Charlemagne, and the weapons of the Franks unfelt in no land, and the earth tamed, and the fierce Longobardi, and impious Tartarus with the horrific punishments of the wretched, and the Elysian grove and the citizens of burning Olympus. We are carried on an unaccustomed road, and the paths of former men show traces to the runner with no signs. Christ, powerful over all things, in the wisdom of the eternal father, breathe inspiration into my beginnings, and, divine Calliope, don't spurn your poet (a difficult thing) who prays to you; open the secret places of Parnassus, relating in brief an abridgement of huge things.

The *Aeneid* comes first: *proelia . . . Carli* echoes *arma virumque* and Verino varies *cano* with *canimus.*[10] The form of the proem is Virgilian, in eleven lines, subject matter followed by invocation, but the subject matter of Dante forms the climax of Verino's list of the poem's content, out of order, coming after the *Longobardi,* who represent the second half of the poem. Nevertheless, the words *Tartara* and *Elysium* emphasize the continuity with *Aeneid* 6, presenting the underworld in fundamentally Virgilian terms. In the invocation, Christ comes first, followed by Calliope, forming a chiastic arrangement of classical and Christian inspiration (Virgil, Dante: Christ, Calliope). Calliope's revelatory role recalls *Aeneid* 6 and the language of opening up secret places.[11] At *Aeneid*, 6.9–12 the Sibyl is represented as a poet figure:

fable regarding the pilgrimage which as a character he pretends to have made with Virgil." On Landino's reading of the *Aeneid*, see also Adam T. Foley's essay in this volume.

[10] Thurn, *Kommentar zur 'Carlias,'* 102.

[11] On the Sibyl and imagery of opening and revealing, see Emily Gowers, "Virgil's Sibyl and the 'Many Mouths' Cliché (*Aeneid* 6.625–7)," *Classical Quarterly* 55 (2005): 176–77. *Pandere* is also a Lucretian word of revelation, used for instance in the proem at Lucretius, *De rerum natura*, 1.55, and again at 5.54. It is also used of poetic inspiration

At pius Aeneas arces quibus altus Apollo
praesidet horrendaeque procul secreta Sibyllae,
antrum immane, petit, magnam cui mentem animamque
Delius inspirat vates aperitque futura.

But dutiful Aeneas seeks the citadels in which high Apollo presides and the deep secrets of the awe-requiring Sibyl, the immeasurable cave in which the Delian prophet inspires her great mind and soul and opens the future.

Verino calls himself *vates* at 1.9 and combines this sense of the poet as Sibyl for whom the Muses open up secret truths with Virgil's similar call for inspiration to be allowed to describe the underworld at the moment when Aeneas and the Sibyl enter it (*Aeneid*, 6.264–67):

Di, quibus imperium est animarum, umbraeque silentes
et Chaos et Phlegethon, loca nocte tacentia late,
sit mihi fas audita loqui, sit numine vestro
pandere res alta terra et caligine mersas.

Gods, who hold power over souls, silent shades and Chaos and Phlegethon, soundless spaces wide in night, may it be right for me to speak what I have heard, by your power may it be right for me to open up matters buried in the deep earth and the dark.

By asking Calliope to open the secret places of Parnassus, Verino represents his poetic enterprise as a *katabasis*, or descent, into the classical past, in which the initiatory rhetoric of Virgil and the Sibyl in accessing the afterlife is transferred onto his own engagement with ancient poetry. Thus, Verino puts the underworlds of Virgil and Dante at the heart of his poem. As we will see, he uses Dante to give spiritual meaning to Virgil, and Virgil to go beyond Dante in an authentically classical vision.

Structures: Dante in Virgil and Virgil in Dante

The large-scale narrative structure of the *Carlias* largely follows the *Aeneid*. It begins with Satan, as Juno, stirring up a storm that wrecks Charlemagne's fleet at Buthrotum, where he is welcomed and invited to tell his story (Book 1). Charlemagne narrates his crusade and the storming of Jerusalem, the conquest of Egypt, Babylon, and Persia (Books 2–4). During their enforced stay at Buthrotum, the Franks mend their fleet, go hunting, and celebrate games (Book 5). Table 1 shows the structures of Books 5–8 with their main models.

---

in general at Virgil, *Georgics*, 1.34, and, for instance, *Aeneid*, 7.641, but without the connotation of revealing hidden places.

Table 1.	Major sources of *Carlias* 5–8[12]
Book 5: 1–173: Hunt	*Aeneid*, 4.129–72
174–225: Vision of Pippin	*Aen.* Dream of Mercury: 4.238–78; Dream of Anchises: 5.721–45. Detail of prophecy also evokes *Aen.*, 6.83–97.
226–427: Games	*Aen.*, 5.104–603
428–458: Vision of Pippin	Second dream of Mercury: *Aen.*, 4.554–70
459–490: Forest	*Inferno*, 1
491–513: Animals	*Aen.*, 6.268–94; *Inf.*, 1
514–540: Intervention of Astraea	
541–569: Entrance to the underworld	*Aen.*, 6.295–336: Acheron, Charon, the unburied
570–601: Charon, boat	
Book 6: 1–19 Entrance inscription	*Inf.*, 3.1–9; *Aen.*, 6.548–59
20–51: Binding of Cerberus	*Aen.*, 6.417–25; Hercules myth
52–55: court and judge	*Aen.*, 6.282–94
76–94: Confrontation with Minos	*Inf.*, 5.1–24
95–204: Luxuria. Setting:	*Inf.*, 5.25ff.; *Inf.*, 18
Punishments:	*Purgatorio*, 25–26; *Inf.*, 12
205–65: Gula. Setting:	*Inf.*, 6
Punishments:	*Purg.*, 22–24
266–331: Invidia. Setting:	Ovid, *Metamorphoses*, 2.760–86
Punishments:	*Inf.*, 3, 32; Ovid.
332–62: Demon ride.	*Inf.*, 27; La Spagna 21–22
363–456: Ira I. Setting:	*Inf.*, 12
Punishments:	*Inf.*, 24
457–505: Ira II. Setting:	*Inf.*, 13; *Aen.* 6.434–39
Punishments:	*Inf.*, 3.65; *Inf.*, 24
506–622: Avaritia. Setting:	*Inf.*, 7
Punishments:	*Purg.*, 22–24; *Aen.*, 6.602–7
623–59: Inertia. Setting:	*Inf.*, 3; *Inf.*, 7
Punishments:	*Aen.*, 6.616
660–813: Centrum.	*Inf.*, 31–34; *Aen.*, 6.893–99

[12] Drawn from N. Thurn, *Kommentar zur 'Carlias,'* 304, 363, 418–19.

Book 7: 1–16: Carlus's purification	*Purg.*, 1.121–29; *Inf.*, 3.22–27; *Aen.*, 6.635–36
17–74: Topography	*Purg.*, 2; *Aen.*, 6.535–47
75–135: Superbia	*Purg.*, 3–4; Trajan: *Paradiso*, 20
136–90: Chlodwig	*Purg.*, 9; Sordello: *Purg.*, 6
191–311: Dream of Carlus	*Purg.*, 9, 15, 19, 22, 25. Revelation.
312–44: Morning	*Purg.*, 9
345–99: Avaritia	*Purg.*, 19
400–53: Invidia. Setting:	*Purg.*, 11–14
Punishments:	*Purg.*, 13–14
454–79: Ira. Setting:	*Purg.*, 15–17
Punishments:	*Inf.*, 13; *Par.*, 20; *Aen.*, 3.22–48; Ovid, *Met.*, 2.358.
480–91: Inertia	*Purg.*, 4. Punishments: *Purg.*, 12
492–545: Statius	*Purg.*, 22
546–603: Entrance to Elysium	*Purg.*, 9
603–793: Elysium	*Aen.*, 6.613–887; *Purg.*, 28–33; *Inf.*, 4

Book 8 (mainly follows the *Anticlaudianus* of Alain de Lille. See Thurn, *Kommentar zur 'Carlias'*)	
1–58: The Sun	*Purg.*, 27; *Par.*, 1
59–204: The firmament	
205–324: To the palace of God	
325–363: The palace of God	
364–512: The celestial hierarchy	
513–609: The heavenly Jerusalem	
610–708: Pippin	*Aen.*, 6.679–94
709–783: The Virgin Mary	*Aen.*, 8.31–65
784–877: The holy	*Aen.*, 6.752–901
878–902: The gates of heaven	

In Book 5, Verino splices the beginning of *Aeneid* 4 into Books 5 and 6. The two dreams of Charlemagne's father Pippin stand in for the apparition of Anchises, which leads Aeneas to travel down to the underworld, as well as the two apparitions of Mercury, which put Aeneas back on the right track after the Dido episode. This combination figures the fundamental quest of the *Carlias* as a spiritual quest, in which the central books are not just a means of providing inspiration for the rest of the poem but the point of the whole endeavor. The forest then leads us into Dante, and the arrival of Astraea evokes both the arrival of Virgil in *Inferno* 1 and the arrival of the Sibyl at *Aeneid*, 6.35–42. The next three books recapitulate Dante within the *Aeneid*, as Charlemagne travels through Hell, Purgatory, and Paradise (Books 6–8). He then undertakes a military campaign against the Longobardi in Italy and Spain, which equates to the Iliadic second half of the *Aeneid*, although there is much reminiscence of Silius Italicus' *Punica*. This second half includes a river-battle for the hero Rinaldus (10.526–615), heroes called Hector and Ajax, a battle of Cannae, and a battle with the Moors, whose general is called Hasdrubal. Finally, Charlemagne is crowned king in Rome and returns to Aachen to celebrate a triumph, as Scipio finishes the *Punica* - and Aeneas did not finish the *Aeneid* (unless we take Verino to be transplanting the Augustan triumph at the end of Book 8 into its rightful chronological position at the very end of the poem). Dante, then, forms the central panel of the poem, spilling over from the single book of *Aeneid* 6, and essentially squeezing out the Dido episode. However, the progression towards military victory does reassert a Virgilian concern with the governance of this world: although Dante is the heart of the poem, Virgil provides the overall shape, suggesting that spiritual enlightenment is a step on the journey to ideal monarchy.

On the smaller scale, Verino's Books 5 to 8 take the structure of Dante's *Divine Comedy* and map onto it episodes from *Aeneid* 6 on which parts of Dante were already based. *Aeneid* 6 is thus read through Dante, Dante is read through *Aeneid* 6. The two texts are interwoven and interdependent. The ways in which Verino reorganizes the material from *Aeneid* 6 in his Dantean schema reveal the complexities of his engagement with both poets.

Pippin's prophecy to Carlus in the first of the two dreams in Book 5 shows how Verino conceptualizes Dante's tripartite journey as a reworking of *Aeneid* 6. Let us look at it in some detail (*Carlias*, 5.209–20):

> At sunt infernae sedes et Averna fragosis
> Stagna prius visenda vadis Stigiique liquoris
> Atra palus sulcanda tibi. Gyrosque per omnes
> Inferni incolumem et per inhospita Tartara Ditis
> Te summo delapsa polo Titania virgo
> Ducet et Elysios campos Astrea docebit.
> Mox te gemmiferis pennis demissus ab astris
> Suscipiet Seraphis, portam qui pandet Olympi.
> Alite quo vectus super ardua culmina caeli,
> Quanta sit aeternae, spectabis, gloria gentis,
> Aliferasque novem circum praetoria turmas
> Meque iterum aspicies nostrosque ab origine reges.

But first you must see the infernal places and the pools of Avernus with broken-up shallows and you must plow the black marsh of Stygian liquid.

> Through all the circles of the Inferno, safely, and through the unwelcoming Tartarus of Dis, the Titanian virgin, slipped down from the highest axis, will lead you and Astraea will teach you about the Elysian fields. Soon, sent down from the stars with bejeweled wings, Seraphis will take you up, who opens the gate of Olympus. On whose wing borne above the high peaks of the sky, you will see how great is the glory of the eternal race, nine winged squadrons around the court, and you will see me again and our kings from the beginning.

Pippin begins with the entrance to the underworld; he then moves on to Hell, which is doubled with Tartarus (in the same way that Virgil's Tartarus forms a separate part of his underworld, only described in an ekphrasis by the Sibyl). The climax of Astraea's teaching takes place in the Elysian Fields, where Carlus engages with the classical world, set at the end of Verino's Purgatory. This is one version of the high point of *Aeneid* 6: Aeneas meets Anchises and sees the glorious future of the Roman race in the Elysian Fields. Verino's Elysian Fields combine Virgil's Elysium with Dante's Limbo and Earthly Paradise. In Verino, the transfer from Astraea to the Seraph, from one guide to another, takes place at the beginning of Book 8 and symbolizes a movement from *Aeneid* 6 to the transcendence of Dante's *Paradise*. However, in Pippin's speech, Paradise is called Olympus, and what Carlus will see in Paradise is not revealed, except for the section that corresponds to Virgil's Elysium: the meeting with Pippin and the roll-call of the holy, a second version of Virgil's Parade of Future Heroes, for Carlus straightforwardly looking back. This speech puts a strongly Virgilian slant on what Verino actually does: the sections on the palace of God, the celestial hierarchy, the heavenly Jerusalem, and the Virgin Mary are all omitted. Pippin's speech therefore presents Verino's reworking of Dante as fundamentally Virgilian.

The relationship between literary time and historical time in Verino's *Carlias* also gives a sense of his engagement with Virgil and Dante. Each of the three texts has a discrepancy between the dramatic setting and the perspective of the contemporary audience. While the *Aeneid* makes Aeneas look forward to Roman history as the Roman readers look back, Dante sets his poem only a few years before it was written, so that his prophecies look forward to the political turmoil and exile that he was shortly to experience. Verino, in contrast, inserts himself between Dante and Virgil, in the (near-fantasy) time of Charlemagne. The past for Charlemagne is almost entirely the classical and Christian past, with hardly any opportunity for direct reference to Verino's own times. This shows how important the religious and philosophical aspects of poetry are to Verino; his relationship to the classical past and to his literary forebears foregrounds his spiritual and intellectual journey.

The richness and complexity of Verino's engagement with both poets, often through the lens of contemporary exegeses of both by Landino, offers enough material for many years of study.[13] Thurn's hefty commentary on the *Carlias* (one volume on fifteen books of poetry) can only scratch the surface. In the rest of this paper, I offer three key aspects of Verino's poetic self-fashioning in his reworking of Dante: first, the figure of Astraea, who replaces Dante's Virgil; secondly, the meeting with Statius, another Dantean character who is also a poetic successor of Virgil, and their admittance to Elysium; third, a brief discussion of Carlus's revelation and encounter with the Virgin.

Astraea

The *katabasis*, or descent into the underworld, of Carlus is a Dante-like digression from what is fundamentally a Virgilian plot. Yet Virgil has a more tangible presence in Dante than in Verino. As guide through the Inferno and companion through Purgatory, Virgil is an important character in his own right: Jacoff calls him "the affective heart of the *Commedia* . . . the source of the poem's purest pathos."[14] When Dante makes Virgil his Sibyl, he brings out the poetic side of the Sibyl as *vates*, rather than priestess and prophet. He also emphasizes the role of poetry in creating an emotional engagement with religion. Landino's commentary on Dante gives a sense of the different approaches taken by those reading Dante's Virgil. Landino innovates with respect to the earlier tradition of commentary on Dante by creating an overall philosophical framework based on the characters of Dante and Virgil. "Dante" is taken to represent sensuality, while "Virgil" stands for human reason. However, Landino used allegory with sensitivity (gloss to *Inferno*, 1.61–66, trans. Gilson):

> . . . let it be known to us that Virgil is used both with a single and with many meanings. And sometimes his name will mean nothing other than this poet. Sometimes it will mean human reason alone, and Dante

[13] On Landino's allegorizations of Virgil, see Craig Kallendorf, "Cristoforo Landino's *Aeneid* and the Humanist Critical Tradition," *Renaissance Quarterly* 36 (1983): 519–46; on Landino's Dante commentary and its context, see Gilson, *Dante and Renaissance Florence*, 163–231. Books 3 and 4 of the *Disputationes Camaldulenses* gave an allegorical reading of the first half of the *Aeneid* as part of a discussion of the *summum bonum*: Aeneas moves from the sensual pleasures of Troy to the active life in Carthage and finally to an understanding of the divine in Book 6; see n. 9. Landino was lecturing on the *Aeneid* in 1462–1463; the *Disputationes* were published in 1480 and were widely read. In 1488 Landino published a line-by-line commentary on the whole *Aeneid* which was subsequently included in nineteen of the thirty-five editions of the *Aeneid* published between then and 1500 (Kallendorf, "Cristoforo Landino's *Aeneid*," 522).

[14] Rachel Jacoff, "Vergil in Dante," in *A Companion to Vergil's* Aeneid *and its Tradition*, ed. Joseph Farrell and Michael C. J. Putnam (Malden, MA, Oxford, and Chichester: Wiley-Blackwell, 2010), 247–57.

> will be sensuality. At other times we will interpret his name as the intellect illuminated by many and various doctrines. At other times through his name we will express superior reason, and then Dante will not signify sensuality alone, but also inferior reason.[15]

What is the significance of this reading in the light of what Verino does with Dante's Virgil and Virgil's Sibyl? Verino writes Virgil out of Dante. Instead he offers us Astraea, the *virgo* of *Eclogue* 4, who has links with the figure of the Sibyl. *Eclogue* 4 was read by Augustine as a true prophecy of the coming of Christ, which Virgil had repeated without understanding it from the prophecies of the Cumaean Sibyl.[16] Astraea is a symbol of empire and justice, not least in Dante's *De Monarchia*, 1.11.1.[17] Dante the poet has Virgil the poet for his guide; Carlus the emperor has imperial power and justice for his guide. Verino asserts his poetic credibility by de-emphasizing poetics.[18]

But how is Astraea represented and how does she compare to Dante's Virgil? Astraea appears, like Dante's Virgil, at the moment when the traveler is panicked and unable to face the beasts around him (5.514–29):

> Martius at ductor, quamvis fatalibus armis
> Tectus erat, timuit tamen et conterritus ensem
> Fulgentem eduxit **frustra**que immania monstra
> Aggreditur. Vanae deceptus **imagine formae**
> Nequicquam **tenues** gladio **diverberat** auras.
> Ceu qui per somnum **venientes** viderit hostes,
> Protinus exclamat pugnamque lacessit inanem,
> Haud aliter Carlus circum fera monstra vagatur,
> Incertusque animi nunc huc, nunc fluctuat illuc,
> Cum circumfusus prorupit ab aethere fulgor

---

[15] Gilson, *Dante and Renaissance Florence*, 198: "ci sia noto che non *univoce* ma *equivoce* sarà posto Virgilio, et alchuna volta non sonerà altro che questo poeta. Alchuna volta significherà la ragione humana semplicemente, et Danthe sarà la sensualità. Altra volta lo interpreterremo per lo intellecto illustrato di varie et molte doctrine. Altra volta exprimerremo per quello la ragione superiore, et allora Danthe significherà non la sensualità solo, ma anchora la ragione inferiore."

[16] Frances Yates, *Astraea: The Imperial Theme in the Sixteenth Century* (London: Routledge, 1975). 35.

[17] *'Virgo' namque vocabatur Iustitia, quam etiam Astraeam vocabant; 'Saturnia regna' dicebant optima tempora, que etiam 'aurea' nuncupabant* ("For Iustitia is called 'Maiden,' and they also used to call her Astraea; they used to say 'The Reign of Saturn' for the best times, which they also declared 'The Golden Age'").

[18] Thurn, *Kommentar zur 'Carlias,'* 295–97, discusses the importance of Astraea, whom he refers to as Iustitia throughout. She represents the justice of God, on display in *Inferno*; *iustitia* is the most important virtue for a monarch; it is also one of the names of God. He also cites its importance in Plato.

> Discissumque supra caelum resonantibus alis
> Intonuit. Tum lapsa polo Titania virgo
> Nuda pedes, niveo circumdata pectora velo
> Ignea ceu lampas **prestrinxit lumina** Carli,
> Maiestasque in fronte sedet, mitemque rigorem
> Sidera bina **vomunt** mixta gravitate nitori.

> But the warrior leader, although he was protected by death-bringing weapons, nevertheless he was afraid and terrified drew out his shining sword and attacks the enormous monsters **in vain.** Deceived by **the picture of** an empty **shape** he pointlessly beat apart the **slender** breezes with his sword. As one who has seen enemies coming in a dream immediately shouts out and provokes an empty fight, not otherwise did Carlus wander around the wild monsters, and uncertain in his mind he turned now here, now there, when overflowing radiance broke forth from the aether and thundered above the sundered sky with resounding wings. Then the Titanian virgin slipped down from the axis, with naked foot, chest surrounded with a snowy veil as if a fiery lamp **grazed the eyes** of Carlus, and majesty resides in her brow, gentle sternness mixed with a serious gleam **spews out** from her twin stars.

The two main passages that underlie this encounter are Dante's first meeting with Virgil and the episode at *Aeneid*, 6.290–94, in which Aeneas strikes out in irrational fear at the dreams gathered in the entrance to Orcus and the Sibyl calms him and restrains his hand. The following passage contains verbal echoes of Verino's above (see bolded words here and above):

> corripit hic subita trepidus formidine ferrum
> Aeneas strictamque aciem **venientibus** offert
> et ni docta comes **tenuis** sine corpore vitas
> admoneat volitare cava sub **imagine formae,**
> inruat et **frustra** ferro **diverberet** umbras.

> Aeneas trembling in sudden fear snatches his sword and presents his drawn blade **against those approaching,** and if his learned companion had not warned him that they were **slender** lives without a body that flit about in the hollow **image of a shape,** he would have attacked and **beaten about** the shadows with his sword **in vain.**

Aeneas is terrified by dreams, and the dreams are mythological monsters (Centaurs, Scyllas, the hundred-handed Briareus, the Lernaean hydra, the Chimaera, the Gorgons, and the Harpies); this suggests a Lucretian evocation of true religion replacing the empty superstitions of mythology. In this passage the Sibyl rescues Aeneas, but their first encounter is the moment when she sternly removes him from gazing at Daedalus's *spectacula* (*Aeneid*, 6.33–39).[19] She is not described until she falls under the inspiration of Apollo at 6.45–51.

When Dante meets Virgil, he is terrified by leopard (lust), lion (pride), and wolf (avarice). The wolf stalks him, and in his terror he retreats, but "dinanzi a li occhi mi si fu offerto | chi per lungo silenzio parea fioco" ("suddenly appeared one who seemed faint through the long silence," *Inferno*, 1.62–63). Dante calls for his help and asks whether he is a shade or a man. The poetry of Virgil thus rescues Dante from avarice: the intense emotional connection between the two is established by dialogue, in which Virgil gives an account of his life and Dante expresses his love for Virgil's poetry (*Inferno*, 1.79–87).

In the appearance of Astraea, then, we have a frame from Dante filled with Virgilian imagery and emotion. Another Virgilian passage seems to me important: the arrival of Aeneas at the battle in Book 10, rescuing the Trojans when they are under pressure from the Latins. As he arrives he burns like Achilles approaching Hector: *ardet apex capiti tristisque a vertice flamma | funditur et vastos umbo vomit aureus ignis* ("The peak of his head burns and grim flame pours from the top and the golden boss spews immense flames," *Aeneid*, 10.270–71). The key word *vomunt* above at *Carlias*, 5.529, describing light pouring out, in a situation of rescue and revelation, is enough to activate the connection. This connection intensifies the emotional link between Carlus and Astraea, who is not just a guide but also a leader and role model for Carlus as king. Further, the fear of Carlus here is not fear *at* a dream, but rather fear as if in a dream. Most famously this image is used of the fear of Turnus during the final duel with Aeneas (*Aeneid*, 12.908–12). In this unusual simile, Virgil calls on the reader to be personally involved (*videmur*, 'we seem'), to remember what it is like to dream that you want to run but cannot, that tongue, strength, and speech fail. Virgil's underworld is, in any case, a place of dreams: not just those nightmare creatures against whom Aeneas lashes out, but the gates of dreams with which the book closes (6.893–99).

As we have seen, Renaissance readings of Virgil and Dante treat both the Sibyl and Dante/Virgil allegorically. Astraea's description as a personification with naked feet, snowy chest, fiery eyes and "gentle rigor," "serious shine," puts her into the category of allegory incarnate. In particular, her presentation here evokes that of the figure of *Virtus* in Statius's *Thebaid*: Virtus, too, comes down from the pole to earth where she rarely goes (*Thebaid*, 10.632–37). She takes on the appearance of the prophet (*vates*) Manto (10.641–43):

abiit horrorque vigorque
ex oculis, paulum decoris permansit honosque
mollior . . . .

[19] This moment is recapitulated much later in Verino's Paradise when the Seraph moves Carlus on from viewing the spectacles of a triumphal arch at 8.312–20.

> The horror and energy went away from her eyes; a little stateliness and a gentler honor remained.

Finally, the phrase *prestrinxit lumina* strongly evokes the simile which compares Caesar to a thunderbolt at Lucan, *Civil War*, 1.151–57; at 1.154, *terruit obliqua praestringens lumina flamma*, the phrase *praestringens lumina* is in the same metrical position, in which the light of Astraea's eyes temporarily blinds Carlus. In Statius the transfigured Virtus hits Menoeceus like a lightning strike hitting a cypress tree (*Thebaid*, 10.674–77), a process of violent inspiration like that of Apollo inspiring Virgil's Sibyl. Further, she holds back his hand from fighting (10.661) and inspires him instead to take his own life as a sacrifice for his city. This could be seen as leaving behind the mundane world of epic for a higher, more noble calling, just as Lucan's destructive but powerful Caesar goes beyond the bounds of normal epic heroism and normal military success. It is notable that Verino does not take over the worrying and extreme nature of Statius's Virtus: Astraea is not a thunderbolt; she is not like cross-dressed Hercules; instead the light in her eyes is genuinely, not deceptively, gentle.

Astraea has something about her of both Virgil's Sibyl and Dante's Virgil. Dante's Virgil is an important part of his poetic self-positioning: he becomes a Virgil for his own age, using what is best of the classical tradition as his guide and going beyond it in his progress towards God. Verino, by using a personification, and one important from Virgil's fourth Eclogue, as his main character's guide, is being more like Virgil than Dante. However, he does not entirely abandon the sense of Astraea as poet figure. The Sibyl is both prophet and divine messenger: her knowledge of the future and the underworld creates authority for Virgil's own poetic voice. In Verino, Astraea is not just a figure of Justice, but also a *vates* (poet/prophet).[20] Thurn finds the use of *vates* to describe Astraea "ungewöhnlich" (unusual). He explains it through Landino's reading of the Sibyl as *rerum divinarum doctrinam* ("learning of divine matters," *Disputationes*, 4.205), and Boccaccio's allegorization of Dante's Virgil as *doctrina* or *philosophia*. We could also see it as a blurring of Dante's use of Virgil's poetic wisdom with the Sibyl's prophetic knowledge. Dante stretches the figure of Virgil into more than a poet; so the figures of Sibyl and of Astraea are poetic as well as prophetic. It is worth remembering that Statius's personification of *Virtus* disguised herself as the *vates* Manto. Further, at 7.510 Astraea and Carlus will be joined by the poet Statius himself. Verino's Astraea may not present such a close personal connection between Verino and the classical past as presented by Dante's relationship with Virgil, but neither is Verino his own main character.

The emotional intensity of Carlus's relationship with Astraea is intensified when she rescues him from Minos's minions. Verino points out that if she had

---

[20] Astraea as *vates*: 6.787 (*dixit vates Titania*); 7.100 (*vates alma*); 7.109 (*sic vates*); 7.136 (*Traiano Carlus vatesque relicto*): see Thurn, *Kommentar zur 'Carlias,'* 297.

not done so he might have ended up another Amphiaraus, a living body who actually died in the underworld (6.76–85):

> "Arripite," exclamat violenta concitus ira,
> "Hunc," Minos, "legem sic nam despexit Averni."
> Nec mora, mille enses et mille sonantia tela
> Explicuit rabiosa cohors. Tum mille dracones
> Horrida tergeminis vibrarunt sibila linguis.
> Quod nisi Tartareis virgo Titania monstris
> Occlusisset iter spumantiaque ora colubrum
> Fregisset gladio, nunquam remeasset ad astra
> Carlus et Oeclide prope busta miserrima vatis
> Aeternum infoelix tristi iacuisset in urbe.

> "Seize him!," shouts Minos, struck by violent anger. "For he so despised the law of Avernus." No delay, and the maddened cohort unwound a thousand swords and a thousand sounding weapons. Then a thousand dragons brandished bristling hissing with tri-forked tongues. But if the Titanian virgin had not shut the way for these Tartarean monsters and had not broken the foaming mouths of the snakes with her sword, Carlus would never have returned to the stars and near the most wretched tomb of the prophet Amphiaraus he would have lain forever, unlucky in that grim city.

Amphiaraus is a poet figure in Statius's *Thebaid* who is swallowed alive by an earthquake; he goes down to the underworld alive, like Aeneas, but is unable to come back, instead fading from metaphorical into literal death. Amphiaraus is both prophet and king, priest and warrior, an apt predecessor for Carlus as he follows in the footsteps of Dante. Amphiaraus appears in *Inferno,* 20.31–39, the key example of the passivity of prophets, who are represented as twisted in the middle so their top halves face backwards, looking back to the future. Dante's Virgil chastises Dante for pitying them. This reference shows Verino's sophisticated use of Statius's underworld in conjunction with those of Dante and Virgil, all aligned together in relevance to the education of an effective king. Virgil's Sibyl similarly rescues Aeneas from Cerberus at 6.417–23; however, she drugs him with a honeyed cake rather than fighting him, more like Medea putting the dragon to sleep with drugs in Apollonius than Astraea confronting the demons and dragons of Minos with her sword. Thurn interprets this episode of Astraea and Minos as pointing out that *speculatio* (speculation) is dangerous without the help of *doctrina* (learning).[21] It also shows the masculinity of Astraea, again more like Statius's Virtus than Virgil's Sibyl.

The most affectionate moment between Astraea and Carlus comes in Purgatory, when he has spent half the night reminiscing with his ancestor Clodoveus,

---

[21] Thurn, *Kommentar zur 'Carlias,'* 321.

whom he is not able to embrace, and he finally falls asleep *subnixus sinu* ("leaning on the lap/breast") of Astraea. This leads into a surreal dream in which he foresees the Apocalypse (7.191–95):

> Dimidium iam noctis erat, seramque quietem
> Accepit vatisque sinu Mavortius heros
> Subnixus tandem vigilantia lumina clausit.
> Plurimaque ante oculos miris portenta figuris
> Delusos trepida implebant formidine sensus.

> Now it was the half-way point of the night, and the warlike hero accepted late rest and resting on the lap of the poet/prophet at last he closed his watchful eyes. Before his deluded eyes many portents with wondrous figures were filling his senses with panicked fear.

Astraea is here called *vates* again and provides the comfort and safety to allow Carlus to escape from one dream into another, a prophetic dream. This emotional connection is rather unlike the instances of dreaming in Dante, in which Dante moves quite fluidly between waking vision and sleeping dream, and there is much more emphasis on the waking up. Virgil either wakes him up rather sternly or is awake before him.[22] Similarly, Virgil's Sibyl takes an astringent line with Aeneas: she frequently hurries him along, instructs him loftily, and occasionally rebukes him.[23] Poetic ancestors are not easy companions: the sense of inadequacy in the attempt to reach the sublime is conveyed by the anxiety in the relationship between guide and traveler. For Dante this is not just an anxiety of influence, but an anxiety of spiritual inadequacy; for Aeneas and Carlus spiritual inadequacy might lead to inadequacy in their military and political roles.

The portrayal of the relationship between Astraea and Carlus builds on the relationships between guide and traveler in both Virgil and Dante. When she leaves, abruptly in the final line of Book 7, she flies away more swiftly than the winds, in a way that evokes the vanishing of Creusa in *Aeneid* 2 (*Carlias*, 7.790–93, plus M793b-c):

> "Iam remeo," Titanis ait, "prope plaustra Boete
> Ascendoque tronos sublimis cardinis, unde
> Ad te perveni tenues delapsa per auras."
> Dixit et in caelum rapidis volat otior Euris.
> [Substulit et liquidum crepitantibus aethera pennis
> Subsecuit nusquamque oculis post reddita Carli est.]

[22] Dreams in Dante: *Purg.*, 15.85–138; 19.1–36 (preparatory somnolence at 18.76–87); 27.91–120.

[23] Ordering Aeneas away from viewing Daedalus's artwork: 6.37–39; briskly hurrying Aeneas on: 6.539, 629–30; breaking off the dialogue with Palinurus: 6.372–81.

> "Now I return," Titanis said, "near the plow of Bootes, and I climb up to the high thrones of the turning point, from which I reached you, slipping down through the thin breezes."
>
> She spoke and flies into heaven more swiftly than the quick East winds. [She took herself away and cut the liquid aether with flapping wings and did not return to Carlus's eyes anywhere thereafter.]

Thurn reads the departure of Astraea (or Iustitia, as he calls her) as an indication that worldly wisdom and moral philosophy are not needed in the third stage of the ascent to heaven.[24] But the allegorical level is not the only one in operation. The earlier version (M) contained a line with a direct evocation of Creusa's disappearance in *Aeneid* 2. The phrase *nusquamque oculis post reddita Carli est* (M7.793c) adapts *nec post oculis est reddita nostris* ("nor did she return afterwards to our eyes," *Aeneid*, 2.740). Thurn calls this line "absurde" (413) and is not prepared to acknowledge the other dimensions (literary, emotional) of the character Astraea. As the abrupt final line of the book, line 793 of version R also evokes the death of Turnus (*Aeneid*, 12.952).[25] Carlus is certainly abandoned, alone, and disorientated at the beginning of Book 8 (8.5–6), in the first few lines of which Astraea is re-established in the stars and Statius too vanishes back to Purgatory (8.1–4). Verino's Carlus is significantly more self-sufficient, more Aeneas-like than Dante-like. He must go on, on his own, like Aeneas after the loss of Creusa, and he does not head towards a new love (or an old one). The seraph who later becomes his guide is an even more alien creature than Astraea (arrival: 8.61–78).

What does this analysis of the figure of Astraea tell us about Verino's relationship to Dante and Virgil and his reflections on literary ancestry? First, it shows further the ways in which Verino creatively combines Dante and Virgil to produce a final result indebted to Renaissance allegorical readings of both poets but sensitive to the multiple levels on which such figures function. The emotion of reading and engaging with the literary past has become something with not just personal but spiritual and political significance, in the end perhaps more like Virgil than Dante.

Statius

As in Dante's *Divine Comedy*, the traveler and his companion are joined by a third person: the poet Statius, who encounters Carlus and Astraea just outside Elysium. In *Purgatorio* 22 Statius is a secret Christian converted by the fourth Eclogue, made both poet and Christian by Virgil. Verino had thought, as Dante

[24] Thurn, *Kommentar zur 'Carlias,'* 413.

[25] Though not with verbal echoes: *vitaque cum gemitu fugit indignata sub umbras* ('and his angered life flees with a groan to the shades below,' 12.952).

did, in earlier versions of the *Carlias*, that the author of the *Thebaid* was from Toulouse and hence a countryman of Carlus.[26] By the time of version R, however, Poliziano had published his commentary on Statius's *Silvae*. In this later version we see an uneasy mix of the two understandings of Statius's life.

The character of Statius gives us another perspective on Verino's use of Dante and Virgil and his engagement with his literary ancestry. In this case, we have an actual poet figure, and in Dante the relationship between Statius and Virgil, like that between Dante and Virgil, is characterized by strong emotions. What difference does it make when, instead of three poets, we have one poet, one ruler, and his guide?

First, a reminder about Dante's Statius: he appears in *Purgatorio* 21 and continues with Dante after Virgil disappears at the arrival of Beatrice in *Purgatorio* 33. He vanishes from the text without comment later in the same canto (last mentioned at 33.134). Statius confesses his great love of Virgil by saying that he would willingly have endured another year in Purgatory, exiled from heaven and God, if he could have lived at the same time as Virgil (*Purgatorio*, 21.100–2). The gradual process of revelation, in which Dante first smiles at this and then finally reveals that his companion is Virgil, intensifies this emotional impact. Virgil then reveals that he returns the high regard of Statius, loving him in return for his love (*Purgatorio*, 22.13–18). This is a model of allusion as embrace, intertextual discipleship, love shared between master and followers. The Dante-poet's Christian ambivalence towards the classical past is offset by the Dante-protagonist's deep emotional connection with it.

How is Verino's triangulation of these relationships different? What can it tell us about Verino's attitude to the classical past and to his literary ancestors, including Dante? In Verino's earlier version, Statius's link to the travelers would have been provided by the fact that he was a countryman of Carlus, but it is revealing that Verino chooses to keep him in later versions of the poem despite losing this connection. He is also an emblem of shared literary ancestry, a model for Dante, and Verino himself, in his love of Virgil and his belatedness in the literary tradition. Verino's Statius joins the others and tells a compressed version of his life story which combines Dante with the *Silvae*. His overriding longing is to enter Elysium, the next stage on their journey. Verino's Elysium combines Dante's Limbo (in which the pagan authors are exiled) with his Earthly Paradise, the last stop in Purgatory before moving to Paradise. Elysium is the final destination of Aeneas in *Aeneid* 6, so Verino is going back to Virgil by situating

[26] Thurn, *Kommentar zur 'Carlias,'* 396–97, explains the relationship between Verino, Landino, and Poliziano, and the developing understanding of Statius's life as best as can be worked out. Landino seems to have held onto the idea that Statius was born in Toulouse in his commentary on *Purgatorio* 21, even though later he mentions the *Silvae* to point out that Statius's father was born in Naples.

his Elysium at this point, as well as upgrading the importance of classical learning and emphasizing its role in the process of spiritual growth.

Statius's exclusion from Elysium renders him a locked-out lover, desiring to join his compatriots but excluded by his hypocrisy in not being brave enough to declare his Christianity; he supplicates the doorman, Phocion, in vain (7.541–44):

> Tentavi quotiens supplex, ut limina pandat,
> Ut semel aegregias animas clarosque poetas
> Aspicerem; surdus verbum non reddidit ullum.
> Sed quid cessamus? Quid frustra tempora perdo?

> How many times have I begged him as suppliant to open the threshold, so that I might once see the outstanding souls and the bright poets; deaf, he did not return a word. But why have we stopped? Why do I destroy time in vain?

Statius is the only soul to accompany Astraea and Carlus, and this is the most difficult crossing of a threshold in the three books. The guardian refuses to open the gate even to Astraea, and an angel comes down to let them in. This episode suggests a profound anxiety about the poet's ability to inhabit the classical past, to truly connect with his predecessors. Despite the eloquence of his poetry, Statius is unable to achieve his desire, like Virgil's Orpheus (7.570–78):

> Sed perpetuo sub pondere vatem
> Curvarant humeri, caelum vix fronte supina
> Suspicere ut posset. Sed erat facundia tanta
> Vatis Apollinei, rabidas ut flectere tigres
> Posset et infernas cantu mulceret Erinnes,
> Dum septem Argolicos reges Thebanaque bella
> Et placidas Silvas et Cadmi narrat Agavem
> More Sophocleo, Latio dum tradit Homerum,
> Grandia suspenso recitat dum carmina regi.

> But under his perpetual weight his shoulders bent the poet, his face was so bowed to the ground that he could scarcely look up. But so great was the eloquence of the Apolline poet, that he could turn maddened tigers and soothe the infernal Furies with his song, while he tells of the seven Argive kings and the Theban wars and the peaceful *Silvae* and Agave, daughter of Cadmus, in Sophoclean style, while he hands Homer over to Latium, while he recites great songs for the waiting king.

Statius's power as a poet is not enough even to bridge the gap between his age and that of Virgil; on the other hand, this passage shows not only Verino's positive evaluation of Statius but his knowledge and understanding of his poetry, even imitating Statian style with the hyperbolic tone and the accumulation of Greek names and epithets. Only the grace of God, and not the power of poetry, allows access to Elysium. Further, once the trio (Astraea, Carlus, and Statius) arrive in Elysium, they are shown the spirits of the classical past from an elevated viewpoint, just as Anchises shows the future heroes of Rome to Aeneas. They do not go among them and become part of their company, as Dante does at *Inferno*, 4.97–102, with Homer, Horace, Ovid, and Lucan. However, here too desire is not sated: we do not hear the conversation of Dante with his poetic comrades. Verino takes this alienation a step further by allowing his characters only to look and not to converse with the representatives of the classical past. He clearly goes beyond Virgil, however, by starting with the heroes, generals, and statesmen who form the entirety of Anchises's parade in *Aeneid* 6 (for Verino they represent the active life) and moving towards the contemplative life, in which the next stage of the ascent is formed by poetry. It is also noteworthy that Verino does not bring into his historical parade the mythical characters from poems; he emphasizes his learning in contrast to Dante by insisting on a more particular definition of the classical past: not literature come to life but historical personages. Statius thus functions to model and intensify the desire of the poet and reader to make real contact with the past, a desire that will always ultimately be frustrated by the textuality through which it is fulfilled, expressed here in aptly Virgilian manner by the fact that we as readers see the Greek and Roman heroes on display only through the description presented by Astraea (7.623–709).

In the section on poetry, finally focalized through the eyes of Carlus and Statius, there is little more than a bare list, with Homer and Virgil at its head, in competition, but not in conversation (7.711–18):

> Silva fuit myrto et viridi densissima lauro
> Qualis Apollineis statio gratissima Musis
> Dicitur Aemathiae circum Penneia Tempe.
> Illic purpureis precinctos crura coturnis
> Aspiciunt vates. Ante omnes maior Homerus
> Emicat, hunc aliis longe post terga relictis
> Aequat Virgilius, primo nec cedit honori,
> Ut dubitent, prime cui dentur premia laudis.

> There was a wood, thickly grown with myrtle and green laurel, just like the place which is said to be most welcome to the Apolline Muses, Penneian Tempe around Emathia. There, legs girded with purple boots, they see the poets. Before all greater flashes out Homer; this man, with all others left far behind his back, Virgil equals, and does not cede the first prize, so that they are not sure to whom the rewards of supreme praise are given.

This is a sophisticated reworking of Homer's epiphany to Scipio at Silius's *Punica*, 13.778–97.[27] Like Virgil's Venus (*Aeneid*, 1.337: *purpureo cothurno*), the poets wear tragic boots (*purpureis coturnis*, 714), and like Virgil's Venus their epiphany is not satisfactory.[28] Verino plays with Silius's passage, in which the build-up leads us to expect a manifestation of Virgil, but the key poet turns out not to be Virgil, but Homer instead. In Verino's version, Homer is first and greatest, faithfully following Silius, but Virgil somehow still equals him, trumping the famous assertion of Quintilian that Virgil comes second to Homer, but "nearer first than third" (*Institutio oratoria,* 10.1.86: *proprior tamen primo quam tertio*). In contrast, when Pippin finally appears to his son both a physical and an emotional connection are allowed. Unlike Anchises, he can take his son by the hand and kiss him (8.661–64):

> Nec mora fit, dat turba locum, dextraque prehensa
> Oscula dat nato roseoque haec exprimit ore:

---

[27] *Atque hic, Elysio tendentem limite cernens | effigiem iuvenis, caste cui vitta ligabat | purpurea effusos per colla nitentia crines, | "dic," ait, "hic quinam, virgo? nam luce refulget | praecipua frons sacra viro, multaeque secuntur | mirantes animae et laeto clamore frequentant. | qui vultus! quam, si Stygia non esset in umbra, | dixissem facile esse deum!" "non falleris," inquit | docta comes Triviae, "meruit deus esse videri, | et fuit in tanto non parvum pectore numen. | carmine complexus terram, mare, sidera, manes | et cantu Musas et Phoebum aequavit honore. | atque haec cuncta, prius quam cerneret, ordine terris | prodidit ac vestram tulit usque ad sidera Troiam." | Scipio, perlustrans oculis laetantibus umbram, | "si nunc fata darent, ut Romula facta per orbem | hic caneret vates, quanto maiora futuros | facta eadem intrarent hoc," inquit, "teste nepotes! | felix Aeacide, cui tali contigit ore | gentibus ostendi! crevit tua carmine virtus."* (And now Scipio saw a figure moving along the Elysian path, whose hair rippled over his shining shoulders and was duly confined by a purple fillet. "Say who is this, Maiden," he asked; "for his sacred brow shines with a light beyond compare, and many souls follow him and escort him with cries of wonder and delight. What a countenance is his! Were he not in the darkness of Hades, I should have said confidently that he was a god." "You are right," answered the wise handmaid of Trivia; "he deserved to seem divine; a great genius dwelt in his mighty mind. His poetry embraced earth and sea, the sky and the nether world; he rivalled the Muses in song and Apollo in glory. All this region also, before he ever saw it, he revealed to mortals; and he raised the fame of Troy to heaven—Troy the mother of Rome." Scipio gazed with joyful eyes at the ghost of Homer and said: "If Fate would suffer this poet now to sing of Roman achievements, for all the world to hear, how much deeper an impression the same deeds would make upon posterity, if Homer testified to them! How fortunate was Achilles, when such a poet displayed him to the world! The hero was made greater by the poet's verse": Silius Italicus, *Punica*, 13.778–97).

[28] Aeneas complains at 1.407–9. On Venus, see K. J. Reckford, "Recognising Venus (I): Aeneas Meets His Mother," *Arion* 3 (1995–1996): 1–42; on epiphany and desire, see Helen V. Lovatt, *The Epic Gaze: Vision, Gender and Narrative in Ancient Epic* (Cambridge: Cambridge University Press, 2013), 78–85.

> "Nate, meis oculis et vita carior ipsa,
> Dum vixi, regni et nostrae spes una senectae!"
>
> No delay: the crowd gives space, and grasping his right hand he gives kisses to his son and expresses these things with shining face: "Son, dearer than my eyes and my life, while I lived, the one hope of my rule and my old age!"

He does so again before he leaves at 8.876–77: *nec plura locutus | Oscula dat nato, tenuesque recedit in auras* ("No more was said; he gives kisses to his son and goes away into the slender breezes"). Pippin offers Carlus a prophecy of the immediate future similar to that which the Sibyl gives in the *Aeneid* and combines it with Anchises's advice to the Roman race about how to rule: *Pontifices venerare sacros, haec cura, memento | Sit tibi praecipua* ("revere the sacred high-priests/popes; remember, make this care the most important for you," 8.679–80). He also promises Carlus the "ever-living name of Magnus" (*nomen perenne . . . Magni*) and echoes Apollo's exhortation to Ascanius from *Aeneid* 9: *sic itur ad astra* ("That's how to reach the stars," 8.684 = *Aeneid*, 9.641). When Carlus reaches the holy city of Jerusalem, he is baptized in "charisma," a miraculous liquid, which allows the scales to fall from his eyes (8.583–609), as if his revelation is a permanent version of Venus's grant of the divine gaze to Aeneas at *Aeneid*, 2.604–33. The poet does stand back from fully describing the triumph of heaven, the second parade of heroes, as it were (8.610–18), using the Sibyl's declaration of inadequacy from her ekphrasis of Tartarus (6.625–27, see page 166 above). Finally, however, it is up to Carlus himself to pray to the Mother of God for success in his military campaigns and for the grace to be a good ruler. He asks not for *imperium sine fine* ("rule without end," *Aeneid*, 1.279) but *imperium sine labe* ("rule without fault," *Carlias*, 8.729). He is emotionally and spiritually fulfilled by his encounters in a way that Aeneas is not, and does not leave by the gate of false dreams. To reach for the stars is not to reach for epic fame but immortal life in the company of God—a genuinely moving vision, of a ruler whose *pietas* is based on emotional connections with the past, with religion and beloved family members. Verino eschews Dante's romantic love but considerably intensifies the emotional engagement which Virgil denies to Aeneas.

Literary Ancestry

Virgil is everywhere in Verino's three-book reworking of Dante, the ground upon which we walk, the words we speak, the air we breathe; but he is not a character, an emotional being with whom one might have a relationship. The poet's longing for a connection with his literary ancestors is embodied in the character of Statius, allowing Verino to combine Dante's exploration of emotional engagement with the classical past and spiritual engagement with the Christian present, with Virgil's focus on leadership and *imperium*. The ultimate return to *Aeneid* 6, as end-point of both Purgatory and Paradise, shows how important Virgil is in Verino's reworking.

This essay has traced something of the richness of Verino's engagement with his literary ancestors, both classical and non-classical, and the way that Dante is interwoven with Virgil. While Astraea replaces Virgil as guide, Verino adopts and adapts Dante's Statius as an alternative model of belatedness and engagement with Virgil. As Thomas Greene argues, "the increase of humanist knowledge heightened ironically the sense of the unknown; the wider the diameter of light, the greater the circumference of darkness—and the keener the awareness of potential estrangement."[29] Virgil is everywhere, like the air, but ungraspable, like the breeze: although we can see traces of the *Aeneid* it is often hard to pin down their significance. Verino's engagement with Virgil is more belated than Dante's, even though his story is set before his and, in fact, more like that of Statius, whose story is set before both *Aeneid* and *Iliad*. Verino's detachment from Virgil allows room for a reconciliation of humanist learning with Christian faith, in which Virgil's personification of justice leads Carlus, as well as Statius, to God.

[29] Thomas M. Greene, *The Light in Troy: Imitation and Discovery in Renaissance Poetry* (New Haven: Yale University Press, 1982), 149.

11

Virgil Reborn, Reconfigured, Reinvented in the Early Modern Verse-*Cento*

George Hugo Tucker
University of Reading

Our subject is the sixteenth- to seventeenth-century Virgilian verse-*cento*, an ancient literary form (κέντρων in Greek, *cento* in Latin; "patchwork" coverlet), which was by name and composition a patchwork of verse-fragments lifted from a canonical author (Homer in Greek, Virgil in Latin) to generate a new poem typically described as being "sewn" together from verse-fragments endowed with new meaning.[1] For this reason it was compared to *parodia* ("song sung beside") in the *Poetics* (1561) of Julius Caesar Scaliger, who also linked it to *r*[*h*]*apsodia* ("stitched-song") because of its similarly "sewn" stitchings.[2] Yet the *cento* was not to be confused with parody, though sharing a transformative (mis)appropriation of source-text, affecting *verba* and *res*. Unlike parody, the *cento* did not respect

[1] See Octave Delepierre, *Tableau de la littérature du centon*, 2 vols. (London: Nicholas Trübner, 1874–1875); Giovanni Salanitro, ed., "La poesia centonaria greco-latina," in Osidio Geta, *Medea*, Bibliotheca Athena 24 (Rome: Edizioni dell' Ateneo, 1981), 9–60; Jean Lafond, "Le Centon et son usage dans la littérature morale et politique," in *L'Automne de la Renaissance, 1580–1630*, ed. idem and André Stegmann (Paris: Vrin, 1981), 117–28; Mark D. Usher, "Prolegomenon to the Homeric Centos," *American Journal of Philology* 118 (1997): 305–21; idem, *Homeric Stitchings: The Homeric Centos of the Empress Eudocia* (New York: Rowman & Littlefield, 1998); Christoph Hoch, *Apollo Centonarius: Studien und Texte zur Centodichtung der italienischen Renaissance*, Romanica et Comparatistica 26 (Tübingen: Stauffenburg, 1997); Hélène Cazes, "Le Livre et la lyre: grandeur et décadence du centon virgilien au Moyen-Âge et à la Renaissance" (Thèse de doctorat, Paris X-Nanterre, 1998; 2 vols., Lille: ANRT, 2003); Scott McGill, *Virgil Recomposed: The Mythological and Secular Centos in Antiquity* (Oxford and New York: Oxford University Press, 2005); Martin Bažil, *Centones Christiani: métamorphoses d'une forme intertextuelle dans la poésie chrétienne de l'Antiquité tardive* (Paris: Études Augustiniennes, 2009).

[2] J. C. Scaliger, *Poetices libri septem* (Lyons: Antonius Vincentius, 1561), Lib. I, Cap. XLIII: "Centones."

the structure of its source,[3] nor did it alter or add to the verses it borrowed. It was a compositional technique lending itself to different ends.[4]

A *cento* resembles a mosaic, and verse-centos were described as such in the Renaissance.[5] This lapidary metaphor was a variant upon the comparison that Ausonius (fourth century) had drawn between the verse-*cento* and the Greek puzzle-game *Ostomachion* (involving the combination of bone *tesserae* to make human, animal, or other shapes) when explaining his Virgilian *Cento nuptialis*, a parodic epithalamium written for the Emperor Valentinian, in a letter to the rhetor Assius Paulus.[6] The mosaic metaphor of the High Renaissance hearkened back to the parallel Byzantine traditions of composing mosaics and Homeric verse centos to common Christian ends, pointing to an aesthetic of colorful "bedazzlement" common to Byzantine mosaics and late or "silver" Latin poetry, as Michael Roberts has suggested of the "jeweled" poetic "style" of late antiquity.[7]

Above all, the metaphor of a verbal mosaic tapped into the classical topos that speech or writing constituted a variegated, potentially uneven, mosaic of words,[8] and into a Renaissance conception of knowledge as fragmentary and

---

3 On the close relation to parody, see Margaret A. Rose, *Parody: Ancient, Modern, and Post-Modern*, Literature, Culture, Theory 5 (Cambridge: Cambridge University Press, 1993), 16–17, 78; Hoch, *Apollo*, 43–58 on Lilio G. Giraldi, *Historiæ poetarum . . . dialogi decem* (Basel: M. Isingrinius, 1545), J. C. Scaliger, *Poetices*, and Henri Estienne, *Parodiæ* (1575; see below, n.10), for whom parody, unlike the *cento*, respects its source's structure (cf. Bažil, *Centones*, 22).

4 See Bažil, *Centones*, 12.

5 E.g., in Antonio Possevino (1533–1611; secretary to Cardinal Ercole Gonzaga), "Ioachimo Belaio Antonius Possevinus Mantuanus S.P.D." dedicatory letter describing the *cento*-compiler as a mosaicist, prefacing Possevino's edition of the *Centones ex Virgilio* of fellow Mantuan, Lelio Capilupi (1497–1560): with verses of Benedetto Egio, postface of Fulvio Orsini (Rome: Valerius Doricus, 1555; additions, V. and Aloysius Doricus, 1555–1556), fols. [i]v–[ii]v (fol. [i]v).

6 "Ausonius Paulo S.," ll. 42–61, *Cento nuptialis*, in Ausonius, *Opuscula*, ed. Rudolf Peiper (Leipzig: Teubner, 1886; Sesto Prete edition, 1978), 206–19, at 206–8; Hugh G. Evelyn White, trans., *Ausonius*, Loeb Classical Library, 2 vols. (London: Heinemann, and New York: G. P. Putnam's Sons, 1919), 1:370–77, at 374–77, and "Appendix" (395–97) on this *loculus Archimedius* ("Archimedes's box," *Stomachion / Ostomachion*), named in the *fragmentum* "De Metris" of C. Caesius Bassus (ca. AD 60); see Alexandre Burnier, "Démonter Virgile et bâtir un classique: le *Centon nuptial* d'Ausone comme jeu de reconstruction," *Ítaca: Quadernas Catalans de Cultura Clàssica* 21 (2005): 79–93, at 85.

7 Michael Roberts, *The Jeweled Style: Poetry and Poetics in Late Antiquity* (Ithaca, NY and London: Cornell University Press, 1989), 70–91, at 72–73.

8 Eric MacPhail, "The Mosaic of Speech: A Classical Topos in Renaissance Aesthetics," *Journal of the Warburg and Courtauld Institutes* 66 (2003): 249–64. This parallel is traceable back to Lucilius's fragments (*C. Lucili Carminum Reliquiae*, ed. Friedrich Marx, 2 vols [Leipzig: Teubner, 1904–1905], 1:84–85) satirizing the peppering of Latin with Greek words. It resurfaces as a metaphor for composition in Cicero (*De Oratore*,

composite. Notable for its application of the mosaic metaphor is the dialogue *Profugiorum ab aerumna libri* (c. 1441–1442) of Leon Battista Alberti (1404–1472) at the moment of Niccola de' Medici's disquisition therein upon his interlocutor Agnolo Pandolfini's prose-style (and so, in passing, upon the composite, recycled nature of Renaissance thought, of the spoken or written word, and of new artistic images); Niccola de' Medici compares this eclectic style to the first Greek floor-mosaic, assembled from architectural fragments for the decoration of the Temple of Artemis at Ephesus.[9]

Because, in the sixteenth and seventeenth centuries, the Latin verse-*cento* was still based preponderantly upon Virgil, it gave broad currency to the term *Virgiliocento*, enshrined by the philologist-printer Henri Estienne in his *Parodiæ morales* (1575), devoted to parodies and centos.[10] This term was hijacked by Reformers such as Estienne, and so treated with caution by Catholic Virgilian centonists such as Andreas Fabri Wethulensis (in his preface [(1589)] to his *Centones* (1609),[11] where Fabri defends his practice of the Virgilian *cento* against those "who . . . despising the easy elegance of Cicero and the grave eloquence of Virgil, only delight in overblown and archaic words," and against their "slanderous accusations of textual theft and falsehood."[12] The term *Virgiliocento* had

3.172; *Orator*, 149–50; *Brutus*, 274) and Quintilian (*Institutio Oratoria*, 9.4.113, 2.4.27), to be revived by Leonardo Bruni (1369–1444; *De interpretatione recta*, c. 1421–1424) on Plato's style being reminiscent of a floor-mosaic; Leon Battista Alberti (see below, n.9); and Erasmus in his mosaic-like *Moriæ Encomium* (1511) and *De duplici copia verborum ac rerum* (1512), on the "interweaving" of archaisms in Latin; then in Montaigne's pronouncements on writing and quotation in his mosaic-like, *cento*-like *Essais*. See George H. Tucker, "Montaigne et les néo-latins: 'Capilupus' et l'art du centon dans les *Essais*," in *Montaigne et les Anciens*, ed. Catherine Magnien, *Montaigne Studies* 17.1–2 (2005): 163–74, at 173–74.

[9] Leon Battista Alberti, *Opere volgari*, ed. Cecil Grayson, 3 vols., Scrittori d'Italia 218, 234, 254 (Bari: Giuseppe Laterza, 1960–1973), vol. 2 (1966: *Rime e trattati morali*), 105–83 (*Profugiorum ab aerumna libri III*), at 160–62. I am indebted to Hans Aurenhammer for this reference in his paper "*Liberalitas*: The Image of a Friendly Virtue as Hidden Self-Portrayal in Leon Battista Alberti's *Della pittura*," presented at the Renaissance Society of America's Annual Meeting in Venice, 8–10 April 2010.

[10] Henri Estienne, *Parodiæ morales H. Stephani, In poetarum vet*[*erum*]. *Sententias celebriores, totidem versibus Gr*[æcè] *ab eo redditas* (s.l.: H. Estienne, 1575); cf. Cazes, "Le Livre et la lyre," 604. Part 2 of Estienne's work is titled *Centonum et parodiarum exempla, ab Henrico Stephano selecta & illustrata*.

[11] See Cazes, "Le Livre et la lyre," 596–613, at 604, referring to and translating Fabri's preface: Fabri distances himself from the term *Virgilio-cento* because of its association with Protestant hijacking of Lelio Capilupi's *cento* (*De vita monachorum*) and of the Virgilian *cento* form in general.

[12] Andreas Fabri Wethulensis (André Le Fèvre de Vétheuil), "Benigno proboque lectori Andræas Fabri W. Salutem" (preface dated January 1589), in idem, *Centones, cum Diana, et iuvenilibus* (Paris: David Douceur, 1609), 3–7, at 4–5.

a long pedigree, however, having been coined by St Jerome (*Epistolae*, 53.7; c. AD 395) in a letter to Paulinus of Nola, deploring those who "twist meanings to draw Scripture to their own will," as in (Homeric) Greek or (Virgilian) Latin verse *centones.*[13]

In the early modern period, a Latin verse *cento* could also be based on an alternative canonical Roman poet (Ovid, notably, but also Horace, Lucilius, Persius, Plautus, or Lucan); it sometimes employed a combination of two (Virgil and Ovid, typically, or, more rarely, Horace and Lucan). Occasionally, it drew on three (e.g., Virgil, Claudian, and Statius) or more (e.g., Juvenal or Seneca). The early modern Latin verse *cento* thus exploited elegiac, lyric, or dramatic meters, as well as dactylic hexameters, and so, a wide generic range (epic, or mock-epic, satirical, didactic, political-polemical, amatory, dramatic comic or tragic).

Although there were numerous early modern *centos* in Latin exploiting this large range of possibilities, there were not many examples of *cento* composition in Greek. A notable instance was an early seventeenth-century French Virgilian-Homeric *cento* on the early reign of Louis XIII following the assassination of Henri IV.[14] There was the keenest interest, however, in the fourth- to fifth-century, Christianizing Byzantine *Homerocentra*, attributed nowadays to the Empress Eudocia and her predecessors.[15] Published by Henri Estienne in 1578,[16] these *Homerocentra* had been printed by Aldus Manutius in Venice in 1501, so as to accompany the fourth-century Virgilian *Cento* of Falconia Proba on the life and passion of Christ; they were even thought, according to Aldus's preface of 1501, to have been inspired by Proba's Virgilian *Cento.*[17]

---

[13] See Delepierre, *Tableau*, 1:16–17; Usher, "Prolegomenon," 316–17; McGill, *Virgil*, xvi, 155, n.17; Bažil, *Centones*, 19.

[14] *Scena Motuum in Gallia nuper excitatorum Virgilianis et Homericis versib*[*us*] *expressa* (s.l.: s.n., 1616), attributed (Delepierre, *Tableau*, 2:229) to "Jacques Capel, seigneur de Tilloy" (d. 1624), and attached to the Virgilian *cento* of "Pasquinus Passavanti" (Pasquinade and quasi-theatrical *sortes virgilianae*; see Cazes, "Le Livre et la lyre," 578–79, 735), *Sortes Virgilianæ quibus Æstuantis Galliæ Theatridium instruxit Pasquinus Passavanti patricius Romanus Archireferendarius Catholicus. Sors omnia versat* ("Veronæ" [Bern / Geneva?], 1616). Both were composed after the assassination of Henri IV (1610) and the revolt (1614) in the early reign of Louis XIII.

[15] *Patricius, Eudocie, Optimus, Côme de Jérusalem: Centons Homériques (Homerocentra)*, ed. André-Louis Rey, Sources Chrétiennes 437 (Paris: Éditions du Cerf, 1998); Usher, "Prolegomenon," passim; idem, *Homeric Stitchings*; Brian P. Sowers, "Eudocia: The Making of a Homeric Christian" (PhD diss., University of Cincinnati, 2008); cf. Delepierre, *Tableau*, 1:96–114.

[16] *Homerici Centones, à veteribus vocati* Ὁμηρόκεντρα *Virgiliani Centones. Vtrique in quædam historiæ sacræ capita scripti* ([Geneva]: Henricus Stephanus, 1578).

[17] Aldus Manutius, "VITA Probæ mulieris Romanæ," *Probæ Falconiæ Cento ex Virgilio de novo et veteri testamento. Homerocentra, hoc est Centones ex Homero . . .* , in *Poetæ Christiani veteres*, vol. 2 (Venice: Aldus, 1501).

In the early modern period, the looser, multi-citational prose-*cento* was also pioneered in Latin by Justus Lipsius in his *Politica* (1589).[18] Together with Virgilian *Centones* composed in the 1540s and 1550s by Lelio Capilupi of Mantua (1497–1560),[19] Lipsius's prose-*cento*, a commonplace-book[20] based on multiple sources, principally Tacitus, was admired by Montaigne, with whose citational and compositional techniques Lipsius' *Politica* had chimed. In the late sixteenth and early seventeenth centuries the prose-*cento* also spilled into the vernacular, notably in French,[21] as well as "macaronically" (Latin-English) in Robert Burton's *The Anatomy of Melancholy* (1621–1651),[22] a *cento*-"rhapsody" conceived in imitation of Lipsius and of Montaigne's multi-citational *Essais*.[23]

However, in incorporating and combining prose and verse quotations within an authorial prose frame, such prose-centos were quite different from verse ones, which were characterized by an exclusive, strict metrical combination of lifted verse fragments. If the so-called rules for this stricter verse-method had been established by Ausonius for the Virgilian verse-*cento* in his letter "To Paulus" (reproduced in Aldus's 1501 edition of Proba and the *Homerocentra*), they were highlighted by Erasmus in his adage *Farcire centones* (1506).[24] They thus achieved

---

[18] Justus Lipsius, *Politicorum, sive civilis doctrinæ libri sex* (Leiden: ex off. Plantin., Franciscus Raphelengius, 1589); Delepierre, *Tableau*, 1:257–61; George H. Tucker, "Justus Lipsius and the *Cento* Form," in *(Un)masking the Realities of Power: Justus Lipsius and the Dynamics of Political Writing in Early Modern Europe*, ed. Erik De Bom et al., Brill's Studies in Intellectual History 193 (Leiden and Boston: Brill, 2010), 163–92.

[19] Lelio Capilupi, *Centones ex Virgilio* (Rome, 1555–1556), containing centos of the 1540s and 1550s, plus new ones; repr. in *Carmina illustrium poetarum italorum*, ed. Giovanni M. Toscano, 2 vols. (Paris: Ægidius Gorbinus, 1576–1577), vol. 2: fols. 308r–340v, and *Capiluporum* [Hippolyti, Lælii, Camilli, Alphonsi, Iulii] *carmina*, ed. Giulio Capilupi and Giuseppe Castiglione, letter-postface of Giulio Rossi (Rome: ex typogr. hæredum Io. Lilioti, 1590), 153–250. See Claudio Mutini, "CAPILUPI, Lelio," in *Dizionario biografico degli Italiani* (Rome: Istituto dell' Enciclopedia Italiana, 1960-), 18:542–43; Dennis E. Rhodes, "Lelio Capilupi and the 'Centones ex Virgilio'," *The Library* 16 (1994): 208–18; George H. Tucker, "Mantua's 'Second Virgil': Du Bellay, Montaigne and the Curious Fortune of Lelio Capilupi's *Centones ex Virgilio* [Romæ, 1555]," in *Ut granum sinapis: Essays on Neo-Latin Literature in Honour of Jozef IJsewijn*, ed. Dirk Sacré and Gilbert Tournoy, *Humanistica Lovaniensia* Supplementa XII (Leuven: Leuven University Press, 1997), 264–91.

[20] See Ann Moss, "The *Politica* of Justus Lipsius and the Commonplace-book," *Journal of the History of Ideas* 59 (1998): 421–36; Tucker, "Justus Lipsius," passim.

[21] See Lafond, "Le Centon," passim.

[22] Consult Robert Burton, *The Anatomy of Melancholy* [1632, collated with 1638 and 1651 editions], ed. Thomas C. Faulkner et al., intro. J. B. Bamborough, Oxford English Texts, 6 vols. (Oxford: Clarendon Press, 1989–2000).

[23] See Tucker, "Justus Lipsius," passim.

[24] Desiderius Erasmus, *Adagia* [1506] 58 "Farcire centones," in idem, *Opera Omnia*, ed. Jean Leclerc, 10 vols. (Leiden: 1703–1706; repr. Hildesheim: Georg Olms, 1961–

wide currency alongside Ausonius's comparison of the Virgilian verse-*cento* with the *Ostomachion* and his related views of the *cento* as ludic, a memory-game. Indeed, like Ausonius's Virgilian *Cento nuptialis*, the (predominantly Virgilian) Latin verse-*cento* was occasional in nature, engaging satirically, or descriptively, with contemporary issues, people, and places, to which canonical texts had been ingeniously or wittily adapted; like the Latin *silva*, it was almost invariably also ex tempore in style.[25]

Eventually, in the Counter Reformation post-1555, the Virgilian verse-*cento* fell into discredit for its use of Virgil's pagan language. This disfavor was also the particular result of the 1543 *cento* by Lelio Capilupi, *De vita monachorum*, an obscene satire "Upon the Life of Monks,"[26] reproduced as anti-Roman propaganda in Reformist editions of 1545 (Wittemberg, Zurich, and Basel) and later seized upon by Mathias Flacius Illyricus for his *Varia doctorum piorumque virorum de corrupto Ecclesiæ statu poemata* ("Various Poems of Learned, Pious Men on the Corrupt State of the Church") of 1556–1557.[27] Indeed, this was compounded by Lelio's *De vita monachorum* also being paraded by Calvinist Henri II Estienne in the second part of his *Parodiæ morales* (1575, 104–18). For Capilupi's anti-monastic *cento* was followed there (124–26) by two extracts from a hybrid *cento* of Pierre Viret (1511–1571), *De theatrica Missæ saltatione ceuto* [i.e., *cento*] (1553, without these two extracts), which not only satirized the sacrament of the Mass but also borrowed verses from Lelio's Virgilian *cento* as well as from Falconia Proba, Virgil, and Ovid. (Viret's *cento* was cast, unusually, in elegiac distichs, deriving hexameters and pentameters from this Virgilian-Ovidian mix).[28]

1962), 2:542D; quoted by Henri Estienne, *Thesaurus Linguæ Græcæ*, 4 vols. (Lyons: Henricus Stephanus, 1572), 2: cols. 1293–94 (on Ὁμηρόκεντρα / Ὁμηροκέντρωνες), repr. in idem, *Parodiæ morales* 2nd part, 3–4.

[25] See George H. Tucker, "La Poétique du centon, une poétique de la silve?," in *La Silve: histoire d'une écriture libérée en Europe de l'Antiquité au XVIIIe siècle*, Latinitates: culture et littérature latine à travers les siècles 5, ed. Perrine Galand and Sylvie Laigneau-Fontaine (Turnhout: Brepols, 2013), 525–64.

[26] Lelio Capilupi, *Cento ex Virgilio de vita monachorum et Gallus* (Venice: Paulus Gerardus, 1543); repr. "Venetiis," actually, Lyons: Gioanni Pullon da Trino, 1550.

[27] Mathias Flacius Illyricus, *Varia doctorum piorumque virorum de corrupto Ecclesiæ statu poemata* (Basel: Ludovicus Lucius, 1557); dedicatory preface dated May 1556. Pages 355–70 contain Lelio Capilupi's *De vita monachorum*. See Tucker, "Mantua's 'Second Virgil'," passim, and below n.29.

[28] Viret's *cento* closes his *De Vero Verbi Dei, Sacramentorum et Ecclesiæ ministerio, lib. II. De adulterinis sacramentis, lib. I. De adulterato baptismi sacramento, et de sanctorum oleorum usu et consecrationibus, lib. I. De adulterata cœna Domini, et de tremendis sacræ missæ mysteriis, lib. VI. De theatrica Missæ saltatione ceuto* [*cento*] *ex veteribus poetis latinis consarcinatus* (Geneva: Robertus Stephanus, 1553). On this *cento*'s unusual verse-form [cf.? H. Estienne, *Parodiæ*], its *bricolage* (filtering Virgil through Capilupi and Proba, in combination with Ovid), and the absence of the two extracts quoted by Estienne in the 1553

The Latin Verse Centonist Lelio Capilupi (1497–1560), Mantua's *Virgilius redivivus*

In sixteenth-century Italy the most celebrated practitioner of the Latin verse-*cento* was without a doubt the above mentioned Lelio Capilupi, Mantua's "Second Virgil." His various *Centones ex Virgilio* were first published individually or in small clusters in the 1540s and early 1550s,[29] then more completely in 1555 in Rome, and dedicated by his Mantuan editor Antonio Possevino to the Pléiade poet Joachim Du Bellay (1523–1560).[30] In 1557, as a result of the scandal of the *De vita monachorum*, that *cento* and Lelio's other *centones* (by association) were placed by Paul IV on the universal Roman *Index librorum prohibitorum* ("Index of forbidden books" of 1557, then 1559; Tridentine revision 1564), and then on the Indexes of Liège and Antwerp (1569), and of the Spanish Inquisition (1583). However, a proviso of expurgation was introduced in 1564, thanks to Lelio's brother, Ippolito Capilupi, papal nunzio in Venice from May 1561, who had enlisted the Patriarch of Venice to argue before the Commission of the Index (Council of Trent, 18 January 1562 to 4 December 1563) for a relaxation of the total ban of 1557 and 1559.[31] As a result, Lelio's Virgilian *Centones* appeared, expurgated or modified, twenty years later in Giovanni Matteo Toscano's Parisian anthology (1576–1577) of the *Carmina* of Italian neo-Latin poets,[32] and subsequently in the Roman edition (1590) of the *Capiluporum Carmina*, which drew together the Latin verses and Virgilian *centones* of the Capilupi brothers, Lelio, Ippolito (1511–1580),[33] Camillo (1504–1548), and Alfonso (1500–1519), and of

edition, see Cazes, "Le Livre et la lyre," 567–68, 645–53, 733, 1103–8. On Viret, see Melchior Adam, *Decades duæ continentes Vitas theologorum exterorum principum* (Frankfurt: sumpt. Jonæ Rosæ viduæ, 1653), 120–23.

[29] (a) *Cento ex Virgilio de vita monachorum et Gallus* (Venice, 1543; repr. "Venetiis," 1550); (b) [just *De vita*] (Wittemberg, 1545; [Zurich, c.1545?]; [Basle, c.1545?]; Edinburgh, 1565; "Romæ" [Geneva: Jacob Stoer], 1575); (c) [just *De vita*], in Flacius Illyricus (ed.), *Varia doctorum piorumque virorum . . . poemata* (Basel, 1557), 355–70; (d) *Centonum ex Virgilio libri tres* [= *Ad principes Christianos Aristæus*; *Ad Rainutium Farnesium Damon*; *In fœminas*] ([Venice: Michael Tramezinus, c.1545–1550]).

[30] See above, n.5.

[31] See Tucker, "Mantua's 'Second Virgil'," 287–88; J. M. De Bujanda, *Index de livres interdits*, 10 vols. (Sherbrooke: Centre d'études de la Renaissance, and Geneva: Droz, 1984–1996), 8:107.

[32] See above, n.19.

[33] On Ippolito Capilupi, agent of the pro-Imperial Gonzagas of Mantua and secretary to Cardinal Ercole Gonzaga, see Gaspare De Caro, "CAPILUPI, Ippolito," in *Dizionario biografico*, 18:536–42; Giovanni B. Intra, "Di Ippolito Capilupi e del suo tempo," *Archivio Storico Lombardo*, 2nd series, 10 (1893): 76–142. Ippolito's *Rime*, like Lelio's and Camillo's, are in *Rime del S. Lelio, e fratelli de Capilupi. Nuovamente poste in luce* (Mantua: Francesco Osana, 1585; repr. Mantua: Padus, 1973).

their nephew-editor Giulio Capilupi (Ippolito's illegitimate son, b. 1544),[34] a renowned Virgilian verse-centonist like Lelio.[35]

In the *Capiluporum Carmina*, Lelio's Latin verses contained few independent poems (just ten occasional or amatory *Epigrammata*). For they mainly comprised his *Centones ex Virgilio* as they had appeared in Rome in 1555. This included two important early Virgilian *centones* of Lelio's that had been re-printed in the 1555 volume: his wittily erotic *Gallus* (Venice, 1543; Lyons, 1550), recounting the lost *Amores* of Virgil's poet-friend Gallus;[36] and his misogynistic *In fœminas* (Venice, c. 1545–1550),[37] dedicated to the historian Paolo Giovio (1483–1553), and inspired by Girolamo Fracastoro's poem *Syphilis sive morbus Gallicus* ("Syphilis, or the French Disease"; Verona: Stefano Nicolini da Sabio, 1530). Lelio's Roman *Centones ex Virgilio* also ranged to occasional pieces added in 1555–1556, reflecting the changing cultural-political context of Rome under three popes in rapid succession (Julius III, r. February 1550 to March 1555; Marcellus II, r. April 1555; Paul IV, r. May 1555 to August 1559), and relating in particular to the pro-Imperial faction in Rome and to the cardinal of Trent, Cristoforo Madruzzo (d. 1578), appointed Imperial governor of Milan in 1556. These additional occasional pieces thus reflected, above all, the pro-Imperial alignment of Lelio and Ippolito Capilupi's Mantuan Gonzaga patrons.[38] Conspicuously absent, how-

[34] See Tiziano Ascari, "CAPILUPI, Giulio," in *Dizionario biografico*, 18:535–36.

[35] On the four brothers and "nephew" Giulio, see Cazes, "Le Livre et la lyre," 506–52; and Delepierre, "Les Capilupi," in idem, *Tableau*, 1:170–223.

[36] Cf. Ovid, *Amores*, 3.9.63 and Virgil, *Eclogues*, 10.6 (*Galli dicamus amores* ["let us tell of the loves of Gallus"]) and 10.10 (*cum Gallus amore periret* ["when Gallus was dying of love"]). Lelio Capilupi's's *Gallus* is reprinted, without title, as "Cento I." in his *Centones ex Virgilio* (1555), then as "Cento XVI." in the *Capiluporum Carmina* (1590); ed. and trans. Reinhold F. Glei in *›Parodia‹ und Parodie: Aspekte intertextuellen Schreibens in der lateinischen Literatur der Frühen Neuzeit*, ed. idem and Robert Seidel, Frühe Neuzeit 120 (Tübingen: Niemeyer, 2006), 287–320 (Glei, "Vergil am Zeug flicken: Centonische Schreibstrategien und die *Centones ex Virgilio* des Lelio Capilupi"). Cf. George H. Tucker, "Érotisme, parodie, et l'art du centon dans le *Gallus* (1543; *Centones ex Virgilio*, 1555) de Lelio Capilupi," in *Syntagmatia: Essays on Neo-Latin Literature in Honour of Monique Mund-Dopchie & Gilbert Tournoy*, ed. Dirk Sacré and Jan Papy, *Humanistica Lovaniensia* Supplementa XXVI (Leuven: Leuven University Press, 2009), 329–43.

[37] Appearing as "In fœminas" in Lelio Capilupi's *Centonum ex Virgilio libri tres* (c. 1545–1550), as "Cento III. In fœminas . . . ad Paulum Iovium" in his *Centones ex Virgilio* (1555), and as "Cento XVII" in *Capiluporum Carmina* (1590). See Stephen Murphy, "Maro mutatus in melius? Lelio Capilupi's *Cento in feminas*," in *Acta Conventus Neo-Latini Bonnensis*, dir. Rhoda Schnur, ed. Perrine Galand-Hallyn et al., Medieval and Renaissance Texts and Studies 315 (Tempe, Arizona: ACMRS, 2006), 611–17.

[38] See Intra, "Di Ippolito Capilupi," passim, on the Capilupi's pro-Imperial, pro-Spanish leanings, and their relationship with the Gonzagas of Mantua (and Cardinal Ercole Gonzaga). See Tucker, "Mantua's 'Second Virgil'," passim; idem, "Neo-Latin

ever, in the later Roman volume of 1590, was Lelio's *De vita monachorum*, suppressed there, because re-written (re-centonized) by Giulio Capilupi as a new, more edifying Counter Reformation piece *De Ætate aurea, & ferrea* ("On the Age of Gold, and of Iron"), dealing with human decadence and salvation by the Catholic liturgy.[39]

Indeed, this process of rehabilitation of Lelio and his Virgilian *centones*[40] would be continued, through further apologetic re-presentation of both Lelio and of the Virgilian *cento* form more broadly, by his former editor Possevino in the latter's *Bibliotheca selecta* of 1593 and 1603.[41] In the *Capiluporum Carmina* of 1590, the sanitized contents of this Roman volume were crowned, moreover, by technical explanation of the Latin (Virgilian) verse *cento*-form in a letter-postface by Giulio Rossi (or Roscio, or Rosso; Julius Roscius Hortinus), poet-orator of Orte,[42] where Rossi commented upon the metrical rules for the Virgilian verse-*cento* set out by Ausonius, and so, inherently, upon Lelio's and Giulio's Virgilian *centones* contained in the 1590 volume. Entitled "Camillo ac Prospero Capilupis

---

Literary Monuments to Rome and the Papacy 1553–1557," in *Acta Conventus Neo-Latini Bonnensis*, 81–120; idem, "Strategies of argument, politics and poetics in the *Centones ex Virgilio* (1555–56) of Lelio Capilupi of Mantua," in *The Art of Arguing in the World of Renaissance Humanism*, ed. Marc Laureys and Roswitha Simons, *Humanistica Lovaniensia* Supplementa XXXIV (Leuven: Leuven University Press, 2013), 151–86.

39 See Stephen Murphy, "The Metamorphoses of *De vita monachorum*," in *Acta Conventus Neo-Latini Cantabrigiensis*, dir. Rhoda Schnur, ed. Jean-Louis Charlet et al., Medieval and Renaissance Texts and Studies 259 (Tempe, Arizona: Arizona Center for Medieval and Renaissance Studies, 2003), 377–82; Delepierre, *Tableau*, 1:203–13. Lelio-Giulio's *De Ætate* would be reproduced in vol. 2 (Helmstedt, 1600, fols. H[4]r–K[2]v) of Heinrich Meibom's compendium of *Virgiliocentones*, even if Lelio's original, satirical *De vita monachorum* had been paraded by Meibom as a restored text (based on previous Italian, French, and German editions), with appended marginal source references, in vol. 1 (Helmstedt, 1597), fols. G[1]r–H[4]v. See below, n.53.

40 On Lelio Capilupi's and the *cento*'s problematic status, censorship, and eventual re-habilitation, see Tucker, "Mantua's 'Second Virgil'," 289–90; Cazes, "Le Livre et la lyre," 524–31.

41 See Cazes, "Le Livre et la lyre," 544–55, at 50, for whom this re-writing of Capilupi's poem was no less a form of *censure* than Possevino's "selection" and partial re-writing of Lelio's *centones* in his *Bibliotheca selecta*, 2 vols. (Rome: ex Typogr. Apost. Vat., 1593; repr. 1603), bk. 17, chap. 16.

42 Rossi's own *Carmina* had featured, along with six of Giulio Capilupi's *Centones*, in the 1588 edition by Damianus Grana (Professor of Theology at Verona, d. 1596) of Falconia Proba and other Virgilian verse-centonists: *Probæ Falconiæ Hortinæ fœminæ Cl. Cento ex Virgilio In vetus ac novum testamentum*, etc., ed. Damianus Grana and Giulio Rossi (1588)], appended to the *De origine et rebus Faliscorum Liber. Ad Ludovicum Madruccium S.R.E. Cardinalem amplissimum. Et alia aliorum opuscula*, ed. Damianus Grana, 2nd edition (Rome: ex Typogr. Sanctii, & Soc., 1588) of Antonio Massa di/da Gallese (1500–1568).

clariss. adolescentibus Julius Roscius Hortinus S.P.D.," this letter-postface of Rossi's was addressed, moreover, to the grandsons of Lelio and Ippolito's brother Camillo, and it contributed pedagogically to the 1590 Roman volume's rehabilitation and sanitization of the Virgilian *cento*-form.[43] Indeed, Rossi's pedagogic letter would reappear a few years later, together with all of Giulio Capilupi's thirty-one and Lelio's nineteen or so Virgilian *centones*, in the Virgilian verse-*cento* compilations (2 vols., 1597 and 1600, discussed below) of Heinrich Meibom, a Professor of Poetry and History in Helmstedt, crowned poet laureate by Rudolph in 1590.[44]

In Rome, in the *Capiluporum Carmina* of 1590, Lelio's *Centones ex Virgilio* were therefore skillfully presented and re-packaged by his editor-nephew Giulio in juxtaposition with Giulio's own new-style, sanitized corpus of Virgilian *centones*, after what had been virtually twenty-five years of partial censorship since the Tridentine Index of 1564 and after more than three decades since the original Roman universal prohibition of 1557 and 1559. In this endeavor, Giulio was aided and lent authority, moreover, by an influential co-editor from Ancona, linked to the papacy, Giuseppe Castiglione (Josephus Castalio), the poet-humanist and commentator upon Symphosius's *Ænigmata*, often juxtaposed with Proba's Virgilian *Cento*.[45] Giuseppe Castiglione supplied a highly significant admonitory preface "To the Reader" for the section of the *Capiluporum Carmina* devoted to the Virgilian *Centones* of Lelio Capilupi; Castiglione's edito-

---

[43] See Cazes, "Le Livre et la lyre," 120nn1–2.

[44] A poetic coronation marked by the *Laurea poetica ab invictissimo et potentissimo Imperatore, Cæsare Rudolpho II. Aug. Germanico, P.P. Pio, Felici, Henrico Meibomio Lemgoviensi, in IVLIA academia professori publico, virtutis ergô clementissimè donata, & amicorum clarissimorum carissimorumquè scriptis celebrata* (Helmstedt: in officina Iacobi Lucii Transylvani, 1591). On Meibom, his Latin verses, centos and parodies, see Lothar Mundt, ed., "Einleitung," *Heinrich Meibom d.Ä: Poemata selecta—Ausgewählte Gedichte (1579–1614)*, Fruhe Neuzeit 174 (Berlin and Boston: De Gruyter, 2012), xi–xcvii.

[45] See Cazes, "Le Livre et la lyre," 526–30, on Castiglione; Cazes also indicates (597–99, 722–23) that Castiglione's *Ænigmata Symphosii poetæ cum scholiis Iosephi Castalionis Anconitani* (Rome: Franciscus Zanettus, 1581; repr. Aloysius Zanettus, 1597) was bound, in Paris, Bibl. Mazarine A10848, with Proba's *Cento*; works of/on anagrams, acrostichs, palindromic verses; Estienne de Pleurre, *Sancti Victoris Victoria Virgiliocentonibus descripta* (Paris: Denys Langlois, 1610; on St. Victor, where de Pleurre was canon); and two other pseudo-"prophetic" Virgilian *centones*, on Henri III's assassination in 1589 and on Henri de Navarre's accession as Henri IV: *Cassandra, sive Præconium anni 1589 bellorumque in Gallia sequentûm . . . Carmen . . . . . . separatim depromptum ex sola Æneide Virgiliana. Ad Henricum II. Regem Navarræ futurum Francorum . . . 1588*; and *Cento lugubris vel Cenotaphium Henrici Tertii . . . depromptum ex sola Æneide Virgiliana . . . Ad Henricum Quartum . . . 1589* (onomastic anagrams, acrostichs, and prophetic *Carmen figuratum* of twelve hexameters). The last two were published in Andreas Fabri (Le Fèvre), *Centones, cum Diana* (1609), 9–44 and 45–63.

rial apologia speaks volumes about the Counter Reformation climate in Italy and about the problematic status, within that climate, of the *cento*'s re-cycling and re-deployment of Virgil's pagan poetic language:

> Utinam ille [Lælius Capilupus] aut ad Virgilii versus non ita se adstrixisset, aut non tam soluto seculo floruisset. Multa scripsit ut illa tempora ferebant licenter, poetarum etiam more. Centonum quoque coactus legibus nonnulla Virgiliana usurpavit verba, quibus nobis interdictum est. Hæc quamquam non essent Lælii ipsius sed temporis, & facultatis vitia, tamen nostri sæculi gravitas minime ferenda esse censuit. Quare opus illud cæteroquin ingeniosissimum . . . Iulii Capilupi eius nepotis . . . opera & studio quàm maximè fieri potuit expurgatum est. Si qua in eo verba sunt reliqua à nostræ religionis more quae aliena esse videantur vt fata, fortuna, Dii, Divi, Iuppiter, Mars, Venus, & alia huiusmodi meminisse nos oportet Virgilii esse verba, deinde posse per allegoriam aliter accipi . . . . Propter quam difficultatem factum est ut annorum vigintiquinque ferè spatio hi Centones interdicti extiterint. Hoc volebam[,] Lector optime[,] nescius ne esses. Vale.

> Would that he [Lelio Capilupi] had not enslaved himself thus to the verses of Virgil, nor had lived in such a dissolute age! He wrote much after the fashion of poets, certainly, when those times freely accepted such writings. Constrained also by the rules for centos, he made use of several Virgilian words now forbidden us. Although these were not Lelio's own faults, but those of the time, and of eloquence, nevertheless the seriousness of our own age has deemed them unacceptable. Therefore, that work of his, for the rest most ingenious . . . has been expurgated as much as was possible through the care and efforts . . . of his nephew Giulio Capilupi. If there remain in it any words that seem foreign to the usage of our religion, such as *fate*, *fortune*, *gods*, *divinities*, *Jupiter*, *Mars*, *Venus*, and others of this type, we should remember that these are the words of Virgil, and, secondly, that they can be understood differently, allegorically . . . . It is on account of this difficulty that these *Centones* have come to be prohibited [on the Index] over the space of almost twenty-five years. My intention, dearest Reader, was that you should not be ignorant of this. Farewell.[46]

No less revealing of this Counter Reformation climate is the manuscript testimony about Lelio Capilupi's poetic talents and privately wise, virtuous character, written by his nephew Camillo (1531–1603), son of younger brother Camillo and a friend of Lelio's earlier Mantuan editor Possevino.[47] Camillo recounts a

[46] Giuseppe Castiglione (co-ed. with G. Capilupi), "Lectori" ("Lælii Capilupi Centones ex Virgilio"), in *Capiluporum carmina* (1590), 153–250, at 154 (my translation).

[47] See Gaspare De Caro, "CAPILUPI, Camillo," in *Dizionario biografico*, 18:531–35. On the two nephews' (Camillo's and Giulio's) links with the fellow Mantuan Possevino, see Cazes, "Le Livre et la lyre," 532–33.

secret "act of goodness and discernment" by his late uncle "for the salvation of the honor, and for the disburdening, of the soul of a deceased friend:"

> Lelio Capilupi huomo di mirabil giuditio et di rara acutella [~~*belleza*~~] d'ingegno, come si po conoscer dalli xiii centone<*s*> de versi di Virgilio ch' egli compose che fecero stupir al mondo dell'arte et della destrezza dell'ingegno suo, senza che le rime [~~*versi*~~?] scritte da lui fanno anchor fede quanto egli fosse [~~*andasse*~~?] copioso di concetti et polito et culto [~~*osservante*~~] nella lingua Italiana . . . Argomento non tanto della sua bontà quanto della prudenza nel conservar l'honore dell'amico, documento assai raro a ciascuno qual debba esser l'amico vero, et come conviene all'huomo da bene operar sempre integramente cosi quando l'attione e pubblica come quando ha da esser secreta essendo la firma della virtù l'operar bene compiacersi nel fatto, et non nella vanita della gloria . . . come facevano questi che mentre scrivevano i libri de contemnenda gloria vi apponevano il nome loro. cose ordinarie degli Hippocriti et huomini finti che tutte le operationi loro publiche parono santissime le occulte poi diaboliche.[48]
>
> Lelio Capilupi, a man of wonderful judgment and rare sharpness [~~beauty~~] of mind. As one may realise from the *xiii centones* of Virgil's verses composed by him, which astounded the world by the art and skillfulness of his wit, even if the lyric poems [~~verses~~] written by him show how copious he was [~~would be~~] in conceits, and how polished and cultivated [~~observant~~] in the Italian language . . . This tells us not so much about his goodness as about his prudence in safeguarding the honor of a friend, demonstrating to each and all how to be a true friend and how it befits a man ever to act well with integrity in exactly the same way when the deed is public as when it has to be done in secret, for the hallmark of virtue is to do well taking pleasure in the deed itself and not in vain glory . . . as would be the case with those who, while writing books *de contemnenda gloria* ['on despising glory'], would add their names thereunto. Such is the stuff ordinarily of hypocrites and false men, that their public acitivities seem most holy, but their hidden doings are then diabolical.

This poetic-hagiographic account rehabilitates Lelio in parallel, mutually reinforcing ways, literary and ethical, both demonstrating his "judgment" and "sharpness" ("beauty") "of mind." Camillo stresses Lelio's credentials as an ingenious, overt, famous Virgilian centonist, but he also proclaims him to be a "polished"

[48] Camillo Capilupi, "Atto di gran bonta et di avvedimento di Lelio Capilupi per salvezza dell'honor et scarico dell'anima d'un suo amico morto," in MS Rome Bibl. naz. Vitt. Em. 1009 [idem, "Raccolta di aneddoti"], fols. 12v–13v; see Tucker, "Mantua's 'Second Virgil'," 265, 290.

Petrarchist poet in his own right,[49] for Camillo is at pains to correct any imbalance between Lelio's competing reputations as a centonist in Virgilian Latin and as a "cultivated" Petrarchist poet in the vernacular. Camillo goes on, likewise, to portray Lelio's private character as that of a man of genuine moral "virtue" and a "true friend" by stressing the "secret" nature of his deed of "wisdom" and "goodness," contrasting it with religious hypocrites' feigned show of virtue in public, belied by their private vice. Camillo's literary rehabilitation of his centonist-uncle and his moral rehabilitation of the same as a private individual, despite his notoriety as a censored centonist placed on the Index, seem thus to go hand-in-hand, alongside a broader cultural-moral rehabilitation of the Virgilian *cento*-form itself happening in the same period, as we shall see below. Indeed, for Montaigne and for Robert Burton, similarly, the condition for artistic and intellectual acceptance of the overtly derivative and composite *cento*-form itself would be its lack of *textual* hypocrisy.[50]

Giovanni Battista Spada, Successor to and Emulator of Lelio and Giulio Capilupi

Despite Lelio's persistent notoriety and the long shadow cast by the prohibition of his *De vita monachorum*, but in the wake of the noted rehabilitation of Lelio and the Virgilian *cento* by Giulio Capilupi, Giuseppe Castiglione, Antonio Possevino, and others, it was again Lelio who in 1614 would be cited as the key model, together with Giulio, for composing Virgilian Latin verse-centos in the monumental *Succisivarum horarum centones ex Virgilio* ("Virgilian centos of Stolen Hours") of the Catholic theologian and inquisitor Giovanni Battista Spada (Spadius) of Firenzuola (d. c. 1660), a prolific writer of Virgilian religious or ecclesiastical verse-centos in 1606–1628.[51] Moreover, this acknowledgment of

---

[49] Of Lelio's Petrarchist *rime* only three sonnets were *centoni*: "Donne, che ragionando ite per via," "Questa bella d'Amor nemica, & mia," and "Tu che dentro mi vedi, e'l mio mal senti"; see *De le Rime di diversi nobili poeti toscani*, ed. Dionigi Atanagi (Venice: Ludovico Avanzo, 1565), fol. 142r–v, and the latter two sonnets in *Rime del S. Lelio, e fratelli*, 61, 78 / 93, 109. Cf. Hoch, *Apollo*, 321–23, and, more generally, 59–92 on the Petrarchan-Petrarchist *cento*.

[50] See Tucker, "Montaigne et les néo-latins," passim; idem, "Justus Lipsius," passim.

[51] The following published verse-centos are by Spada: 1) *Divi Raimundi a Penafort, ordinis prædicatorum generalis III, vita, ex hemestichiis virgilianis… contexta* (Pavia: Andreas Vianus, 1606, 1607; Piacenza: s.n., 1627); 2) *In Celeberrima mausolei in quo sanctissimum divi patris Dominici corpus conditum est, in honestiorem locum, translatione, de eiusdem divi laudibus cento ex Virgilio* (Pavia: A. Vianus, 1606); 3) *Deiopeia ecloga ex Virgilio, in nuptiis illustrissimorum D.D. Iacobi Auriæ et Brigidæ Spinulæ* (Pavia: A. Vianus, 1606, 1607); 4) [including 1–3] *Succisivarum horarum centones ex Virgilio* (Piacenza: hæredes Io[annis] Baz[achii], 1614); 5) *In Odoardi S.R.E. Cardinalis atque Ranutii Placentiæ, Parmæ &c.*

both Lelio and Giulio Capilupi as the pre-eminent sixteenth-century models for contemporary practice of the Virgilian verse-*cento* was now made in Spada's *cento* volume without any unease about the transposition of a pagan Virgilian poetic language into orthodox Christian verses. For, strengthened by Possevino's intervening *Bibliotheca Selecta* (1593; 1603), Giulio Capilupi's and Castiglione's jointly authoritative editorial rehabilitation of Lelio (and so, of the questionable Virgilian *cento*-form itself) would seem to have made its mark upon Spada's preface-writer of 1614, the Modena-born cabalist Giuseppe Fogliano of Piacenza. In the wake of Ausonius, Rossi, and Possevino, Fogliano supplied an unapologetically laudatory disquisition about Spada's amazing skill in Virgilian *cento*-composition, which recalled and even surpassed for strictness and brilliance Lelio's and Giulio's own exceptional compositional prowess so admired by Possevino, transforming utterly the pagan sense of Virgil's verses. Indeed, according to Fogliano, such an awe-inspiring Christianizing transformation of the original sense of Virgil's words by "Father Spada" was "divinely inspired" and so, implicitly, divinely sanctioned:

> adfui, vidi Centones concinnantem, rei felicitate obstipui: lætatusque sum, quòd ei Virgiliana carmina quasi ultrò deservirent; . . . Virgiliana hemistichia tanquam ad digiti crepitum præsto erant, quibus tam lepidè, & eruditè sententias disponebat, ut Virgilius ipse, alius factus, prope nitidior videretur. Quod si Antonius Possevinus . . . Lælium & Iulium Capilupos mirabiles appellat, eorumque Centones veteribus anteponens laudibus extollit; profectò, si Spadianos lusus vidisset, non omnem laudem Capiluporum studio adiudicaturum fuisse crediderim . . . . Immò . . . ille [Spadius] non omnia, quæ usurparunt alii, sibi licere arbitratus est, qui vel arctiorem sibi legem præscripserit. Quippe cum in alienis Centonibus non modò integri versus legantur, sed hemistichia quoque iis adnectantur: Spadius autem quò recentior, eò ingeniosior, ne versum quidem integrum in tanto volumine usquam adhibuit. Hic de eorum faciendorum ratione quidquam præcipere, ne actum agamus, minimè aggrediemur. Satis enim de iis præ-

---

Ducis, Farnesiorum fratrum ad Placentinos adventu Eridanus ex Virgilio (Piacenza: hæredes Io. Bazachii, 1615); 6) *De Federico Borromæo . . . idyllium ex Virgilio* (Milan: Ioannes Iacobus Comus, 1619; repr. Piacenza: Iac. Ardizzonus, 1628); 7) *De Ludovico Ludovisio S.R.E. cardinali, atque archiepiscopo Bononiensi, idyllium ex Virgilio* (Milan: her. q. Pacifici Pontii & Ioannes Baptista Piccaleus, 1621; repr. Piacenza: Iac. Ardizzonus, 1628); 8) *De Francisco Sacrato S.R.E. cardinali anagrammaton numericorum corona ex Virgilianis conserta flosculis, aliisque numericis lemniscata* (Milan: Iacobus Lantonus, 1621; repr. Piacenza: Iac. Ardizzonus, 1628); 9) *De Nicolao Ludovisio et Isabella Gesualda Venusiæ principp. corona nuptialis ex Virgilio* (Piacenza: typis Alexandri Bazachii, apud Iacobum Ardizzonum, 1622; repr. Piacenza: Iacobus Ardizzonus, 1628); 10) *S.R.E. Triumphus ab Urbano VIII P.O.M. actus Francisco cardinali Barberino . . .* (Piacenza: Iac. Ardizzonus, 1623 and 1628); (11) *De Urbano VIII P.O.M. Erato et Clio ex Virgilio* (Piacenza: Iac. Ardizzonus, 1627); see Cazes, "Le Livre et la lyre," 685, 776–77.

ceperunt primùm Ausonius, tum Iulius Roscius Hortinus, deinde verò Antonius Possevinus: . . . Quæ omnia vel à Virgilio fuisse unquam somniata; vel ex eius scriptis elici potuisse ab ullo putabis? Aut à Patre Spadio divinitùs collecta legens, non obstupesces?

I was there, and saw him [Spada] composing his *Centones*, dumbstruck by the felicity of his composition; I rejoiced that Virgil's verses utterly served his purpose as if of themselves, . . . As if at the snap of his fingers Virgilian half-verses were at his disposal, by means of which he so charmingly and eruditely set out his arguments that Virgil himself, in becoming another, almost appeared more elegant. In fact, if Antonio Possevino . . . calls Lelio and Giulio Capilupi amazing, and praises their *Centones*, preferring them to those of antiquity, certainly, if he had seen Spada's amusements, I believe not all his praise would have been allotted to the studiousness of the Capilupis . . . . Rather, . . . he [Spada] has judged not licit for himself all the licenses employed by others, given that he has prescribed for himself a set of rules, which is even stricter. Since in the *centones* of others not only are complete verses reproduced, but also half verses are joined to these: Spada, however, the more ingenious as he is the more recent, has not even taken over a single complete verse anywhere in so large a volume. We shall not undertake here to teach anything about the method of composing *centones*, lest we do what is already done. For Ausonius firstly, then Giulio Rossi of Orte, and indeed thirdly, Antonio Possevino, have taught about them enough; . . . Would you have thought that all these things were ever dreamt of by Virgil, or could have been elicited from his writings by anyone? Or, on reading them assembled together by Father Spada, through divine inspiration, would you not be dumbstruck?[52]

Heinrich Meibom, Otho Gryphius, and the Centonist Milieu of Emperor Rudolph II

As already noted, Lelio and Giulio Capilupi's *centones* reappeared in the second volume (1600) of two (Helmstedt, 1597 and 1600) of *Virgiliocentones*[53] compiled by Rudolph II's poet laureate of 1590 Heinrich Meibom, and in the Cologne

[52] Giuseppe Fogliano, "Iosephus Folianus Lectori S." [preface], in Spada, *Succisivarum horarum centones ex Virgilio*, fols. A2r–[3]v (fols. 2r–v), [3]v (my translation).

[53] Heinrich Meibom, ed. and author, vol. 1: *Virgilio-centones auctorum notæ optimæ, antiquorum & recentium. Probæ Falconiæ Hortinæ: D. Magni Ausonii, Burdigal.: Lælii Capilupi Mantuani: Iulii Capilupi Mantuani . . . Accesserunt eiusdem Meibomii Centones aliquot uno libro comprehensi* (Helmstedt: excud. Iacobus Lucius, 1597); idem, ed. (with Marx Welser), vol. 2: *Centonum Virgilianorum Tomus alter: Continens Capiluporum Italorum*

1601 reprint of that second volume.[54] Meibom's two volumes also included the *centones* of a new generation of Virgilian verse-centonists associated with the court of Emperor Rudolph II at Vienna and Prague. Meibom's second *cento*-volume contained, notably, a "Protean" Virgilian *cento* (*Vergilius Proteus*) composed by his own patron, the antiquarian historian Marx Welser (Marcus Velserus, 1558–1614), mayor (*Stadtpfleger*) of Augsburg and an admirer of Justus Lipsius, under the pseudonymous anagram "Saulus Mercerus," based on "Marcus Velserus."[55] Similarly, Meibom's first volume paraded his own Virgilian *centones*, notably, "On the single combat of David and Goliath" (1589) and on the

---

centones: Lælii quidem omnes; Iulii eos, qui in priore tomo non extant. His subiunctus est Savli Merceri Augustani [of Marcus Velserus] *Vergilivs Protevs* [dedicatory letter-preface: "Illustri & generoso viro Marco Velsero, Reipublicæ Augustanæ Ex-consuli & septemviro &c. Patrono & Mæcenati meo, S.D. Henricus Meibomius"] (Helmstedt: excud. Iac. Lucius, 1600). In addition to containing "all of Lelio Capilupi's *centones*" and "those of Giulio Capilupi not in the first volume," and "appending" Welser's *cento*-work "Virgil-as-Proteus," this second volume also contains the letter-postface of Giulio Rossi, "Camillo ac Prospero Capulupis clariss. adolescentibus Julius Roscius Hortinus S.P.D.," previously appended to the Roman *Capiluporum Carmina* of 1590 (discussed above).

[54] *Virgilio-centones Probæ Falconiæ Hortinæ, Lælii Julii Capiluporum, et aliorum quorumdam recogniti & purgati, quibus . . . præfixa est epistola Julii Roscii Hortini ad Camillum ac Prosperum Capilupos texendorum centonum præcepta complectens* (Cologne: sumpt. B. Gualtheri, 1601). This volume constitutes Part 2 of Michel Coyssard (Coysardus), re-ed. F. Petit, *P. Virgilii Maronis Opera in locos communes ad Academiæ turnoniæ iuventutis utilitatem digesta . . . Quibus adiecti sunt Virgilio-centones variorum auctorum* (Cologne: sumpt. Bernardi Gualtheri, 1601), catalogued as Paris, Bibl. Nat. Yc-12892 / Yc-12893, Yc-12894, Yc-12895, Rés. P-Yc-1818; and London, BL 1001.b.14(3). This last London copy comprises the 2nd pt only, with different title-pages: *Probæ Falconiæ Hortinæ feminæ clarissimæ Virgilio-centones ab Aldo Manutio olim editi, nunc recogniti* (Cologne: B. Gualtherius, 1601); *Lælii Capilupi Mantuani Virgilio-centones: ante annos aliquot editi, a Iulio Capilupo eius Nepote, nunc recogniti & purgati* (Cologne: B. Gualtherius, 1601); *Iulii Capilupi Mantuani Virgilio-centones triginta & unus* (Cologne: B. Gualtherius, 1601). Cazes, "Le Livre et la lyre," 659–73, 750–58, stresses the pedagogic nature of Coyssard / Petit's 1601 volume with its appended centos as "un recueil sententiel."

[55] On Welser, his Roman antiquarian interests, and links with Lipsius, see Jan Papy, "Lipsius and Marcus Welser: The Antiquarian's Life as *via media*," in *The World of Justus Lipsius: A Contribution towards his Intellectual Biography*, ed. Marc Laureys, *Bulletin de l'Institut Historique belge de Rome* 68 (1998): 173–90; idem, "Justus Lipsius and the German Republic of Letters," in *Germania latina. Latinitas teutonica. Politik, Wissenschaft, humanistische Kultur vom späten Mittelalter bis in unsere Zeit*, ed. Eckhard Kessler and Heinrich C. Kuhn, Humanistische Bibliothek. Texte und Abhandlungen 54 (Munich: W. Fink, 2003), 523–38 (and nn64–66). See Melchior Adam, *Vitæ Germanorum iureconsultorum et politicorum* ([Frankfurt]: heredes Jonæ Rosæ & Heidelberg: Johannes G. Geyder, 1620), 480–82 ("Marcus Velserus").

Austrian Habsburg Emperors (1589).[56] Mention should also be made of Meibom's earlier Virgilian *cento* (1580) "On the ministry and decapitation of St. John the Baptist."[57] Meibom was also the poetic associate of another Virgilian verse-centonist of Prague and Habsburg panegyricist, Jan Černovický (1569–1633).[58]

Meibom's contribution to the *cento*-form in its Virgilian manifestation and, through it, to Habsburg panegyric would be continued by other verse-centonists and imperial poet laureates producing Virgilian centos devoted to Habsburg politics. A key example was Urbanus Hantschmann of Leipzig,[59] who supplied a Virgilian *cento*-apostrophe addressed to the deceased Rudolph II (d. 10 January 1612),[60] as well as a substantial funereal Virgilian *cento* (in 1612 also) on the illness and death on 23 June 1611 of twenty-seven-year-old Christian II, Elector of Saxony.[61]

Parallel to the pro-Habsburg use of the Virgilian *cento*-form as a vehicle for politico-religious reflection, there also ran the current of Reformist religious or political engagement using the same newly fashionable compositional form.

---

[56] Meibom's 1597 volume of *Virgiliocentones* included the following *centones* by him, already published: 1) *Cento Vergilianus De Monomachia Davidis Israelitæ et Goliathi Philistæi* (Helmstedt: excud. Iac. Lucius, 1589); 2) *Imperatorum ac Cæsarum Romanorum ex familia Austriaca oriundorum Descriptiones breves & succinctæ Vergiliano carmine contextæ* (Helmstedt: excud. Iac. Lucius, 1589), which also included (fol. B[1]r) Meibom's *cento* "Ad invictissimos pervetustæ familiæ Austriacæ Cæsares." See Cazes, "Le Livre et la lyre," 98–99.

[57] *Cento Virgilianvs De ministerio & decollatione Iohannis Baptistæ præcursoris Domini* (Helmstedt: Iac. Lucius, 1580).

[58] On Meibom's laudatory *cento*-poetry for the Habsburgs and that of his Prague-educated poetic associate Jan Černovický / Černovský (Czernovicenus / Czernovicius a Lybeo Monte, born Černovice, 1569–1633; cf. Delepierre, *Tableau*, 2:292), see Johannes Amann-Bubenik, "Centodichtung als Habsburg-Panegyrik," *Humanistica Lovaniensia* 48 (1999): 235–50, esp. 240 n50, on Černovický's Habsburg *cento*-volume, *Decas augustissimorum ex amplissima florentissimaque Archiducum Austriæ familia Imperatorum breviter Virgiliano carmine contexta.* (Prague: Typis Schumanianis, 1605), which included a poem of Meibom's. Both Meibom and Černovický wrote Virgilian centos titled "Ad invictissimos pervetustæ familiæ Austriacæ Cæsares Augustos, Romanorum Imperatores."

[59] See Christian G. Jöcher, *Allgemeines Gelehrten-Lexicon*, 4 vols. (Leipzig: Johann F. Gleditsch, 1750–1751), 2: col. 1355: "HANTSCHMANN (Urbanus)," and *Soteria, pro fausto et felici ex Italia in patriam reditu. Clarissimi Viri Dn. VRBANI HANTSCHMANI MISNENSIS, I. V. Doctoris, et Poëtæ Laureati Cæsarei. De quo tristissimus Rumor passim sparsus fuerat, eum miserabili quodam fato interisse* (Leipzig: Abraham Lamberg, 1595), in which Hantschmann, the dedicatee, is styled Imperial poet laureate, and described as safely returned from Italy in 1595 despite rumors of his death.

[60] Urbanus Hantschmann, *Ad Sacratissimos Manes Divi Rudolphi II. Romanorum Imperatoris . . . Apostrophe Cento Virgiliana.* (Leipzig: A. Lamberg, 1612).

[61] Urbanus Hantschmann, *Cupressus Saxonica, Hoc est, De Morbo, Morte, Luctu, & Exequiis . . . Christiani II. Ducis Saxoniæ . . . Historia Integra Cento Virgiliana, Accurato studio descripta* (Leipzig: Valentinus Am Ende, sumpt. Johannis Borneri & Eliæ Rehefeldi, 1612).

A late sixteenth-century example is furnished by the extensive Virgilian *cento*-writing of Otho (Otto) Gryphius of St. Goar, Hessen (1561–1612), a Reformist theologian from Tübingen.[62] Gryphius became Rektor of the Gymnasium Poeticum in Ratisbon (Regensberg), where he composed eight major Virgilian *cento*-works, including, Proba-like, *Virgiliocentones* "Containing the Life of our Saviour Christ" (Ratisbon, 1593),[63] and a piece on "suppliant Hungary," *Hungaria supplex*, for the Imperial Diet of Ratisbon in 1598, addressed to Emperor Rudolph II.[64] His other occasional or celebratory pieces included a quadruple institutional *Cento Virgilianus* for his Gymnasium on "the union of good intention with good fortune," in which Gryphius commends it to "the Senate and People of Ratisbon" and marks its solemn autumn ceremonies of 1591, culminating in a gathering of "men of letters" "in honor of the august, free Imperial City of Ratisbon."[65] Otho Gryphius's other public or celebratory Virgilian *centones* included a congratulatory epithalamium in 1604[66] and a major historical-political piece of 1609, the *Wirtembergias*, a history of the dukes of Württemberg.[67]

Given the above links between the *cento*-form and panegyric surrounding the Habsburg Holy Roman Emperors, it is no coincidence perhaps that even

---

[62] On Gryphius, see Delepierre, *Tableau*, 1:287–301; Jöcher, *Allgemeines Gelehrten-Lexicon*, 2: col. 1226.

[63] Otho Gryphius, *Virgiliocentones continentes Vitam Salvatoris Nostri, Domini Iesu Christi* (Ratisbon: typis excusus ab Andrea Burgero Ratisponensi, 1593). Contemporary and later German Christic Virgilian *centones* include: 1) Johann Andreæ (1554–1601), *Vergilius christianus sive Novum Iesu Christi Testamentum, ad imitationem Vergilii, carminice redditum* (Cologne: Bertramus Bucholtz, 1595): see W. Leonard Grant, "Neo-Latin Verse Translations of the Bible," *The Harvard Theological Review* 52 (1959): 205–11, at 210; and 2) Johann F. Heckel, *Jesus patiens Virgiliani carminis flore convestitus* (s.l.: Baumannianis litteris, 1678; repr. Halle, 1692).

[64] Otho Gryphius, *Pannonia divo Rudolpho secundo, Imperatori Romano . . . & illustrissimis ut & illustribus Imperii Romani ordinibus, A.D. M.D.IIC. Ratisbonam ad Comitia Imperialia evocatis, supplex, habitu ex laciniis Maronis contexto* (Nuremberg: Paulus Kaufmannus, [1598]).

[65] Otho Gryphius, *Cento Virgilianus continens bonorum animi & fortunæ collationem, Gymnasii Poetici S. P. Q. Ratisponensis commendationem, & ad eiusdem IV. Id. Septemb: usque ad VI. Cal. Octob. institutam lustrationem Autumnalem, pridieque Calend. Octob: solennem plantarum Seminarii Ratisponensis γνησίου transpositionem condecorandam, literatissimorum virorum in hac Repub: convocationem, in honorem Augustæ liberæ Imperialisque S.P.Q. Ratisponensium Reipublicæ* ([Ratisbon]: typis excusus ab A. Burgero Ratisponensi, 1591).

[66] Otho Gryphius, *Centone Virgiliano, Ampliss. & doctiss. viro, Dn. Sigismundo Theoph. Richio, Consiliario Brandeburgico, Et Annæ Mariæ Holbecciæ, Virgini pudicissimæ, Sponsis Lectissimis, 24. Aprilis In Electorali Ambergæ combinandis gratulatur Otho Gryphius Goarinus* (s.l.: s.n., 1604).

[67] Otho Gryphius, *Wirtembergias. Hoc est illustrissimorum inclytæ VVirtembergiæ & Tecciæ Ducum, etc. & in ea rerum memorabilium breves descriptiones, Virgiliano carmine confectæ* (Ratisbon: ex typographæo Matthiæ Mylij, 1609).

the surviving engraved portrait of a Reformist verse-centonist such as Gryphius was executed by an artist in the service of Rudolph II, Dominicus Custos (1559/60–1615).[68] Described in that portrait's legend as "aged thirty-three in 1594," Gryphius was presented in its two accompanying Latin elegiac distichs, as a verse-centonist whose poetic "talent" was "approved of" by no less than Hesiod's Ascra and Virgil's Mantua, "beloved of Apollo" (*Ingenium Ascra probat, dilectaq[ue] Mantua Phoebo*). Indeed, it was proven, beyond "doubt," by "either [type of] *cento*" (in Hesiod's Greek or Virgil's Latin) "fulfilling its promise" (*Si dubitas: Cento præstat uterque fidem*). In this eulogistic portrait of Gryphius, any distinction in status or "talent" between poet-author and verse-centonist was thus deemed to have been abolished. The *cento* had come of age.

By way of a coda to this necessarily brief, selective survey of the early modern Virgilian verse-*cento* and of the key exemplars and turning points in its technical conception, historical and socio-literary status, and practice—from Aldus, Erasmus, Scaliger and Estienne to Giuseppe Castiglione, Possevino and Fogliano, from the Capilupis to Otho Gryphius, Meibom and Spada, from Renaissance and Counter Reformation Rome to Reformist France or Germany and turn-of-the-century Habsburg Holy Roman Empire, from controversy and censorship to acceptance as a valid, useful form of "divinely inspired" poetry, consonant with Christianity in its transformative re-cycling of the words and sense of Virgil's pagan language and verses—we can usefully return to the crowning example of "Father" Giovanni Battista Spada. Not just because of Spada's status as a major Latin Virgilian verse-centonist, heir to the Virgilian art of Lelio and Giulio Capilupi; rather, because Spada, alive in that capacity to the unceasing transformations of language and textual matter that characterized the *cento*-form (as but one manifestation of the mutability and flux that also characterized the

[68] Dominicus Custos, portrait of Otho Gryphius (1561–1612) [Regensburger Porträtsammlung, Sign: 9994/PoS MF No. 1985]: (Top left) ÆT[*ATIS*]. *SVÆ*. | *XXXIII*. || *A*[*NNO*]. *D*. *XCIV*. || (Bottom left) *D*[*ominicus*] *C*[*ustos*] *sculp*[*tor*]. || (Bottom Right) *N. Regius M. f.* || (Beneath Portrait) *In effigiem Cl. Et Doctiss. Viri. D. M. Othonis Gryphii:* | *Goarini, Catti. Poetici Ratisponensiv*[*m*] *Gymnasii Rectoris.* || *Cùm faciem spectes: facie datur Otho serena* | *Gryphius! Hassiaci viuida fama soli.* | *Ingeniu*[*m*] *Ascra probat, dilectaq*[*ue*] *Mantua Phoebo:* | *Si dubitas: Cento præstat uterq*[*ue*] *fidem*. ["When you look at this face, you see, of serene countenance, Otho | Gryphius! The living glory of the Hessian land. | [Hesiod's] Ascra and [Virgil's] Mantua, beloved of Apollo, approve of his talent; | If you doubt that, either *cento* fulfills the promise."] On Custos, see Walter Dietl, *Die Elogien der Ambraser Fürstenbildnisse: Die Kupferstiche des Dominicus Custos (1599): Leben und Werk ihres Autors Marcus Henning*, Commentationes Aenipontanæ 32, Tirolensia Latina II (Innsbruck: Universitätsverlag Wagner, 2000).

whole terrestrial world of matter), went on in 1648 to compile and publish a thesaurus of Italian epithets, in which just such an awareness of the protean mutability of all matter surfaced, significantly, in one of its entries (on *polpo,* "octopus," and its epithets). Spada furnished there a striking image, drawn from a linked pair of French-Italian cosmological intertexts, by which we might usefully grasp and represent to ourselves the similarly protean nature of the *cento*-form in general, in both its mutability and adaptability, and in its particular Virgilian manifestation surveyed here.

It was Guillaume Du Bartas's *La Sepmaine ou Creation du Monde* (1578)—in the passage describing the uniquely "eternal" "matter" of the universe as "wax" because "more-than-Protean" in its unceasing transformations, albeit "eternal" and "immutable" in its material "essence": "La Matiere du monde est céte cire informe | . . . | Mais la seule Matiere immortele demeure" ("Second Jour," lines 197, 206)—that supplied the verses to Spada for an appropriate epithet to use for his entry on *polpo*; these verses compared that quintessentially protean world of change to octopuses on the sea-shore:

> Immuable d'essance, & muable de front
> Plus que n'est un Prothée, & plus qu'encor ne sont
> Les poulpes cauteleus, qui sur l'ondeus rivage
> Changent pour butiner châque heure de visage.[69]
>
> Immutable in its essence, but changeable in its aspect
> More than a Proteus, and even more than
> The cunning octopi, which on the wave-swept shore,
> In order to prey, change at each moment their appearance.

More precisely, these verses of Du Bartas's were cited by Spada from the Italian translation of Ferrante Guisone, Mantua's ambassador in Paris (1575–1597).[70] In his *Giardino de gli epiteti* ("Garden of epithets") of 1648 and 1665, Spada thus drafted his lemma on the substantive *polpo* by applying to it the epithet *astuto* ("crafty"; "wily") culled from Guisone's Italian rendering (*gli astuti* | *Polpi*; "the wily octopi") of Du Bartas's marvelously camouflaged *poulpes cauteleus* ("cunning [dissembling] octopi"):

> Polpo, e polipo. *Spetie di pesce senza scaglie.* Astuto. *Guis*[oni]. *Immutabil d'essenza, mà di faccia | Via più che Proteo varia, e che gli astuti | Polpi, i*

[69] Guillaume de Salluste, seigneur Du Bartas, *La Sepmaine, ou creation du monde, de Guillaume de Salluste, Seigneur du Bartas* (Paris: Jean Fevrier, 1578), 33: "Second Jour," lines 211–14.

[70] G. Du Bartas, *La Divina Settimana*, trans. Ferrante Guisone (Guisoni) (Tours: Giametto Metaieri [Jamet Mettayer], 1592; repr. Venice: Giovanni B. Ciotti, 1593 and 1613).

> *quai per predar lungo le rive | Hor questo volto, hor quel prendendo vanno. D[ivina] Sett[imana] 2.*[71]
>
> Octopus. A kind of fish without scales. *Wily.* Guisoni. 'Immutable in its essence, but in its aspect | More changeable than Proteus himself, and than the wily | octopi, who, in order to prey along the shores, | Continually change their appearance, from this to that.'

In Du Bartas's French poem, as in Guisone's Italian version of it, these "cunning octopi" had been explicitly used to symbolize the myriad transformations and adaptations of cosmic "matter," and so arguably, by extension, of textual poetic matter. If, for Du Bartas, such an octopus-like, "crafty," "dissembling" nature had characterized the "eternal" ever changing "matter" of the physical world, this would have been no less true of the textual universe of words and verse-fragments for a *cento*-author or encyclopedic collector-compiler of Italian verse fragments such as Spada.

Indeed, one can imagine that for the strict Virgilian verse-centonist Spada, as for looser prose-centonists such as Burton, Lipsius, Montaigne, or as for Spada's models Giulio and Lelio Capilupi, the universe's unceasing adaptations and transformations, ever taking new form from an enduring finite body of matter, would have inevitably thus constituted a cosmological paradigm for the similarly "crafty," "octopus"-like transformations and adaptations of textual matter and its meanings that were the hallmark of the *cento*-form.

This would never have been more obviously or aptly the case than in the early modern age of Virgil's multiple rebirth(s) through the successive textual recyclings and re-incarnations of the Virgilian verse-*cento*: from Proba and Ausonius in late antiquity and from the Capilupis in the Italian High Renaissance to the new golden age of the Virgilian verse-*cento* at the close of the sixteenth century and at the beginning of the seventeenth century, embodied by a Gryphius, by a Meibom, or by a Spada, and by their many fellows and heirs.

---

[71] Giovanni Battista Spada, *Giardino de gli epiteti, traslati, et aggiunti poetici* (Bologna: l'erede di Vittorio Benacci, 1648 [and 1665]), 685, col. 2, where Spada quotes Guisone's rendering of Du Bartas from its 1613 edition; the Guisone 1592 edition varies: ". . . i quai per *far* lungo le rive | *Lor prede, prendon mille vari aspetti*"; ". . . which along the shores, in order to | Hunt their prey, take on a thousand different appearances."

12

Virgil and the Idea of a Renaissance

L. B. T. Houghton[1]
University of Reading

That engagement with the poetry of Virgil formed a persistent and pervasive thread in European culture during the period traditionally known as the Renaissance has long been established. Some of the contexts in which the Roman poet's works were appropriated, adapted, and interpreted are revealed by the studies of Vladimiro Zabughin, Craig Kallendorf, and David Wilson-Okamura,[2] while the depth and breadth of Renaissance interactions with the *Eclogues*, *Georgics*, and *Aeneid* will be readily apparent from the papers that make up the rest of this collection. The present study considers an aspect of Virgil's reception in the Renaissance that has received rather less attention, although it has potentially important implications for the entire historiography of the period in question: namely, the contribution made by poetic imagery derived from the work of Virgil and, in particular, from one especially influential section of the Virgilian corpus, the fourth Eclogue, to contemporary formulations of the concept of the Renaissance itself. I shall not be concerned here with how far that paradigm represents an accurate reflection of historical reality: that perennially contentious subject has been raked over so thoroughly that it is difficult to see how anything sub-

---

[1] My thanks to Marco Sgarbi, Alexander Lee, and other participants in the Mantua conference of October 2012, generously hosted by the Accademia Nazionale Virgiliana di Scienze Lettere e Arti; also to the Warburg Institute, where much of the research for this chapter was carried out, for the award of a Frances A. Yates visiting fellowship in early 2011.

[2] Vladimiro Zabughin, *Vergilio nel rinascimento italiano*, 2 vols. (Bologna: Zanichelli, 1921–1923; repr. Trento: Editrice Università degli studi di Trento, 2000); Craig Kallendorf, *In Praise of Aeneas: Virgil and Epideictic Rhetoric in the Early Italian Renaissance* (Hanover, NH and London: University Press of New England, 1989); idem, *Virgil and the Myth of Venice. Books and Readers in the Italian Renaissance* (Oxford: Oxford University Press, 1999); David Scott Wilson-Okamura, *Virgil in the Renaissance* (Cambridge: Cambridge University Press, 2010). See also the bibliographical survey in the introduction to this volume.

stantially new can be added to the debates that have raged over the nature, duration, and extent of the episode or movement generally designated by the term Renaissance.[3] Rather, I shall argue that, whatever the validity of the Renaissance as a conceptual template, the ways in which this idea was articulated by commentators at the time are heavily (though not exclusively) indebted to the long tradition of encomia modeled on Virgil's declaration of epochal renewal, which was already profoundly embedded in the literary and political culture of Italy and beyond centuries before the first glimmerings of Renaissance humanism, whenever we may suppose these to have appeared. Although the appropriation of Virgil's poem by partisans of the Medici in Florence forms the subject of a short but deservedly celebrated article by E. H. Gombrich,[4] the position occupied by the fourth Eclogue in the development and proliferation of a theory of temporal and cultural rebirth has not always been sufficiently recognized by historians of the Renaissance,[5] with the result that previous assessments of contemporary "awareness" of the phenomenon have arguably failed to take full account of the literary and intellectual contexts that underlie the humanists' assertions of the onset of a new age, an appreciation of which might add significant nuances to our understanding of these authors' presentation of themselves and their historical situation, and of how that self-presentation should be interpreted by modern scholars.

Let me repeat at the outset that I do not intend to pass judgment here on whether or not the Renaissance as traditionally defined ever actually occurred, or to speculate on what form it might have taken; nor am I interested for the purposes of this investigation in how far those who promulgated the concept of a Renaissance genuinely believed their own claims of revival and regeneration, or expected their intended audiences to accept such claims at face value.[6]

---

[3] For an historical overview, see Wallace K. Ferguson, *The Renaissance in Historical Thought: Five Centuries of Interpretation* (New York: Houghton Mifflin Co., 1948; repr. Toronto, Buffalo, and London: University of Toronto Press, 2006); also *Zu Begriff und Problem der Renaissance*, ed. August Buck (Darmstadt: Wissenschaftliche Buchgesellschaft, 1969), esp. 1–36; William Kerrigan and Gordon Braden, *The Idea of the Renaissance* (Baltimore and London: The Johns Hopkins University Press, 1989).

[4] E. H. Gombrich, "Renaissance and Golden Age," *Journal of the Warburg and Courtauld Institutes* 24 (1961): 306–9; repr. in Gombrich, *Norm and Form: Studies in the Art of the Renaissance* (London: Phaidon, 1966), 29–34.

[5] See however Buck, ed., *Zu Begriff und Problem*, 2, 5; note also Harry Levin, *The Myth of the Golden Age in the Renaissance* (London: Faber and Faber, 1970), 145, "The conception of a Renaissance itself, the metaphor of renascence, was derived from the evangelical doctrine of rebirth and had its harbingers in Dante and Petrarch. It came into its own when it was blended with the Vergilian rhetoric of congratulation at the Medici courts."

[6] On contemporary attitudes towards (or "awareness of") the phenomenon of the Renaissance, see especially B. L. Ullman, "Renaissance—The Word and the Underlying Concept," *Studies in Philology* 49 (1952): 105–18 (repr. in Ullman, *Studies in the Italian Renaissance*, 2nd ed. [Rome: Edizioni di Storia e Letteratura, 1973], 11–26); M. L.

It cannot be denied, moreover, that the range of metaphors used to express the renewal of classical antiquity extends far beyond the vocabulary employed by Virgil to celebrate the wonders that will be set in motion by the consulship of Pollio: return from exile, awakening from a lengthy period of sleep, resurrection from the dead, and excavation from burial in the dim recesses of the earth are all standard images in humanist writing for the recovery of ancient culture,[7] and display no obvious obligation to the distinctive imagery of the messianic eclogue. But it is nonetheless inescapable, as I hope to demonstrate in the examples that follow, that adoption and manipulation of the language and symbolism of Virgil's poem is a significant and immediately recognizable feature of many of the most emphatic declarations of temporal rebirth, and this element should be acknowledged as a characteristic and recurring expression of the mental habits and the cultural milieu that generated—or at least gave such widespread currency to—the idea of a Renaissance.

Furthermore, this use of the fourth Eclogue has a long and distinguished pedigree stretching back to antiquity itself, the progress of which can be witnessed from almost immediately after the composition of the poem and continued throughout the centuries of imperial rule at Rome, beyond the fall of the city to waves of invasion by Huns, Goths, and Vandals, and into what might now be called the early Middle Ages.[8] With the institution of the Holy Roman Empire

McLaughlin, "Humanist Concepts of Renaissance and Middle Ages in the Tre- and Quattrocento," *Renaissance Studies* 2 (1988): 131–42; Cesare Vasoli, "Il concetto di *Renascentia* nelle prime generazioni umanistiche," in *Saeculum tamquam aureum: Internationales Symposion zur italienischen Renaissance des 14.-16. Jahrhunderts am 17./18. September 1996 in Mainz*, ed. Ute Ecker and Clemens Zintzen (Hildesheim: Olms, 1997), 39–57; Andreas Kablitz, "Renaissance—Wiedergeburt. Zur Archäologie eines Epochennamens (Giorgio Vasari—Jules Michelet)," ibid., 59–108; Alejandro Coroleu, "On the Awareness of the Renaissance," in *Il latino nell'età dell'Umanesimo. Atti del convegno di Mantova, 26–27 ottobre 2001*, ed. Giorgio Bernardi Perini (Florence: Olschki, 2004), 3–15; Jon Usher, "Metempsychosis and 'Renaissance' between Petrarch and Boccaccio," *Italian Studies* 60 (2005): 121–33. For discussion of the sincerity or otherwise of those claims, see, e.g., Erwin Panofsky, *Renaissance and Renascences in Western Art* (Stockholm: Almqvist & Wiksell, 1960; repr. New York: Harper & Row, 1972), 1–41; Levin, *The Myth of the Golden Age*, 144–45; Henry Kamen, "Golden Age, Iron Age: A Conflict of Concepts in the Renaissance," *The Journal of Medieval and Renaissance Studies* 4 (1974): 135–55.

[7] On these and other metaphors see Ullman, "Renaissance"; T. M. Greene, *The Light in Troy: Imitation and Discovery in Renaissance Poetry* (New Haven and London: Yale University Press, 1982), 30–33, 92–93; McLaughlin, "Humanist Concepts"; Vasoli, "Il concetto di *Renascentia*."

[8] For some echoes and adaptations, see Symmachus, *Orationes*, 3.9; Claudian, *In Rufinum*, 1.45–57, 372–87; Sidonius Apollinaris, *Carmina*, 2.102–15; Venantius Fortunatus, *Carmina*, 6.2.41–48.

and the cultural resurgence of the so-called Carolingian Renaissance, the fourth Eclogue's proclamation of the return of the Golden Age was being channeled in much the same way as it had been to salute the accession of successive Roman emperors;[9] and the successors of Charlemagne, however brief their ascendancy and however exiguous their accomplishments turned out to be, were regularly hailed with prophecies of universal regeneration couched in similar terms.[10] The application of Virgilian eulogy to contemporary dignitaries conferred on the recipients of such accolades the cultural prestige that attached in the eyes of later ages to the exemplary incarnation of the imperial ideal, the great Augustus, and asserted the return of ancient glories to the modern world through the process of *translatio* or *renovatio imperii.*[11] When Peter of Eboli in the late twelfth century greeted the newborn boy who was destined to become the Emperor Frederick II as *Iovis proles, Romani nominis heres,* | *Inmo reformator orbis et inperii* ("Jove's offspring, heir of the Roman name—nay, refashioner of the world and the empire"), and affirmed that under his father Henry VI *iam redit aurati Saturnia temporis etas,* | *iam redeunt magni regna quieta Iovis* ("Now the Saturnian age of gilded time returns, now the tranquil reign of great Jove returns"),[12] the poet's choice of literary models was dictated by the presumed Augustan associations of the ancient archetype. Whether or not Virgil's lines were originally intended to allude to Octavian, later Augustus, is of course an entirely different question, but his candidacy for the status of the miraculous child of the eclogue had been proposed at an early date, and was encouraged by the poet himself through his

---

[9] For a tabulated survey, see Bodo Gatz, *Weltalter, goldene Zeit und sinnverwandte Vorstellungen* (Hildesheim: Olms, 1967), 138–39.

[10] See, e.g., Walahfrid Strabo on Louis the Pious: *Aurea, quae prisci dixerunt saecula vates* | *Tempore, magne, tuo, Caesar, venisse videmus* ("the age which the ancient poets called golden we see has come in your time, great Caesar"): *Monumenta Germaniae Historica: Poetae Latini Aevi Carolini*, vol. 2, ed. Ernst Dümmler (Berlin: Weidmann, 1884), 373, ll 94–95.

[11] On *translatio imperii* see especially Werner Goez, *Translatio Imperii. Ein Beitrag zur Geschichte des Geschichtsdenkens und der politischen Theorien im Mittelalter und in der frühen Neuzeit* (Tübingen: Mohr, 1958); J. G. A. Pocock, *Barbarism and Religion, vol. 3: The First Decline and Fall* (Cambridge: Cambridge University Press, 2003), 127–50; Cary J. Nederman, *Lineages of European Political Thought* (Washington, DC: The Catholic University of America Press, 2009), 177–89.

[12] Peter of Eboli, *Liber ad honorem Augusti*, 1411–1412, 1512–1513. For the text see *Il* Liber ad honorem Augusti *di Pietro da Eboli*, ed. Giovanni Battista Siragusa (Rome: Forzani, 1906); also *Petri Ansolini de Ebulo de rebus Siculis carmen*, ed. Ettore Rota (Città di Castello: Lapi, 1904); on the Virgilian echoes in Peter's verses, see Teresa Sampieri, "La cultura letteraria di Pietro da Eboli," in *Studi su Pietro da Eboli* (Rome: Istituto storico italiano per il Medio Evo, 1978), 67–87; F. J. E. Raby, *A History of Secular Latin Poetry in the Middle Ages*, 2 vols. (Oxford: Clarendon Press, 1957), 2:168 ("a kind of Messianic eclogue").

reworking of the eclogue to pay tribute to the reign of Augustus in the parade of Roman heroes in *Aeneid* 6.[13]

That such imagery was still current in the rhetoric of imperial homage in the early fourteenth century is apparent from Dante's famous letter to the Emperor Henry VII, in which the author encourages his addressee to extend his intervention in Italian affairs by telling him that on the occasion of the emperor's earlier incursion into the peninsula "very many people, anticipating their wishes in their joy, began to sing with Maro both of the reign of Saturn and of the Virgin returning" (*plerique vota sua praevenientes in iubilo, tam Saturnia regna quam Virginem redeuntem cum Marone cantabant*)[14]—and indeed, Dante based his theoretical justification of the principle of imperial monarchy itself on a reading of the sixth line of *Eclogue* 4.[15] But what has this to do with the Renaissance? After all, nowhere in the fourth Eclogue does Virgil actually use the Latin verb *renasci*, to be reborn, unlike Horace, whose observation on the mutability of linguistic usage is quoted in a truncated form by Wilson-Okamura as an epigraph to his study of Virgil's fortunes in the Renaissance.[16] It does occur, however, in precisely the kind of laudatory context in which we shall find it being used in later centuries, in two subsequent passages of Latin poetry,[17] in each of which the latent presence of Virgil can be inferred from the surrounding lines, although it is likely that the later of these two texts also engages with the other, earlier formulation. The first of these instances appears in the eclogues of Calpurnius Siculus, an antique pastoral poet of disputed date,[18] who, in complimenting either Nero

[13] See Virgil, *Aeneid*, 6.791–94.

[14] Dante, *Epistolae*, 7.1; for the text of the letter see *Dantis Alagherii epistolae. The Letters of Dante*, ed. Paget Toynbee (Oxford: Clarendon Press, 1966), 82–105. For discussion see, e.g., Gustavo Costa, *La leggenda dei secoli d'oro nella letteratura italiana* (Bari: Laterza, 1972), 6; Frances A. Yates, *Astraea: The Imperial Theme in the Sixteenth Century* (London: Routledge and Kegan Paul, 1975), 11, 37.

[15] See *De monarchia*, 1.11.1–2, text and translation in *Dante: Monarchia*, ed. and trans. Prue Shaw (Cambridge: Cambridge University Press, 1995); discussed by, e.g., Yates, *Astraea*, 9–10, 36–37; Marie Tanner, *The Last Descendant of Aeneas: The Hapsburgs and the Mythic Image of the Emperor* (New Haven and London: Yale University Press, 1993), 92–93.

[16] Wilson-Okamura, *Virgil in the Renaissance*, v; cf. Horace, *Ars poetica*, 70–71. The verb occurs only once in the Virgilian corpus, in the participial form *renatis* at *Aeneid*, 6.600, where it is used of the eternally self-regenerating liver of the tormented sinner Tityos in the underworld.

[17] The participle *renascens* also appears in conjunction with an allusion to the return of a Saturnian age at [Seneca], *Octavia*, 394–96.

[18] For the debate see Edward Champlin, "The Life and Times of Calpurnius Siculus," *The Journal of Roman Studies* 68 (1978): 95–110; G. B. Townend, "Calpurnius Siculus and the *Munus Neronis*," *The Journal of Roman Studies* 70 (1980): 166–74 (with Roland Mayer's note in the same issue, 175–76); T. P. Wiseman, "Calpurnius Siculus and the

or an emperor of the Severan dynasty, observes the return to earth of *alma Themis* and proclaims *aurea secura cum pace renascitur aetas* ("the Golden Age is born again together with untroubled peace").[19] The second is to be found in an eclogue by the Carolingian bishop and court poet Modoin, who puts into the mouth of one of his speakers the assertion that through the triumphs of Charlemagne *aurea Roma iterum renovata renascitur orbi* ("Golden Rome, renewed once more, is reborn to the world").[20] Now it seems quite probable that Modoin's line, with its initial *aurea* and penultimate *renascitur*, is modeled principally on the hexameter of Calpurnius, rather than referring directly to the messianic eclogue, although the second part of Modoin's poem arguably does contain recollections of the latter.[21] But where did Calpurnius get his terminology? Given the apparent echoes of Virgil's piece in this verse and in the lines immediately following, it is not unreasonable to suggest that Calpurnius's *renascitur* is a modification of the emphatic fifth line of the fourth Eclogue, which announces the beginning of a new cycle of ages: *magnus ab integro saeclorum nascitur ordo* ("the great sequence of the ages is born anew"). It is no great distance from Virgil's phrase *ab integro . . .nascitur* ("is born anew") to the compound verb *renascitur* ("is reborn"), and so even if Modoin's expression derives primarily from the Calpurnian model (in addition to drawing on vocabulary from Ovid and Claudian), the ultimate origin of this imagery of renaissance is the very prominent proclamation of temporal "rebirth" in one of the most celebrated passages in the work of the most canonical poet of antiquity.

There is considerable precedent, therefore, in literature prior to the era of the Renaissance for appropriation of the language of the fourth Eclogue to assert in a celebratory fashion the birth of a new age, and variations on the expression and dominant motifs of Virgil's poem pass through countless permutations in encomiastic settings during the centuries between antiquity and the age of the humanists. It is perhaps partly for this reason that reports and revelations of the return of the Golden Age, or of the reign of Saturn, appear with such regularity—even, it should probably be admitted, with such monotony—in the panegyrical productions of the Italian courts and beyond during the period with which

Claudian Civil War," *The Journal of Roman Studies* 72 (1982): 57–67; E. Courtney, "Imitation, chronologie littéraire et Calpurnius Siculus," *Revue des Études Latines* 65 (1987): 148–57; Barry Baldwin, "Better Late than Early: Reflections on the Date of Calpurnius Siculus," *Illinois Classical Studies* 20 (1995): 157–67; Nicholas Horsfall, "Criteria for the Dating of Calpurnius Siculus," *Rivista di Filologia e di Istruzione Classica* 125 (1997): 166–96.

[19] Calpurnius, *Eclogues*, 1.42–45.

[20] Modoin, *Eclogues*, 1.27.

[21] See R. P. H. Green, *Seven Versions of Carolingian Pastoral* (Reading: Department of Classics, Reading University, 1980), 73 ("A powerful combination of Calpurnius, Claudian and Ovid"); also Helen Cooper, *Pastoral: Mediaeval into Renaissance* (Ipswich: Brewer, 1977), 10–12.

we are here concerned. Indeed, it is striking how many "Renaissance" authors cite material (primarily the sixth and seventh lines) directly from the text of the fourth Eclogue or incorporate Virgilian imagery in their writing by means of the closest possible paraphrase. Giovanni Boccaccio has often been seen as one of the earliest cheerleaders of the Italian Renaissance, not least for his acclamation of his friend and correspondent Petrarch as the latter-day reviver of the civilization of the ancients.[22] And how does Boccaccio express the contemporary sense of this accomplishment, heralding the dawn of a restoration of letters and learning, in his biography of Petrarch? *id nempe omnibus visum puto, iam multo ante lapsa felicia tempora ac regna saturnia rediisse* ("I think that it undoubtedly seemed to everyone that the happy times, which by then had ended long before, and the reign of Saturn had returned").[23] There can be no doubt at all that in the last three words of this statement, Boccaccio is alluding to Virgil's famous announcement of the return of *Saturnia regna* in the sixth line of *Eclogue* 4. Again, when Boccaccio writes to Iacopo Pizzinga in 1372 in praise of the part played by the latter in promoting contemporary poetry to a position of prestige comparable to that which it had enjoyed in ancient Rome, the terms he uses to applaud this achievement, allowing for a minor modification or misrecollection of the exact wording of the first half of the Virgilian line, are more or less a direct quotation of *Eclogues* 4.6: *et ego, choris immixtus festantium tuumque nomen meritis laudibus extollentium, canam: Iam virgo rediit, redeunt saturnia regna* ("and I, in the midst of the throngs of those celebrating and exalting your name with the praises you deserve, shall sing: Now the virgin has returned, the reign of Saturn returns").[24]

---

[22] See, e.g., Denys Hay, *The Italian Renaissance in its Historical Background*, 2nd ed. (Cambridge: Cambridge University Press, 1977), 93–95; Jane E. Everson, *The Italian Romance Epic in the Age of Humanism: The Matter of Italy and the World of Rome* (Oxford: Oxford University Press, 2001), esp. 21 ("Boccaccio too, though not glorified with the title of father of Humanism, is one of the earliest exponents of the ideals, practices, and aspirations of the humanists and the *studia humanitatis*"). For a recent argument for Boccaccio's status as a guiding light of the Renaissance, see Michaela Paasche Grudin and Robert Grudin, *Boccaccio's Decameron and the Ciceronian Renaissance* (New York: Palgrave Macmillan, 2012), and on Boccaccio and the Petrarchan Renaissance, see Usher, "Metempsychosis and 'Renaissance'."

[23] Boccaccio, *De vita et moribus Domini Francisci Petracchi de Florentia*, 16–17; for the text see Giovanni Boccaccio, *Opere latine minori*, ed. Aldo Francesco Massèra (Bari: Laterza, 1928), 241. Boccaccio's use of Virgilian imagery here is discussed by Martin Eisner, *Boccaccio and the Invention of Italian Literature* (Cambridge: Cambridge University Press, 2013), 25 ("Boccaccio's use of Virgil's fourth eclogue in this letter is quite extraordinary") and 136n110; also Tobias Foster Gittes, *Boccaccio's Naked Muse: Eros, Culture, and the Mythopoeic Imagination* (Toronto, Buffalo, and London: University of Toronto Press, 2008), 52.

[24] Boccaccio, *Epistole*, 18; for the text see Boccaccio, *Opere latine minori*, 197. Discussion in Eisner, *Boccaccio*, 25; Gittes, *Boccaccio's Naked Muse*, 246n3; Buck, *Zu Begriff*, 5.

Even Boccaccio, however, was a relatively late arrival on the scene when it came to exploiting the millenarian symbolism of the fourth Eclogue to endorse a particular view of the present state of affairs. Earlier in the fourteenth century the tribune Cola di Rienzo, who in his enthusiasm for the revival of antique customs and institutions has sometimes been seen as a forerunner of certain tendencies later manifested by the champions of humanist culture,[25] had written from Avignon to the Senate and People of Rome, relating in portentous tones the pope's authorization of the Jubilee for 1350:[26]

> Precipua tamen et speciali veneracione alma sancta Roma prorumpat in laudes, et tantorum filiorum adopcione fecunda iam Virginem et Saturnia regna redire et agnum Dei in apostolico trono sedentem mundi scelus auferre supplici devocione proclamet.

> With particular and special veneration, however, let nurturing holy Rome burst forth into praises, and let her proclaim with humble devotion that through the fruitful adoption of so many sons the Virgin and the reign of Saturn are now returning and the lamb of God sitting on his apostolic throne is taking away the sin of the world.

If the reference here to the return of the Virgin and the restoration of the reign of Saturn—as might be expected in view of the occasion of Cola's bulletin—evokes primarily the religious connotations that by this date had long attached to Virgil's "messianic" verses,[27] it is nonetheless difficult not to detect in the tribune's proclamation of a new era a suggestion of his own wider program of political and civic renewal, particularly since Rienzo elsewhere explicitly rejects the Christianizing interpretation of the Virgilian passage.[28] And given the adoption of this imagery by Rienzo himself, it is surely no accident that Petrarch, who had at one stage lent his support to the revolutionary's activities, should have had recourse to the same model when referring to Rienzo's ill-fated enterprise, even after his initial sympathy for the cause had faded.[29] In a letter of November 1353

---

[25] For an overview of scholarship, see Ronald G. Musto, *Apocalypse in Rome: Cola di Rienzo and the Politics of the New Age* (Berkeley, Los Angeles, and London: University of California Press, 2003), 1–20.

[26] Rienzo, *Epistulae*, 1.6–10; text in *Briefwechsel des Cola di Rienzo*, ed. Konrad Burdach and Paul Piur, 5 vols. (Berlin: Weidmann, 1912–1929), 3:1–2. For discussion see, e.g., Musto, *Apocalypse in Rome*, 73.

[27] See the introduction to this volume, note 3.

[28] See Rienzo, *Epistulae*, 70.262–68 (Burdach, ed., *Briefwechsel*, 3:393). On Rienzo and the fourth Eclogue, see Costa, *La leggenda*, 15–20; Zabughin, *Vergilio nel rinascimento italiano*, 1:39.

[29] On Petrarch and Rienzo, see especially Mario Emilio Cosenza, *Francesco Petrarca and the Revolution of Cola di Rienzo* (Chicago: University of Chicago Press, 1913; 2nd ed.,

to the Emperor Charles IV, Petrarch notes the effect produced at Rome by a figure of so little social distinction as Rienzo, thereby encouraging Charles's own involvement in Italian politics, which might be expected to yield greater results; his somewhat optimistic account of what had appeared to be the establishment of a new order under the self-proclaimed tribune glosses Virgil's returning *Virgo* as *iustitia*, in accordance with the interpretation of this figure given by Servius in his commentary on the line, and joins her supposed reappearance on earth—as later adaptations of the fourth Eclogue regularly do—with that of *pax* and *fides*, whose association with the inception of a new *saeculum* is broadcast in Horace's *Carmen saeculare* (57–60) and in the prophecy of Jupiter in the opening book of the *Aeneid* (1.291–93). The climax of this utopian pageant is the emergence of *vestigia* of the Golden Age itself, foreshadowing the fulfillment of the new dispensation that Rienzo was unable to bring to completion, but which might very well ensue, Petrarch implies, from further exertions on the part of the emperor:[30]

> Nudiustertius caput extulit quidam e plebe humili, non romanus rex, non consul, non patritius, et vix bene cognitus romanus civis, nullis titulis suorum, nullis maiorum imaginibus, denique nullis ad id tempus virtutibus suis clarus, qui vindicem se romane libertatis assereret: obscuri hominis clara professio. Illico, ut scis, Tuscia cupide manus dedit, imperia excepit. Iam sensim omnis Italia sequebatur, iam Europa, iam totus orbis in motu erat. Quid multis est opus? non legimus ista, sed vidimus; iam rediisse iustitia et pax et harum comites, alma fides, tranquilla securitas, ad postremum aurei seculi vestigia videbantur.

> Only the day before yesterday someone from the lowly masses lifted up his head—not a king of Rome, nor a consul, nor a patrician, and scarcely a well-known Roman citizen, not distinguished by any titles held by his people, by any portraits of his ancestors, or even by any qualities of his own up to that time—to claim for himself the part of champion of Rome's liberty: the glorious declaration of an obscure man. Straightaway, as you know, Tuscany eagerly gave in, and submitted to orders. Now little by little all Italy was starting to follow, now Europe, now the whole world was in motion. What need to go on at length? We haven't read about these things—we've seen them; now justice and peace and their companions, kindly good faith, unruffled security, and ultimately the traces of the Golden Age, seemed to have returned.

New York: Italica Press, 1986); Innocente Toppani, "Petrarca, Cola di Rienzo e il mito di Roma," *Atti dell'Istituto Veneto di Scienze Lettere ed Arti* 135 (1977): 155–72.

30 Petrarch, *Rerum familiarium libri*, 18.1.17–18; text from Francesco Petrarca, *Le familiari*, ed. Vittorio Rossi and Umberto Bosco, 4 vols. (Florence: Sansoni, 1933–1942), 3:268.

If Rienzo's spectacular schemes to restore the values and usages of antiquity in the political arena came to nothing, assertions of a revival of classical ideals in the sphere of learning and culture have proved more enduring. In any consideration of the evolution of Renaissance scholarship, a significant place must be granted to the pugnacious humanist, apostolic secretary, and manuscript hunter Poggio Bracciolini, whose rediscovery of the text of Lucretius's *De rerum natura* in 1417 has recently been identified by Stephen Greenblatt as one of the motive forces in the process of the Renaissance.[31] Such an assessment perhaps raises more questions than it answers, but the central position accorded to Poggio in the classic accounts of the Renaissance rediscovery of the Greek and Latin classics remains difficult to ignore, even if some of his codicological coups turn out to have been rather less clear-cut than has sometimes been assumed.[32] Once again, the link between Poggio's literary labors and the dawn of a new age of intellectual endeavor can be traced back to the scholar's own lifetime, as is apparent from the following glowing, but wistful, appreciation in a letter of 1 August 1447 to Poggio from the celebrated humanist educator Guarino of Verona:[33]

[31] Stephen Greenblatt, *The Swerve: How the Renaissance Began* (London: The Bodley Head, 2011); despite his subtitle, Greenblatt does acknowledge that "[t]here is no single explanation for the emergence of the Renaissance and the release of the forces that have shaped our own world. . . . One poem by itself was certainly not responsible for an entire intellectual, moral, and social transformation—no single work was, let alone one that for centuries could not without danger be spoken about freely in public" (11).

[32] In the Life of Poggio contained in his *Vite di uomini illustri*, the fifteenth-century librarian and book-dealer Vespasiano da Bisticci talks of Florence's debt to the humanist as follows: ". . . essendogli la città e tutti questi della lingua latina molto obligati, avendo illustrata e lui e messer Lionardo e frate Ambrogio, che furono de' primi, la lingua latina, che per tutti i secoli era stata oscurata; e trovossi in questo secolo aureo insieme con tanti dotti uomini" ("the city, and all those who possessed the Latin language, being much in debt to them; for Latin, which throughout the ages had lain in obscurity, had been illuminated by him and Messer Leonardo [Bruni] and Fra Ambrogio [Traversari], who were among the pioneers—and it found itself in this golden age along with so many learned men"): text in Vespasiano da Bisticci, *Vite di uomini illustri del secolo XV*, ed. Ludovico Frati, 3 vols. (Bologna: Romagnoli-Dall'Acqua, 1892–1893), 2:208. On Poggio's discoveries, see the remarks of Michael D. Reeve, "Classical Scholarship," in *The Cambridge Companion to Renaissance Humanism*, ed. Jill Kraye (Cambridge: Cambridge University Press, 1996), 26–27.

[33] Guarino Veronese, *Epistolario*, 806.52–67, in *Epistolario di Guarino Veronese*, ed. Remigio Sabbadini, 3 vols. (Turin: Bottega d'Erasmo, 1915–1919), 2:495; see Costa, *La leggenda*, 37. Guarino's name is juxtaposed with that of Poggio in Enea Silvio Piccolomini's list of contemporary authors whose *volumina tersa sunt legentibusque frugifera* ("volumes are polished and fruitful for readers"): see *De liberorum educatione*, 72, in *Humanist Educational Treatises*, ed. Craig W. Kallendorf, I Tatti Renaissance Library 5 (Cambridge, MA and London: Harvard University Press, 2002), 222–24.

> Cum tuum istud elegans contemplor ingenium, Poggi vir clarissime, non exclamare non possum: "o mores, o tempora!" "O totam sub arma coactam Hesperiam!" cum locus non est ingeniis, non artibus honestis praemia, cum etiam si velis, bene beateque vivere vix liceat. Quam facile factu esset, ut pares priscis illis reviviscerent homines et animi paene divini et illustria quondam studia, Antonios, Crassos dico, Cottas, Scaevolas. Modo solitus accederet honos et merces, qui praeclaras alunt artes, non diffido fore ut paria efflorerent opera, quando nostratibus non vis non ardor non facultas ipsa, sicuti favor et alimonia, desit. Id documento est: nam sicubi quasi theatrum disciplinarum ullo cum praemiolo praestitum est, videmus eruditos emergere et romanis et graecis doctrinis imbutos eximia de se polliceri et novum propemodum exoriri velle saeculum. Gratulari liceret et illud vociferari "iam nova progenies caelo demittitur alto," nisi silere musae cogantur inter arma.

> When I contemplate that refined genius of yours, most famous Poggio, I can't help exclaiming, "Ah, the customs, the times! [Cicero, *Catilinarians*, 1.2] Ah, all Italy forced into arms! [Virgil, *Aeneid*, 7.43]," when there is no place for genius, no rewards for honorable arts, since even if you wanted to it is scarcely possible to live well and in happiness. How easy it would be to bring it about that people equal to those great characters of old should come back to life, along with spirits almost divine and pursuits that were once illustrious—I mean the Antonies, the Crassi, the Cottas, the Scaevolas. If only the accustomed honor and remuneration that give sustenance to the foremost arts were to be granted, I have no doubt that it would come about that comparable works would flourish, since our people do not lack the power, nor the zeal, nor the capacity itself, as they do support and sustenance. Here's the proof: wherever a stage for the branches of learning (as it were) is supplied along with some little recompense, we see learned men appearing and those steeped in Roman and Greek teachings promising outstanding achievements on their part and practically a new age wishing to come into being. We would have cause to rejoice and to bawl out that tag "Now a new offspring is sent down from heaven on high," were the Muses not compelled to keep silent in the midst of conflict.

The revival of learning, the resurrection of the spirit and genius of past civilizations, the advent of a new era spearheaded by the progress of erudition in the wisdom of the ancients: what could be more evocative of the idea of the Renaissance as propagated in later narratives of historical development? And at the end of this effusive estimate of the heights attainable by the brilliance of Poggio and his contemporaries, as a final acknowledgment of the burgeoning cultivation of *praeclarae . . . artes* currently impeded by the turmoil of the times, we have a direct citation of Virgil's vision of a wondrous new generation sent down from heaven. There could scarcely be a clearer illustration of the interdependence of the conceptual apparatus of the doctrine of cultural rebirth and the terminology of the fourth Eclogue—or at the very least of the mutual reinforcement of each of these two eminently compatible phenomena by the other.

Poggio was by no means alone in attracting this kind of accolade. Among the luminaries of Renaissance thought, one of the most distinguished names will always be that of the pioneering Florentine Neoplatonist Marsilio Ficino, supreme proponent of the Renaissance revival of interest in the teachings of the ancient philosopher (see Adam Foley's chapter in this volume).[34] And sure enough, a letter from Giles of Viterbo to Ficino dating from around summer 1499 applies to the latter's advances in the field of Platonic exegesis the same unmistakably Virgilian vocabulary that we saw Boccaccio adopt to celebrate the (literally) epoch-making contribution of Petrarch:[35]

> Hec sunt, mi Marsili, Saturnia regna, hec toties a Sibylla et vatibus etas aurea decantata, hec Platonis illa tempora quibus fore precinuit, ut sua quam optime studia nota fierent.

> This, my dear Marsilio, is the reign of Saturn, this the Golden Age sung so many times by the Sibyl and the poets, these are those times of Plato in which he prophesied that it would come about that his studies would be most excellently known.

It is perhaps no coincidence that Ficino himself provides one of the most definitive identifications of his own *seculum* with the Golden Age proclaimed in classical literature,[36] although the sequence of four metallic ages he attributes to the utterances of *poetae* goes rather beyond anything we find in the fourth Eclogue, which mentions only the displacement of the immediately preceding race of iron by the reinstated *gens aurea*.

---

[34] On Ficino see, e.g., *Marsilio Ficino e il ritorno di Platone: studi e documenti*, ed. Gian Carlo Garfagnini, 2 vols. (Florence: Olschki, 1986); *Ficino and Renaissance Neoplatonism*, ed. Konrad Eisenbichler and Olga Zorzi Pugliese (Toronto: Dovehouse Editions, 1986); Paul Oskar Kristeller, *Marsilio Ficino and his Work after Five Hundred Years* (Florence: Olschki, 1987); *Marsilio Ficino: His Theology, his Philosophy, his Legacy*, ed. Michael J. B. Allen and Valery Rees with Martin Davies (Leiden, Boston, and Cologne: Brill, 2001).

[35] Giles of Viterbo, *Lettere familiari*, 15; text in Egidio da Viterbo OSA, *Lettere familiari*, ed. Anna Maria Voci Roth, 2 vols. (Rome: Institutum Historicum Augustinianum, 1990), 1:104.

[36] See Marsilio Ficino, *Opera omnia*, 2 vols. (Basel: Petri, 1576; repr. Turin: Bottega d'Erasmo, 1959), 1:944, discussed in Alessandra Tarabochia Canavero, "Marsilio Ficino e l'età dell'oro: *saeculum aureum ab ingeniis aureis*," in *Millenarismo ed età dell'oro nel Rinascimento. Atti del XIII Convegno internazionale (Chianciano-Montepulciano-Pienza 16–19 luglio 2001)*, ed. Luisa Secchi Tarugi (Florence: Cesati, 2003), 207–20.

Similar compliments could be paid to patrons as well as to scholars, by those who enjoyed or hoped to enjoy the financial support of those at the social and economic pinnacle of the Renaissance pyramid. The following highly rhetorical tribute by Guarino to Francesco Sforza, the *condottiere* who had come into possession of the duchy of Milan and married into the previous ruling dynasty, the Visconti, resembles the humanist's earlier homage to Poggio in its deployment of classical tags to advertise contemporary merit. Once again it builds up to a triumphant enunciation of Virgil's ubiquitous lines on the reversion of the ages and descent of a celestial progeny, this time as the climax of an elaborate volley of expressions denoting restoration, regeneration, and renewal (*renovasti*, *restituisti*, *revocasti*, *redintegrasti*), making this convoluted glorification a veritable roll-call of Renaissance metaphors:[37]

> Ut autem intermissis bellis togam suscipere pro tua sapientia aggressus es, facile omnes docuisti Minervam ipsam, ut gentiles dicerent, non minus pacis quam belli praesidem deam tibi ducem tibi comitem tibi sociam accedere; adeo vastatos belli calamitate agros, fessos mortales, labefactatas civitates tua prudentia aequitate animi magnitudine renovasti roborasti restituisti, leges iudicia magistratus revocasti, artes redintegrasti ut te, quem antea maximum belligerandi ductorem noverant, nunc demum admirandum pacis magistrum verumque patriae parentem experiantur; quo fit ut prae felicitate gratulantes illud sibyllinum clamitent: "iam redit et virgo, redeunt Saturnia regna, iam nova progenies caelo demittitur alto." Proinde "cedant arma togae. . . ."

> But since, putting a stop to wars, you have made a move to take up civil life in accordance with your wisdom, you have easily taught everyone that Minerva herself, as the pagans would say, the presiding goddess no less of peace than of war, is joining you as your leader, you as your comrade, you as your ally; to such an extent have you renewed, reinforced, and restored the fields, ravaged by the disaster of war; weary mortals; and fallen states, by your prudence, fairness, and greatness of soul, to such an extent have you recalled the laws, the courts, and the offices of state, and have revived the arts, that you, whom previously people had known as the mightiest leader in waging war, they now at last experience as the admirable author of peace and the true parent of your country. Thus it comes about that, rejoicing on account of their good fortune, they keep on calling out that Sibylline tag,

---

[37] Guarino Veronese, *Epistolario*, 932.17–29 (Sabbadini 2:681); noted by Costa, *La leggenda*, 37–38. Guarino's expression *prae felicitate gratulantes . . . clamitent* ("on account of their good fortune, they keep on calling out . . .") might be taken as an indication that the author is thinking rather of the earlier allusion to these lines in Dante's epistle to Henry VII (*vota sua praevenientes in iubilo . . . cantabant*, "anticipating their wishes in their joy, began to sing/were singing"; see above, p. 207) than of the fourth Eclogue in isolation.

"Now the Virgin too returns, the reign of Saturn returns; now a new offspring is sent down from heaven on high." Hence, "let arms give way to the toga. . . ." (Cicero, *De officiis*, 1.77)

These instances of direct quotation from the text of the fourth Eclogue in statements of cultural and political rebirth and restoration raise the question of whether the conceptual and linguistic template bequeathed by Virgil to later exponents of the notion of temporal renewal might not also underlie other manifestations of "Renaissance" imagery, many of which display discernible parallels to the treatment of the subject in *Eclogue* 4, even if they do not reproduce the Roman poet's formulae verbatim. So, in a passage from the second redaction of the infamous collection of a hundred elegies, the *Hecatelegium* of Pacifico Massimi of Ascoli,[38] the forecast of a gilded future is pressed into service to salute the papacy of Julius II, a scion of the della Rovere dynasty, whose emblematic oak tree had obvious associations (frequently evoked by other panegyrists of Julius and his uncle Sixtus IV, and by Massimi himself elsewhere) with the diet of acorns traditionally ascribed to the population of the primitive Golden Age:[39]

Prima renascentur saturni saecula, quamvis
    Aurea non illo tempore quercus erat.
Pax fuit atque fides verumque aetate sub illa
    Aurea mentito nomine dicta fuit.
A re nomen habent haec saecula, flumen ut aurum
    Currit et auratas in mare volvit aquas.
Fert nemus auratas frondes et campus aristas
    Proque uvis aurum pingue racemus habet.

The first age of Saturn will be reborn, although at that time the oak wasn't golden. There was peace and faith, but in that era it was called golden by a counterfeit name. *This* age takes its name from the fact, the river runs like gold and rolls gilded waters to the sea. The grove bears gilded leaves and the plain gilded ears of corn, and in place of grapes the vine-cluster has plump gold.

Here the "rebirth" (cf. *renascentur*, 17) of *Saturni saecula* is marked by the appearance of gold in all areas of the natural environment. Lest it be objected that by this stage the sheer familiarity of prognostications of the return of the age of Saturn had eclipsed any specifically Virgilian connotations the image might originally have carried, it is worth noting the line-ending *campus aristas* in the

[38] For the text see Pacifico Massimi, *Hecatelegium II: Les cent nouvelles élégies*, ed. and trans. Juliette Desjardins Daude (Paris: Les Belles Lettres, 2008).

[39] Pacifico Massimi, *Hecatelegium* B, 5.5.17–24 (Desjardins Daude, ed., *Hecatelegium II*, 157–58).

penultimate line of the extract, recalling Virgil's collocation *campus arista* in his description of the features of the resurgent *Saturnia regna* (*Eclogues*, 4.28). Quite explicitly, then, Massimi's papal panegyric introduces the vocabulary of renaissance in conjunction with verbal reminiscence of the language of *Eclogue* 4, reinforcing the impression that these two elements were felt by Renaissance authors to complement each other in communicating the desired impression of historical time regained.

One theme from Virgil's text that is repeatedly reflected in claims of literary and artistic renascence is that of the recurrence of episodes or, more commonly, individuals from previous eras, for which the prototype can be found in the prediction in *Eclogues*, 4.34–36 of a repeat of the legendary expeditions of the heroic age, with its prophecy of *alter . . . Tiphys* ("a second Tiphys"), *altera . . . Argo* ("a second Argo") and *altera bella* ("other wars"), the last of these involving a reprise of the Trojan War, when Achilles will again be sent to Troy. This replay of archaic exploits and long-distant upheavals is used in the eclogue to signify the gradual stages through which the process of renewal must pass before the full realization of the new order is effected; in later adaptations, by contrast, these reanimated celebrities are no longer a consequence of the lingering residue of ancient transgression (*veteris vestigia fraudis*: *Eclogues*, 4.31), but symptoms of the restored Golden Age itself, the profession of which in association with the recursion of past events or personalities arguably serves to confirm the Virgilian pedigree of this literary trope. The poet Bernardo Bellincioni, who served in turn the Medici of Florence, the Gonzaga of Mantua, and the Sforza of Milan, notes the presence at the court of Lodovico Sforza (Lodovico il Moro) of "[u]n novo Marzïal" ("a new Martial") in the person of the writer Antonio Peloto, and a Florentine Apelles, no doubt to be identified with Leonardo da Vinci, along with a triumvirate of latter-day avatars of venerable figures from the history of medicine ("Galieno, Avicenna, e Ipocrate") whose identity is less easy to ascertain.[40] For Bellincioni, the enlightened patronage of these resurrected sages by Lodovico and his secretary Bartolomeo Calco, the latter branded here a new and greater Maecenas ("quel Calco è Mecenate, e ben n'ha 'l vanto"), truly heralds the return of the Age of Gold ("Veramente ha a tornar l'età dell'oro").

A similar message is conveyed by Ugolino Verino in the second half of a long piece from his collection of Latin elegies, the *Flametta*, in which the poet hails the achievements of his age in the fields of art, science, and morality, not least among which are the distinctions earned by contemporary ventures in poetry and the visual arts:[41]

---

40 See Costa, *La leggenda*, 57–58. For the text of Bellincioni's *Visione*, in which these lines occur, see *Le Rime di Bernardo Bellincioni*, ed. Pietro Fanfani, 2 vols. (Bologna: Romagnoli, 1876–1878), 1:26.

41 Ugolino Verino, *Flametta*, 2.45.99–110. For the text see *Ugolini Verini Flametta*, ed. Luciano Mencaraglia (Florence: Olschki, 1940), 95 (punctuation altered in 109);

Innumeras artes hodie florere videmus
saecula per Latium quae latuere decem.
Nunc Zeusis rediit qui quondam pinxerat uvas
ad quas deceptae saepe volastis, aves;
nunc alter Phidias rediit, nunc alter Apelles,
picturam quorum vivere nempe putes.
Spirantem hic Pario vultum de marmore ducit,
aera alius fundit, fingit at ille rota.
Praeterea florent aliae sine nomine multae
quas lucro intentum vulgus ubique colit.
Pace mihi liceat vestra dixisse, priores,
temporibus cedant aurea saecla meis.

Today we see countless arts flourishing, which for ten centuries lay shtum throughout Latium [note the etymological pun *Latium / latuere*, following *Aeneid*, 8.322–23]. Now Zeuxis has returned, who at one time painted grapes to which you, birds, often flew deluded; now a second Phidias has returned, now a second Apelles, whose painting you would certainly think was alive. One man molds breathing features from Parian marble, another casts bronze [cf. *Aeneid*, 6.847–48], yet another fashions clay on a wheel. Moreover many other [arts] without name are flourishing, which the masses practice everywhere, intent on profit. May I say it—begging your pardon, men of earlier centuries: the golden age should give way to my own times.

The claim advanced is the familiar one of the reincarnation of antiquity, as demonstrated in the media of paint, marble, bronze, and ceramics, which, the elegist maintains, exhibit the same naturalistic qualities as the fabled works of the ancient masters.[42] So the age of Cosimo's son Piero de' Medici, acclaimed later in the poem as *Maecenas . . . alter* ("a second Maecenas," 2.45.135), has been blessed with the return of Zeuxis, to whom Verino elsewhere remarks that his own contemporary da Vinci is not inferior;[43] and both Phidias and Apelles, compared by

also *Poeti latini del Quattrocento*, ed. Francesco Arnaldi, Lucia Gualdo Rosa, and Liliana Monti Sabia (Milan and Naples: Ricciardi, 1964), 862–63.

[42] For the stories about Zeuxis fooling birds by his realistic representations of grapes, see Pliny, *Natural History*, 35.65–66.

[43] Ugolino Verino, *Epigrammata*, 3.23.25–26: *Eracleota licet Zeusis bene pinxeris uvas, | haud tamen est tuscus Vincius arte minor* ("Although you, Zeuxis of Heraclea, painted grapes masterfully, nonetheless da Vinci of Tuscany is not inferior in his art"); text in Ugolino Verino, *Epigrammi*, ed. Francesco Bausi (Messina: Sicania, 1998), 328; *Poeti latini*, 872–75; and *Renaissance Latin Verse: An Anthology*, ed. Alessandro Perosa and John Sparrow (London: Duckworth, 1979), 91–92.

Verino in Book 3 of his epigrams to Verrocchio and Botticelli respectively,[44] are said to have their modern-day counterparts. What is perhaps most significant for our purposes is the Virgilian idiom in which this assertion of parity with the ancients is cast: not only do *alter Phidias* and *alter Apelles* evoke *alter Tiphys* and the other recurring phenomena of *Eclogues*, 4.34–35, but the insistent repetition of *nunc* alongside the emphatic iteration of the verb *redeo* (*rediit* . . . *rediit*, 101–3) might also be taken to reflect the syntax of *Eclogues*, 4.4–7, with its triple *iam* and duplication of *redit/redeunt*. If so, the implicit parallel with the earlier proclamation of a new Golden Age is made apparent in Verino's affirmation of the superiority of his own time to the *aurea saecla* of previous ages in the lines that round off this exaltation of the artistic splendors of the Quattrocento.

By way of a finale, I would like to examine an encomium of the pontificate of Leo X, the grandson of Verino's patron Piero, which brings together a number of the Virgilian motifs, the presence of which we have observed in the passages considered earlier, combining within the space of a few lines a series of themes deriving ultimately from the model of the fourth Eclogue. Towards the end of his survey of the contemporary representatives of poetic activity at Rome, Francesco Arsilli looks forward to a time when peace will flourish, sanctity will be preserved, and the world will experience a miraculous renovation:[45]

> Vaticinor, dis grata cohors, felicius aevum
>   Pectora fatidico murmure Phoebus agit;
> Venturus novus Augustus, venturus et alter
>   Moecenas, divum candida progenies.
> Aurea Principibus novaque illis saecula fient,
>   Saecula, queis aetas ferrea victa cadet;
> Pacificae grave Martis opus tunc cedet olivae;
>   Romano cedent arma cruenta foro.
> Pinguis humus passim nullis cultoribus, ultro
>   Et Cererem, tuaque munera, Bacche, dabit.
> Arva pede incerto pessundare sancta profanos
>   Non sinet, arva sacris caste adeunda choris.
> Tunc virides lauri sudabunt roscida mella,
>   Flumina perpetuo nectare lenta fluent;

44 Verino, *Epigrammata*, 3.23.17, *Nec minor est Phydia noster Verrochius* ("Nor is our Verrocchio inferior to Phidias"); 23–24, *Aequarique sibi non indignetur Apelles* | *Sandrum* . . . ("Apelles should not think it unworthy that Sandro is compared to him . . .").

45 Francesco Arsilli, *De poetis urbanis*, 641–56; text from William Roscoe, *The Life and Pontificate of Leo the Tenth*, 5th ed., revised Thomas Roscoe, 2 vols. (London: Bohn, 1846), 2:519; see also Rosanna Alhaique Pettinelli, "Francesco Arsilli e i '*poetae urbani*,'" in *L'umana compagnia. Studi in onore di Gennaro Savarese*, ed. Rosanna Alhaique Pettinelli (Rome: Bulzoni, 1999), 33, who comments on "il tema dell'età dell'oro, così caro all'umanesimo romano."

Altricemque novus quando instaurabitur orbis,
Tellurem repetent numina prisca Deum.

I foretell, troupe pleasing to the gods, a happier age; Phoebus stirs my breast with prophetic murmur. There will come a new Augustus, there will come a second Maecenas, fair offspring of gods. Under those princes there will be an age golden and new, an age by which the era of iron shall fall defeated. Then the grievous work of Mars shall yield to the peace-bringing olive; bloodstained arms shall yield to the Roman forum. The fertile ground everywhere, with no cultivators, shall of its own accord offer up Ceres's grain, and your gifts, Bacchus. He shall not allow the profane to destroy the holy fields with uncertain foot, fields to be approached chastely by sacred choruses. Then green laurels shall sweat dewy honey, the rivers flow sluggish with unceasing nectar; and when the new world is restored, the ancient divinities shall return to the sustaining earth.

Here we find once more the notion of historical recurrence, in the anticipation of a new Augustus (*novus Augustus*, 643) and a second Maecenas (*alter | Moecenas*, 643–44; cf. Verino above). The latter of these is identified—like the *nova progenies* of the eclogue (who is addressed by the speaker of *Eclogue* 4 as *cara deum suboles*, "dear offspring of gods," 4.49 and will take on the life of the gods, *deum vitam*, 4.15)—as *divum candida progenies* ("fair offspring of gods," 644). The iron age, overcome, will give way to a new Golden Age (645–46; cf. *Eclogues*, 4.8–9), which will be accompanied by an end to warfare and the capitulation of the weapons of war to the more civilized pursuits of the forum, a clear reworking of Cicero's exhortation *cedant arma togae* ("let arms yield to the toga," *De officiis*, 1.77), as paired with the quotation from *Eclogues*, 4.6 in the letter of Guarino to Francesco Sforza considered earlier. This age of peace will witness a burst of spontaneous productivity in the natural world, as the bountiful soil dispenses crops and the *munera* ("gifts") of the vine *nullis cultoribus* ("with no cultivators," 649), like the diminutive *munuscula* ("little gifts") yielded *nullo . . . cultu* ("with no cultivation") by the earth in *Eclogues*, 4.17. These intimations of the literary ancestry of Arsilli's prophecy are crowned at line 653 with a direct incorporation of the entire second half of line 30 of Virgil's poem, the sweating of dewy honey here transferred (with equal botanical improbability) from oaks to laurels (653), before the symptoms of the new era culminate in an expectation of the return to earth of *numina prisca Deum* ("the ancient divinities," 656). One of these, presumably, is none other than the *Virgo* Astraea, whose terrestrial reappearance signals the restoration of the Golden Age under the Medici pope, in keeping with the Virgilian mythology so copiously deployed in praise of his Florentine forebears.[46]

[46] See especially Gombrich, "Renaissance and Golden Age"; Costa, *La leggenda*, esp. 43–55; Janet Cox-Rearick, *Dynasty and Destiny in Medici Art: Pontormo, Leo X, and the Two Cosimos* (Princeton: Princeton University Press, 1984).

It would be rash to suggest that the theory of temporal and cultural rebirth owed its origin and subsequent diffusion solely to its advocates' awareness of and participation in the already extensive afterlife of Virgil's celebration of the return of the Golden Age in the consulship of Pollio;[47] but it can nonetheless be demonstrated, I think, that evocation of the fourth Eclogue and its distinctive prophecies played an integral part in the articulation of the idea of a Renaissance, which was to prove so influential in the conceptualization of this period both at the time and over the course of the following centuries.[48] Recognition of the strong Virgilian current pervading these expressions of regeneration and renewal does not necessarily entail the conclusion that the humanists' exploitation of these formulae represents no more than a perfunctory posture, a convenient vehicle for self-promotion or mutual congratulation, or a cynical bid for subsidy from actual or potential sponsors. In at least some instances—perhaps many—this may indeed have been the case, but conventionality of expression is by no means incompatible with sincerity of belief. It should perhaps serve to modify, however, some of the more extravagant generalizations that have been extrapolated from the frequently tendentious, generally conventional, and almost always highly literary pronouncements of Renaissance authors. This expository template, it can be argued, far from arising suddenly in response to an unprecedented set of historical circumstances, derived at least in part from a long tradition of adaptations of one particular Roman poem (often accompanied by additional elements from other related ancient texts) to sound the praises of patrons both sacred and secular; and to divorce this nexus of ideas from its implication with the wider history of Virgilianizing panegyric must inevitably result in a profoundly deracinated view not only of the rhetoric of Renaissance humanism, but of the historical process itself.

---

[47] For wider manifestations of such conceptions, see especially G. W. Trompf, *The Idea of Historical Recurrence in Western Thought: From Antiquity to the Reformation* (Berkeley, Los Angeles, and London: University of California Press, 1979). Further bibliography in Gombrich, "Renaissance and Golden Age," 307n10.

[48] See especially Levin, *The Myth of the Golden Age*, 144–45 (quoted above, note 5); Costa, *La leggenda*, 35–36 (on Poggio); also Yates, *Astraea*, 38, "The whole process of the 're-naissance' of art and letters is intimately bound up with the return to a classical golden age, or rather with the more vital idea of the eternal survival and living rebirths of that age"; James Hankins, "The Popes and Humanism," in *Rome Reborn: The Vatican Library and Renaissance Culture*, ed. Anthony Grafton (Washington, New Haven, London, and Vatican City: Library of Congress and Yale University Press in association with the Biblioteca Apostolica Vaticana, 1993), 58–59, ". . . the boldest stroke of all, they [the humanists] invented a highly seductive historical myth: the myth of the Renaissance itself. For with the dawn of the fifteenth century the humanists began to announce that Petrarch's Dark Ages at length had passed away, and that, thanks to the work of wise patrons and great geniuses (such as themselves), the golden age, a new classical age, had been reborn" (see also 66, "the central myth of the Renaissance, the myth of renewal, of the new golden age").

Index